VOLUME 674

NOVEMBER 2017

THE ANNALS

of The American Academy of Political
and Social Science

The State of Unequal Educational Opportunity: The Coleman Report 50 Years Later

Special Editors:
MARGOT I. JACKSON
Brown University
SUSAN L. MOFFITT
Brown University

⑤SAGE

Los Angeles | London | New Delhi
Singapore | Washington DC | Melbourne

The American Academy of Political and Social Science

202 S. 36th Street, Annenberg School for Communication, University of Pennsylvania,
Philadelphia, PA 19104-3806; (215) 746-6500; (215) 573-2667 (fax); www.aapss.org

Origin and Purpose. The Academy was organized December 14, 1889, to promote the progress of political and social science, especially through publications and meetings. The Academy does not take sides in controverted questions, but seeks to gather and present reliable information to assist the public in forming an intelligent and accurate judgment.

Meetings. The Academy occasionally holds a meeting in the spring extending over two days.

Publications. THE ANNALS of The American Academy of Political and Social Science is the bimonthly publication of the Academy. Each issue contains articles on some prominent social or political problem, written at the invitation of the editors. These volumes constitute important reference works on the topics with which they deal, and they are extensively cited by authorities throughout the United States and abroad.

Subscriptions. THE ANNALS of The American Academy of Political and Social Science (ISSN 0002-7162) (J295) is published bimonthly—in January, March, May, July, September, and November—by SAGE Publishing, 2455 Teller Road, Thousand Oaks, CA 91320. Periodicals postage paid at Thousand Oaks, California, and at additional mailing offices. POSTMASTER: Send address changes to The Annals of The American Academy of Political and Social Science, c/o SAGE Publishing, 2455 Teller Road, Thousand Oaks, CA 91320. Institutions may subscribe to THE ANNALS at the annual rate: $1129 (clothbound, $1275). Individuals may subscribe to the ANNALS at the annual rate: $126 (clothbound, $185). Single issues of THE ANNALS may be obtained by individuals for $39 each (clothbound, $54). Single issues of THE ANNALS have proven to be excellent supplementary texts for classroom use. Direct inquiries regarding adoptions to THE ANNALS c/o SAGE Publishing (address below).

All correspondence concerning membership in the Academy, dues renewals, inquiries about membership status, and/or purchase of single issues of THE ANNALS should be sent to THE ANNALS c/o SAGE Publishing, 2455 Teller Road, Thousand Oaks, CA 91320. Telephone: (800) 818-SAGE (7243) and (805) 499-0721; Fax/Order line: (805) 375-1700; e-mail: journals@sagepub.com. *Please note that orders under $30 must be prepaid.* For all customers outside the Americas, please visit http://www.sagepub.co.uk/customerCare.nav for information.

THE ANNALS

Editorial Office: 202 S. 36th Street, Philadelphia, PA 19104-3806
For information about individual and institutional subscriptions address:
SAGE Publishing
2455 Teller Road
Thousand Oaks, CA 91320

For SAGE Publishing: Peter Geraghty (Production) and Mimi Nguyen (Marketing)

From India and South Asia,
write to:
SAGE PUBLICATIONS INDIA Pvt Ltd
B-42 Panchsheel Enclave, P.O. Box 4109
New Delhi 110 017
INDIA

From Europe, the Middle East,
and Africa, write to:
SAGE PUBLICATIONS LTD
1 Oliver's Yard, 55 City Road
London EC1Y 1SP
UNITED KINGDOM

International Standard Serial Number ISSN 0002-7162
ISBN 978-1-5443-2283-4 (Vol. 674, 2017) paper
ISBN 978-1-5443-2282-7 (Vol. 674, 2017) cloth
First printing, November 2017

Information about membership rates, institutional subscriptions, and back issue prices may be found on the facing page.

Advertising. Current rates and specifications may be obtained by writing to The Annals Advertising and Promotion Manager at the Thousand Oaks office (address above). Acceptance of advertising in this journal in no way implies endorsement of the advertised product or service by SAGE or the journal's affiliated society(ies) or the journal editor(s). No endorsement is intended or implied. SAGE reserves the right to reject any advertising it deems as inappropriate for this journal.

Claims. Claims for undelivered copies must be made no later than six months following month of publication. The publisher will supply replacement issues when losses have been sustained in transit and when the reserve stock will permit.

Change of Address. Six weeks' advance notice must be given when notifying of change of address. Please send the old address label along with the new address to the SAGE office address above to ensure proper identification. Please specify the name of the journal.

THE ANNALS

OF THE AMERICAN ACADEMY OF
POLITICAL AND SOCIAL SCIENCE

Volume 674

November 2017

IN THIS ISSUE:

The State of Unequal Educational Opportunity: The Coleman Report 50 Years Later

Special Editors: MARGOT I. JACKSON
and SUSAN L. MOFFITT

FORTHCOMING

*Developing the Basis for the Secure and Accessible Use of Data for High Impact Program
Management, Policy Development, and Scholarship*
Special Editors: ANDREW REAMER, JULIA LANE, DAVID ELLWOOD,
and IAN FOSTER

Migrant Smuggling as a Collective Strategy and Insurance Policy: Views from the Margins
Special Editors: SHELDON X. ZHANG, GABRIELLA E. SANCHEZ,
and LUIGI ACHILLI

Keywords: Coleman Report; inequality; social policy

The State of Unequal Educational Opportunity: Introduction to the Special Issue on the Coleman Report 50 Years Later

Sponsored by the U.S. Office of Education, pursuant to Title IV of the 1964 Civil Rights Act, the Equality of Educational Opportunity survey (EEOS)—commonly known as the Coleman Report (Coleman et al. 1966)—was tasked with assessing inequality in American schools and its consequences for student achievement. In the 50 years since the EEOS first appeared in print, tens of thousands of articles and studies have taken up the questions that Coleman raised, the methods that he used, and the conclusions that he reached. The provision of public education remains bedrock to domestic and international social and economic policy. Much political debate and scholarship focuses on how to reduce the gaps in achievement that appear along socioeconomic, racial, and ethnic lines by improving schools: how to improve teacher quality, how to improve the distribution of financial resources, and how to introduce rigorous curricula. A largely separate body of research simultaneously attends to the out-of-school factors that affect inequality in student achievement; revealing strong inequalities in children's skill development well before school entry; and

By
MARGOT I. JACKSON
and
SUSAN L. MOFFITT

Margot I. Jackson is an associate professor of sociology at Brown University. Her work focuses on social stratification and social demography, with an emphasis on inequality of educational opportunity, health, and children and families.

Susan L. Moffitt is an associate professor in the Department of Political Science and the Watson Institute for Public and International Affairs at Brown University. Her work focuses on state capacity to implement policy in the domains of public education and public health.

Correspondence: margot_jackson@brown.edu

DOI: 10.1177/0002716217733711

ANNALS, *AAPSS*, 674, November 2017

demonstrating the importance of children's circumstances outside school, including the design and operation of American socioeconomic and political institutions.

The anniversary of the Coleman Report affords an opportunity to invite different research traditions to engage with each other, to deepen understanding of some of the issues that the EEOS opened up, and to build on Coleman's insights and findings. To reflect on the influence that the EEOS and its ideas have had across disciplines, this special issue brings together scholarship from sociologists, political scientists, psychologists, education economists, legal scholars, and other education scholars. This broad array of scholars seeks to advance the study of inequality and educational opportunity while drawing on some of the ideas that motivated and arose from the Coleman Report. Rather than a retrospective tribute, each article in this issue addresses different dimensions of the sources and state of current inequality of educational opportunity. Some articles focus on ideas that connect closely with those that Coleman raised. Other articles examine issues that bear on the fundamental problem of inequality and address aspects of inequality that Coleman's report raised but that were not specifically part of Coleman's inquiry.

This special issue begins with an historical overview of the Coleman Report that illuminates its origins and assesses the status of knowledge and debate in some of the core domains of inquiry that the EEOS helped to fuel. One such domain probes the ways in which families contribute to children's learning. Building on EEOS ideas, articles in this volume examine how children's familial circumstances and parental engagement bear on skill development and student achievement, and how literacy development opportunities at home contribute to summer learning. Articles in this volume then probe the intersection of schools and families to examine how families differentially experience school policies that are ostensibly designed to improve equity, and how the interaction among families, schools, and the criminal justice system bear on students' educational trajectories.

Moving from families to schools, subsequent articles examine the status of knowledge on how school finances contribute to educational opportunities and consider evidence from school policies, such as voucher policies, from other countries. This issue then offers a series of articles on the impact of communities on educational opportunity. Segregation was a prominent feature in American schools at the time of Coleman's study, as it is today. Scholarship in this volume takes up the issue of segregation in the context of rural schools. Other scholarship examines how aspects of communities, including violence, can bear on and manifest in schooling. Contributors to this issue also build on and move beyond Coleman's considerations of communities by examining policy approaches such as extended school years and collective impact. This issue concludes by synthesizing core themes that emerge across the expanse of scholarship conducted on educational opportunity and by highlighting lines of inquiry that hold promise for advancing knowledge on educational opportunity in the future. This volume's interdisciplinary approach to examining the sources and state of current inequality of educational opportunity in the United States demonstrates the complexity of the problems that the EEOS raised, reveals some areas of progress in our knowledge, highlights the tremendous durability of inequality in educational opportunity, and suggests both the promise and limits of U.S. policy approaches to addressing those inequalities.

Reference

Coleman, James S., Ernest Q. Campbell, Carol J. Hobson, James McPartland, Alexander M. Mood, Frederic D. Weinfeld, and Robert L. York. 1966. *Equality of educational opportunity*. Washington, DC: U.S. Government Printing Office.

The Coleman Report, 50 Years On: What Do We Know about the Role of Schools in Academic Inequality?

By
HEATHER C. HILL

Achievement outcomes for U.S. children are overwhelmingly unequal along racial, ethnic, and class lines. Whether and how schools contribute to educational inequality, however, has long been the subject of debate. This article traces the debate to the Coleman Report's publication in 1966, describing the report's production and impact on educational research. The article then considers the field's major findings—that schools equalize along class lines but likely stratify along racial and ethnic lines—in light of current policy debates.

Keywords: Coleman Report; sociology of education; inequality; social policy

Achievement outcomes for U.S. children are overwhelmingly unequal. The National Assessment of Education Progress regularly reports that white students' proficiency rates on mathematics and reading exams are double or even triple those of African American and Hispanic students, and the size of gaps is similar when comparing students based on family income and parental education. Whites also lead in high school completion and college attendance rates, and they average double-digit advantages in four-year college completion (U.S. Department of Education, National Center for Education Statistics 2014, 2015, 2016).

News outlets carry near-daily reports that implicate numerous and varied sources for

Heather C. Hill is the Jerome T. Murphy Professor in Education at the Harvard Graduate School of Education. Her primary work focuses on teacher and teaching quality and the effects of policies aimed at improving both.

NOTE: The author would like to thank David K. Cohen and Mike (Marshall) Smith for their help and support, and also thanks the many researchers who were interviewed for the piece. Helpful readers included the staff at Chalkbeat, where an earlier version of this piece appeared.

Correspondence: heather_hill@gse.harvard.edu

DOI: 10.1177/0002716217727510

these gaps—unequal school financing, racism in schools, differences in parenting practices, the stresses of poverty, crumbling school facilities, ineffective teachers, and so on. Reading these accounts, it is easy to imagine a crushingly dysfunctional public education system, one in which schools bring about declines in student achievement for low-income students of color as they progress through their K–12 years. Others (e.g., Downey, Gamoran) view schools as compensating for the disadvantages of poverty, offering educational experiences superior to those available in the homes and neighborhoods in which children live.

Discerning the relative importance of these views—and ultimately, the extent to which schooling, writ large, contributes to social inequality—requires reading a research literature that dates back to a report released just prior to the July 4th weekend, 1966. In its 50 years, this report has been covered up, scrutinized, corroborated, used as evidence in the making of social policy, and, ultimately, dramatically improved upon. In all of this, the report has profoundly influenced how scholars have unraveled, and are still unraveling, the relationship among race, income, schools, and children's academic achievement. It has prompted scholars to ask and answer the question: Are schools to blame for unequal student outcomes?

The Beginning

Congress commissioned the Equality of Educational Opportunity Study (EEOS), colloquially known as the Coleman Report after its lead author James S. Coleman, as part of the 1964 Civil Rights Act. In many ways, Coleman was a logical choice to lead the study. A polymath with interests in sociology, mathematics, and economics, he had completed a PhD in Columbia University's prestigious sociology department, where distinguished names in the field—Robert Merton, Paul Lazarsfeld—reportedly wrangled for his attention (Kilgore 2016). Coleman had recently finished a survey and then a book on adolescent culture (Coleman 1961), providing him experience with the collection of large-scale survey data and quantitative analysis, experience unique among 1960s-era education researchers. Coleman was also known to support civil rights; in 1963, he and his family had been arrested for demonstrating outside an amusement park that refused to admit African Americans (Grant 1973; Kilgore 2016).

The study itself was massive. In fall 1965, Coleman and his team collected data from 4,000 schools, 66,000 teachers, and almost 600,000 first-, third-, sixth-, ninth-, and twelfth-graders (Coleman 1966)—one of the largest standalone testing and survey efforts ever undertaken in U.S. schools. Coleman and his team also produced the data and subsequent report within a remarkably compact timeline. By way of comparison, modern studies that enroll more than a few hundred students can take up to two years or more to conceptualize and design. By contrast, Coleman's EEOS took just over a year to fashion from stem to stern—including its conceptualization and design, questionnaire and test development, school and student sampling, data collection, data analysis, and writing (Grant 1973). The looming July 1966 deadline led Coleman, according to David

K. Cohen, a professor emeritus at the University of Michigan's School of Education, to "hole himself up in a hotel with a very large supply of bourbon and deliveries of printouts" to finish his portion of the report.[1] The resulting tome was well north of 700 pages, much of it devoted to thorough analysis of statistical tables and graphs.

In some respects, Coleman's analysis found what you would expect looking backward to 1960s America: mostly segregated schools across all geographic regions and the urban/nonurban divide (an issue taken up by Logan and Burdick-Will, this volume); disparities favoring white children in some resources such as class size, school facilities, and the availability of advanced coursework; and heavy race-based inequality on tests of academic achievement. To a small group of educators and civil rights activists who knew schools, this last finding felt familiar; earlier evidence had shown wide disparities in student test scores, and the Elementary and Secondary Education Act (ESEA), intended to provide aid to impoverished schools, had passed Congress in 1965 in part to alleviate this gap. Yet the achievement gap had been kept quiet, "sort of like your demented aunt in the attic," according to Cohen.[2]

Surprising to many, however, was the news that that schools serving African American and white children looked little different on a bundle of other measures, including the age of school facilities and textbooks, the availability of extra-curricular clubs, and many teacher and principal characteristics. Even more surprising was Coleman's assertion that inequities in school resources did not explain the observed inequalities in school-average student achievement. And where differences among schools serving African American and white students did exist—in the availability of resources like science laboratories, advanced curricula, textbooks, and qualified teachers—these differences explained little in terms of student achievement once other factors were taken into account. Instead, family background—specifically, parental income, education, wealth, and aspirations for their children—proved a strong influence on student test scores. As Coleman noted midway through the report:

> One implication stands out above all: That schools bring little influence to bear on a child's achievement that is independent of his background and general social context; and that this very lack of an independent effect means that the inequalities imposed on children by their home, neighborhood, and peer environment are carried along to become the inequalities with which they confront adult life at the end of school. (Coleman 1966, 325)

The analysis also identified students' peers as a powerful influence on their academic achievement.

These conclusions were initially slow to penetrate public discourse. The Johnson administration sought to limit, and largely succeeded in limiting, media coverage to the report's findings on racial segregation in schools, in part to protect federally driven desegregation efforts then under way, and in part to shield the ESEA's funding of high-poverty schools—funding that was of questionable value, according to the report (Grant 1973). Yet in 1967, Daniel Patrick

Moynihan, the urban policy scholar who went on to become a U.S. senator, began to deliver speeches and write articles about the report, which he saw as buttressing his views regarding the importance of families in reproducing inequality (Grant 1973). Moynihan even managed to get Coleman called before a congressional committee that, among other things, entertained the possibility that Johnson staffers had covered up the report (Grant 1973).

Once evident, the EEOS findings set off a strong reaction in the policy world. They defied conventional wisdom among liberals and progressives, which leaned toward the view that differences in school quality either reinforced or magnified racial and socioeconomic stratification. "Everybody knew that the schools were worse for black kids than for white kids, just like everybody knew that Communism was a threat," said Christopher (Sandy) Jencks, then a reporter for the *New Republic* and fellow at the Institute for Policy Studies in Washington, D.C.[3] Yet when data failed to bear this out, scholars and others were at a loss. "Holy mackerel, what are you going to do when school's not working?" said Marshall (Mike) Smith, a principal data analyst for a subsequent reexamination of Coleman's results. "And the way they don't work in this report was that they didn't equalize outcomes."[4]

Less obvious to the public was the seismic shock the EEOS set off in the world of education research. At the time of the report's release, quantitative analyses occurred mostly in educational psychology departments, where investigators conducted small-scale experimental studies.[5] Though psychologists possessed the statistical tools to relate schooling inputs to student outcomes and had in fact conducted a large-scale study on the effects of schooling, Project TALENT, only a few years earlier, they had no natural interest in social stratification—the idea that schools and schooling might play an important role in reproducing racial and class differences. Sociologists of education did think of schools along these lines, but at the time few tackled such questions with more than anecdotes or philosophical arguments. But with the EEOS came a sea change: Children could be tested, and those test scores could be explained by a host of family, classroom, and school features. The report reshaped the way educational research questions were asked.

Molding this new field's growth was scholars' general consternation over—and, to some degree, suspicion of—the report's findings. In particular, evidence that school resources did little to predict student test scores cut against commonsense assumptions that more money could buy better student outcomes. When faced with controversial findings, scholars generally lock themselves up, either alone or in groups, to check and recheck the data. At Harvard, a group of scholars led by Moynihan and Tom Pettigrew, a young social psychologist whose work focused on race and the impacts of integration, did just this, convening a yearlong seminar to reanalyze the EEOS data. Originally designed to be small, the seminar eventually attracted dozens of regularly attending faculty, graduate students, and public intellectuals. In typical Harvard style, the main work of the seminar occurred after dinner and drinks at the Harvard Faculty Club. "We'd sit around and analyze data," said Smith. "I would give them data sheets. I'd give them data analysis, looking at some hypothesis that they'd come up with in prior meetings. And we'd pore over these tables."[6]

Seminar attendees were a who's who of educational research at the time, and a who-would-be-who in educational research and policy over the following decades. Ted Sizer, a public intellectual and also, at the time, the dean of the Harvard Graduate School of Education, led a policy committee. Frederick Mosteller, a widely respected Harvard statistician, contributed analytic expertise. Smith, the data analyst, later served as a key education advisor to three administrations and became a leading architect of the 1990s standards-based reforms, a precursor to the Common Core. Jencks, the reporter for the *New Republic*, participated in and wrote about the reanalysis, as did Eric Hanushek, then a graduate student in the economics department at MIT. It is likely that at no other time in the history of education research did so much intellectual firepower work collectively and in a sustained way toward a common goal. Jencks ended up at Harvard and Hanushek at Stanford, and both have been widely influential in education policy. Hanushek credits the seminar with moving him toward a career in quantitative education research: "It was formative. It got me into this whole area of research. And I continue to be there."[7]

Seminar participants—and by extension, the field more broadly—had a lot of work to do to understand schools' impact generally, and to understand schools' impact on social inequality specifically. One reason was that the EEOS collected only a snapshot of student test score outcomes at a single time point, not documentation of changes in those scores as students aged. Snapshot data do not allow analysts to disentangle the many factors that might contribute to student outcomes including schools themselves, but also families, neighborhoods, health care, and childcare access—a fact that Coleman knew and carefully navigated in his report to Congress. Instead, information about students' rates of learning would eventually be necessary to address the question of whether schools served to reduce or exacerbate achievement equality.

A second issue related to the structure of Coleman's dataset. To get clearance from what later became the U.S. Office of Management and Budget, a body that oversees the manner in which federally funded researchers may conduct business in schools, the EEOS team could not link students to their teachers, only to the schools they attended.[8] Although Coleman had measured teacher knowledge on a thirty-question SAT-like test, and school-average teacher scores did correlate with student test scores, that correlation was small, and he could not identify the extent to which teachers overall—not just their test scores—contributed to students' outcomes. This problem was symptomatic of a wider issue, too, as the EEOS dataset could only correlate school-average resources and school-average student outcomes, rather than exploring how resources were differentially distributed among students within schools, for instance within ability groups or academic tracks.

The third problem with EEOS related to the relatively underdeveloped methods in the social sciences for answering complex questions. Coleman conducted his analyses by reporting the extent to which school characteristics and student background variables generally explained why some students scored well and others poorly. This technique was roundly criticized by the Harvard seminar attendants and rapidly replaced with methods popular in economics that estimated the relationship between achievement and *specific* school and student background characteristics, and that allowed for testing to see whether each characteristic's relationship to student outcomes was larger than what could reasonably be explained by chance alone. Techniques for properly handling missing data—extensive in the EEOS dataset—did not appear until the 1970s (Schafer and Graham 2002). Even a lack of computing power played a role; Coleman's IBM-7094 at Johns Hopkins had strained mightily to churn out the relatively simple statistics it did produce (Grant 1973); only in the 1980s did computing power and statistical software become available to run more complex models.

A fourth problem concerned what the EEOS did—and did not—measure. The main student outcomes were basic tests of vocabulary, comprehension, and computation, rather than a more robust set of indicators of student success (say, for instance, "grit" or high school graduation). And the indicators of school quality tended toward easily counted objects, like the number of books in the library or whether the school had a science lab. In a recent interview, Jencks described the sense of the seminar on this point: "Everybody knew you had to worry about the things that were left out. You had to be a moron not to know that, 'Well, if you're looking at the class size, there's a lot of things that probably go with that and they might be what's explaining what looks like an effective class size and so forth.'"[9]

Participants in the Harvard seminar argued over these issues and more. Remarkably, however, at the end of the day their collective reanalyses largely showed that Coleman's original findings stood: schools appeared to exert relatively little pull—explaining only 10 to 20 percent of the variability in student outcomes—while family background, peers, and students' own academic self-concept explained much more of the variability in test scores (Smith 1972).

Yet the process of critiquing, reanalyzing, and, ultimately, inventing helped seminar attendees and others to shape the path that the larger field of education research took forward. Over the years, the federal government funded and collected an alphabet soup of new datasets—High School and Beyond (HSB), National Longitudinal Study (NLS), and several waves of later data collected under the moniker Early Childhood Longitudinal Study (ECLS). These datasets tracked students over time, better allowing scholars to separate home and school effects. Scholars cast about for methodologies that would solve the EEOS report's analytic problems, then applied them to these datasets. And new thinking about how schools, classrooms, and families contributed to child outcomes led to innovative and improved measures—in fact, almost as many measures as there were assistant professors to write papers about them. Cohen summarized: "From one perspective, the EEOS was a very, very clumsy and crude instrument, and probably not to be believed. But from another perspective, even if that was true, it set off a whole stream of research, which greatly improved the understanding of how schools do work."[10]

School Resources and Student Outcomes

Scholars focused on improving the measurement of what the field calls *purchased school inputs*—what Coleman had explored in the EEOS data and found largely unrelated to student outcomes. Throughout the 1970s and 1980s, scholars, mostly economists, found new things to count and more accurate ways to count them (for a review, see Monk 1992). Coleman's measures related to spending, for instance, had been obtained only at the district level, yet considerable evidence existed that schools' funding levels differed within districts, and economists obtained and analyzed such data. Some studies even followed the dollars within schools, measuring the number of square feet in classrooms, the number and types of books in classroom libraries, and the journals that teachers read (e.g., Thomas and Kemmerer 1983). "We've gotten much more sophisticated about our ability to match resources to the individual students who are exposed to them," said Aaron Pallas, a sociologist at Teachers College, Columbia University.[11]

Yet even with better measurement techniques, more complete datasets, and more sophisticated modeling techniques, dozens of studies conducted through the late 1990s failed to consistently link tangible school inputs to student test scores (see, e.g., Hanushek [2003] for a review and Rebell [this volume for an overview of how these arguments have played out in states' school finance court cases). Schools in impoverished communities are demonstrably worse, in terms of facilities, access to textbooks, and many measures of teacher quality, than schools serving nonimpoverished communities. Standing alone, the relationships appear quite consistent. However, once controlled for family background and students' previous-year test scores, allowing analysts to estimate how the resources influenced student test score gains, the relationship typically disappeared.

"At some level, money does matter. You can't run a school without a building, a teacher, and a textbook. And maybe an iPad," remarked Eric Hanushek of Stanford University. But based on the lack of a relationship between resources and student outcomes, said Hanushek, simply adding more money to schools is unlikely to raise performance. "You can't just write a bigger check to each school and expect to get much out of it, because there's no evidence, on average, that schools will find good ways to use that money."[12] To many, Hanushek's assertion makes sense: measures of countable things—the age of books, the condition of the school, class size, and even teachers' salaries and certification—do not capture what happens in the classroom. In my own work, I have seen many skilled, committed, and compassionate teachers do excellent work despite poor facilities and large class sizes.

By 2000, scholars had moved toward a new view of resources, arguing that how schools use dollars to create learning opportunities for students appears to matter more than the mere presence of dollars (Cohen, Raudenbush, and Ball 2003; Hanushek 1996). For instance, recent studies have suggested that adopting effective curriculum materials and helping teachers to learn to use them show consistently positive effects (e.g., Llosa et al. 2016; Penuel, Gallagher, and Moorthy 2011; Roschelle et al. 2010; Saxe, Gearhart, and Nasir 2001). Dollars, steered toward the right purchased school inputs, do make a difference.

Yet even here, the ability of resources to explain gaps in student outcomes is limited. For the average student, the difference between an effective and ineffective instructional program is about one-tenth of a standard deviation, which corresponds to roughly one-tenth of the black-white achievement gap on most standardized tests (Lipsey et al. 2012). To fully explain achievement gaps, scholars began formulating complex models that took into account both school and nonschool factors.

Family and Community Contexts

One set of factors that did explain student outcomes, with force, was *family background*—a term scholars use to refer to factors including race and ethnicity as well as parental income and education. Coleman's analysis showed that despite that parents of all races held similar educational aspirations for their children (for more, see N. Hill, Jeffries, and Murray, this volume), race-based differences in academic achievement not only existed but were in fact quite large in the first grade. Again and again over the subsequent decades, scholars replicated Coleman's finding. Federal data collected in 2010, for instance, showed the average black child roughly one-half of a standard deviation behind the average white child in mathematics at kindergarten entry, and one-third of a standard deviation behind in reading (Quinn 2015). Comparisons of families in the top and bottom of the income distribution found similar gaps.

These differences were striking and occurred, obviously, prior to any formal schooling. As better datasets and more advanced statistical models became available in the decades after the EEOS, scholars set to work identifying and evaluating potential explanations for these gaps. One such explanation refers to genetic differences among children: a fair portion of intelligence is inherited, and perhaps low-income or minority children were less lucky in terms of their genetic endowment. Yet rigorous studies of intelligence and genetics discount such a theory, as does evidence from intelligence tests performed with infants.

An example from the Early Childhood Longitudinal Study–Kindergarten Cohort (ECLS-K) illustrates the latter point. Using this nationally representative sample of children tracked from birth through age five, Roland Fryer and Stephen Levitt (2013) show that the average black-white difference in nine-month-olds' mental functioning—a metric that measures infants' exploration, expressive babbling, and problem-solving—was about one-tenth the typical differences found by kindergarten, almost vanishingly small in absolute size. When the authors used statistical techniques to account for differences in family demographics and children's home environments, the relationship became even smaller; when the authors further accounted for children's birthweight and prematurity in their analyses, the direction of the relationship flipped, nominally favoring black children over white. By the time children were two years of age, however, the situation looked markedly different according to Fryer and Levitt's analysis. At that age, the typical black-white score difference had grown to about half the size of the kindergarten gap, with the difference favoring white children. Controlling for home environment, birthweight, and family demographics, however, only halved the size of the gap, rather than reversed it. Asian and Hispanic toddlers also showed a similar disadvantage versus white toddlers (Fryer and Levitt 2013).

The appearance of the achievement gap in the second year of life—and related evidence that heredity has little to do with intelligence—led investigators to other potential explanations. "It's certainly the case that from birth, and actually before birth if you think about the prenatal environment that kids in different socioeconomic strata are exposed to, children have different challenges and opportunities to learn," said Greg Duncan, an economist at the University of California, Irvine, whose work has focused on explaining early childhood outcomes. "Over the course of five years up to kindergarten entry, these accumulate to very dramatic differences in both reading achievement and numeracy."[13]

The list of ways that family background influences student outcomes is long, including family income, family structure, and maternal depression (see Jackson, Kiernan, and McLanahan, this volume). Parenting practices form one conduit. Middle- and upper-income parents tend to be more authoritative, setting boundaries but explaining those boundaries to their children, responding to their needs, and encouraging independence and growth—all activities made easier by the time and peace of mind that money can supply. Low-income parents tend to be more authoritarian, emphasizing rules and punishing disobedience. There's some sense that this approach may be adaptive to families' context, says Peg Burchinal, an early childhood researcher at the University of North Carolina: "If you live in inner city Baltimore, it's really important that the child do the right thing at the right time or that child could end up dead."[14]

Parents living at or below the poverty level also typically have less time to engage in activities that lead to positive school outcomes—reading storybooks, tracking schoolwork, and even just carrying on extended conversations with children—and are less likely themselves to have been raised in households that featured these parenting activities. Kraft and Monti-Nussbaum (this volume) explored a low-cost intervention designed to promote these literacy skills during the summer months. Poverty and its related stressors also appear to double the incidence of maternal depression, which itself has been further negatively linked to child pre-K outcomes. Immigrant status may also shape parental engagement, as detailed in Liu and White (this volume). Says Burchinal: "If you're very secure economically, it's very easy to devote time to your children. If you are worried about every aspect of your life, your relationship, your income, your relationships with your employer, it's very difficult."[15]

Family income—how many dollars a family accumulates, and what those dollars can purchase in families' neighborhoods—forms another conduit between social status and student outcomes. Dollars buy childcare of either better or worse quality, and although low-income families' access to better quality care has increased in the past three decades with the expansion of subsidized childcare, Head Start, and district-based pre-K programs, says Burchinal, these programs often differ from those available in more affluent communities. In programs serving high-income families, teachers tend to engage in extended conversations with children and to design classroom activities with an eye toward enhancing child development in the long term. In programs serving low-income families, these elements are less often present.[16] Dollars also enable families to purchase child enrichment activities: Duncan estimates that families earning $25,000 a year spend roughly $1,300 per child per year on summer camp, vacations, outings, and educational programming; families earning $135,000 a year spend almost ten times that amount.[17]

Perhaps unsurprisingly, once scholars correct for these economic differences among families, including income, the black-white test score gap diminishes in size, and sometimes reverses in direction. Fryer and Levitt showed in a 2004 study that black students outperform whites on reading at kindergarten entry once only a relatively small set of family background factors is taken into account. In the preschool years, income—and, by extension, the wider set of social background characteristics associated with families —appears to be a driving factor in children's outcomes.

Schools and Schooling

Once in school, students experience the influence of both families and schools, yet identifying the unique effect of each was largely out of scholars' grasp in the first decades after the EEOS. Although most scholars and policy-makers intuitively believed that schools and teachers led students to learn—for lack of a better word—"stuff," the scholarly archives were far from teeming with evidence regarding schools' impact on students' cognitive growth. This situation even led several prominent sociologists of education to publish a paper in 1985 looking for proof that schools caused students to learn *at all*. (The answer? Yes; see Alexander, Natriello, and Pallas 1985.)

Meanwhile, however, educational statisticians were fashioning a new way to think about and model the effect of schools and teachers on student learning. The EEOS and similar studies had correlated tangible school resources with student outcomes, finding few relationships. Yet the data also suggested substantial differences among schools that could not be explained by observed differences in resources. Thus, beginning in the 1980s, scholars began to ask whether and how much assigning students to school A versus school B versus school C (and so on) might impact their test scores, and to use statistical models appropriate to answering this question.

A hypothetical walk through what statisticians call "student growth curves"— student test performance plotted over time—helps to illustrate this modeling technique. Say that plots of hundreds of elementary students' performance over the early grades show that students gain, on average, seven or eight points every year. In late elementary and the middle school years, students learn, on average, only five or six points each year, leading to a downward bend (deceleration) in average student growth rate. Now say that grouping these children by school, as this modeling technique can do, shows that students in school A gain one extra point per year while students in school B grow only at the sample average. Further, students in school A may experience less deceleration of their growth in the later grades than school B. By doing this over enough students and schools, these models estimate the extent to which students' school assignments deflect them from typical growth patterns.

Initial findings from such models agreed with the 1966 Coleman estimates regarding the influence of schools on student outcomes. Tony Bryk and Stephen Raudenbush, who literally wrote the book on these newer modeling methods, used another Coleman dataset, an early version of the statistical techniques in 1988, to show that differences among schools accounted for about 21 percent of the variability in student outcomes, an upper bound that has held over the years, even through marked improvements to the modeling techniques (Bryk and Raudenbush 1988). In another two decades, experiments using lottery data from oversubscribed urban schools—in other words, the most desirable schools in the eyes of city parents—began to clarify the size of this advantage. In a study of oversubscribed Boston charters, for instance, economists estimated that these schools made up between one-half and two-thirds of the black-white test score gap each year of middle school (Angrist et al. 2016). In New York, newly configured small high schools improved students' probability of high school graduation by nearly 7 percent (Bloom, Thompson, and Unterman 2010).

What drives these schools and other high performers is still a matter of debate. Both early and recent evidence suggests that successful schools meet the most basic needs of their inhabitants: students and faculty report feeling safe, teachers have high expectations for students, and students attend to their studies seriously (Ingersoll 2001; Purkey and Smith 1983). Many of the urban charters included in lottery studies have a "no excuses" philosophy, which focuses on maximizing instructional time, minimizing behavioral disruptions, and improving test scores. Beyond this, key school characteristics have been hard to measure. Many of these characteristics—school trust, teacher collaboration, principal leadership, teacher working conditions, teacher efficacy, academic optimism—appear to positively predict student outcomes, but studies have yet to understand whether these are related to or distinct from one another, and which are causally related to student outcomes.

Yet whether anyone can explain it, something associated with differences between schools *does* appear to explain student outcomes. But this research has also shown that in the context of the overall variability in child outcomes, schools still pack a weaker punch than many imagine. Even in the most sophisticated models, differences in family background, students' intelligence, temperaments, and childhood experiences explained the majority—and in some datasets, the vast majority—of children's trajectories across the school years. Bryk and Raudenbush's (1988) methodology, when applied to datasets available in the 1980s and 1990s, also generally failed to disentangle child- and school-level contributions to growth in educational inequality.

Summer Recess

To complete the disentangling, scholars made clever use of an artifact of the U.S. school system: summer recess. Observing students' academic growth over the summer, reasoned sociologists like Barbara Heyns, author of an influential early study on this topic (Heyns 1978), provides insight into how students' natural rates of learning differ by race and social class. Comparing these summer benchmarks to the corresponding school-year rates of growth would make visible the unique impact of schools.

Although Heyns and others had designed studies based on this logic since the 1970s, the best datasets for answering these questions were not created until nearly 30 years later, when the 1999 ECLS followed a nationally representative sample of children through their first years of school. A second ECLS began tracking a new cohort of kindergartners in 2010.[18] Both studies tested young students in the fall and spring, a key condition for differentiating summer from school-year growth. Analyses of both clearly show that students steadily learn during the school year, but that the rate of learning drops to zero in some subjects and grades over the summer recess (Downey, von Hippel, and Broh 2004; Quinn et al. 2016). Schools, when all is said and done, are fairly effective in teaching students at least some math, reading, and science each year.

Answering the question about the role of schools in social stratification required asking how student growth rates differed over time. One version of this question simply focuses on the dispersion of student growth rates, regardless of student background: when plotted over time, do kids' growth rates look more parallel to one another during the school year as opposed to the summer? The answer is yes—during the school year, student growth resembles telephone wires tracking steadily up a hill. During the summer months, however, those learning rates resemble more of a fan, with some children learning quickly, others not at all, and still others losing ground. Schools reduce overall variability in academic outcomes by making students' growth look more similar during the school year than over the summer (Downey, von Hippel, and Broh 2004).

A second version of this question focuses on the role of family income and parental education in explaining these summer and school year growth rates. Here, the results are again unequivocal. Douglas Downey, a sociologist at Ohio State University who has conducted the most extensive work on seasonal differences in children's growth rates, reports that "The best evidence suggests that schools reduce those [income] gaps. We observe the gaps in reading and math skills grow in the summer when students are not in school, and then those gaps don't change much while school is in session."[19] In other words, the students losing ground during the summer tend to come from poor families; children in nonpoor families either hold their ground or gain, probably owing to the array of resources nonpoor families marshal both within and outside the home. Schools, somewhat remarkably given the wide differences in resources across schools, notes Downey, manage to make advantaged and disadvantaged students' rates of growth more similar to one another during the academic year.

Skeptics argue that the school-year parallel lines do not necessarily mean schools are compensatory; parallel does not close the achievement gap. But Downey and others disagree. If children did not attend schools at all—a seemingly ridiculous counterfactual, but arguably the correct one if the question of interest is the impact of schooling on inequality—students' growth rates would continue fanning out indefinitely, and where children ended up in the fan would be heavily determined by their family background. U.S. elementary schools, in other words, compensate for the disadvantages experienced by poor children.

For race and ethnicity, the story is more complicated. In Downey, von Hippel, and Broh's 2004 analysis of the original ECLS, African American children's rate of learning (corrected for family income) kept pace with whites over the summer, but fell about 10 percent behind during the school year. An analysis of a more recent wave of ECLS data by David Quinn and colleagues suggests that African American children learn more rapidly than or at the same pace as white students in some grades and subjects, but lag in others (Quinn et al. 2016).

Similar to the story on why some schools perform better than others, there are no clear-cut explanations for these slower school-year growth rates among African Americans and Latinos. Coleman's report pointed to peer effects—essentially the impact of attending school with other students of similar academic background and ambitions—but many other explanations might hold: a slower-paced curriculum, lower-quality instruction, lower teacher expectations, implicit racism. The explanations may be interactive—characteristics of schools, neighborhoods (as shown in Pelletier and Manna, this volume), and related social institutions, such as the criminal justice system, that combine to negatively impact student outcomes (as shown in Haskins, this volume). It is likely that sorting among these explanations will take yet another set of studies and measures.

The data also tell an interesting story regarding another ethnic group. "There's a hint that schools are potentially not a favorable institution for Asian Americans," said Downey. "This is puzzling, because Asian Americans perform well in schools on average. Is their performance good *because* of schools or *in spite* of schools?" The seasonal comparisons seem to be trending toward the "in spite of" explanation: in both ECLS cohorts, Asian American students' summer growth rates are often stronger than white students', but Asian American students' growth either resembles or even lags behind whites' during the school year. Downey continued: "There may be some processes in schools that are undermining the gains of Asian American students. What exactly those are—it's kind of speculation."[20]

One explanation may be an artifact of the ways schools compensate for out-of-school social inequality. Downey notes that schools classify students by age into grades, then teach them a common curriculum regardless of child ability level—a process likely to help low-performing students by simply exposing them to grade-level content, and also to stymie high-performers' growth by returning them to material they have already mastered. In surveys and interviews, most teachers also report directing most of their attention to struggling children rather than high performers—another compensatory mechanism (Booher-Jennings 2005; Loveless, Parkas, and Duffett 2008). Thus, Asian Americans, who arrive in kindergarten far ahead of their non-Asian peers, may see their school-year growth slowed by these same forces that boost low-income children's achievement.

Educational Inequality and Public Policy

The narrative describing schools as equalizers differs considerably from that in public discourse, which often focuses on schools' shortcomings. Adam Gamoran, a sociologist who is now the president of the William T. Grant Foundation, explained why: "People focus on raw numbers. We look at schools for poor kids and rich kids, and we see that achievement rates are different. Graduation rates are different. College-going rates are different. And then we simply attribute those differences to schools."[21] Aaron Pallas of Teachers College agrees: "Seeing a spanking new building and a falling apart building," said Pallas, "those inequalities are more visible than the inequalities that come from being in school vs. not being in school."[22]

Another reason for the mismatch between the academic and public images of schooling may be that high schools, which include the years most vividly remembered by students and most proximal to students' labor market entry, may exacerbate inequality. Without fall/spring testing, as is done in ECLS, said Gamoran, "we don't know as much about growth and inequality for kids out of elementary school."[23] The best evidence that exists suggests that high schools in Texas and Massachusetts are largely neutral regarding inequality, with traditionally advantaged students only slightly more likely to attend high schools that are better at boosting student achievement (Jennings et al. 2015).

Yet Gamoran's and others' research on the effects of high school tracking, the practice of separating students into general, advanced, and remedial courses, shows that this practice tends to exacerbate within-school racial and income inequality (for a recent review, see Gamoran 2009). Whether student assignments to tracks are themselves overtly racially biased or they simply result from prior student achievement patterns is a topic on which scholars have waged long and loud arguments. But income, race, and ethnicity are correlated with track assignment, and students in higher tracks have opportunities to learn more challenging content from more qualified teachers, resulting in inequality in growth rates. Other recent data show that high school students' access to Advanced Placement courses varies by the racial, ethnic, and income composition of the schools that they attend—gaps very much similar in size to those reported by Coleman 50 years ago (U.S. Department of Education, Office of Civil Rights 2016).

This points to the role that social choices play in the production of inequality. Tracking is viewed as a way to ensure that instruction matches students' prior skill level and to prepare qualified students for the demands of college; middle school marks the beginning of mathematics tracking in most districts and humanities tracking in some (Loveless 2013). Exposing all students to a similar curriculum over those middle years, however, is a viable option; curricular differentiation could still occur in high school, and delaying tracking would preserve the equalizing effects of schools over the early adolescent period. Yet this is not a choice most states and districts make. Similarly, Johnson and Wagner (this volume) show that year-round schools can mitigate neighborhood-based stratification of test scores. Major changes to the school calendar and school funding, and enhanced services to schools, however, are difficult choices for localities to make.

The same can be said of the targeting of resources to at-risk students, though Gamoran agrees that general infusions of money appear not to matter: "Additional resources, wisely spent, can make a difference."[24] Separate studies by Fryer and Gamoran, for instance, have found that allocating enhanced services to schools, including intensive school-based tutoring and social services programs, appear to help return many low-performing students to close to grade-level norms (Fryer 2014; Gamoran and An 2016).

The United States makes social choices regarding families and early childhood as well. Downey points to a recent study that uncovered a modest gap between U.S. and Canadian high school sophomores on the test associated with the Programme for International Student Assessment (PISA). The author of this study, Joseph Merry, also compared Canadian and U.S. children in their late preschool years on the Peabody Picture Vocabulary Test, a standard assessment used to measure children's reading aptitude. The United States–Canada gap near kindergarten entry? The exact same size.

"That suggests to me that it's easier to be poor in Canada than in the U.S. I don't think Canadian kids are ahead of us for genetic reasons; Canada has made a wide range of social policy decisions differently," said Downey. "The kind of society that we live in really shapes what we see at kindergarten entry. And we can make policy decisions that change that."[25] Such policy decisions would surely have to address income inequality, which itself is related to a complex set of social factors. Recent studies strongly suggest continuing racism in private firms' hiring and landlords' rental decisions, for instance (for a review, see Bertrand and Duflo 2017), and minimum-wage jobs fall far short of allowing parents to provide the support they desire for their children. Such policy decisions would also surely have to encourage a more robust social safety net for struggling families, as detailed in Riehl and Lyon's article (this volume) on cross-sector collaborations.

Such a wide-ranging discussion of the role of schools, families, race, and public policy choices would be unusual in U.S. education politics today. In the years since Coleman's report, public debates about solutions to poverty have narrowed, and academics have become shy of stating any position with what Coleman once called "illiberal implications" (Coleman 1975). But widening the debate, and more accurately rendering public assessments about the role of schooling in students' academic outcomes, is necessary to stop blaming schools and families separately and to understand the path forward. Schools can mitigate social inequality, but they govern only a fraction of students' lives and eventual outcomes. Families matter, and families are profoundly shaped by the contexts in which they find themselves. Finding policy solutions that work in both realms presents the challenge that the next generation of scholars must solve.

Notes

1. David K. Cohen (John Dewey Professor of Education, University of Michigan), interview with the author, June 22, 2008, Cambridge, MA.

2. Ibid.

3. Christopher Jencks (Malcolm Wiener Professor of Social Policy, Kennedy School of Government, Harvard University), interview with the author, March 19, 2010, Cambridge, MA.

4. Marshall (Mike) Smith (senior fellow, Carnegie Foundation for the Advancement of Teaching), interview with the author, June 14, 2010, Washington, DC.

5. For a review of early research, see Stodolsky and Lesser (1967).

6. Smith, interview.

7. Eric Hanushek (Paul and Jean Hanna Senior Fellow, Hoover Institution, Stanford University), interview with the author, March 3, 2010, Washington, DC.

8. Cohen, interview.

9. Jencks, interview.

10. Cohen, interview.

11. Aaron Pallas (Arthur I. Gates Professor of Sociology and Education, Teachers College, Columbia University), interview with the author, April 20, 2016.

12. Hanushek, interview.

13. Greg Duncan (distinguished professor, University of California, Irvine), interview with the author, April 13, 2016.

14. Margaret Burchinal (senior scientist, Frank Porter Graham Child Development Institute), interview with the author, April 13, 2016.

15. Ibid.

16. Ibid.

17. Duncan, interview.

18. Both datasets and accompanying documentation can be found at https://nces.ed.gov/ecls/.

19. Douglas Downey (professor of sociology, Ohio State University), interview with the author, April 15, 2016.

20. Ibid.

21. Adam Gamoran (president, William T. Grant Foundation), interview with the author, April 18, 2016.

22. Pallas, interview.

23. Gamoran, interview.

24. Gamoran, interview.

25. Downey, interview.

References

Alexander, Karl L., Gary Natriello, and Aaron M. Pallas. 1985. For whom the school bell tolls: The impact of dropping out on cognitive performance. *American Sociological Review* 50 (3): 409–20.

Angrist, Joshua D., Sarah R. Cohodes, Susan M. Dynarski, Parag A. Pathak, and Christopher R. Walters. 2016. Stand and deliver: Effects of Boston's charter high schools on college preparation, entry, and choice. *Journal of Labor Economics* 34 (2): 275–318.

Bertrand, Marianne, and Esther Duflo. 2017. Field experiments on discrimination. In *Handbook of economic field experiments*, eds. Esther Duflo and Abhijit Banerjee, 309–84. Amsterdam: Elsevier.

Bloom, Howard S., Saskia Levy Thompson, and Rebecca Unterman. 2010. *Transforming the high school experience: How New York City's new small schools are boosting student achievement and graduation rates*. New York, NY: MDRC.

Booher-Jennings, Jennifer. 2005. Below the bubble: "Educational triage" and the Texas accountability system. *American Educational Research Journal* 42 (2): 231–68.

Bryk, Anthony S., and Stephen W. Raudenbush. 1988. Toward a more appropriate conceptualization of research on school effects: A three-level hierarchical linear model. *American Journal of Education* 97 (1): 65–108.

Cohen, David K., Stephen W. Raudenbush, and Deborah Loewenberg Ball. 2003. Resources, instruction, and research. *Educational Evaluation and Policy Analysis* 25 (2): 119–42.

Coleman, James S. 1961. *The adolescent society*. Westport, CT: Greenwood Press.

Coleman, James S. 1966. *Equality of educational opportunity*. Washington, DC: National Center for Educational Statistics.

Coleman, James S. 1975. Social research and advocacy: A response to Young and Bress. *The Phi Delta Kappan* 57 (3): 166–69.

Downey, Douglas B., Paul T. von Hippel, and Beckett A. Broh. 2004. Are schools the great equalizer? Cognitive inequality during the summer months and the school year. *American Sociological Review* 69 (5): 613–35.

Fryer, Roland G., Jr. 2014. Injecting charter school best practices into traditional public schools: Evidence from field experiments. *Quarterly Journal of Economics* 129 (3): 1355–1407.

Fryer, Roland G., Jr., and Steven D. Levitt. 2004. Understanding the black–white test score gap in the first two years of school. *Review of Economics and Statistics* 86 (2): 447–64.

Fryer, Roland G., Jr., and Steven D. Levitt. 2013. Testing for racial differences in the mental ability of young children. *American Economic Review* 103 (2): 981–1005.

Gamoran, Adam. 2009. Tracking and inequality: New directions for research and practice. In *The Routledge international handbook of the sociology of education*, eds. Michael W. Apple, Stephen J. Ball, and Luis Armando Gaudin, 213–28. New York, NY: Routledge.

Gamoran, Adam, and Brian P. An. 2016. Effects of school segregation and school resources in a changing policy context. *Educational Evaluation and Policy Analysis* 38 (1): 43–64.

Grant, Gerald. 1973. Shaping social policy: The politics of the Coleman report. *Teachers College Record* 75 (1): 17–54.

Hanushek, Eric A. 1996. A more complete picture of school resource policies. *Review of Educational Research* 66 (3): 397–409.

Hanushek, Eric A. 2003. The failure of input-based schooling policies. *Economic Journal* 113 (485): F64–F98.

Haskins, Anna R. 2017. Paternal incarceration and children's schooling contexts: Intersecting inequalities of educational opportunities. *The ANNALS of the American Academy of Political and Social Science* (this volume).

Heyns, Barbara. 1978. *Summer learning and the effects of schooling*. New York, NY: Academic Press.

Hill, Nancy E., Julia R. Jeffries, and Kathleen Murray. 2017. New tools for old problems: Inequality and educational opportunity for ethnic minority youth and parents. *The ANNALS of the American Academy of Political and Social Science* (this volume).

Ingersoll, Richard M. 2001. Teacher turnover and teacher shortages: An organizational analysis. *American Educational Research Journal* 38 (3): 499–534.

Jackson, Margot, Kathleen Kiernan, and Sara McLanahan. 2017. Maternal education, changing family circumstances, and children's skill development in the United States and UK. *The ANNALS of the American Academy of Political and Social Science* (this volume).

Jennings, Jennifer L., David Deming, Christopher Jencks, Maya Lopuch, and Beth E. Schueler. 2015. Do differences in school quality matter more than we thought? New evidence on educational opportunity in the twenty-first century. *Sociology of Education* 88 (1): 56–82.

Johnson, Odis, Jr., and Michael Wagner. 2017. Equalizers or enablers of inequality? A counterfactual analysis of racial and residential test-score gaps in year-round and nine-month schools. *The ANNALS of the American Academy of Political and Social Science* (this volume).

Kilgore, Sally B. 2016. The life and times of James S. Coleman. *Education Next* 16 (2). Available from http://educationnext.org/life-times-james-s-coleman-school-policy-research/.

Kraft, Matthew A., and Manuel Monti-Nussbaum. 2017. Can schools empower parents to prevent summer learning loss? A text messaging field experiment to promote literacy skills. *The ANNALS of the American Academy of Political and Social Science* (this volume).

Lipsey, Mark W., Kelly Puzio, Cathy Yun, Michael A. Hebert, Kasia Steinka-Fry, Mikel W. Cole, Megan Roberts, Karen S. Anthony, and Matthew D. Busick. 2012. *Translating the statistical representation of the effects of education interventions into more readily interpretable forms* (NCESR 2013-3000). Washington, DC: National Center for Special Education Research, Institute of Education Sciences, U.S. Department of Education.

Liu, Zhen, and Michael J. White. 2017. Education outcomes of immigrant minority youth: The role of parental engagement. *The ANNALS of the American Academy of Political and Social Science* (this volume).

Llosa, Lorena, Okhee Lee, Feng Jiang, Alison Haas, Corey O'Connor, Christopher D. Van Booven, and Michael J. Kieffer. 2016. Impact of a large-scale science intervention focused on English language learners. *American Educational Research Journal* 53 (2): 395–424.

Loveless, Thomas. 2013. *The 2013 Brown Center report on American education: How well are American students learning?* Washington, DC: Brookings Institution Press.

Loveless, Tom, Steve Parkas, and Ann Duffett. 2008. *High-achieving students in the era of NCLB*. Washington, DC: Thomas B. Fordham Institute.

Monk, David H. 1992. Education productivity research: An update and assessment of its role in education finance reform. *Educational Evaluation and Policy Analysis* 14 (4): 307–32.

Pelletier, Elizabeth, and Paul Manna. 2017. Learning in harm's way: Neighborhood violence, inequality, and American schools. *The ANNALS of the American Academy of Political and Social Science* (this volume).

Penuel, William R., Lawrence P. Gallagher, and Savitha Moorthy. 2011. Preparing teachers to design sequences of instruction in earth systems science: A comparison of three professional development programs. *American Educational Research Journal* 48 (4): 996–1025.

Purkey, Stewart C., and Marshall S. Smith. 1983. Effective schools: A review. *Elementary School Journal* 83 (4): 427–52.

Quinn, David M. 2015. Kindergarten black–white test score gaps: Re-examining the roles of socioeconomic status and school quality with new data. *Sociology of Education* 88 (2): 120–39.

Quinn, David M., North Cooc, Joe McIntyre, and Celia J. Gomez. 2016. Seasonal dynamics of academic achievement inequality by socioeconomic status and race/ethnicity: Updating and extending past research with new national data. *Educational Researcher* 45 (8): 443–53.

Rebell, Michael A. 2017. The courts' consensus: Money does matter for educational opportunity. *The ANNALS of the American Academy of Political and Social Science* (this volume).

Riehl, Carolyn, and Melissa A. Lyon. 2017. Counting on context: Cross-sector collaborations for education and the legacy of James Coleman's sociological vision. *The ANNALS of the American Academy of Political and Social Science* (this volume).

Roschelle, Jeremy, Nicole Shechtman, Deborah Tatar, Stephen Hegedus, Bill Hopkins, Susan Empson, Jennifer Knudsen, and Lawrence P. Gallagher. 2010. Integration of technology, curriculum, and professional development for advancing middle school mathematics: Three large-scale studies. *American Educational Research Journal* 47 (4): 833–78.

Saxe, Geoffrey B., Maryl Gearhart, and Na'ilah Suad Nasir. 2001. Enhancing students' understanding of mathematics: A study of three contrasting approaches to professional support. *Journal of Mathematics Teacher Education* 4 (1): 55–79.

Schafer, Joseph L., and John W. Graham. 2002. Missing data: Our view of the state of the art. *Psychological Methods* 7 (2): 147–77.

Smith, Marshall S. 1972. *Equality of educational opportunity: The basic findings reconsidered*. Cambridge, MA: Center for Educational Policy Research, Harvard Graduate School of Education.

Stodolsky, Susan, and Gerald Lesser. 1967. Learning patterns in the disadvantaged. *Harvard Educational Review* 37 (4): 546–93.

Thomas, J. Alan, and Frances Kemmerer. 1983. *Money, time and learning. Final report*. Washington, DC: National Institute of Education.

U.S. Department of Education, National Center for Education Statistics. 2014. *Digest of education statistics*. Available from https://nces.ed.gov/programs/digest/d14/tables/dt14_326.20.asp.

U.S. Department of Education, National Center for Education Statistics. 2015. *Digest of education statistics*. Available from https://nces.ed.gov/programs/digest/d15/tables/dt15_326.10.asp.

U.S. Department of Education, National Center for Education Statistics. 2016. *Digest of education statistics*. Available from https://nces.ed.gov/programs/digest/d16/tables/dt16_302.60.asp.

U.S. Department of Education, Office of Civil Rights. 2016. *2013–2014 civil rights data collection: A first look*. Washington, DC: U.S. Department of Education, Office of Civil Rights.

Education Outcomes of Immigrant Youth: The Role of Parental Engagement

By
ZHEN LIU
and
MICHAEL J. WHITE

Using the 2009 to 2012 waves of the High School Longitudinal Survey, this article examines the role of parental engagement in academic achievement in the United States. Specifically, we examine the influence of parental engagement while also investigating the academic trajectories of racial/ethnic and immigrant groups, controlling for other standard factors. Results suggest that the progression of students' academic performance varies substantially by race/ethnicity and by immigrant generational status. After controlling for ninth-grade test scores and family and other school-level characteristics, we find that first-generation immigrant youth generally have higher eleventh-grade test scores and lower probability of dropping out compared to native-born students who are second or third generation. Greater levels of parental engagement predict superior test scores and lower rates of dropout for youth of various racial and immigrant generation backgrounds, even in the presence of a variety of controls.

Keywords: immigrant minority youth; educational outcomes; parental engagement

The proportion of children in immigrant families in the United States has increased dramatically during the past two decades. The percentage of children with one or more foreign-born parents has increased to approximately 25.5 percent of all children under age 18 in 2015 (Migration Policy Institute 2017). As more and

Zhen Liu is a PhD candidate in the Department of Sociology at Brown University and an adjunct research fellow at the Asia Demographic Research Institute. Her current work examines assimilation of children in immigrant families in the United States and the impacts of internal migration on children in China.

Michael J. White is the Turner Distinguished Professor of Population Studies at Brown University, where he also directs Spatial Structures in the Social Sciences. White is author (with J. Glick) of Achieving Anew *(Russell Sage Foundation 2009). He also edited the* International Handbook of Population Distribution and Migration *(Springer 2016).*

Correspondence: zhen_liu@brown.edu

DOI: 10.1177/0002716217730009

more immigrants from Latin America and Asia have come to the United States and have settled in new immigrant destinations (places that previously had very little immigration), both the composition and geographic distribution of immigrants has become more diverse (Fischer 2010; Donato et al. 2008; Iceland 2009; Lichter and Johnson 2009; Lichter 2012; Logan and Zhang 2010). The impact of increasing numbers of first- and second-generation immigrant children on school systems is also felt by communities across a broader set of geographic contexts, particularly those new destinations in small cities or rural places that are adapting to absorb children from immigrant families (Fischer 2010). Consequently, the educational outcomes of children of recent immigrants has attracted increasing attention from social researchers, since educational attainment is so closely linked to perceived upward immigrant mobility and assimilation (Alba and Nee 2009; Hirschman 2001; Portes and Rumbaut 2001; White and Glick 2009).

The original concerns of James Coleman, seen in the range of his work from the 1966 Coleman Report itself (Coleman et al. 1966), through the longitudinal analysis of the 1980s, are also manifest in our work. What has changed since that time is the composition of American schools, which now reflect the increasing diversity of the U.S. population, driven by immigration. In this article, our analysis and approach owes much to that of Coleman; in fact, we use a longitudinal U.S. educational dataset—the High School Longitudinal Study—a successor to the High School and Beyond study, the source for Coleman's work in the 1980s on schooling and achievement (Coleman, Hoffer, and Kilgore 1982; Coleman and Hoffer 1989).

This new immigration and the varied performance of first- and second-generation students in U.S. schools further invigorates questions about the role of immigration and ethnicity in school achievement and suggests a reexamination of the mechanisms through which families and schools translate resources from one generation to the next. To be sure, how immigrants do and particularly how well the children of immigrants do in school or, in other words, whether they experience educational inequality, has sweeping consequences for educational policy and immigration policy in the United States and other immigrant-receiving nations.

Previous research has suggested various mechanisms for how race, ethnicity, generational status, and family resources may lead to disparate educational outcomes among children. Following the early Equality of Educational Opportunity study (Coleman Report) in 1966, there continued a long debate on how schools and family resources affect child well-being (Parcel, Dufer, and Zito 2010). The original Coleman Report argued for the importance of student background and family socioeconomic status in determining school achievement, whereas much prior discussion had emphasized inputs to the school environment itself. Coleman's

NOTE: This article and associated figures and tables have undergone disclosure review by the IES Data Security Office, U.S. Department of Education. Approval for dissemination was received on 23 August 2017. We are grateful to the Population Studies and Training Center at Brown University, which receives funding from the NIH (P2C HD041020), for general support. A previous version of this article was presented at the 2016 annual meetings of the Population Association of America in Washington, D.C. We thank Margot Jackson and Susan Moffitt and the external reviewers for their helpful comments.

own later writing questioned the advisability of the phrase "equality of educational opportunity," but did argue for refocusing the role of schooling to reduce inequality (Coleman 1975). Since that time many studies, including ours, have sought to determine the relative importance of various factors—family background, demography, student's in-school performance, peer characteristics, school organization— in predicting achievement within and beyond school. Coleman is also noted for his early and extensive attention to social capital (Coleman 1988). In an oft-observed phrase, Coleman argued that "social capital inheres in the structure of relations between actors and among actors" (Coleman 1988, S98). In our analysis, we give attention to the impact of "social capital" on educational outcomes while controlling for school-level characteristics, but in doing so, our approach concentrates on specific indicators of the parent-child relationship and parental school involvement (directly measured in the High School Longitudinal Survey [HSLS]) to capture elements of parental engagement.

There remains uncertainty about whether first- and second-generation individuals outperform or, instead, lag behind later-generation U.S.-born children in academic performance. Some researchers have found that children of immigrants, particularly some subgroups of East and Southeast Asian immigrants, are doing as well as or even better than their U.S.-born counterparts despite their low initial socioeconomic status and language barriers (Glick and White 2004; Kao 1995; Kao and Tienda 2005; Kao and Rutherford 2007; White and Glick 2000, 2009). Other researchers have found that children of immigrants, particularly second-generation Hispanic immigrants from Caribbean origins, are disadvantaged in terms of both family resources and economic resources and thus are experiencing downward assimilation (Portes and Rumbaut 2001, 2006; Portes and Vickstrom 2015; Portes and Fernández-Kelly 2008; Haller, Portes, and Lynch 2011). Moreover, it is unclear to what degree the variation in educational outcomes among youth of differing race/ethnicity/generation groups is due to differential family social capital.

Coleman (1988) argues that family background can be divided into three components: financial capital, human capital, and social capital (p. 109). Coleman (1988) also suggests that parental social capital reflected through time and effort that parents spend on children, or social capital of the family defined as (strong) relations between children and parents is essential for transferring human capital of parents to children and that human capital such as parents' education is relevant to children's educational growth only when it is complemented by social capital in the family. Parcel and Menaghan (1993) and Parcel and Dufur (2001) also provide empirical evidence for the positive impact of family social capital on child well-being. However, there might be significant differences in parental practices among race/ethnic groups, as well as differences between immigrant and native populations (Kao 2004a). Children in immigrant families might experience different levels and forms of family social capital in terms of parental interaction and parental school involvement due to cultural differences or language proficiency of immigrant parents (Kao 2004a; Kao and Rutherford 2007).

Using the 2009 and 2012 waves of the HSLS, we examine the extent to which parental engagement impacts high school students' academic performance and, further, the extent to which that impact varies by the race/ethnicity and generational status. In our approach, we consider the mediating effect of parental engagement on educational outcomes along race/ethnicity and immigrant generation lines. We consider the educational outcomes of high school dropout and standardized test score progression across waves of the survey. Parental engagement, which can be seen as a form of or linked to family social capital, is measured here through parental school involvement, parent-child communication, and parental participation in activities with students. This article refers to *first-generation students* as students who are born outside of the United States with foreign-born parents. *Second-generation students* refers to students who are born within the United States but with at least one foreign-born parent. *Third (or higher order)-generation students* refers to all students who are born in the United States to native-born parents. The use of two waves of the HSLS gives us the considerable advantage of longitudinal, nationally representative data— collected with the dedicated goal of measuring educational achievement—to investigate these issues.

Previous research has shown that the assimilation of immigrants and children of immigrants may not follow the same paths for all racial/ethnic groups. Parental engagement has long been identified as an important factor influencing educational achievement, but whether parental engagement, in terms of parent-child interaction and school involvement, operates differently by race/ethnicity and generation status remains unclear (Kao 2004a; Kao and Rutherford 2007). Thus, we also extend previous research by examining whether there are systematic differences in levels of parental engagement among racial/ethnic/generation groups and whether such groups of students experience differential returns to levels of parental school involvement, parent-child communication, and parent participation in activities with students.

In sum, this article aims to answer the following research questions: (1) What is the role of parental engagement in affecting educational performance (as measured by change in standardized math test scores from ninth to eleventh grade and dropout status)? (2) Does the effect of this engagement on educational outcomes differ by race/ethnicity and generational status? Figure 1 shows key presumed determinants of educational outcomes, with attention to the pathways through which race/ethnicity and generational status might affect those outcomes. We aim to understand the links between race/ethnicity/generational status and educational performance as well as the distinct and mediating effect of parental engagement on educational outcomes.

Parental Engagement and Education Outcomes

Parental engagement as a form of social capital

The concept of social capital has gained broad currency throughout the research and policy worlds. At the same time, what exactly constitutes social capital has been broadly interpreted (Bankston and Zhou 2002a, 2002b; Bankston 2004; Kao 2004b; Kao and Rutherford 2007; Turney and Kao 2009; Portes 2014).

FIGURE 1
How Race/Ethnicity, Generational Status, and Parental Engagement May Affect
Educational Outcomes

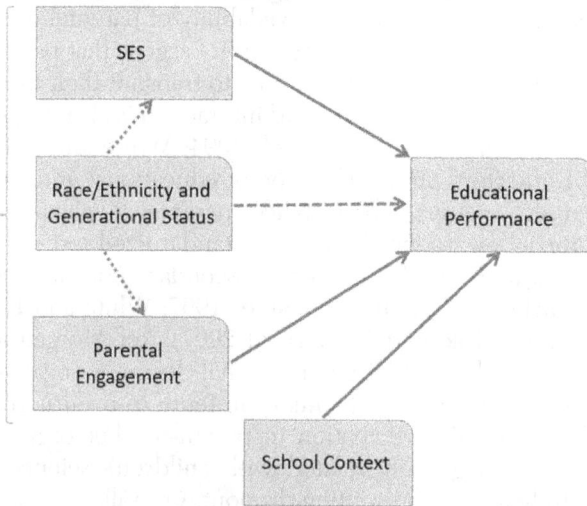

What is more, the application of the concept of social capital to immigrant and minority populations, while quite relevant, also enjoys no singular interpretation. The concept of social capital is widely recognized to originate in the work of Bourdieu and of Coleman (Portes 2000a, 2000b; Kao and Rutherford 2007). Both Bourdieu's and Coleman's definitions of social capital focus on the benefits of ties between individuals, though there is significant variation (Bourdieu 1985; Coleman 1993; Portes 2000b). As summarized by Portes (2000b, 2), sociologists have focused on exploring three aspects of social capital: social capital as "a source of social control," "a source of family-mediated benefits," and as "a source of resources mediated by nonfamily networks." It is noteworthy that Coleman's own theoretical treatise admits a key role for family ties among the features of social capital (Coleman 1990, 300 ff.). What is more, Coleman's empirical work on educational achievement quite explicitly discussed family social capital, even going so far as to provide an example of immigrant families harnessing family social capital to help a child do well in school (Coleman and Hoffer 1987, 223).

As a likely consequence of these various interpretations, there is no standard measure of social capital. The concept has been operationalized with various measures, such as community-level networks and interaction within families (Portes 2000b; Kao and Rutherford 2007). In studies of education outcomes, researchers have measured social capital using parent-school involvement (Kao and Rutherford 2007; White and Glick 2000; Yan 1999), intergenerational closure (Carbonaro 1998; Morgan and Sørensen 1999; Kao and Rutherford 2007; Portes 2000b), the parent-child relationship (Muller and Ellison 2001; Kao 2004a), intact families (White and Kaufman 1997), and networks in the community (Bankston and Zhou 2002a; Zhou and Kim 2006).

Our approach follows the reasoning of several scholars who suggest that parental engagement is likely to impact education outcomes, especially for children of immigrant families that are economically disadvantaged. For those groups faced with economic disadvantage, upward mobility and successful assimilation likely depends more on the availability of parental involvement and the wider set of social ties. Coleman (1988, 1991) argues that parent-child interactions and parental involvement help parents to transmit their human capital to children. The positive effect of parent-child interaction is also supported in other empirical work (Valenzuela and Dornbusch 1994; White and Glick 2000; Kao 2004a; Kao and Rutherford 2007). The type of educational outcomes and social capital measured also matters. For instance, parental involvement is found to have a positive impact on students' GPA and standardized test scores, continuation in high school, and enrollment in postsecondary education (Goyette and Conchas 2002; Teachman, Paasch, and Carver 1997; White and Kaufman 1997; White and Glick 2000; Kao and Rutherford 2007). Yet Morgan and Sørensen (1999) found that a high level of intergenerational closure is negatively associated with gains in math test scores of students from tenth to twelfth grades. McNeal (1999) found that parents' participation in parent-teacher organization (PTO) meetings in school is negatively related with children's science achievement though it seems to help with preventing dropout. Overall, previous studies provide mixed evidence on the impact of parental engagement on education outcomes, depending on both the type of parental engagement and the indicator of academic achievement used.

Varied levels of parental engagement and parenting styles by race/ethnicity and immigrant status

Previous studies not only suggest that parental engagement could impact education outcomes, but they also find that there are significant differences in parental practices among race/ethnic groups, as well as differences between immigrant and native populations. Many studies suggest that minority students, particularly minority first- and second-generation students, have lower access to parental social capital compared to white third- and higher-generation students with native-born parents (Sui-Chu and Willms 1996; Kao and Rutherford 2007). But at the same time, there is controversy on whether minority immigrant children indeed have less access to social capital, or they in fact possess more ethnic-specific social capital (Bankston and Zhou 2002a; Fuller and Hannum 2002; Kao 2004b; Lee and Zhou 2015; Zhou and Kim 2006). Zhou and Kim (2006) argue that ethnic social structures, namely, ethnic supplementary education in the Chinese and Korean immigrant communities and the associated ethnic social environments, are important factors contributing to the educational success of Asian immigrant children. Lee and Zhou (2015) suggest that high educational attainment among second-generation Asian students is partly due to a specific "success frame" that puts great emphasis on getting into elite universities and obtaining higher education. Also, this kind of success frame is reinforced within

Asian communities through supporting environments and resources such as college preparation courses and tutoring that might lead to better academic outcomes among Asian students. Lee and Zhou argue further that hyperselectivity, the very high degree of selection for favorable educational characteristics compared to those left behind, characterizes contemporary Asian immigration (Lee and Zhou 2015, 6). While Lee and Zhou concentrate on the case of Asian-origin persons, and while they argue that hypo-selectivity may operate for migrants from Mexico, some degree of positive selectivity for success, even across unobserved characteristics, may operate among several immigrant subpopulations. Both Sui-Chu and Willms (1996) and Kao (2004a) found that Asian parents have lower levels of involvement in school than whites, but they do not have significantly lower levels of school-related discussions. While direct measurement is not possible, one might speculate that those parent-child discussions convey the success frame, even when direct parental engagement in school itself is somewhat muted. Once again, the literature provides mixed evidence about whether immigrant and minority groups are disadvantaged in terms of levels of parental engagement, depending on the form of parental engagement being measured.

More pertinent to our current investigation, we know less about whether parental engagement has a more powerful mediating impact on education outcomes for one immigrant and/or minority group over others. Researchers have started to examine whether particular parenting practices are contributing to the seemingly remarkable academic performance of immigrant children, especially those of Asian origin, given their generally less advantaged socioeconomic status.

Although the literature on parenting styles is vast and there are numerous dimensions of parenting practices, in this article we focus on three aspects of parenting styles that are frequently used in literature and can be operationalized readily in the 2009–2012 HLLS: (1) parent *school involvement* (as measured by participation in school meetings and events), (2) parent-child interaction (measured as parent *extracurricular participation* in activities with their child), and (3) parent-child *communication* (as measured by discussions about school work, college, or careers; or personal problems with their child). These three indicators of involvement are all expected to help translate parental aspiration and resources into student education outcomes. Direct involvement in school programming both shows support for the value of education itself (joining a school fund-raiser) and provides a conduit for information about student performance (PTO meetings). Research suggests that direct communication between parent and child is beneficial for students' academic outcomes (Muller 1998; Glick and White 2004; Kao 2004a). Through open communication with parents, children can learn essential social skills to deal with problems at school or in relationships with peers. Kao (2004a) also argues that frequent discussion about school or college helps parents to communicate to children their educational aspirations. If parental aspiration is to positively influence academic performance, then discussion between parent and child is most likely essential for that aspiration to be realized. Interaction through participation matters as well. This aspect of parental engagement, such as attending museums or school science fairs, is shown to have a positive impact on students' educational outcomes by providing a supportive environment (Muller 1993).

Variation in parenting styles such as parent-child communication, parent participation in activities with students, and parental aspiration has been observed among racial groups and by generational status. Valenzuela and Dornbusch (1994) suggest that cultural differences in parenting style may account for some of the racial and ethnic disparities in educational achievement. Immigrant parents are often found to have high educational aspirations for their children compared to their native counterparts (Glick and White 2004; Kao 1995; Kao and Tienda 2005; Goyette and Xie 1999). But notably, Asian-origin parents are also less likely to share decision-making power with children or to communicate with children compared to white parents (Kao 2004a). It also may be the case that children of different racial groups respond differently to parenting styles. Dornbusch (1989) suggests that while authoritarian parenting is negatively associated with white students' grades, it is positively related to grades for Asian students. However, there is limited evidence on how parent-child discussion and parent participation in activities with students may operate differently among racial/ethnic groups and by generational status. The study by Kao (2004a) is one of the few that has attempted to examine whether children of different race/ethnicity and generation status may respond differently to a particular parent-child interaction. Using the National Education Longitudinal Survey of 1988 (NELS), Kao (2004a) found that while black and Hispanic students respond favorably to general discussions about school, Asian students respond negatively to general discussions about school. Also, discussions about college have a significant positive impact on GPA for Asian students but not for Hispanic or black students. Using the same NELS data, Kao and Rutherford (2007) found that immigrant and minority students experience different returns to parental-school involvement and intergenerational closure. However, neither of the two studies examines the impact of parental social capital on educational outcomes net of school effects. Therefore, our work aims to update and expand on Kao's (2004) and Kao and Rutherford's (2007) studies by incorporating more aspects of parental involvement into and including school-level contextual factors in our analysis.

Data and Methods

Data source

We use data from the 2009 and 2012 waves of the HSLS (HSLS:2009–2012; National Center for Education Statistics [NCES] 2013). The HSLS is a nationally representative study that began in fall 2009 with a cohort of more than 20,000 high school students in the ninth grade. The first follow-up was conducted in spring 2012 when students were in eleventh grade. The HSLS is a superior data source for two reasons. First, many previous studies have used the earlier rounds of similar national educational surveys conducted by NCES such as NELS 1988–2000 to study the relationship between education outcomes and parental engagement (Glick and White 2004; Kao 2004a; Kao and Rutherford 2007). By using the most up-to-date nationally representative survey on education outcomes conducted by the NCES, this article complements those earlier studies while also expanding the literature using the most recent evidence. Moreover, the HSLS 2009 wave collected richer information on parental involvement and participation than previous waves of national educational surveys. The goal of doing so was to understand students' educational trajectories such as how and why students choose certain college majors and careers; at the same time, such data provide a great resource for studying parental engagement and its effects.

Since our central concern is how parental engagement influences adolescents' educational performance, we limit our analysis to participants in the 2009 wave for whom their parents completed the companion parent survey. Many of the key independent variables of interest (parent-school involvement, parent-child communication, parent participation in students' extracurricular activities) are available only from the parent questionnaire. The base sample used for this study therefore includes 13,000 respondents (rounded) for whom values of all key variables are nonmissing. Our analyses are weighted in accordance with NSLS documentation recommendations. Summary statistics of the analytical sample are presented in Table 1.

Key variables

Educational outcomes. We examine two educational outcomes in this article: standardized math test scores (in the eleventh-grade follow-up wave) and dropout status (follow-up wave). The standardized math test score is chosen because it is comparable for measuring students' achievement across schools and states, since it is based on the same computer test given to all interviewees during the time of the survey, and it is standardized to a 100-point scale by the NCES, with a mean of 52 and standard deviation of 10. Dropout status is ascertained at the time of the follow-up survey. Students are asked whether they ever dropped out between the time of the first wave (when students are in ninth grade) and the follow up (when students are or would be in eleventh grade). We argue that it is important to measure both test scores and enrollment status, since they are indicators of different aspects of academic performance. Standardized test scores have been widely used in studies of educational achievement. They have been generally treated as an indicator of both intelligence and learned information (Kao and Thompson 2003), and as "more objective measures of what students have learned" (Kao and Rutherford 2007, 33). We follow a long-standing tradition of examining dropout status, for its obvious value as an academic outcome and the associated public policy concern, since high school dropouts are generally more likely to be unemployed or in contact with the criminal justice system. Math scores are used instead of reading scores because they are less likely to be affected by language barriers.

Race/ethnicity and immigrant status. We categorize students by race/ethnicity (non-Hispanic Asian, non-Hispanic black, Hispanic and non-Hispanic white [reference]), and by generational status (first-generation, second-generation, and third-generation and above [reference]). First-generation youth are classified as those

TABLE 1
Descriptive Statistics of Analytic Sample

Variables	Weighted Means[a]
Key outcome variables	
Student ever dropped out of school (by follow-up year 2012)	7.1%
Follow-up year (11th grade) math score (standardized theta score)	52.2 (10.0)
Base-year (9th grade) math score (standardized theta score)	51.9 (9.8)
Main independent variables	
Generation status	
First generation	5.2%
Second generation	19.0%
Third + generation	75.8%
Gender	
Male	49.4%
Race/ethnicity	
Asian	4.2%
Black	10.7%
Latino	20.9%
Whites and others	64.2%
Family characteristics	
Family socioeconomic status (standardized)	0.03 (0.8)
Family structure (in base year 2009)	
Intact family	63.0%
Single mother (with or without partner)	28.1%
Single father (with or without partner)	6.2%
No parent	2.7%
Parental engagement	
Parent school involvement	
Item: Attended a general school meeting since start of 2009–10 school year	82.9%
Item: Attended a PTO meeting since start of 2009–10 school year	35.8%
Item: Attended parent-teacher conference since start of 2009–10 school year	53.7%
Item: Attended school event since start of 2009–10 school year	65.2%
Item: Served as a school volunteer since start of 2009–10 school year	26.4%
Item: Participated in school fund-raiser since start of 2009–10 school year	49.9%
Item: Met with a school counselor since start of 2009–10 school year	42.3%
Parent participation in extracurricular activities with children	
Item: Went to science or engineering museum with 9th grader in last year	53.0%

(continued)

TABLE 1 (CONTINUED)

Variables	Weighted Means[a]
Item: Worked or played on computer with ninth grader in last year	86.9%
Item: Built or fixed something with ninth grader in last year	47.2%
Item: Attended a school science fair with ninth grader in last year	16.7%
Item: Helped ninth grader with a school science fair project in last year	39.8%
Item: Discussed STEM program or article with ninth grader in last year	65.2%
Item: Visited a library with ninth grader in last year	64.2%
Item: Went to a play, concert or live show with ninth grader in last year	63.2%
Parent-child communication[b]	
Item: Discuss about school course work	66.7%
Item: Discuss about going to college	84.2%
Item: Discuss about jobs/career	86.3%
Item: Discuss about personal problems	63.3%
School-level characteristics	
Percent in public school	92.2%
Percent in non-Catholic private school	3.7%
Percent in Catholic school	4.1%
Percent student body in free-lunch program	36.5 (23.2)
Percent students taking AP courses	16.7 (13.1)
Percent students who are first or second generation	19.1 (15.5)

SOURCE: High School Longitudinal Survey 2009 and 2012 panels ($N \sim = 13{,}000$). The analytical sample used in this article only includes students who participated in both waves and also have parent interviewed in the base year who have answered questions on parental engagement. Key information such as generation status and parental engagement are only available from the parent data.

a. The means and proportions are weighted by W1PARENT, which is defined as "parent weight for student-level analyses involving the parent questionnaire." According to NCES, because of low response rate in parent questionnaires, analysis involving parent information should be adjusted by parent weight.

b. Parent-child communication is measured based on students' responses to a series of ten questions regarding whether they have ever discussed school, college, jobs/careers, and personal problems with mother/father during the academic year. We collapsed the ten items to four. Answers from both mother/father are pooled together due to space constraints.

born outside of the United States, while second-generation students are classified as those born in the United States but with at least one foreign-born parent. Third+ generation youth are those who are born in the United States with both parents also born in the United States. (For ease of exposition we sometimes refer to this final group as "third" generation, recognizing that it also includes all higher-order generational statuses; similarly, we often drop the "non-Hispanic" qualifier for the race-ethnic categories). In our descriptive statistics (means comparison), we represent twelve categories: cross-classifying four race/ethnic groups by three generation groups.

Measures of parental engagement

The score of parental engagement is constructed through principal-component factor analysis as a factor score based on twenty-five items asked in the HSLS 2009 survey. Among the twenty-five items, seven items tap *parental school involvement*: whether parent reported attending a general school meeting, a PTO meeting, or school event; served as a school volunteer; participated in a school fund-raiser; met with a school counselor; or attended a parent-teacher conference since the start of the 2009–2010 school year (when students are in ninth grade). *Parental extracurricular participation in students' activities* is measured based on parents' responses to a series of eight questions regarding whether they went to a science or engineering museum; worked or played on a computer; built or fixed something; attended a school science fair; helped their ninth grader with a school science fair project; discussed a STEM (science, technology, engineering, and mathematics) program or article; visited a library; or went to a play, concert, or live show with a ninth grader in the last year (prior to the time of the base-year survey). *Parent-child communication* is measured based on students' responses to a series of ten questions regarding whether they have ever discussed school work, college, jobs/careers, and personal problems with mother/father during the academic year 2009–2010. Table 1 collapsed the ten items to four. Answers from both mother/father are pooled together due to space constraints. For example, discussion about school work includes four questions: whether ninth grader talked to mother about science, whether ninth grader talked to father about science, whether ninth grader talked to mother about other courses, and whether ninth grader talked to father about other courses. Discussion about college includes two items: whether ninth grader talked to mother about going to college and whether ninth grader talked to father about going to college. Discussion about jobs/careers also includes two items: whether ninth grader talked to mother about adult jobs/careers and whether ninth grader talked to father about adult jobs/careers. Discussion about personal problems also includes two items: whether ninth grader talked to mother about personal problems and whether ninth grader talked to father about personal problems.

In exploratory analysis, we considered developing factor scores based on each of the three a priori groupings. Given the cross-correlation of the three such factors and limited additional information the separation conveyed, we opted for parsimony. We thus conducted factor analysis with all twenty-five items and extracted a single overarching factor to capture parental engagement.

Responses for each item are originally coded as dummy variables, and principal-component factor analysis is conducted to check the consistency among items and to construct the final factor score of social capital. Principal-component analysis is used here because it is believed to be useful for reducing correlated observed variables to a smaller set of important independent composite variables (Abdi 2003; Suhr 2005). Analytical weights are applied for item responses at the individual level. The complete list of items used for constructing the composite score is presented in Table A1 in the appendix. Only one factor index of parental engagement is retained because of its highest eigenvalue of 4.6, which is greater than the conventional criterion (>1). All of the response items are positively related to the final index, while attending school events (fund-raising or volunteering) and parent-child discussion about school have the greatest weights in the parental engagement score.

Control variables

Individual characteristics of gender, base-year math score, family socioeconomic status (SES), family structure, and school-level characteristics are included as control variables in all models. Previous research suggests that those are the measures of individual and family characteristics that influence educational outcomes (Glick and White 2004; Kao and Rutherford 2007). In the HSLS, family SES is a composite measure constructed from the education and occupation (prestige score) of parents and family income. Besides family SES, we also control for family structure. Students living in single-parent households may face extra barriers in accessing social capital and parental attention.

Crucially, we also control for students' prior academic performance (math score in the ninth grade) to accurately capture the effects of parental engagement on achievement trajectory. School-level characteristics, such as school type, share of immigrant students, percent students in free-lunch program, and percent students taking AP courses, are also included as controls to minimize the potential confounding impact of school characteristics on education outcomes.

Methods

We begin with a descriptive comparison (Table 2) of educational outcomes, family background characteristics, parental engagement, and school-level characteristics by generational status and race/ethnicity. We then employ mixed-effects models to estimate the effect of parental engagement on wave 2 math score (Table 3A) and probability of dropping out of high school (Table 3B), after controlling for base year math score and other individual-level, family background, and school context characteristics. We build our models sequentially, to determine how the predictive effects of variables are altered in the presence of additional covariates. Last, stratified models (Tables 4A and 4B) are used to examine whether these processes appear to differ by race/ethnicity.

We employ mixed-effects models to estimate the effects of parental engagement, race/ethnicity, and generational status on education outcomes, while controlling for family background and school characteristics. Mixed-effects models

TABLE 2
Weighted Means of Measures of Academic Performance, Parental Engagement, Family Background, and School Characteristics, by Race/Ethnicity and Generational Status

	Asian			Black			Hispanic			White		
	1st	2nd	3rd	1st	2nd	3rd	1st	2nd	3rd	1st	2nd	3rd
Key outcome variables												
Base-year (9th grade) math score (standardized theta score)	57.57	60.23	55.47	49.20	49.98	46.43	50.40	49.52	49.50	55.58	55.91	53.08
Follow-up year (11th grade) math score (standardized theta score)	58.18	61.55	52.94	50.96	48.36	46.93	49.45	49.24	50.02	57.65	55.94	53.39
Student ever dropped out of school (by follow up year 2012)	0.03	0.05	0.09	0.03	0.02	0.12	0.06	0.10	0.11	0.14	0.04	0.06
Parental engagement index	-0.12	0.03	-0.39	-0.51	-0.24	-0.21	-0.36	-0.35	-0.27	-0.05	0.22	0.17
Household characteristics												
Intact family (both parent present)	0.86	0.83	0.75	0.71	0.59	0.34	0.73	0.68	0.47	0.84	0.77	0.68
Family socioeconomic status (standardized score)	0.30	0.35	0.37	-0.15	0.11	-0.30	-0.72	-0.57	-0.12	0.12	0.47	0.23
School-level characteristics												
Percent in public school	91.39	93.38	93.01	94.66	89.26	96.83	98.11	96.00	94.06	93.53	86.83	90.10
Percent in non-Catholic private school	6.74	3.65	3.01	4.27	3.10	0.96	0.80	1.38	2.29	5.44	5.73	4.84
Percent in Catholic school	1.87	2.97	3.98	1.07	7.64	2.21	1.09	2.62	3.65	1.03	7.44	5.06
Percent student body in free-lunch program	39.40	27.67	31.38	40.67	44.48	50.15	51.49	49.34	43.45	27.89	26.80	30.22
Percent students taking AP courses	22.24	20.75	14.10	17.84	19.82	16.87	21.60	18.89	17.63	19.07	18.04	15.44
Percent students who are first or second generation	36.42	32.19	18.77	39.42	27.20	15.54	37.98	33.61	22.31	34.00	24.98	13.59

NOTE: The number of students who are identified as third-generation Asian, first-generation or second-generation black are relatively small, and thus the mean estimations have large standard deviations. They should be interpreted with caution.

TABLE 3A
Mixed-Effects Model Predicting Eleventh-Grade Math Test Scores

	Model 1	Model 2	Model 3	Model 4	Model 5
Parental engagement	2.262***	0.636***	0.607***	0.310**	0.294*
	(0.179)	(0.142)	(0.150)	(0.155)	(0.154)
Individual characteristics					
2009 (base year) standardized math score		0.684***	0.671***	0.640***	0.638***
		(0.0280)	(0.0262)	(0.0252)	(0.0237)
Males (ref = Females)			0.329	0.239	0.275
			(0.309)	(0.312)	(0.312)
Race/ethnicity (ref = non-Hispanic whites)					
Non-Hispanic Asian			2.032***	1.944***	1.944***
			(0.585)	(0.606)	(0.615)
Non-Hispanic black			−2.145***	−1.702***	−1.686***
			(0.660)	(0.636)	(0.628)
Hispanic			−1.024*	−0.492	−0.549
			(0.562)	(0.522)	(0.537)
Generation status (ref = third+ generation)					
First generation			1.106*	1.335*	1.167*
			(0.669)	(0.698)	(0.686)
Second generation			0.0466	−0.0324	−0.175
			(0.434)	(0.442)	(0.424)
Family background characteristics					
2009 (base year) composite SES score				1.438***	1.317***
				(0.235)	(0.249)
Family composition					
Single mother				−0.503	−0.467
				(0.351)	(0.350)
Single father				−0.817	−0.769
				(0.665)	(0.658)
No parent				−0.326	−0.272
				(0.632)	(0.641)
School-level characteristics					
School type (vs. public school)					
Non-Catholic private school					0.846
					(0.533)
Catholic private school					1.199***
					(0.355)
Percent student body in free lunch program					−0.00341
					(0.00823)

(continued)

TABLE 3A (CONTINUED)

	Model 1	Model 2	Model 3	Model 4	Model 5
Percent students taking AP courses					−0.00713 (0.0137)
Percent students who are first or second generation					0.0142 (0.0119)
Constant (mean of school level intercepts)	51.84	16.77	17.51	19.16	19.07
Random effects					
Variance at the school level	12.89	4.10	3.63	2.73	2.47
Variance at the individual level	71.21	40.49	40.22	39.71	39.74
Intraclass correlation	.15	.09	.08	.06	.06
Observations	~13,000	~13,000	~13,000	~13,000	~13,000
Number of schools	~900	~900	~900	~900	~900

NOTE: Standard errors in parentheses. Results presented in this table are based on complete cases. Weights are used to adjust for missing of parent questionnaires in the survey, following documentation from NECS. Results are consistent when multiple imputation (twenty imputations) is used to impute missing values. Findings also hold when country of origin is added in the models.
$^{\circ}p < .1.$ $^{\circ\circ}p < .05.$ $^{\circ\circ\circ}p < .01.$

are advantageous for their ability to reflect and adjust for influences at the higher level of aggregation (the school). Hearkening back to the early work of Coleman and colleagues, who used High School and Beyond Data (Coleman, Hoffer, and Kilgore 1982), one would expect school type to matter for students' academic performance and students' family background characteristics to impact the types of schools that students attend. Using the Children of Immigrants Longitudinal Study, Portes and Hao (2004) find that school-level SES is associated with higher GPA and lower probability of school attribution. Mixed-effects models have further advantages, since students with similar background characteristics are clustered within school and the errors for individual observations in the same school are likely to be correlated, with education outcomes reflecting school-level context in addition to individual-level characteristics. Students are not at all randomly distributed across schools. In fact, there is substantial variation in school type (and probably choice where able) by race/ethnicity and by generational status. As shown in Table 2, first-generation students regardless of racial and ethnic origin are far more likely to enroll in schools with higher shares of immigrants, compared to their native-born counterparts. The clustering of peers of similar ethnicity and immigrant status might have varied implications for students of different racial and ethnic origin. Portes and Hao (2004) suggest that the disadvantage in academic performance among second-generation Mexicans is

TABLE 3B
Mixed-Effects Logistic Model Predicting Probability of Ever Dropping Out

	Model 1	Model 2	Model 3	Model 4	Model 5
Parental engagement	−0.694***	−0.564***	−0.557***	−0.432***	−0.427***
	(0.0864)	(0.0933)	(0.0933)	(0.115)	(0.112)
Individual characteristics					
2009 (base year)		−0.0506***	−0.0479***	−0.0337***	−0.0319***
standardized math score		(0.00915)	(0.00906)	(0.00975)	(0.00957)
Males (ref = females)			0.167	0.191	0.194
			(0.162)	(0.165)	(0.164)
Race/ethnicity (ref = non-Hispanic whites)					
Non-Hispanic Asian			0.433	0.488	0.485
			(0.390)	(0.400)	(0.382)
Non-Hispanic black			0.327	0.141	0.184
			(0.302)	(0.282)	(0.291)
Hispanic			0.182	−0.0178	−0.0114
			(0.241)	(0.255)	(0.267)
Generation status (ref = third+ generation)					
First generation			−0.619**	−0.745**	−0.756**
			(0.308)	(0.315)	(0.326)
Second generation			−0.357	−0.349	−0.350
			(0.243)	(0.253)	(0.268)
Family background characteristics					
2009 (base year)				−0.616***	−0.636***
composite SES score				(0.165)	(0.153)
Family composition					
Single mother				0.110	0.132
				(0.160)	(0.158)
Single father				0.400	0.413
				(0.297)	(0.299)
No parent				0.717**	0.730**
				(0.321)	(0.325)
School-level characteristics					
School type (vs. public school)					
Non-Catholic private school					0.481*
					(0.283)
Catholic private school					−0.915***
					(0.320)
Percent student body in free lunch program					0.00103
					(0.00416)

(continued)

TABLE 3B (CONTINUED)

	Model 1	Model 2	Model 3	Model 4	Model 5
Percent students taking AP courses					−0.00866 (0.00713)
Percent students who are first or second generation					0.00273 (0.00630)
Constant (mean of school level intercepts)	−3.037	−0.508	−0.732	−1.514	−1.613
Random effects					
Variance at the school level	0.476	0.415	0.389	0.297	0.236
Intraclass correlation[a]	.13	.11	.11	.08	.07
Observations	~13,000	~13,000	~13,000	~13,000	~13,000
Number of schools	~900	~900	~900	~900	~900

NOTE: Standard errors in parentheses.

a. Residual variance is assumed to be $\pi^{2/3}$. Results presented in this table are based on complete cases. Weights are used to adjust for missing parent questionnaires in the survey, following documentation from NECS. Results are consistent when multiple imputation (twenty imputations) is used to impute missing values. Findings also hold when country of origin is added into the models.

$^*p < .1.$ $^{**}p < .05.$ $^{***}p < .01.$

significantly attenuated by attending schools with higher shares of coethnics, while the advantage for Asian second-generation immigrants is also reduced by attending schools with a high concentration of Asian students. Also, minority students, particularly black and Hispanic students, are more likely to be clustered in public schools or schools with lower average SES compared to their white counterparts. School-level characteristics such as learning resources (e.g., teacher quality or teacher-student ratio) that are not measured in the model but could affect students' education outcomes are adjusted with a random constant at the school level to allow variation among schools. In sum, to examine the effects of both individual characteristics and school contexts, while addressing the issue of correlated errors at the school level, we employ two-level mixed-effects models, with the students as level 1 and schools as level 2 observations and random intercepts at the school level. Using the math test score as an example, the full mixed-effects model is specified as:

$$Y_{ij} = \beta_{0j} + \beta_1 X_{1ij} + \beta_2 X_{2ij} + \beta_3 X_{3ij} + \beta_4 X_{4ij} + \beta_5 Z_j + e_{ij},$$

where i is the student level; j is the school level; X_1 includes all combinations of race/ethnicity and generation status; X_2 refers to prior academic performance; X_3

TABLE 4A
Mixed-Effects Model Predicting 11th Grade Math Test Scores, by Race

	Asian	Black	Hispanic	White
Parental engagement	0.646	−0.805	0.696**	0.246
	(0.423)	(0.635)	(0.351)	(0.206)
Individual characteristics				
2009 (base year) standardized math score	0.732***	0.618***	0.653***	0.634***
	(0.0372)	(0.0392)	(0.0393)	(0.0403)
Males (ref = females)	0.488	−1.346*	0.140	0.556
	(0.802)	(0.731)	(0.676)	(0.380)
Generation status (ref = third+ generation)				
First generation	1.005	3.253**	−0.698	4.131**
	(1.784)	(1.414)	(0.843)	(1.748)
Second generation	1.646	−1.279	−0.678	−0.829
	(1.620)	(2.073)	(0.613)	(0.624)
Family background characteristics				
2009 (base year) composite SES score	0.798*	1.444***	0.747	1.603***
	(0.428)	(0.543)	(0.471)	(0.344)
Family composition				
Single mother	−0.716	−1.579*	−0.602	−0.256
	(0.862)	(0.830)	(0.982)	(0.515)
Single father	−4.944	−1.335	−0.867	−0.472
	(3.023)	(1.230)	(1.139)	(0.879)
No parent	−0.297	−1.749**	0.467	0.217
	(1.116)	(0.781)	(1.247)	(0.997)
School-level characteristics				
School type (vs. public school)				
Non-Catholic private school	0.494	1.131	1.491	0.345
	(0.941)	(1.451)	(1.259)	(0.557)
Catholic private school	−2.159**	2.590***	1.431	0.907**
	(1.092)	(0.903)	(0.969)	(0.422)
Percent student body in free-lunch program	−0.0392***	0.0191	0.00862	−0.0180
	(0.0148)	(0.0168)	(0.0143)	(0.0121)
Percent students taking AP courses	0.0103	0.0489	0.0163	−0.0262*
	(0.0250)	(0.0339)	(0.0268)	(0.0149)
Percent students who are first or second	0.00316	0.0282	0.000618	0.0102
generation	(0.0228)	(0.0333)	(0.0210)	(0.0139)
Constant (mean of school level intercepts)	16.11***	17.37***	17.56***	19.91***
Random effects				
Variance at the school level	0	2.439	0.885	2.367
Variance at the individual level	32.31	34.91	40.84	39.46
Intraclass correlation	.000	.065	.021	.057
Observations	~900	~1,100	~2,000	~7,700
Number of schools	~400	~500	~700	~900

NOTE: Standard errors in parentheses.
*$p < .1$. **$p < .05$. ***$p < .01$.

TABLE 4B
Mixed-Effects Model Predicting High School Dropout Status, by Race

	Asian	Black	Hispanic	White
Parental engagement	−0.857***	−1.477***	−0.135	−0.487***
	(0.241)	(0.475)	(0.175)	(0.148)
Individual characteristics				
2009 (base year) standardized	−0.0481**	−0.00723	−0.0653***	−0.0220*
math score	(0.0230)	(0.0347)	(0.0179)	(0.0116)
Males (ref = females)	−0.724	1.005	0.120	0.0442
	(0.471)	(0.684)	(0.267)	(0.194)
Generation status (ref = third+				
generation)				
First generation	−1.928**	−3.840***	−0.528	−0.0129
	(0.849)	(1.472)	(0.413)	(0.803)
Second generation	−1.385***	−3.197**	0.0696	−0.807**
	(0.439)	(1.578)	(0.381)	(0.401)
Family background characteristics				
2009 (base year) composite	0.0464	−1.151**	−0.920***	−0.456**
SES score	(0.359)	(0.564)	(0.258)	(0.210)
Family composition				
Single mother	0.781	0.948	−0.0151	0.140
	(0.521)	(0.801)	(0.352)	(0.198)
Single father	0.388	2.427	0.307	0.653
	(0.691)	(1.754)	(0.661)	(0.406)
No parent[a]	—	−0.527	1.953***	0.836**
		(1.272)	(0.662)	(0.416)
School-level characteristics				
School type (vs. public school)				
Non-Catholic private school	−0.0397	−6.217**	0.625	0.695*
	(0.671)	(2.547)	(0.779)	(0.398)
Catholic private school[b]	—	−2.149	0.265	−0.942**
		(1.652)	(0.558)	(0.465)
Percent student body in	0.00463	−0.0155	0.00293	0.00791
free-lunch program	(0.0122)	(0.0182)	(0.00729)	(0.00662)
Percent students taking	0.00200	−0.0649	−0.00723	−0.0154
AP courses	(0.0149)	(0.0508)	(0.00987)	(0.0121)
Percent students who are first	0.00910	−0.0289	0.00196	0.0149
or second generation	(0.0144)	(0.0265)	(0.00960)	(0.0110)
Constant	0.291	−3.659	−0.454	−2.299***

(continued)

TABLE 4B (CONTINUED)

	Asian	Black	Hispanic	White
Random effects				
Variance at the school level	0	6.453	0.218	0.0532
Intraclass correlation	.00	.66	.06	.02
Observations	~900	~1,100	~2,000	~7,700
Number of schools	~400	~500	~700	~900

NOTE: Standard errors in parentheses.

a. There is no coefficient for no parent for the Asian subgroup because there are only twenty (rounded) Asian students without any biological parent present in the sample and none has dropped out during Grade 9 and Grade 11.

b. There is no coefficient for Catholic private school for the Asian subgroup because there are 130 (rounded) Asian students enrolled in Catholic private school in the sample and none has dropped out during Grade 9 and Grade 11.

$^\circ p < .1.$ $^{\circ\circ} p < .05.$ $^{\circ\circ\circ} p < .01.$

refers to family characteristics such as SES and family structure; X_4 refers to parental engagement; Z refers to school specific context (school type, percent student in free lunch program, percent taking AP courses, immigrant stock); and $\beta_{0j} = \gamma_{00} + u_{0j}$ (random intercept by school).

Results

Descriptive statistics

First, we present the descriptive statistics for the analysis sample in Table 1. The descriptive statistics show that HSLS 2009 provides a diverse sample with about 5.2 percent of student respondents being first generation and 19.0 percent of them being second generation. Table 1 also presents the weighted summary statistics for item measures of the clusters of parental engagement: parent-school involvement, parent participation in extracurricular activities with children, and parent-child communication. As shown in Table 1, parents in general report a fair amount of parent-school involvement and participation. More than half of parents report attending a general school meeting, parent-teacher conference and school event, as well as participation in most extracurricular activities. But parents are less likely to serve as school volunteers, or participate in fund-raisers or PTO meetings, all of which are indictors of higher levels of involvement that require more resources (temporal and perhaps monetary) from the parents. Meanwhile, students also report quite high levels of communication with parents. More than 80 percent of the high school students interviewed report discussing going to college and future careers with parents, though the percentage of them who are willing to discuss personal problems with parents is lower (63.3 percent).

Table 2 presents the weighted means of academic performance, parental engagement, and household characteristics by race/ethnicity and immigrant status. A significant difference (symbols not indicated for reasons of space) is observed between minority first- and second-generation groups and third+-generation whites in terms of education outcomes. With education outcomes measured as math test scores, first- and second-generation Asians on average have higher math test scores in both ninth grade and eleventh grade than native third-generation whites, while immigrant blacks and Hispanics (both first and second generation) perform worse in high school compared to third- or higher-generation whites. Notably, children of Asian and black immigrants all seem to do better than their third-generation counterparts within the same racial/ethnic group, but the generational ordering is not the same for all minority racial groups. For Asians, the second-generation children perform best; while for blacks, the first generation seems to perform best in terms of eleventh-grade math test scores. For Hispanics, the first and second generations seem to lag behind compared to their third+-generation counterparts. Dropout rates increase with generation for all three minority groups. Hispanic and black dropout rates for those in the third (and higher order) generation are almost twice that for comparable whites.

Though immigrant children and children of immigrants have both higher base wave and follow-up wave test scores for all groups except for Hispanics, they are not advantaged in terms of levels of parental engagement. First-generation or second-generation immigrant minority youth tend to have lower parental engagement compared to their third+-generation counterparts, except for Asians. For Asians, third-generation youth have the lowest parental engagement, which could be because the Asian group is more heterogeneous. Also, the number of third-generation Asians is relatively small, and thus the mean estimation has a large standard error, so the mean estimation for third-generation Asians should be interpreted with caution. In terms of racial/ethnic differences, minority groups all have lower levels of parental engagement compared to whites, regardless of generation status.

Children of different racial/ethnic groups and immigrant status are also exposed to varied household and school-level characteristics. As shown in Table 2, first-generation Hispanic children in general have the lowest SES, though the condition improves across generation. Meanwhile, first- and second-generation Asians are not economically disadvantaged compared to third+-generation whites and economic condition improves over time for Asians. Black youth regardless of generational status are economically disadvantaged compared to their third+-generation white counterparts, and the economic disadvantage among black youth seems to amplify over time. Among whites, the second-generation youth seem to have the highest family SES.

In terms of school-level characteristics, first-generation immigrant youth are most likely to enroll in schools with the highest immigrant student stock and least likely to enroll in Catholic private schools, regardless of race and ethnicity. Both first- and second-generation youth are more likely to enroll in schools with relative higher proportions of students taking AP courses compared to their third-generation counterparts among all racial groups. Minority youth are more likely to enroll in less economically advantaged schools (measured by percent student in free lunch program) overall, although there are some differences along generation lines. First-generation Asians and Hispanics are more likely to enroll in less economically advantaged schools, compared to their second- or third-generation same-race counterparts. Yet among black youth, the third-generation students are most likely to end up in schools that are more economically disadvantaged.

Mixed-effects regression analysis

Impact of parental engagement on educational trajectories. Mixed-effects generalized linear model (GLM) regression results predicting the effects of race/ethnicity, immigrant status, and parental engagement on math test scores are presented in Table 3A, and logistic regression results predicting probability of dropping out are presented in Table 3B. All models adjust for school-level clustering. In the tables we present here, we include parental engagement as the key independent variable first, to examine its effect solely, since race/ethnicity, generational status, and other family characteristics are likely to have an impact on the level of parental engagement. In alternative preliminary analyses (tables not presented here), we include race/ethnicity, generational status first before adding in parental engagement. We find that the mediating impact of parental engagement on race/ethnicity and generational status is limited, but the mediating impact of parental engagement on SES, as well as its independent impact, is substantial and statistically significant.

Model 1 in both Tables 3A and 3B shows the effect of parental engagement has highly significant predictive power on wave 2 math test scores and dropping out of high school. Model 2 adds in base-year (ninth grade) math, and the estimated effect of parental engagement decreases, but it is still significant. Base-year math explains over half of the variation in the follow-up year math test score in all of the estimation models. (Appendix Table A2 provides the regression on base-year math test score as the outcome from the equivalent set of covariates.) Model 3 in Tables 3A and 3B adds in gender, race/ethnicity, and generational status. Model 4 in Tables 3A and 3B adds in family composition and SES. The results in model 4, Tables 3A and 3B, suggest that in terms of nativity difference, compared to third-generation and above youth, first-generation youth are more likely to have higher eleventh-grade math scores and lower probability of dropping out after controlling for gender, race/ethnicity, base-year math score, parental engagement, and family SES ($p < .01$). Meanwhile, the impact of being second generation on math test score and probability of dropping out of high school is not significant. (We do find that first- and second-generation youth in general have higher ninth-grade math test scores compared to their third-generation and above counterparts [see appendix Table A2]).

In terms of racial/ethnicity differences, we find that Asian students tend to have higher eleventh-grade math scores, while non-Hispanic black students tend to have lower eleventh-grade math scores compared to non-Hispanic whites ($p <$ .01), after controlling for base-year math and generational status. Hispanic students also tend to have lower eleventh-grade math test scores compared to whites, but the effect is only marginally significant, after controlling for base-year math, gender, and generational status. The racial differences observed for eleventh-grade math scores are also seen in ninth-grade test scores. However, race/ethnicity is notably not appreciably predictive of ever dropping out of high school, after controlling for family SES and composition.

In keeping with the findings of much prior research, our results show that family SES (introduced in models 4 and 5) is a highly significant predictor of academic performance regardless of whether the outcome is measured as math test or dropout status. Children living in economically better-off families are more likely to have higher eleventh-grade math scores and lower probability of dropping out of high school, even after controlling for ninth-grade math test scores.

The lack of a two-parent family (family structure also introduced in models 4 and 5) points to inferior schooling outcomes, although several specific differentials do not achieve statistical significance at conventional levels. Family structure effects are more strongly predictive at base year, as shown in appendix Table A2. We do find that children living in households with no biological or adoptive parents are much more likely to drop out of high school than children living in two-parent families. Meanwhile, even after we include all the measures for family SES and family structure, the predictive effect of parental engagement is still statistically significant for improving math test scores and preventing youth from dropping out of high school at $p < .001$.

To further understand how much school context could alter the measured effects of race/ethnicity, generational status, and family characteristics, we introduce school-level characteristics into the regression models. Model 4 (before the explicit introduction of school-level covariates) in both Tables 3A and 3B suggests that school-level clustering explains about 6 percent of the total variance in twelfth-grade math test scores and about 8 percent of the residual variance in dropout probability, after we control for all individual and family-level characteristics. Model 5 introduces the several school-level measures: school organizational type; poverty (percent free lunch); percent taking AP courses; and immigrant stock. Results in Model 5 indicate that school type has a significant predictive power regarding education outcomes, net of individual and family-level characteristics. Students in Catholic private schools on average have higher eleventh-grade math test scores and lower probability of dropping out, compared to students in public schools. Meanwhile, school-level poverty measured by percent of students in the free lunch program is negatively associated with eleventh-grade math scores and positively associated with probability of dropping out, but the associations are not statistically significant. Other school-level characteristics are not statistically significant in these models.

These results are trajectories, net of base-year circumstance. When we examine base-year conditions (appendix Table A2), we do see some important differences along these lines. Students in schools with a higher percent of students in free-lunch programs have significantly lower ninth-grade math test scores. Student impoverished (large fraction free lunch) schools are predicted to perform less well initially, but those in schools with more advantaged curricula and higher immigrant stock are predicted to do better on the initial math test. Interestingly, students enrolled in private schools (catholic or non-Catholic) are predicted to have lower base-year math test scores, net of the school-level and family background traits entered into the model.

Varied impacts of parental engagement by race/ethnicity and education outcomes. Tables 4A and 4B look at within race/ethnic groups. We estimate these models, stratified by race/ethnicity, to better understand the interactive effect of race/ethnicity, generational status, and parental engagement. We present only models that include all substantive personal, family, and school covariates, as above. The inclusion of parental engagement does not appreciably change the parameter estimates for other variables. (All statistically significant coefficients retain their significance, sign, and approximate magnitude.)

Table 4A reveals that the predictive effect of prior math score is quite strong across all ethnic groups. Generation status is generally nonsignificant in these models (except for immigrant white students), and is in places inconsistent in sign. Family SES operates as expected to predict more favorable math trajectories, although it is not significant in all cases. Students from non-dual-parent homes are predicted to fare less well, although only a fraction of the coefficients achieve statistical significance. Table 4B echoes the predictive effect of early school performance (wave 1 math) on dropout probability. Students who did well in ninth-grade math are less likely to drop out (significant for all but blacks). First- and second-generation students are generally less likely to drop out of high school, with the relationship most pronounced for Asians and blacks. More favorable family background conditions—higher SES and dual-parent household—generally pointed to lower dropout. (Interestingly, the SES effect was near zero for Asians.)

Parental engagement carries only substantively statistically significant predictive power over math trajectory for Hispanics. For Asians and whites, the coefficient on engagement is smaller in size and nonsignificant. For blacks, the coefficient is negative while nonsignificant. Asian, black, and white students from homes with engaged parents were generally much less likely to drop out than their peers ($p < .01$). Oddly, a parental engagement effect was in the same direction but not of statistical significance for Hispanic students.

School-level effects, where they manifest, are inconsistent. For whites and blacks, Catholic school attendance predicts a superior math trajectory, but for Asians, Catholic school attendance (and for peers in free lunch programs) lowers the trajectory. School-level variables are not usually significant in the dropout models. Estimation parameters from the multilevel math trajectory model also shed some interesting light on the school achievement variation by race/ethnicity. Not surprisingly (and consistent with pooled models), variance at the individual level dominates variance at the school level. We do find for blacks, however, that this is the case, and in turn, the intraclass correlation is higher than for the other groups. This would be consistent with higher error correlation (more similarity) within schools among blacks, perhaps in turn reflective of more sorting or academic segregation not otherwise measured by included covariates in these models. Due to the variation in sample size for the different racial groups and variances in standard errors, the results for cross-comparison between racial groups should still be interpreted with caution. All told, parental engagement comes through more strongly in predicting dropout than the trajectory of math. This is consistent with a behavioral mechanism in which the parents are able to translate their aspirations more into school attendance itself than into within-school performance.

Conclusion

While previous research has examined the effect of parental engagement on students' educational outcomes in general, we used the most recent nationally representative education survey to focus on both the overall and conditional (including mediating) effects of parental engagement. We look at parental engagement through a rich set of indicators that include parent-school involvement, parental participation in extracurricular activities, and parent-child discussions, and our analysis considers a host of family background characteristics, including race/ethnicity, immigrant generation status, and characteristics of the school itself. Our models take advantage of the longitudinal nature of the data, predicting eleventh-grade math outcomes while controlling for ninth-grade math performance, thereby giving a better sense of how the covariates influence outcomes. Our approach is in the spirit of Coleman, in that we seek to assess the determinants of stratification in schools and improve our understanding of family social capital. Accordingly, our models include individual demographic characteristics, conventional family background measures, direct measures of parental engagement, and school contextual effects.

We find that higher levels of parental engagement predict improvements in students' math test scores and prevent students from dropping out of high school. This effect persists even when we control for conventional educational attainment variables such as race/ethnicity, family SES, and school-level contextual factors, as well as when interactions of parental engagement with other race/ethnicity/immigrant generation variables are examined. In keeping with prior studies, we find that students from higher socioeconomic backgrounds are less likely to drop out and are more likely to follow superior academic trajectories. Further, we find that greater parental engagement predicts a superior achievement trajectory (as reflected in standardized math test scores) across the high school years.

School-level effects are also discernable in our empirical results. This is evidenced both by direct covariate measures (such as school organizational type and school socioeconomic composition) and by the portion of the variance that remains at the school level. Including these school-level measures reduces the magnitude of the parental engagement effect but notably does not remove it. All told, these findings add weight to arguments for the importance of family social capital.

We do find some variation in the impact of parental engagement by ethno-racial groups. Across all four major groups that we can analyze in the HSLS:2009, we find that greater parental engagement is associated with lower dropout rates. For this fundamental education outcome, our results are quite robust. Effects of parental engagement on predicting math trajectory were weaker and inconsistent across the four groups. Taken together, we interpret these findings to mean that parental involvement translates more easily into children continuing in school, rather than performing well. It also points to potential differences in the way that school engagement is manifest across different race/ethnic groups and is correlated with other achievement variables, such as family socioeconomic background and school type.

Parental engagement, as arguably one window into the broader landscape of family social capital, clearly matters in ways that promote high school achievement. Still, future analysis must do more to understand how different features of engagement may operate to promote success and, equally important, how parental aspirations and their associated behaviors might differentially operate across various race/ethnicity/generation groups. As schools come to have increasing shares of first- and second-generation minority children, it is important to understand how the influences of parenting might operate differently among subpopulations, so that we can develop constructive policies that improve education outcomes for the growing number of children of immigrant minorities in contemporary American society.

Appendix

Input Item	Definition
Parent school involvement	
P1SCHMTG	Attended a general school meeting since start of 2009–10 school year
P1PTOMTG	Attended a PTO meeting since start of 2009–10 school year
P1PTCONFER	Attended parent-teacher conference since start of 2009–10 school year
P1SCHEVENT	Attended school event since start of 2009–10 school year
P1VOLUNTEER	Served as a school volunteer since start of 2009–10 school year
P1FUNDRAISE	Participated in school fund raiser since start of 2009–10 school year
P1COUNSELOR	Met with a school counselor since start of 2009–10 school year
Parental participation in extracurricular activities	
P1MUSEUM	Went to science or engineering museum with ninth grader in last year
P1COMPUTER	Worked or played on computer with ninth grader in last year
P1FIXED	Built or fixed something with ninth grader in last year
P1SCIFAIR	Attended a school science fair with ninth grader in last year
P1SCIPROJ	Helped ninth grader with a school science fair project in last year
P1STEMDISC	Discussed STEM program or article with ninth grader in last year
P1LIBRARY	Visited a library with ninth grader in last year
P1SHOW	Went to a play, concert or live show with ninth grader in last year
Parent-child discussion	
S1MOMTALKS	Ninth grader talked to mother about science courses to take in 2009-2010
S1DADTALKS	Ninth grader talked to father about science courses to take in 2009-2010
S1MOMTALKOTH	Ninth grader talked to mother about other courses to take in 2009-2010
S1DADTALKOTH	Ninth grader talked to father about other courses to take in 2009-2010
S1MOMTALKCLG	Ninth grader talked to mother about going to college
S1DADTALKCLG	Ninth grader talked to father about going to college
S1MOMTALKJOB	Ninth grader talked to mother about adult jobs/careers
S1DADTALKJOB	Ninth grader talked to father about adult jobs/careers
S1MOMTALKPRB	Ninth grader talked to mother about personal problems
S1DADTALKPRB	Ninth grader talked to father about personal problems

TABLE A2
Mixed-Effects Model Predicting Base-Year (9th Grade) Math Test Score

	Model 1	Model 2	Model 3	Model 4
Parental engagement	2.353***	2.251***	1.521***	1.437***
	(0.173)	(0.183)	(0.146)	(0.146)
Individual characteristics				
Males (ref= Females)		0.105	−0.134	−0.0532
		(0.341)	(0.317)	(0.314)
Race/Ethnicity (ref=Non Hispanic whites)				
Non-Hispanic Asian		4.108***	3.592***	3.417***
		(0.879)	(0.831)	(0.824)
Non-Hispanic black		−4.081***	−2.854***	−2.700***
		(0.595)	(0.564)	(0.535)
Hispanic		−2.545**	−1.313	−1.598
		(1.057)	(0.975)	(1.012)
Generation Status (ref= Third+ generation)				
First generation		1.996**	2.787***	1.981***
		(0.818)	(0.762)	(0.753)
Second generation		1.963***	1.961***	1.310***
		(0.485)	(0.463)	(0.458)
Family background characteristics				
2009 (base year) composite SES score			3.331***	3.007***
			(0.329)	(0.303)
Family composition				
Single mother			−0.311	−0.278
			(0.463)	(0.479)
Single father			−1.738**	−1.648**
			(0.840)	(0.836)
No parent			−2.322***	−2.173***
			(0.727)	(0.705)
School-level characteristics				
School type (vs. Public school)				
Non-Catholic private school				−1.975***
				(0.689)
Catholic private school				−1.293**
				(0.509)
Percent student body in free lunch program				−0.0542***
				(0.00974)
Percent student taking AP courses				0.0431**
				(0.0167)
Percent students who are first or second generation				0.0629***
				(0.0156)

(continued)

TABLE A2 (CONTINUED)

	Model 1	Model 2	Model 3	Model 4
Constant (Mean of school level intercepts)	50.99	51.3	51.24	52.36
Random effects				
Variance at the school level	12.70	10.68	6.79	4.47
Variance at the individual level	69.62	68.13	64.38	64.24
Intraclass correlation	.15	.14	.10	.07
Observations	~13,000	~13,000	~13,000	~13,000
Number of schools	~900	~900	~900	~900

NOTE: Results presented in this table are based on complete cases. Weights are used to adjust for missing parent questionnaires in the survey, following documentation from NECS. Results are consistent when multiple imputation (twenty imputations) is used to impute missing values. Findings also hold when country of origin is added into the models.
$*p < .1.$ $**p < .05.$ $***p < .01.$

References

Abdi, Herve. 2003. Factor rotations in factor analyses. In *Encyclopedia for research methods for the social sciences*, eds. M. Lewis-Beck, A. Bryman, and T. Futing, 792–95. Thousand Oaks, CA: Sage Publications.

Alba, Richard, and Victor Nee. 2009. *Remaking the American mainstream: Assimilation and contemporary immigration*. Cambridge, MA: Harvard University Press.

Bankston, Carl L. 2004. Social capital, cultural values, immigration, and academic achievement: The host country context and contradictory consequences. *Sociology of Education* 77 (2): 176–79.

Bankston, Carl L., and Min Zhou. 2002a. Social capital and immigrant children's achievement. *Schooling and Social Capital in Diverse Cultures* 13:13–39.

Bankston, Carl L., and Min Zhou. 2002b. Social capital as process: The meanings and problems of a theoretical metaphor. *Sociological Inquiry* 72 (2): 285–317.

Bourdieu, Pierre. 1985. The social space and the genesis of groups. *Theory and Society* 14 (6): 723–44.

Carbonaro, William J. 1998. A little help from my friend's parents: Intergenerational closure and educational outcomes. *Sociology of Education* 71 (4): 295–313.

Coleman, James S. 1975. What is meant by "an equal educational opportunity"? *Oxford Review of Education* 1 (1): 27–29.

Coleman, James S. 1988. Social capital in the creation of human capital. *American Journal of Sociology* 94:S95–S120.

Coleman, James S. 1990. *Foundations of social theory*. Cambridge, MA: Harvard University Press.

Coleman, James S. 1991. *Parental involvement in education: Policy perspective series*. Washington, DC: Office of Educational Research and Improvement of Practice.

Coleman, James S. 1993. The rational reconstruction of society. *American Sociological Review* 58 (6): 898–912.

Coleman, James S., and Thomas Hoffer. 1987. *Public and private high schools: The impact of communities*. New York, NY: Basic Books.

Coleman, James S., and Thomas Hoffer. 1989. *Public and private schools*. New York, NY: Basic Books.

Coleman, James Samuel, Thomas Hoffer, and Sally Kilgore. 1982. *High school achievement: Public, Catholic, and private schools compared*. New York, NY: Basic Books.

Coleman, James Samuel, and U.S. Department of Health, Education, and Welfare. 1966. *Equality of educational opportunity*, vol. 2. Washington, DC: Office of Education.

Donato, Katharine M., Charles Tolbert, Alfred Nucci, and Yukio Kawano. 2008. Changing faces, changing places: The emergence of new nonmetropolitan immigrant gateways. *New Faces in New Places* 71 (4): 75–98.

Dornbusch, Sanford M. 1989. The sociology of adolescence. *Annual Review of Sociology* 15:233–59.

Fischer, Mary J. 2010. Immigrant educational outcomes in new destinations: An exploration of high school attrition. *Social Science Research* 39 (4): 627–41.

Fuller, Bruce, and Emily Hannum. 2002. *Schooling and social capital in diverse cultures*, vol. 13. Bingley, UK: Emerald Publishing.

Glick, Jennifer E., and Michael J. White. 2004. Post-secondary school participation of immigrant and native youth: The role of familial resources and educational expectations. *Social Science Research* 33 (2): 272–99.

Goyette, Kimberly A., and Gilberto Q. Conchas. 2002. Family and non-family roots of social capital among Vietnamese and Mexican American children. *Research in Sociology of Education* 13:41–72.

Goyette, Kimberly, and Yu Xie. 1999. Educational expectations of Asian American youths: Determinants and ethnic differences. *Sociology of Education* 72 (1): 22–36.

Haller, William, Alejandro Portes, and Scott M. Lynch. 2011. Dreams fulfilled, dreams shattered: Determinants of segmented assimilation in the second generation. *Social Forces* 89 (3): 733–62.

Hirschman, Charles. 2001. The educational enrollment of immigrant youth: A test of the segmented-assimilation hypothesis. *Demography* 38 (3): 317–36.

Iceland, John. 2009. *Where we live now: Immigration and race in the United States*. Berkeley, CA: University of California Press.

Kao, Grace. 1995. Asian Americans as model minorities? A look at their academic performance. *American Journal of Education* 103 (2): 121–59.

Kao, Grace. 2004a. Parental influences on the educational outcomes of immigrant youth. *International Migration Review* 38 (2): 427–49.

Kao, Grace. 2004b. Social capital and its relevance to minority and immigrant populations. *Sociology of Education* 77 (2): 172–75.

Kao, Grace, and Lindsay Taggart Rutherford. 2007. Does social capital still matter? Immigrant minority disadvantage in school-specific social capital and its effects on academic achievement. *Sociological Perspectives* 50 (1): 27–52.

Kao, Grace, and Jennifer S. Thompson. 2003. Racial and ethnic stratification in educational achievement and attainment. *Annual Review of Sociology* 29:417–442.

Kao, Grace, and Marta Tienda. 2005. Optimism and achievement: The educational performance of immigrant youth. In *The new immigration: An interdisciplinary reader*, 331–343. New York: Taylor & Francis.

Lee, Jennifer, and Min Zhou. 2015. *The Asian American achievement paradox*. New York, NY: Russell Sage Foundation.

Lichter, Daniel T. 2012. Immigration and the new racial diversity in rural America. *Rural Sociology* 77 (1): 3–35.

Lichter, Daniel T., and Kenneth M. Johnson. 2009. Immigrant gateways and Hispanic migration to new destinations. *International Migration Review* 43 (3): 496–518.

Logan, John R., and Charles Zhang. 2010. Global neighborhoods: New pathways to diversity and separation. *American Journal of Sociology* 115 (4): 1069–1109.

McNeal, Ralph B. 1999. Parental involvement as social capital: Differential effectiveness on science achievement, truancy, and dropping out. *Social Forces* 78 (1): 117–44.

Migration Policy Institute. 2017. *State immigration data profiles*. Available from http://www.migration-policy.org/data/state-profiles/state/demographics/US (accessed 7 April 2017).

Morgan, Stephen L., and Aage B. Sørensen. 1999. Parental networks, social closure, and mathematics learning: A test of Coleman's social capital explanation of school effects. *American Sociological Review* 64 (5): 661–81.

Muller, Chandra. 1993. Parent involvement and academic achievement: An analysis of family resources available to the child. In *Parents, their children, and schools*, eds. B. Schneider and J. S. Coleman, 77–113. San Francisco, CA: Westview Press.

Muller, Chandra. 1998. Gender differences in parental involvement and adolescents' mathematics achievement. *Sociology of Education* 71 (4): 336–56.

Muller, Chandra, and Christopher G. Ellison. 2001. Religious involvement, social capital, and adolescents' academic progress: Evidence from the National Education Longitudinal Study of 1988. *Sociological Focus* 34 (2): 155–83.

National Center for Educational Statistics (NCES). 2013. *High school longitudinal survey 2009–2012.* Available from https://nces.ed.gov/surveys/hsls09/.

Parcel, Toby L., and Mikaela J. Dufur. 2001. Capital at home and at school: Effects on child social adjustment. *Journal of Marriage and Family* 63 (1): 32–47.

Parcel, Toby L., Mikaela J. Dufur, and Rena Cornell Zito. 2010. Capital at home and at school: A review and synthesis. *Journal of Marriage and Family* 72 (4): 828–46.

Parcel, Toby L., and Elizabeth G. Menaghan. 1993. Family social capital and children's behavior problems. *Social Psychology Quarterly* 56 (2): 120–35.

Portes, Alejandro. 2000a. Social capital: Its origins and applications in modern sociology. In *Knowledge and social capital*, ed. Eric L. Lesser, 43–67. Boston, MA: Butterworth-Heinemann.

Portes, Alejandro. 2000b. The two meanings of social capital. *Sociological Forum* 15:1–12.

Portes, Alejandro. 2014. Downsides of social capital. *Proceedings of the National Academy of Sciences* 111 (52): 18407–8.

Portes, Alejandro, and Patricia Fernández-Kelly. 2008. No margin for error: Educational and occupational achievement among disadvantaged children of immigrants. *The ANNALS of the American Academy of Political and Social Science* 620:12–36.

Portes, Alejandro, and Lingxin Hao. 2004. The schooling of children of immigrants: Contextual effects on the educational attainment of the second generation. *Proceedings of the National Academy of Sciences of the United States of America* 101 (33): 11920–27.

Portes, Alejandro, and Rubén G. Rumbaut. 2001. *Legacies: The story of the immigrant second generation.* Berkeley, CA: University of California Press.

Portes, Alejandro, and Rubén G. Rumbaut. 2006. *Immigrant America: A portrait.* Berkeley, CA: University of California Press.

Portes, Alejandro, and Erik Vickstrom. 2015. Diversity, social capital, and cohesion. In *Migration: Economic change, social challenge*, ed. Christian Dustman, 461–79. New York, NY: Oxford University Press.

Suhr, Diana D. 2005. Principal component analysis vs. exploratory factor analysis. In *SUGI 30 Proceedings*, 203–30.

Sui-Chu, Esther Ho, and J. Douglas Willms. 1996. Effects of parental involvement on eighth-grade achievement. *Sociology of Education* 69 (2): 126–41.

Teachman, Jay D., Kathleen Paasch, and Karen Carver. 1997. Social capital and the generation of human capital. *Social Forces* 75 (4): 1343–59.

Turney, Kristin, and Grace Kao. 2009. Barriers to school involvement: Are immigrant parents disadvantaged? *Journal of Educational Research* 102 (4): 257–71.

Valenzuela, Angela, and Sanford M. Dornbusch. 1994. Familism and social capital in the academic achievement of Mexican origin and Anglo adolescents. *Social Science Quarterly* 75 (1): 18–36.

White, Michael J., and Jennifer E. Glick. 2000. Generation status, social capital, and the routes out of high school. *Sociological Forum* 15:671–91.

White, Michael J., and Jennifer E. Glick. 2009. *Achieving anew: How new immigrants do in American schools, jobs, and neighborhoods.* New York, NY: Russell Sage Foundation.

White, Michael J., and Gayle Kaufman. 1997. Language usage, social capital, and school completion among immigrants and native-born ethnic groups. *Social Science Quarterly* 78 (2): 385–98.

Yan, Wenfan. 1999. Successful African American students: The role of parental involvement. *Journal of Negro Education* 68 (1): 5–22.

Zhou, Min, and Susan Kim. 2006. Community forces, social capital, and educational achievement: The case of supplementary education in the Chinese and Korean immigrant communities. *Harvard Educational Review* 76 (1): 1–29.

Maternal Education, Changing Family Circumstances, and Children's Skill Development in the United States and UK

By
MARGOT I. JACKSON,
KATHLEEN KIERNAN,
and
SARA McLANAHAN

Maternal education influences families' socioeconomic status. It is strongly associated with children's cognitive development and a key predictor of other resources within the family that strongly predict children's well-being: economic insecurity, family structure, and maternal depression. Most studies examine the effects of these variables in isolation at particular points in time, and very little research examines whether findings observed among children in the United States can be generalized to children of a similar age in other countries. We use latent class analysis and data from two nationally representative birth cohort studies that follow children from birth to age five to answer two questions: (1) How do children's family circumstances evolve throughout early childhood? and (2) To what extent do these trajectories account for differences in children's cognitive development? Cross-national analysis reveals a good deal of similarity between the United States and UK in patterns of family life during early childhood, and in the degree to which those patterns contribute to educational inequality.

Keywords: education; inequality; cognitive development; family

Socioeconomic status during childhood has important consequences for children's development and opportunities for social mobility. Among the key findings of the Coleman Report

Margot I. Jackson is an associate professor of sociology at Brown University. Her research focuses on inequality of educational opportunity, health, and children and families. She studies the dynamics of inequality within and across generations, and the ways in which circumstances during childhood have long-reaching effects throughout children's schooling and into adulthood.

Kathleen Kiernan is a professor of social policy and demography at the University of York. Her research interests center on family environments and child well-being in the early years, family change in developed countries, cohabitation and unmarried parenthood, and parental separation and children's well-being.

Correspondence: margotj@brown.edu

DOI: 10.1177/0002716217729471

(1966) was that, much to the surprise of government sponsors and researchers, the strongest predictor of students' performance was their parents' education and social background; in comparison, the influence of educational resources was weak to non-existent (Coleman et al. 1966). The finding that student achievement differences within schools were as large as, or larger than, differences between schools suggested to many observers that schools were not the great equalizers that offset substantial inequalities between children. In that vein, socioeconomic status (SES) inequality in children's skill development is present well before they enter school, and the degree of inequality increases throughout childhood and adolescence (Adler et al. 1994; Currie and Stabile 2003; Finch 2003; Duncan, Ziol-Guest, and Kalil 2010). Among the core dimensions of SES (occupation, income, and education), maternal education shows the strongest association with children's cognitive development (Harding, Morris, and Hughes 2015; Reardon 2011) and is a key predictor of other resources within the family that strongly predict children's well-being: economic insecurity, family structure, and maternal depression. Today, parents with low levels of education not only face more economic insecurity than they did in the past, but they are also more likely to raise their children in unstable family environments (McLanahan 2004). Mothers with low levels of education are also more likely to suffer from mental health problems, such as depression, making it harder for them to care for their child(ren) (Kiernan and Huerta 2008; Meadows, McLanahan, and Brooks-Gunn 2008).

Although existing research documents important associations between maternal education and each of the components described above, most studies examine these circumstances in isolation of one another and at particular points in time, precluding a comprehensive understanding of how the family environment evolves over time and how it contributes to educational disparities in children's skill development. In addition, very little research examines whether findings observed among children in the United States can be generalized to children of a similar age in other countries. Great Britain provides a useful point of comparison to the United States because of country differences in the provision of social services affecting children and families, along with many demographic and cultural similarities. In this article, we use data from two nationally representative birth cohort studies that follow children from birth to age five—the American Fragile Families and Child Wellbeing Study (FFS), and the British Millennium Cohort Study (MCS)—to examine two questions: (1) How do children's family circumstances evolve throughout early childhood? and (2) To what extent do these trajectories account for differences in children's cognitive development? To address these questions, we use latent class trajectory analysis to construct longitudinal measures of family income, family structure, and maternal depression throughout early childhood that take into account the duration and stability of

Sara McLanahan is a professor of sociology and public affairs at Princeton University. She is a principal investigator of the Fragile Families and Child Wellbeing Study and editor-in-chief of The Future of Children, *a journal dedicated to providing research and analysis to promote effective policies and programs for children.*

each circumstance, as well as to examine the extent to which these trajectories explain differences in children's cognitive development.

Background

Maternal education, family circumstances, and child well-being

Although much of our understanding of the educational "gradient" in well-being comes from research on adults, growing evidence points to similar patterns among children. The appearance of disparities so early in life has led to an increased recognition that the reproduction of intergenerational inequality begins at a very young age (Jonsson 2010). Among the core dimensions of SES (occupation, income, and education), maternal education is most strongly associated with children's health, behavior, and cognitive development (Harding, Morris, and Hughes 2015; Reardon 2011). Moreover, parental education is a strong—increasingly strong—predictor of other important developmental resources within the family: education shapes children's cognitive development by shaping their family lives, including their income, family structure, and parents' mental health. The strong contemporary association between parental education and the broader family environment has important implications for children's social mobility.

Rising income inequality in recent decades has motivated research on family income and its relationship with children's development, with some evidence suggesting that the independent effects of income on children's development have increased in recent years (Reardon 2011).

Income-based inequalities in children's learning are present at the beginning of the school years, a troubling fact given the strong correlations between achievement, completed schooling, and economic status (Duncan, Ziol-Guest, and Kalil 2010). While income likely exerts independent effects on children's development, it is also strongly predicted by parents' education (Goldin and Katz 1999).

Alongside research on the effects of income is a rich literature documenting the effects of family structure and stability on children's development in many countries, including the United States, United Kingdom (UK), Australia, Canada, Germany, and Sweden (e.g., Amato 2005; Bernardi, Harkonen, and Boertien 2013; Kiernan and Mensah 2010; McLanahan, Tach, and Schneider 2013; Sigle-Rushton and McLanahan 2004). Children who live apart from their biological father are less likely than their peers to graduate from high school and college (Brown 2004; Cherlin et al. 1991; McLanahan and Sandefur 1994), more likely to be unemployed or out of the labor force, and more likely to become teen parents (Kiernan and Hobcraft 1997; Wu 1996). These children exhibit more withdrawn, anxious, and aggressive behavior in early childhood (Amato 2001; Chase-Lansdale, Cherlin, and Kiernan 1995; Jekielek 1998; McCulloch et al. 2000), and they are more likely to smoke, drink heavily, and use drugs in adolescence (Amato 2001; Estaugh and Power 1991). More recent research indicates that family instability, defined as changes in parents' relationship status, is also associated with a host of negative child outcomes (Fomby and Cherlin 2007; McLanahan and Beck 2010). Part of the association between family structure/ instability and poor child outcomes is due to low levels of education among women who become single mothers. For example, increasing union dissolution, nonmarital childbearing, and single motherhood are now concentrated most heavily among poorly educated families (Edin and Kefalas 2005; Ellwood and Jencks 2004; Loughran 2002; Martin 2004; McLanahan and Percheski 2008). Another part is due to family circumstances that are a consequence of father absence, including poverty, residential instability, and parenting stress (McLanahan, Tach, and Schneider 2013).

Finally, ample research documents the association between maternal depression and children's well-being (National Research Council and Institute of Medicine 2009). Children raised by depressed mothers are also more likely to exhibit behavior problems, particularly externalizing behavior, and to show more problems with educational development, including language and cognitive deficits (Brennan et al. 2000; Pettersen and Albers 2001; Kiernan and Huerta 2008). As is the case for income and family structure, mothers who suffer from depression have lower levels of SES (Kessler 1982), with the association between educational attainment and depression being particularly well documented. Mothers with less education not only experience more depressive symptoms, but their depression is also more severe (McLoyd 1998; Mirowsky and Ross 2003; Meadows, McLanahan, and Brooks-Gunn 2008).

In addition to their independent associations with parental education and child well-being, these different domains of family life—income, family structure, and maternal depression—also affect one another (e.g., Kiernan and Mensah 2009; Meadows, McLanahan, and Brooks-Gunn 2008; Mollborn 2016). Poverty, for example, is associated with greater family instability and maternal depression, both of which independently affect poverty. The disproportionate concentration, and frequent co-occurrence, of poverty, single motherhood, and less supportive relationships among families with less-educated mothers has led to speculation that the composition and content of family life provide the central explanation for large and persistent (or, in some cases, increasing) gaps in cognitive skills between children in different socioeconomic groups (e.g., Heckman 2008).

Temporal Dimensions of the Relationship between Family Circumstances and Child Development

Existing research demonstrates a strong relationship between maternal education and family circumstances, and between family circumstances and children's development, establishing the importance of both material resources and family relationships for children. Implicit in much existing work is the idea that family circumstances play an important role in explaining the differences in early childhood outcomes, and in the persistence of educational gaps throughout childhood. Despite speculation, however, little research takes into account the temporal dimension of children's exposure to multidimensional family circumstances (but see Mollborn 2016), and little is known about whether family circumstances throughout early childhood explain the persistent educational gradient in skill development. Life course theory emphasizes the possibility that circumstances across ages may have differing and combined effects on childhood and adulthood outcomes, pointing to the importance of the timing, duration, and stability of a circumstance (Ben-Shlomo and Kuh 2002; Ferraro and Shippee 2009; Schoon et al. 2002).

With respect to duration and stability, if children in more highly educated families experience a longer duration of positive economic, family structure, and mental health circumstances, as well as greater stability in those resources, they may be less likely to experience the compounding developmental effects of family disadvantage. There is ample evidence, for example, that chronic exposure to poverty is particularly detrimental for children, to the extent that it persistently increases exposure to stressors and limits opportunities for human capital development and social and economic advancement (McLeod and Shanahan 1996; Wagmiller et al. 2006). Similarly, continuously married mothers are in better mental and physical health than single mothers (Meadows, McLanahan, and Brooks-Gunn 2008). Instability in family circumstances during childhood is also associated with poorer development among children several years later—moving in and out of poverty is negatively associated with high school graduation (Lee 2014), and family structure instability during the first few years of childhood is negatively associated with mothers' mental health and stress (Cavanagh and Huston 2008; Meadows, McLanahan, and Brooks-Gunn 2008).

The effects of instability may intersect with those of timing, to the extent that transitioning in or out of a more disadvantaged circumstance (e.g., moving out of poverty) implies exposure to that circumstance during a more or less sensitive period of development. A growing body of evidence demonstrates that disadvantage during very early childhood has a durable impact on development because it hampers cognitive development during critical or sensitive periods of development (Jackson 2010; Palloni 2006; Torche 2011). In this vein, a growing number of studies consider the dynamics of economic disadvantage and child development, demonstrating important effects of the timing of poverty and economic disadvantage (Holmes and Kiernan 2013; Lee 2014; Wagmiller et al. 2006). Similarly, prior work has examined the importance of the timing of different family structures and the types of different transitions (Kiernan and Mensah 2010; Lee and McLanahan 2015; Osborne and McLanahan 2007). While there is compelling evidence that both early childhood and middle/late childhood circumstances are associated with child outcomes, the preponderance of evidence suggests that early exposure to family disadvantage may be more important than later exposure (e.g., Duncan et al. 1998). Because education is associated with greater economic resources, higher levels of biological father involvement, and better mental health among mothers, children in more highly educated families may be less likely to experience economic disadvantage, single motherhood, and maternal depression during early childhood (Duncan, Ziol-Guest, and Kalil 2010).

A Comparative Lens on Family Circumstances and Child Well-Being

An important benefit of this study is its cross-national approach. We reveal whether findings observed among children in the United States—which compose the majority of research on this topic—can be replicated among children of a similar age elsewhere. The UK provides a useful comparison because, despite many demographic and cultural similarities to the United States, the UK provides social services to children and families differently. Both countries have racially and ethnically diverse populations and large immigrant communities, albeit from different sending countries (Hernandez, Mccartney, and Blanchard 2009). In addition, both the United States and the UK have experienced similar economic and demographic changes during the past several decades. The two societies share patterns of family formation: rates of nonmarital birth and divorce are high in both countries (Haskey 1996); both countries also exhibit a strong socioeconomic and racial/ethnic pattern to family structure. The two countries also share trends in social inequality: income inequality is higher in the United States (e.g., Banks, Blundell, and Smith 2003), but levels in both societies are high and have increased over the last several decades.

Despite similar patterns of family formation (Kiernan et al. 2011) and income inequality (Banks, Blundell, and Smith 2003; Wilkinson and Pickett 2009), the two countries have different health care and social welfare systems, resulting in different levels of government support for children and families. The UK provides more universal health services than does the United States, including health care through the British National Health Service, home visits for new mothers, priority in scheduling medical appointments for children, and child centers with integrated childcare services. Welfare state policies in the UK are also more generous than those in the United States with respect to family cash assistance, social housing, and childcare (Meyers and Gornick 2005).

Perhaps because of important institutional differences amid many similarities, many studies compare broad patterns of inequality in the United States and the UK as they relate to family formation, economic inequality, and social mobility (e.g., Banks, Blundell, and Smith 2003; Kerckhoff 1993; Kiernan et al. 2011). While there is more research comparing macro-level processes in the United States and the UK, a growing body of research focuses on how micro-level processes at the family level influence children's development. Cross-sectional research shows that children's skill development is strongly predicted by maternal education, family income, family structure, and maternal depression (Cherlin et al. 1991; Joshi, Paci, and Waldfogel 1999; McCulloch et al. 2000; Parcel, Campbell, and Zhong 2012). In addition, strong socioeconomic gradients in children's development exist in both countries (Banks, Blundell, and Smith 2003).

There is a dearth of research, however, that examines the dynamics of family circumstances in a multidimensional and longitudinal way.

In this article we use longitudinal data and latent class analysis to identify the most prevalent trajectories of family circumstances throughout early childhood, to link these trajectories to children's cognitive development, and to examine their role in mediating the educational differences.

Given existing cross-sectional research showing a strong relationship between family resources and child well-being, one plausible hypothesis is that we will observe a similar association between maternal education and child development across both countries and a similar role of family resources in explaining the educational gradient in child development. In this case, maternal education and family economic and social capital may act as fundamental causes of children's development (e.g., Link and Phelan 1995; Olafsdottir 2007; Parcel, Campbell, and Zhong 2012). At the same time, Esping-Anderson (2002) suggests that countries with stronger government investments in child and family services should exhibit a weaker relationship between family-level factors and child development, since government investments may compensate for a lack of resources among low-SES families. If true, we should observe a weaker relationship between maternal education and both family resources and child development in the UK, as well as a weaker role for family-level processes in explaining the gradient (but see Parcel, Campbell, and Zhong [2012] for contrasting evidence).

Data

Our analysis is based on two surveys: the Fragile Families and Child Wellbeing Study (FFS) in the United States and the Millennium Cohort Study (MCS) in the UK. Both birth cohort studies are representative of national populations; contain rich longitudinal information on children's family environments, health, and development; and oversample disadvantaged and ethnic minority families. The FFS follows approximately 5,000 children born between 1998 and 2000 in large U.S. cities, including a large oversample of births to unmarried parents. Mothers, and most fathers, were interviewed in the hospital soon after birth, with additional interviews when the children were ages one, three, five, and nine. When weighted, FFS data are representative of births in cities with populations of more than 200,000—we use weights in estimating descriptive statistics and trajectories. A key component of the FFS study design was the use of a hospital-based sampling frame. By starting at the hospital, the FFS was able to obtain higher response rates than studies that sample from birth records and interview mothers in their homes.

The MCS is the fourth of Britain's national birth cohort studies. The first wave of the MCS took place during 2001–2002 and included 18,552 families and 18,818 cohort children. Information was first collected from parents when their children were nine months old, with follow-up interviews with the main caregiver (usually the mother) when the children were ages three, five, and seven. The sample design included an overrepresentation of families living in areas with high proportions of child poverty or ethnic minority populations.

In both surveys, we use data through age five to maximize the comparability of the two surveys. Sensitivity analyses using similar outcomes at age nine in the FFS yield highly similar results with respect to both family trajectories, as well as the association between family trajectories and cognitive development. Sensitivity analyses using outcomes at age seven in this MCS data also show highly similar patterns of results, using a slightly different measure of cognitive skill.[1]

Measures

Maternal education

Our focal measure of socioeconomic status is maternal education, given compelling evidence that education predicts other resources in the family, as well as child development. Because education remains relatively fixed over the adult life course, it is also less likely than other measures to be affected by the dimensions of family circumstances that we consider. In the United States, our measure of maternal education separates mothers with less than a high school education, a high school diploma, some college, and a college diploma or higher. In the UK, we use a comparable measure, separating mothers with no qualifications, ordinary level examinations (typically school leaving qualifications taken at age 16), A-level college entrance exams and vocational equivalents, and university degrees.

We treat children's well-being as a function of maternal education around the time of children's birth, plus family circumstances (family income, family structure, and maternal depression) during early and middle childhood. We examine the shape of family trajectories in early and middle childhood, as well as the collective contribution of these dimensions to the size of the educational gradient.

Family income

At each survey wave we measure family income using the household poverty ratio, which adjusts income for number of adults and children in the household. We construct binary categories, differentiating between children living in or near poverty and those with a higher income. Specifically, in both samples we distinguish between families with adjusted incomes below 200 percent of the federal poverty line (reference category) from families with adjusted incomes above the poverty line.[2]

Family structure

To measure family structure at each wave, we use a binary measure in both samples differentiating between mothers who are living with their child's biological father (married or cohabiting) and mothers who are not living with the father. This measure affords clear examination of the composition and stability of family structure throughout early childhood and recognizes the importance of biological father involvement for children's development (Carlson 2006). We explore the sensitivity of the results to several alternative measures of family structure, including a binary measure that makes family structure at each age contingent on marriage (to the biological or social father), compared to cohabiting and single mothers; and a three-category measure of family structure that distinguishes mothers who are married/cohabiting with the biological father, married/cohabiting with a nonbiological father, and living alone. Results using these alternative measures are similar to those based on the original measure, and so we use the binary measure in the final analyses.[3] We also compare results with and without a control for the number of mother's romantic partnerships and observe identical findings. We do not include this measure in the final models because of concerns that it is conflated with our family structure trajectories, which also capture some aspects of relationship stability.

Maternal depression

Finally, in both surveys we examine maternal depression as an indicator of maternal well-being.[4] At each wave we distinguish between mothers who are and are not depressed. In the FFS this measure is constructed from the Composite International Diagnostic Interview (CIDI)–Short Form, which includes items that compose a score for major depression. In the MCS, measures at each age are based on mothers' self-reports about whether they have been diagnosed with depression or anxiety. Maternal mental health is a commonly used indicator of mothers' ability to engage in stimulating parenting behavior, given the strong association between mental health and the content of parent-child relationships (Brooks-Gunn and Markman 2005).

Moreover, maternal mental health is strongly predicted by family circumstances (e.g., Meadows, McLanahan, and Brooks-Gunn 2008). In each survey, we examine the extent to which available measures of mothers' engagement with children at each age correlate with depression and find strong relationships across age and samples.

Child cognitive development

We measure cognitive development using the British Ability Scales Naming Vocabulary Test (MCS) and the Peabody Picture Vocabulary Test (FFS). We convert raw scores to z-scores to enable comparable and relative assessment.

Other variables

We also measure several variables that are expected to be correlated with both family environments and child well-being, including maternal race/ethnicity, child sex, number of children in the household, and mothers' age at the time of the child's birth.

Rather than drop children with missing information from a particular module within a wave, we use multiple imputation (five imputations, estimation via chained equations in Stata) to replace missing values on independent and dependent variables, based on predictions from the variables described above (Allison 2002). Values are not imputed if a child is entirely missing from a wave.

Analysis

The analysis proceeds in several steps. First, we use the measures described above to identify trajectories of family circumstances throughout early childhood that include family income, family structure, and maternal depression. We use longitudinal latent class analysis (LCA) to identify trajectory classes of family types. Rather than analyzing the timing, duration, and stability of exposure to particular family circumstances separately, we apply LCA to simultaneously account for each of these temporal dimensions. Children's family circumstances at each age are time-ordered, permitting differentiation among the temporal dimensions of exposure (Jones and Nagin 2007; Muthén 2004). LCA identifies a latent categorical variable, C, that consists of a limited number of trajectory classes, j. LCA assumes a finite mixture of unobserved groups of individuals (i.e., latent classes), estimating the probability of falling into a trajectory class, j, of the latent variable C. LCA relaxes the assumptions of growth curve modeling, which assumes that all individuals are drawn from a single population and that the degree of deviation from the population mean intercept and slope captures individual variation.

We use this modeling strategy to find the best-fitting number of trajectories of family income, family structure, and maternal depression from birth through age five in the FFS, and ages one through age five in the MCS.[5] To determine the best-fitting number of latent class trajectories, we rely on substantive knowledge from previous research, as well as two statistical criteria: the Bayesian Information Criterion (BIC) and entropy criteria (Raftery 1996). Models that provide a better fit to the data, and that are more parsimonious, produce a lower BIC value, and higher entropy values indicate better differentiation among trajectory classes. We use these criteria to compare models with two through five classes, for each family dimension (economic status, family structure, and maternal depression). All descriptive and LCA results use national weights at age five.

After describing the evolution of family circumstances throughout early childhood, we estimate ordinary least squares (OLS) regression models that examine the relationship between maternal education and children's well-being, while examining the mediating role of the family trajectories in explaining the educational gradient in each sample.

Results

Describing the samples

Table 1 presents weighted descriptive statistics for each sample. Mothers in the FFS are more likely to be poorly educated than MCS mothers—29 percent with less than high school versus 16 percent with no qualifications. FFS mothers

TABLE 1
Weighted Descriptive Statistics, FFS and MCS

FFS		MCS	
Maternal education		Maternal education	
Less than high school	29	No qualifications	16
HS	32	O-levels	39
Some college	19	A-levels	20
College or more	20	Higher education	25
Non-Hispanic white	29	White	84
Non-Hispanic black	35	South Asian	9
Hispanic	29	Black	4
Other	7	Other	3
Child male	54	Child male	50
Mother mean age at birth	27.1	Mother mean age at birth	28.4
Mean number of kids in household, wave 1	1.1	Mean number of kids in household, wave 1	1.1
Mean PPVT Z-score, age 5	0	Mean naming ability Z-score, age 5	0

NOTE: Columns include percentages unless otherwise specified.

are also slightly less likely than MCS mothers to have a college degree. The distribution of race/ethnicity in the FFS reflects the urban composition of the sample, with more than half of mothers identifying as non-Hispanic black (35 percent) or Hispanic (29 percent). (About half of Hispanic mothers are immigrants from Mexico, which accounts for the high prevalence of U.S. mothers with less than a high school degree.) In the MCS, the largest ethnic minority group is South Asians (9 percent), with smaller percentages of black (African and Caribbean, 4 percent) and other (3 percent), largely East Asian, mothers.

How do children's family circumstances evolve throughout early childhood?

Our first goal is to identify trajectories of family income, family structure, and maternal depression that account for the timing, duration, and stability of exposure to each circumstance.

Before presenting the trajectories, Table 2 shows model selection criteria for the LCA analyses. We proceed with the four-class model for family structure in both samples; a four-class model for economic status in the United States, and three-class model in the UK; and a two-class model for maternal depression in both samples. Figures 1 and 2 show results from the longitudinal LCA.

Figures 1A and 2A show the estimated weighted probability of children's living with the biological father by age. For family structure, the best-fitting models include four trajectories in both the FFS and MCS samples. In both samples, inspection of these probabilities reveals four trajectory classes: a group with a

TABLE 2
Latent Class Model Selection for Family Trajectories, FFS and MCS

Number of Latent Classes	BIC	Entropy	Vuong-Lo-Mendell-Rubin Likelihood Ratio Test (LRT)	Lo-Mendell-Rubin Adjusted LRT
FFS				
Family structure				
2	18,244.299	.736	.0000	.0000
3	18,049.989	.694	.0000	.0000
4	**17,855.152**	**.701**	**.0000**	**.0000**
5	18,019.634	.694	.0100	.0100
Economic disadvantage				
2	18,003.820	.821	.0000	.0000
3	17,884.420	.623	.0000	.0000
4	**17,896.078**	**.663**	**.0000**	**.0000**
5	17,938.560	.673	.5000	.5000
Maternal depression				
2	**10,982.960**	**.69**	**.0000**	**.0000**
3	11,016.761	.649	.5000	.5000
4	11,050.562	.454	.0000	.0000
5	11,084.362	.396	.2879	.2879
MCS				
Family structure				
2	73,398.743	.92	.0000	.0000
3	68,684.451	.92	.0000	.0000
4	**67,411.057**	**.92**	**.0000**	**.0000**
5	67,460.452	.704	.0984	.0984
Economic disadvantage				
2	53,200.733	.733	.0000	.0000
3	**52,240.250**	**.744**	**.0000**	**.0000**
4	53,279.760	.541	.0000	.0000
5	53,319.281	.351	.1271	.1330
Maternal depression				
2	**26,771.050**	**.883**	**.0000**	**.0000**
3	26,810.569	.509	.4050	.4050
4	26,850.080	.492	.0000	.0000
5	26,889.590	.568	.0000	.0000

NOTE: Bolded rows indicate preferred models.

consistently high probability of living with the biological father ("always living with the biological father"), a group with a consistently low probability of living with the biological father ("never lives with the biological father"), a group that has a low early probability that increases with age ("transitions to biological

FIGURE 1A
Trajectories of Exposure to Biological Father, FFS 0–5

FIGURE 1A
Trajectories of Exposure to Biological Father, FFS 0–5

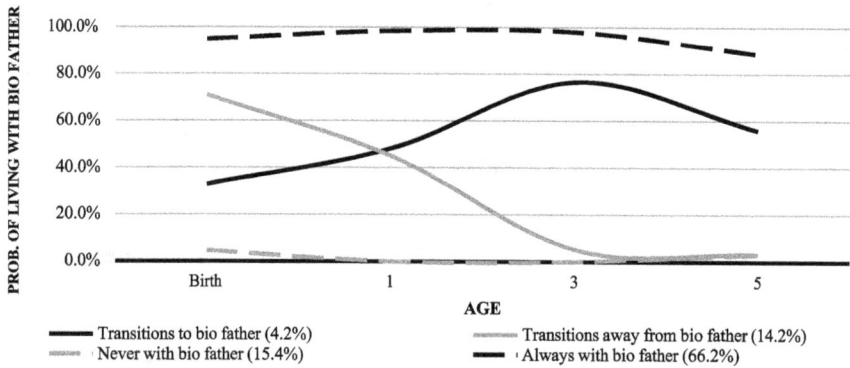

father"), and a group that has a high early probability that decreases with age ("transitions away from biological father"). Both samples experience similar patterns of timing, duration, and stability of exposure to marriage. In the FFS, children who "always" live with the biological father (in either a married or cohabiting household) compose 66 percent of children—among these children, the probability of living with the biological father is close to 1 at every age, meaning that these children experience a long duration with, as well as a stable exposure to, the biological father. In the MCS, this group composes about 58 percent of the sample.

The "never lived with biological father" group is smaller than the previous type but prevalent in both samples, at 15 percent in the FFS and 17 percent in the MCS. This group of children has a very low probability of living with the biological father at every age, meaning that they experience a long and stable duration of single motherhood. In addition to the two largest groups in each sample, the analysis also reveals two smaller groups that experience a greater degree of instability and variation in the timing of exposure. About 4 percent of FFS children and 7 percent of MCS children experience an increase in the probability of moving in with their biological fathers after living apart during the first year of life. This group of children experiences very early childhood biological father absence. About 14 percent of FFS children and 18 percent of MCS children experience the exit of a biological father after age one. For these children, the probability of living without the biological father is lowest around age five, rather than very early childhood.

Figures 1B and 2B show the probability of exposure to economic disadvantage by age. The first comparison to note between the two samples is that the best-fitting model includes four trajectories in the FFS and three in the MCS. Second, the majority of children in both samples live stably in either low-income or higher-income households—36 percent of FFS children and 27 percent of MCS children are "always higher income," with a very low probability of living in/near poverty at all ages. About 44 percent of FFS children consistently live in low-income families between birth and age five, compared to 27 percent of MCS children. Third, there is a greater deal of economic instability among FFS children. While the third group

FIGURE 1B
Trajectories of Exposure to Economic Disadvantage, FFS 0–5

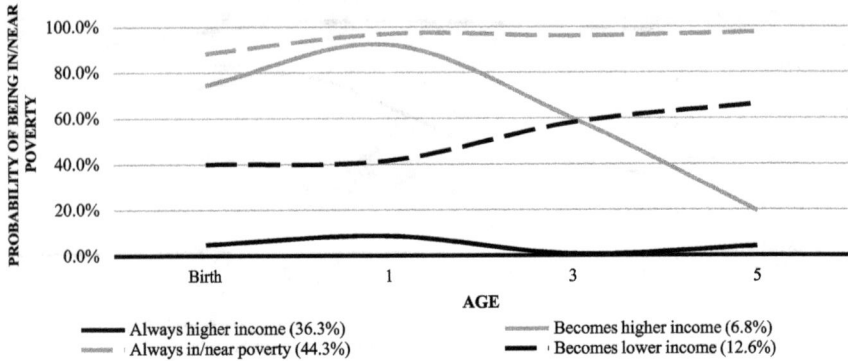

Always higher income (36.3%)
Always in/near poverty (44.3%)
Becomes higher income (6.8%)
Becomes lower income (12.6%)

FIGURE 1C
Trajectories of Exposure to Maternal Depression, FFS 1–5

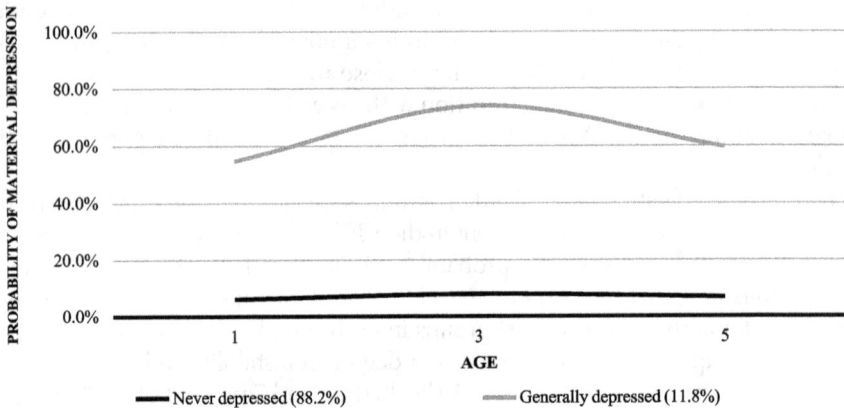

Never depressed (88.2%)
Generally depressed (11.8%)

in the MCS sample comprises children who are consistently "middle income" (though still with a high probability of economic disadvantage), two groups of FFS experience early and late exposure to economic disadvantage, respectively. About 7 percent of children experience early economic disadvantage, with a declining probability after age one, and about 13 percent experience an increase in the probability of economic disadvantage around age three.

Finally, examining trajectories of maternal depression reveals two fairly stable classes in each sample. The majority of children in both samples (88 percent in FFS, 90 percent in MCS) have mothers who consistently have a very low probability of depression, while a smaller group (12 percent in FFS, 9 percent in MCS) lives with mothers who are consistently more likely to be depressed. In both samples, the probability of depression among consistently depressed mothers increases around age three and then gradually declines again by age five.

FIGURE 2A

Trajectories of Exposure to Biological Father, MCS 1–5

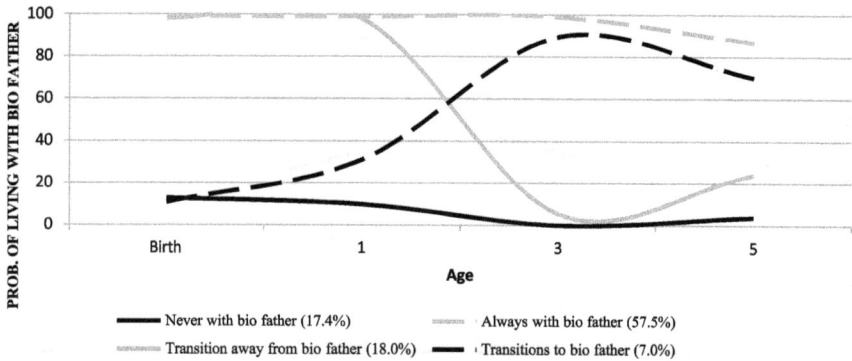

Never with bio father (17.4%)   Always with bio father (57.5%)
Transition away from bio father (18.0%)   Transitions to bio father (7.0%)

FIGURE 2B

Trajectories of Exposure to Economic Disadvantage, MCS 1–5

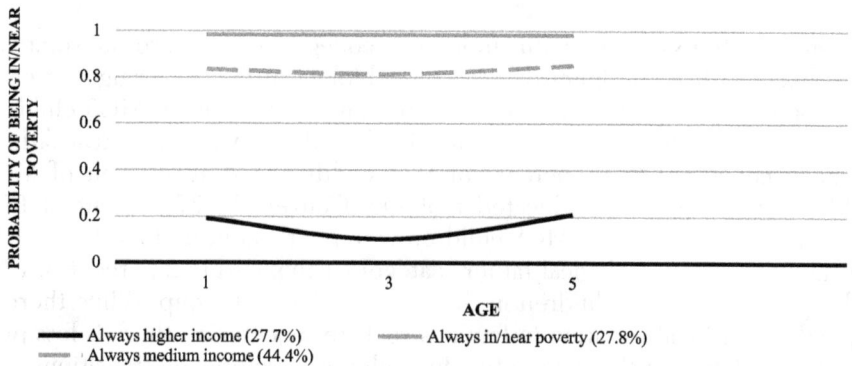

Always higher income (27.7%)   Always in/near poverty (27.8%)
Always medium income (44.4%)

Descriptive LCA results suggest that there are pronounced differences in children's duration of exposure to economic disadvantage, single motherhood, and maternal depression in both countries, as well as variation in the timing of that exposure. While variation in timing produces some instability in children's trajectories, particularly in the case of economic disadvantage in the United States, we do not observe a great deal of instability across early childhood, perhaps because of the relatively long spacing between observed time points.

Educational Variation in Family Trajectories

Table 3 shows the weighted distribution of family trajectories by maternal education. In both samples, there is striking variation in children's duration of exposure to disadvantaged family circumstances. Children of the most highly

FIGURE 2C

Trajectories of Exposure to Maternal Depression, MCS 1–5

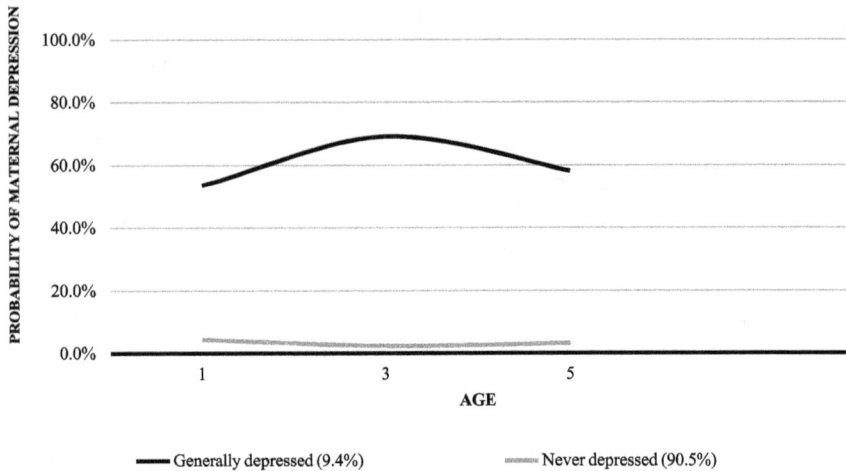

educated mothers—those with at least a college degree—are substantially more likely to live continuously with their biological father throughout early childhood. Ninety percent of FFS children and 78 percent of MCS children with the highest educated mothers are in the "always with biological father" category, compared to 53 percent of FFS children and 40 percent of MCS children with the lowest educated mothers. Conversely, 27 percent of FFS children and 30 percent of MCS children with poorly educated mothers are in the "always without biological father" category, compared to 2 percent of FFS and 5 percent of MCS children in the highest educated group. While there is marked educational variation in family structure trajectories, there is less pronounced variation in the degree to which children experience transitions into living with and away from their biological father, though children with highly educated mothers are less likely to experience instability and transitions away from or to the biological father.

Examining income trajectories reveals similarly large educational variation in the duration of children's exposure to economic disadvantage. Among children in highly educated families, 81 percent of FFS and 61 percent of MCS children live in consistently higher income families, compared to 6 percent (FFS) and 3 percent (MCS) of children in the lowest educated families. As is the case with family structure trajectories, there is less educational variation among the economically unstable groups in the FFS, with children in middle-educated families (high school and some college) slightly more likely to experience increasing or decreasing income than children in the extreme categories. Finally, in both samples there is a small educational gradient in trajectories of maternal depression, whereby higher educated mothers are the least likely to be depressed.

TABLE 3
Educational Variation in Weighted Family Trajectories, FFS and MCS (in percentages)

FFS	Less than HS	HS	Some College	College+
Family structure trajectories				
Always with biological (bio) father	53	59	70	90
Always without bio father	27	17	11	2
Transitions away from bio father	14	19	13	8
Transitions to bio father	6	5	5	0
Income trajectories				
Consistently high income	6	23	53	81
Consistently low income	83	50	22	7
Decreasing income	6	17	19	11
Increasing income	6	11	7	2
Depression trajectories				
Consistently depressed	16	11	10	9
Generally not depressed	84	89	90	91

MCS	No Qualifications	O-Levels	A-Levels	Higher Ed.
Family structure trajectories				
Always with biological (bio) father	40	55	65	78
Always without bio father	30	20	13	5
Transitions away from bio father	22	20	18	15
Transitions to bio father	8	6	4	2
Income trajectories				
Consistently high income	3	16	29	61
Consistently low income	49	44	34	14
Consistently middle income	48	40	37	24
Depression trajectories				
Consistently depressed	9	8	6	4
Generally not depressed	91	92	94	96

Do family trajectories explain differences in children's cognitive development?

Tables 4 and 5 present results from OLS regressions of cognitive development on maternal education and family trajectories. Tables 4 and 5 show the findings for the FFS and MCS samples, respectively. The first column in each panel presents results that control for sociodemographic variables, but not for trajectories of income, family structure, and maternal depression. In both countries, there is a strong gradient in cognitive development, consistent with previous research. Controlling for sociodemographic variables, the difference between children in

TABLE 4
OLS Regressions of Age 5 Cognitive Development on Maternal Education and Family
Circumstances, FFS

	PPVT Z-Score	
HS	.186°	.133°
	(.05)	(.04)
Some college	.560°	.421°
	(.05)	(.06)
College or more	.760°	.477°
	(.08)	(.08)
Income trajectories		
Consistently low income		−.488°
		(.06)
Decreasing income		−.247°
		(.06)
Increasing income		−.232°
		(.08)
Family structure trajectories		
Always without biological (bio) father		.015
		(.05)
Transitions away from bio father		−.015
		(.05)
Transitions to bio father		.023
		(.06)
Depression trajectories		
Consistently depressed		−.034
		(.05)
Intercept	.771°	.396°
	(.09)	(.00)

NOTE: Robust standard errors in parentheses. Controls included.
°$p < .01$ (two-tailed test).

the highest and lowest educated groups is almost one standard deviation in both countries—.760 in FFS and .798 in MCS.

Including family trajectories in the models demonstrates how each family trajectory is related to children's development, and considers its role in mediating educational differences. With respect to economic disadvantage, there is evidence in both countries that children who experience a consistent and long duration in low-income households have significantly lower cognitive development than their peers living in consistently higher-income households. FFS children who live in consistently low-income households from birth through age five score almost 0.5 standard deviations below their peers in consistently higher-income households on the cognitive assessment, on average. In the MCS, this difference

TABLE 5
OLS Regressions of Age 5 Cognitive Development on Maternal Education
and Family Circumstances, MCS

	Naming Vocabulary Z-Score (N = 14,562)	
O-levels	.386°	.341°
	(.02)	(.02)
A-levels	.570°	.480°
	(.03)	(.03)
Higher education	.798°	.635°
	(.03)	(.03)
Income trajectories		
Consistently low income		−.285°
		(.02)
Always medium income		−.177°
		(.02)
Family structure trajectories		
Always without biological (bio) father		−.101°
		(.02)
Transitions away from bio father		−.125°
		(.02)
Transitions to bio father		−.121°
		(.03)
Depression trajectories		
Consistently depressed		−.082°
		(.03)
Intercept	−.740°	−.326°
	(.05)	(.06)

NOTE: Robust standard errors in parentheses. Controls included.
°p < .01 (two-tailed test).

is almost one-third of a standard deviation (−.285), with a smaller but still sizable difference (−.177) between children in middle-income households and their higher-income peers. FFS children who experience economic instability also perform worse than their stably advantaged peers, including children who experience both decreasing (−.247) and increasing (−.232) income during early childhood. Because children who experience increasing income live in or near poverty in the first few years of life (Figure 1B), this finding is consistent with evidence linking exposure to economic disadvantage in very early childhood to poorer development (e.g., Duncan et al. 1998; Lee 2014).

With respect to the association between trajectories of family structure and children's skill development, the findings in the UK reveal that a long duration of residence without the biological father is associated with lower cognitive skill development. Transitioning away from the biological father (which, as shown in Figure 2A, also indicates exposure to single motherhood closer to age five) is also associated with poorer outcomes as compared to children in stable biological father family structures, as is transitioning to a biological father structure (early childhood exposure to single motherhood). In the FFS, family structure coefficients work in a similar direction but do not reach statistical significance after controlling for income trajectories.

The lack of a significant difference between stable, biological-parent families and other families is inconsistent with prior research, including research using these data (e.g., Waldfogel, Craigie, and Brooks-Gunn 2010). One possible explanation for the different pattern of findings here is that we combine cohabiting parents with married parents, focusing instead on the presence of the biological father, whereas Waldfogel, Craigie, and Brooks-Gunn (2010) treated cohabiting-parent families as a separate group and found that children living in stable, cohabiting-parent families score lower on cognitive tests than children in stable, married-parent families. Before controlling for income trajectories, family structure trajectories are significantly negatively related to children's cognitive development in both FFS and MCS, with coefficients of a similar magnitude in both countries. Finally, there is a significantly negative association between maternal depression—specifically, a long duration of maternal depression—and cognitive skill development in the MCS but not the FFS.

Considering the contribution of family trajectories to the magnitude and significance of the educational gradient in children's cognitive development reveals a modest explanatory role in both countries. For cognitive development, family trajectories reduce the gap between children in the highest- and lowest-educated families by about one-third (.760 vs. .477) in the FFS, and by about 20 percent in the MCS (.798 vs. .635). The vast majority of mediation of the educational gradient is driven by income trajectories, suggesting that the strong relationship between education and income throughout early childhood, and between income and child development, is particularly important in explaining the advantages of children in highly educated families. In addition, because income, family structure, and maternal mental health have reciprocal effects at each age (e.g., Lee and McLanahan 2015), it is possible that the large mediating role of income across age partially reflects prior effects of family structure and maternal depression on income.

Conclusion

There is considerable speculation that the resources and content of family life explain the striking degree of educational inequality in children's early development and the persistence of that inequality as children age. But we know very little about the degree to which children's family environments remain stable or unstable as they age, and how variation in the timing, duration, and stability of particular resources contributes to the educational gradient.

In this article, we used high-quality, population-based data to move beyond a cross-sectional and unidimensional account of children's family environments. We provide a nuanced account of the stability of family circumstances by using family income, family structure, and maternal depression to evaluate the association between family trajectories and children's development, and evaluate the contribution of cumulative family circumstances to differences in children's cognitive development.

Cross-national analysis of two longitudinal data sources yields several important findings:

- First, we find a good deal of similarity between the United States and the UK in patterns of family life during early childhood, and in the degree to which those patterns contribute to educational inequality in terms of children's skill development. Children in the United States and UK experience similar patterns of timing, duration, and stability of exposure to their biological fathers.
- Second, the majority of children in both samples experience stability in their family circumstances over time, living consistently with or without their biological father, with mothers who are consistently depressed or not, and in families that are consistently high or low income. While there is striking educational variation in which stable trajectory children fall into, there is less educational variation in the instability of family structure, family income, and maternal depression.
- Third, there is consistent evidence across both countries that family trajectories account for some, but not all, of the differences in children's cognitive skills at the end of early childhood.
- Fourth, these analyses demonstrate a strong negative impact of long durations of exposure to disadvantaged family circumstances on children's outcomes, consistent with the importance of cumulative exposure processes for children's development.

It is important to weigh the merits of this research against some limitations and caveats that will be useful to pursue in future research. First, while we examine the sensitivity of our findings to more refined measures of family structure and family economic status, in final analyses we condensed these complex constructs into simpler measures that can be safely compared over time and countries. Maternal depression, for example, can be consistently measured across ages and samples, unlike some correlated parenting behaviors that vary in content and meaning with age.

It will be valuable in future research to further examine differences and synergies among various dimensions of family financial and social capital (e.g., Harding, Morris, and Hughes 2015). It is also important to note that the research presented here is descriptive by design; we do not claim that the relationships that we observe between maternal education, family circumstances, and child outcomes are causal. Rather, we hope to provide a more complex description of the dynamics of children's family arrangements than exists in previous research, and to understand the associations between these trajectories and children's development. Certainly, family income, family structure, and maternal depression are highly correlated, and the associations that we observe between any one trajectory and child well-being may, in part, reflect reciprocal effects of each family circumstance at each age.

That we observe largely similar relationships among maternal education, cumulative family circumstances, and children's development across the United States and the UK is striking. Important differences in the two countries' health care and social welfare systems create varying landscapes of government support for children and families, suggesting that socioeconomic differences in children's development might be weaker and less persistent in the UK, and that associations between family resources and child outcomes might be less pronounced. In contrast, maternal education is strongly associated with children's cognitive development and health in the UK, as are trajectories of income, family structure, and maternal depression throughout early childhood—in fact, maternal education remains a strong predictor of children's outcomes even after accounting for variation in family trajectories across educational groups. These findings are not consistent with the argument that government investments in health and family services, while vital for affording access to care and resources, offset the role of parental resources in impacting children's development.

Of course, the large number of differences in population composition and policy across the United States and UK does not allow us to attribute cross-national variation to a particular source. However, the largely similar findings across the two countries point to parental circumstances as a fundamental determinant of children's well-being. Moreover, while the three dimensions of family life examined here act as an important pathway linking maternal education to children's development, there are still important associations unexplained by the factors observed here. It will be useful in future research to examine the larger set of circumstances that become relevant as children age, including not only their family environments, but their child care, school, and peer interactions.

Notes

1. The measure of cognitive development in the MCS at age seven is the British Ability Scales Pattern Construction and Word Reading tests.

2. Substantive results do not change when we use a slightly stricter definition of poverty/near poverty (17 percent).

3. Analyses using a three-category family structure measure identify a small cluster of children who experience a transition from a single-mother living arrangement to an arrangement with a nonbiological father in the household, and larger clusters of children who are in stable family structure arrangements with or without the biological father. Regression results using three-category family structure trajectories, instead of binary marriage trajectories, produce identical results with respect to the magnitude of the educational gradient before and after measuring family structure trajectories.

4. We also examine maternal physical health (on a self-reported scale) and results are similar to those examining depression.

5. We also estimate latent class growth analysis (LCGA) models, a variant of LCA models that impose a stricter functional form by estimating growth curve factors among each class, and specifying a functional

form of the growth parameters prior to estimation. While the results are generally quite similar, we present LCA results because of their more flexible estimation.

References

Adler, Nancy E., Thomas Boyce, Margaret A. Chesney, Sheldon Cohen, Susan Folkman, Robert L. Kahn, and S. L. Syme. 1994. Socioeconomic status and health: The challenge of the gradient. *American Psychologist* 49:15–24.

Allison, Paul D. 2002. *Missing data*. Thousand Oaks, CA: Sage Publications.

Amato, P. R. 2001. Children of divorce in the 1990s: An update of the Amato and Keith (1991) meta-analysis. *Journal of Family Psychology* 15:355–70.

Amato, Paul. 2005. The impact of family formation change on the cognitive, social, and emotional well-being of the next generation. *The Future of Children* 15:75–96.

Banks, James, Richard Blundell, and James P. Smith. 2003. Understanding differences in household financial wealth between the United States and Great Britain. *Journal of Human Resources* 38 (2): 241–79.

Ben-Shlomo, Yoav, and Diana Kuh. 2002. A life course approach to chronic disease epidemiology: Conceptual models, empirical challenges and interdisciplinary perspectives. *International Journal of Epidemiology* 31 (2): 285–93.

Bernardi, Fabrizio, Juho Harkonen, and Diederik Boertien. 2013. Effects of family forms and dynamics on children's well-being and life chances: Literature review. Families and Societies Working Paper Series. Available from: http://www.familiesandsocieties.eu/wp-content/uploads/2014/12/WP04Bernard iEtal2013.pdf.

Brennan, Patricia A., Constance Hammen, Margaret J. Andersen, William Bor, Jake M. Najman, and Gail M. Williams. 2000. Chronicity, severity, and timing of maternal depressive symptoms: Relationships with child outcomes at age 5. *Developmental Psychology* 36 (6): 759–66.

Brooks-Gunn, Jeanne, and Lisa B. Markman. 2005. The contribution of parenting to ethnic and racial gaps in school readiness. *The Future of Children* 15 (1): 139–68.

Brown, S. 2004. Family structure and child well-being: The significance of parental cohabitation. *Journal of Marriage and Family* 66:351–67.

Carlson, Marcia. 2006. Family structure, father involvement, and adolescent behavioral outcomes. *Journal of Marriage and Family* 68 (1): 137–54.

Cavanagh, Shannon E., and Aletha C. Huston. 2008. The timing of family instability and children's social development. *Journal of Marriage and Family* 70 (5): 1258–70.

Chase-Lansdale, P. Lindsay, Andrew Cherlin, and Kathleen E. Kiernan. 1995. The long-term effects of parental divorce on the mental health of young adults: A developmental perspective. *Child Development* 66:1614–34.

Cherlin, Andrew, Frank F. Furstenberg Jr., P. Lindsay Chase-Lansdale, Kathleen E. Kiernan, Philip K. Robins, Donna R. Morrison, and Julien O. Teitler. 1991. Longitudinal studies of effects of divorce on children in Great Britain and the United States. *Science* 252:1386–89.

Coleman, James, Ernest Campbell, Carol Hobson, James McPartland, Alexander Mood, Frederick Weinfield, and Robert York. 1966. *Equality of educational opportunity*. Washington, DC: U.S. Department of Health, Education, and Welfare, Office of Education.

Currie, Janet, and Mark Stabile. 2003. Socioeconomic status and child health: Why is the relationship stronger for older children? *American Economic Review* 93:1813–23.

Duncan, Greg J., W. Jean Yeung, Jeanne Brooks-Gunn, and Judith R. Smith. 1998. How much does childhood poverty affect the life chances of children? *American Sociological Review* 63 (3): 406–23.

Duncan, Greg J., Kathleen Ziol-Guest, and Ariel Kalil. 2010. Early-childhood poverty and adult attainment, behavior, and health. *Child Development* 81 (1): 306–25.

Edin, Kathryn J., and Mara Kefalas. 2005. *Promises I can keep: Why poor women put motherhood before marriage*. Berkeley, CA: University of California Press.

Ellwood, David T., and Christopher Jencks. 2004. The uneven spread of single-parent families: What do we know? Where do we look for answers? *Social Inequality* 1:3–77.

Esping-Anderson, Gosta. 2002. *Why we need a new welfare state*. Oxford: Oxford University Press.

Estaugh, V., and C. Power. 1991. Family disruption in early life and drinking in young adulthood. *Alcohol and Alcoholism* 26 (5–6): 639–44.

Ferraro, Kenneth F., and Tetyana Pylypiv Shippee. 2009. Aging and cumulative inequality: How does inequality get under the skin? *The Gerontologist* 49 (3): 333–43.

Finch, Brian K. 2003. Early origins of the gradient: The relationship between socioeconomic status and infant mortality in the United States. *Demography* 40:675–99.

Fomby, Paula, and Andrew J. Cherlin. 2007. Family instability and child well-being. *American Sociological Review* 72 (2): 181–204.

Goldin, Claudia, and Lawrence F. Katz. 1999. Human capital and social capital: The rise of secondary schooling in America, 1910–1940. *Journal of Interdisciplinary History* 29 (4): 683–723.

Harding, Jessica F., Pamela A. Morris, and Diane Hughes. 2015. The relationship between maternal education and children's academic outcomes: A theoretical framework. *Journal of Marriage and Family* 77 (1): 60–76.

Haskey, John. 1996. Population review: (8). The ethnic minority and overseas-born populations of Great Britain. *Population Trends* 88:13–30.

Heckman, James J. 2008. Schools, skills, and synapses. *Economic Inquiry* 46 (3): 289–324.

Hernandez, Donald James, Suzanne E. Macartney, and Victoria Lael Blanchard. 2009. *Children in immigrant families in eight affluent countries: Their family, national, and international context*. Florence: UNICEF Innocenti Research Centre.

Holmes, J., and K. Kiernan. 2013. Persistent poverty and children's development in the early years of childhood. *Policy and Politics* 41 (1): 19–42.

Jackson, Margot I. 2010. A life course perspective on child health, cognition and occupational skill qualifications in adulthood: Evidence from a British cohort. *Social Forces* 89 (1): 89–116.

Jekielek, S. M. 1998. Parental conflict, marital disruption, and children's emotional well-being. *Social Forces* 76:908–35.

Jones, Bobby L., and Daniel S. Nagin. 2007. Advances in group-based trajectory modeling and an SAS procedure for estimating them. *Sociological Methods & Research* 35 (4): 542–71.

Jonsson, Jan J. O. 2010. Child well-being and intergenerational inequality. *Child Indicators Research* 3 (1): 1–10.

Joshi, Heather, Pierella Paci, and Jane Waldfogel. 1999. The wages of motherhood: Better or worse? *Cambridge Journal of Economics* 23 (5): 543–64.

Kerckhoff, Alan C. 1993. *Diverging pathways: Social structure and career deflections*. New York, NY: Cambridge University Press.

Kessler, R. 1982. A disaggregation of the relationship between socioeconomic status and psychological distress. *American Sociological Review* 47 (6): 752–64.

Kiernan, Kathleen, and John N. Hobcraft. 1997. Parental divorce during childhood: Age at first intercourse, partnership and parenthood. *Population Studies* 51 (1): 41–55.

Kiernan, Kathleen, and M. C. Huerta. 2008. Economic deprivation, maternal depression, parenting and children's cognitive and emotional development in early childhood. *British Journal of Sociology* 59 (4): 781–806.

Kiernan, Kathleen, Sara McLanahan, John Holmes, and Melanie Wright. 2011. Fragile families in the US and UK. Fragile Families Working Paper WP 11-04-FF, Center for Research on Child Well-Being, Princeton University, Princeton, NJ.

Kiernan, Kathleen, and Fiona K. Mensah. 2009. Poverty, maternal depression, family status and children's cognitive and behavioural development in early childhood: A longitudinal study. *Journal of Social Policy* 38 (4): 569–88.

Kiernan, Kathleen, and Fiona K. Mensah. 2010. Parternship trajectories, parent and child well-being. In *Children of the 21st century: From birth to age 5*, eds. Kristine Hansen, Heather Joshi, and Shirley Dex, 77–96. Bristol, UK: Policy Press.

Lee, Dohoon. 2014. Age trajectories of poverty during childhood and high school graduation. *Sociological Science* 1:344–65.

Lee, Dohoon, and Sara McLanahan. 2015. Family structure transitions and child development: Instability, selection, and population heterogeneity. *American Sociological Review* 80 (4): 738–63.

Link, Bruce G., and Jo Phelan. 1995. Social conditions as fundamental causes of disease. *Journal of Health and Social Behavior* 35:80–94.

Loughran, David S. 2002. The effect of male wage inequality on female age at first marriage. *Review of Economics and Statistics* 84:237–50.

Martin, Steven P. 2004. Women's education and family timing: Outcomes and trends associated with age at marriage and first birth. In *Social inequality*, ed. Kathryn M. Neckerman, 79–119. New York, NY: Russell Sage Foundation.

McCulloch, Andrew, Richard D. Wiggins, Heather E. Joshi, and Darshan Sachdev. 2000. Internalising and externalising children's behaviour problems in Britain and the U.S.: Relationships to family resources. *Children and Society* 14:368–83.

McLanahan, Sara. 2004. Diverging destinies: How children are faring under the second demographic transition. *Demography* 41 (4): 607–27.

McLanahan, Sara, and Audrey N. Beck. 2010. Parental relationships in fragile families. *The Future of Children* 20 (2): 17–37.

McLanahan, Sara, and Christine Percheski. 2008. Family structure and the reproduction if inequalities. *Annual Review of Sociology* 34:257–76.

McLanahan, Sara, and Gary Sandefur. 1994. *Growing up with a single parent: What hurts, what helps.* Cambridge, MA: Harvard University Press.

McLanahan, Sara, Laura Tach, and Daniel Schneider. 2013. The causal effects of father absence. *Annual Review of Sociology* 39 (1): 399–427.

McLeod, Jane D., and Michael J. Shanahan. 1996. Trajectories of poverty and children's mental health. *Journal of Health and Social Behavior* 37 (3): 207–20.

McLoyd, V. C. 1998. Socioeconomic disadvantage and child development. *American Psychologist* 53:185–204.

Meadows, Sarah O., Sara S. McLanahan, and Jeanne Brooks-Gunn. 2008. Stability and change in family structure and maternal health trajectories. *American Sociological Review* 73 (2): 314–34.

Meyers, Marcia, and Janet Gornick. 2005. Policies for reconciling parenthood and employment: Drawing lessons from Europe. *Challenge* 48 (5): 39–61.

Mirowsky, John, and Catherine E. Ross. 2003. *Education, social status, and health.* New York, NY: Aldine de Gruyter.

Mollborn, Stephanie. 2016. Young children's developmental ecologies and kindergarten readiness. *Demography* 53:1853–82.

Muthén, Bengt. 2004. Latent variable analysis. In *Handbook of quantitative methodology for the social sciences*, ed. D. Kaplan, 345–68. Thousand Oaks, CA: Sage Publications.

National Research Council and Institute of Medicine. 2009. *Depression in parents, parenting and children.* Washington, DC: National Academies Press.

Olafsdottir, Sigrun. 2007. Fundamental causes of health disparities: Stratification, the welfare state, and health in the United States and Iceland. *Journal of Health and Social Behavior* 48 (3): 239–53.

Osborne, Cynthia, and Sara McLanahan. 2007. Partnership instability and child well-being. *Journal of Marriage and Family* 69 (4): 1065–83.

Palloni, Alberto. 2006. Reproducing inequalities: Luck, wallets, and the enduring effects of childhood health. *Demography* 43:587–615.

Parcel, Toby L., Lori Ann Campbell, and Wenxuan Zhong. 2012. Children's behavior problems in the United States and Great Britain. *Journal of Health and Social Behavior* 53 (2): 165–82.

Pettersen, S. M., and A. B. Albers. 2001. Effects of poverty and maternal depression on early child development. *Child Development* 72 (6): 1794–1813.

Raftery, Adrian E. 1996. Approximate Bayes factors and accounting for model uncertainty in generalised linear models. *Biometrika* 83 (2): 251–66.

Reardon, Sean F. 2011. The widening academic achievement gap between the rich and the poor: New evidence and possible explanations. In *Whither opportunity: Rising inequality and the uncertain life chances of low-income children*, eds. R. Murnane and G. Duncan, 91–116. New York, NY: Russell Sage Foundation.

Schoon, Ingrid, John Bynner, Heather Joshi, Samantha Parsons, Richard D. Wiggins, and Amanada Sacker. 2002. The influence of context, timing, and duration of risk experiences for the passage from childhood to midadulthood. *Child Development* 73 (5): 1486–1504.

Sigle-Rushton, W., and Sara McLanahan. 2004. Father absence and child wellbeing. In *Public policy and families*, eds. E. L. Rainwater, Timothy Smeeding, and Daniel P. Moynihan, 116–55. New York, NY: Russell Sage Foundation.

Torche, Florencia. 2011. The effect of maternal stress on birth outcomes: Exploiting a natural experiment. *Demography* 48 (4): 1473–91.

Wagmiller, Robert L., Jr., Mary Clare Lennon, Li Kuang, Philip M. Alberti, and J. Lawrence Aber. 2006. The dynamics of economic disadvantage and children's life chances. *American Sociological Review* 71 (5): 847–66.

Waldfogel, Jane, Terry-Ann Craigie, and Jean Brooks-Gunn. 2010. Fragile families and child wellbeing. *Future of Children* 20 (2): 87–112.

Wilkinson, R., and K. Pickett. 2009. *The spirit level: Why more equal societies almost always do better.* London: Allen Lane.

Wu, Lawrence L. 1996. Effects of family instability, income, and income instability on the risk of a premarital birth. *American Sociological Review* 61 (3): 386–406.

Can Schools Enable Parents to Prevent Summer Learning Loss? A Text-Messaging Field Experiment to Promote Literacy Skills

By
MATTHEW A. KRAFT
and
MANUEL MONTI-NUSSBAUM

The vast differences in summer learning activities among children present a substantial challenge to providing equal educational opportunity in the United States. Most initiatives aimed at reversing summer learning loss focus on school- or center-based programs. This study explores the potential of enabling parents to provide literacy development opportunities at home as a low-cost alternative. We conduct a randomized field trial of a summer text-messaging pilot program for parents focused on promoting literacy skills among first through fourth graders. We find positive effects on reading comprehension among third and fourth graders, with effect sizes of .21 to .29 standard deviations, but no effects for first and second graders. Texts also increased attendance at parent-teacher conferences but not at other school-related activities. Evidence to inform future efforts to reverse summer learning loss is provided by parents' responses to a follow-up survey.

Keywords: parent engagement; summer learning loss; text messaging; literacy skills; achievement gap; randomized control trial

Over half a century since the release of the Equality of Educational Opportunity report (the "Coleman Report"), James Coleman's work

Matthew A. Kraft is an assistant professor of education and economics at Brown University. His research and teaching interests include the economics of education, education policy analysis, and applied quantitative methods for causal inference. His primary work focuses on efforts to improve educator and organizational effectiveness in K–12 urban public schools.

Manuel Monti-Nussbaum is a research manager at Brown University where, alongside faculty in education and economics, he works on the design, implementation, and analysis of programs aimed at improving effectiveness and equity in public schools. His broader interests lie in education and health care policy and program analysis in developing regions.

NOTE: We are grateful for the support of Jeremy Chiappetta; Chiv Heng; and the students, teachers and parents of Blackstone Valley Prep. Melissa Lovitz provided outstanding research assistance on this project. All errors and omissions are our own.

Correspondence: mkraft@brown.edu

DOI: 10.1177/0002716217732009

continues to influence social science and public policy. Among its most important and surprising findings was that "schools account for only a small fraction of differences in pupil achievement," after taking into account students' socioeconomic backgrounds (Coleman et al. 1966, 21). Coleman found that family background factors such as parents' level of educational attainment as well as the amount of reading materials and types of reading practices in the home had far more predictive power than any school characteristics. This seminal finding was received with disappointment by many at the time who hoped to document large gaps in school quality and resources as the primary sources of educational inequality. The report has stood the test of time, though, with reanalyses replicating Coleman's results (e.g., Konstantopoulos and Borman 2011) and a large literature documenting how factors outside of school explain the majority of variation in student achievement (Goldhaber and Brewer 1997; Goldhaber, Brewer, and Anderson 1999; Nye, Konstantopoulos, and Hedges 2004; Altonji and Mansfield 2011).

In our view, the Coleman Report and subsequent studies on school effects should not be interpreted to mean that schools do not or cannot matter. Despite the limitations of the public education system, it has long been and remains the primary vehicle for social investment in the United States (Steffes 2012). For example, programs such as Head Start, a free federally funded and nationwide preschool program for poor children, has been shown to close a significant portion of the earnings gap in adulthood between children from poor and middle-income families (Deming 2009). School finance reforms between the early 1970s and 1990s that raised state funding levels for low-income school districts substantially increased students' achievement (Lafortune, Rothstein, and Schanzenbach 2016) and earnings in adulthood (Jackson, Johnson, and Persico 2016). Schools matter, particularly for children from families with limited resources to invest in supplemental educational opportunities.

We interpret Coleman's findings and the larger school-effects literature as highlighting the need and potential for schools to broaden their influence by more directly engaging parents as active partners in students' learning. The positive relationship between parental involvement in their children's education and students' success in school is widely documented (Barnard 2004; Cheung and Pomerantz 2012; Fan and Chen 2001; Houtenville and Conway 2008; Todd and Wolpin 2007). Studies have identified positive learning environments at home; integration of parents into school programs; and strong relationships between school, family, and the community as distinct ways that parental engagement supports student achievement (Hoover-Dempsey et al. 2005; Henderson 1987). However, research has been less successful at identifying how to promote greater parental involvement in students' education both at home and at school (Mapp and Kutner 2013; Anderson and Minke 2007; Hoover-Dempsey et al. 2005). One study found that parents of students attending urban elementary schools reported that direct invitations from teachers to attend school events and encouragement to engage in their students' learning process had the largest influence on their involvement (Anderson and Minke 2007).

Research in recent decades has also helped to identify the roles that schools and home environments play in the time dynamics of educational inequality. We now know minority students and students from disadvantaged backgrounds enter kindergarten well behind their white and more advantaged peers and that these initial achievement gaps at school entry have lasting effects on students' educational attainment (Fryer and Levitt 2004; Quinn 2015). Research also shows that while these achievement gaps continue to grow as students pass through primary and secondary schooling, this widening is driven primarily by different rates of learning during the summer months when students are exposed to vastly different learning opportunities and home and neighborhood environments (Atteberry and McEachin 2016; Alexander, Entwisle, and Olson 2001; Cooper et al. 1996; Downey, von Hippel, and Broh 2004; Downey, von Hippel, and Hughes 2008; Quinn et al. 2016). While estimates of summer learning loss differ between studies and student populations, Atteberry and McEachin (2016) found that, on average, public school students across an unidentified southern state lost between 25 percent and 30 percent of the learning growth that they had gained in the preceding school year in both reading and math. Studies also consistently document large differences in summer learning loss rates across socioeconomic groups amounting to as much as three months of learning (Alexander, Entwisle, and Olson 2007; Burkam et al. 2004; Cooper et al. 2000; Downey, von Hippel, and Broh 2004).

In this article, we describe and evaluate a school-based pilot text-messaging program intended to engage parents as partners in reducing summer learning loss. The program developed out of a research-practitioner partnership with a public charter school network in Rhode Island with the goal of extending educational supports to families beyond the academic year. We piloted the text-messaging program with two elementary schools in the network that serve a diverse student body where 59 percent of the students are minorities and 63 percent of students are eligible for free or reduced price lunch (FRPL). Figure 1 illustrates the nature and magnitude of summer learning loss among students at these elementary schools. In 2015, student performance on the Standardized Test for the Assessment of Reading (STAR) decreased by an average of 9.89 scaled score points between June and September, a loss of approximately 8 percent of the preceding year's learning growth.

We estimate the causal effect of the text-messaging program by conducting a field experiment in which half of the 183 families that volunteered to participate in the study were randomly assigned to receive a series of eighteen text messages in July and August 2015. The messages, developed by school personnel and the research team, encouraged parents to promote summer reading and provided suggestions for specific literacy development techniques and resources. The focus on reading and use of text-messages as the delivery mechanism were informed by several literatures. Efforts to provide more academically enriching summer opportunities to students and reduce summer learning loss have traditionally overlooked the potential role of parents and taken the form of resource intensive school- or center-based programs costing around $1,500 per student. Evidence on the effect of such programs on student achievement is decidedly mixed (Matsudaira 2008; Jacob and Lefgren 2004; Borman and Dowling 2006;

FIGURE 1
Summer Learning Loss on the STAR Reading Assessment

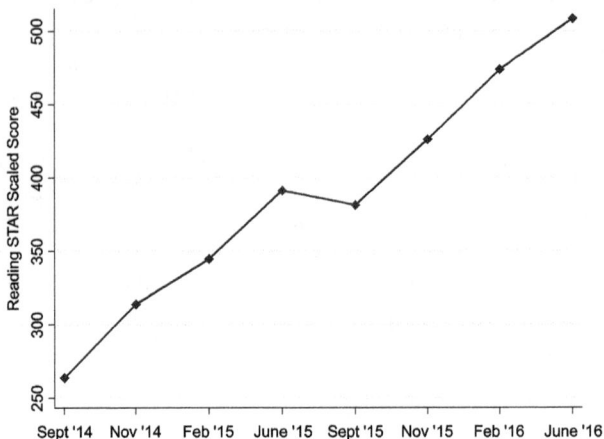

NOTE: Average STAR scaled scores for students in the second through fourth grade from beginning of the 2014/15 academic year to end of the 2015/16 academic year. Students that were assigned to the treatment group are not included in the figure, as their 2015/16 scores were potentially influenced by the treatment. Students included in the figure are those with complete test data across all testing periods ($n = 366$).

Chaplin and Capizzano 2006; Schacter and Jo 2005; Borman, Goetz, and Dowling 2009).

A growing body of research suggests that summer reading programs that provide books and scaffolded reading strategies for students can be a cost-efficient (~\$100 per student) and effective way to raise student achievement in reading (Kim 2006, 2007; Kim and White 2008; Allington et al. 2010; Kim and Guryan 2010; White et al. 2014). Fryer (2014) found that paying students to read books during the school year increased reading achievement among second graders. An emerging body of literature also points to the potential of school-based efforts to engage parents more directly in students' learning by communicating with them more frequently (often via text message) and providing them with more detailed information about their students' performance (Bergman 2015; Bergman and Chan 2017; Kraft and Dougherty 2013; Kraft and Rogers 2015). Finally, the frequency and framing of the text messages are motivated by research in behavioral economics that posits that relevant reminders and positive messaging can nudge parents to engage in activities with their children that they intend to do but that happen infrequently due to competing demands, distractions, and other challenges (Thaler and Sunstein 2008; Castleman 2015).

Two recent studies that examined the effects of sending text messages to parents of preschoolers during the academic year helped to inform the design of our intervention. York and Loeb (2014) evaluated the effect of READY4K!, a text-messaging campaign implemented among a sample of 440 parents. Parents in the treatment group received three text messages per week that provided facts, tips, and encouragement on how to help preschool children develop their literacy skills. The program increased the frequency of home literacy activities as reported by parents, increased the likelihood that parents asked questions about their children's learning as reported by teachers, and increased student performance on several subdomains of the Phonological Awareness Literacy Screening (PALS) assessment. Hurwitz et al. (2015) evaluated the effect of a six-week intervention where 253 parents of children enrolled in Early Head Start centers were randomly assigned to receive daily tips about parent-child activities that promote learning across a range of domains. The authors found that the intervention increased the total number of learning activities that parents reported engaging in with their children by approximately one-fourth of a standard deviation.

Our study provides the first causal evidence of the effect of a school-based text-messaging program aimed at supporting parents to promote literacy skills during the summer. This field experiment allows us to explore the potential for literacy-focused text-message interventions to support parents to reduce summer learning loss and enhance parents' engagement in school-based activities. Our study is also the first to examine the effects of any type of text-messaging intervention for parents aimed at increasing student achievement among elementary school students. Prior studies have focused on preschool and kindergarten students (Doss et al. 2016; Hurwitz et al. 2015; York and Loeb 2014) or middle and high school students (Bergman 2015; Bergman and Chan 2017; Kraft and Dougherty 2013; Kraft and Rogers 2015). In our primary analyses, we estimate effects on student achievement captured by two complementary standardized assessments of early literacy and reading skills administered four times across the school year. These multiple vertically equated test administrations allow us to examine the time dynamics and potential for compounding effects of the intervention. We complement these analyses by assessing program effects on multiple measures of parent engagement in school-related activities. We conclude by exploring potential mechanisms using parent responses to surveys and discussing how future programs can address implementation challenges and enhance program design features.

Context and Procedure

Setting

We conducted this research in partnership with Blackstone Valley Prep Mayoral Academy (BVP) located in Cumberland, Rhode Island, during summer 2015. BVP is a network of public charter schools serving students from across four school districts in Rhode Island: Central Falls, Cumberland, Lincoln, and Pawtucket. First opened in 2009, the BVP network has expanded to six schools including three elementary schools, two middle schools, and one high school. Drawing students from across four diverse sending districts allows BVP to serve a more racially and socioeconomically diverse student population than many urban charter schools. Two of the sending districts, Cumberland and Lincoln, are home to more affluent and homogenous populations where less than 30 percent of students are eligible for FRPL and between 80 and 90 percent are white. In comparison, in the Central Falls and Pawtucket districts 85 percent of students are eligible for FRPL and two-thirds are African American or Latino. Consequently, relative to state averages, BVP schools serve an especially diverse student population. BVP schools are also known for their high academic standards and have consistently outperformed the state average as well as their four sending districts on state standardized tests.

Sample

Principals at two of the elementary schools opted to take part in the study. BVP administrators recruited the parents of students rising into first through fourth grades to participate in the program. Out of 522 parent households, 183 opted into the study. This represented an opt-in rate of 35 percent of potential households with a total of 232 students rising into the first through fourth grades. Among the 183 participating families, 137 had one child enrolled in the two participating elementary schools, 43 had two students, and 3 had three students.

In Table 1, we report the demographic characteristics and previous academic performance of students participating and not participating in the study. Participating students were relatively evenly distributed across first through fourth grades with a racial composition of 32 percent Hispanic, 12 percent African American, 52 percent white, and 3 percent Asian. Nearly 50 percent of the students came from households eligible to receive FRPL and 8 percent were receiving special education services. Students of households that opted into the study, on average, earned higher scores on standardized reading assessments than those of nonparticipant households. Minority, especially Hispanic and African American, students, English language learners, and those eligible for FRPL were less likely to opt-in. These lower take-up rates among minority, nonnative English speaking, and lower socioeconomic status families point to the importance of targeted recruitment efforts or opt-out enrollment policies for parent engagement programs.

Text-messaging program

Over the course of the spring semester, the research team worked with BVP administrators and lead teachers to design and develop the content of the text-messaging intervention. Parents of the 118 students randomly assigned into the treatment group received a total of 18 text messages from the schools' communication management system, roughly 2 per week, throughout the months of July and August 2015. Text messages were translated into Spanish for parents who indicated a preference to receive communication in Spanish. All parents, including parents of the 114 students in the control group and those not involved in the study, received ongoing texts and recorded messages from the schools about school-related summer events.

TABLE 1

Student Characteristics among Study Participants and Nonparticipants

	All Students	Students in Study	Students Not in Study	Difference	p-Value
STEP June 14/15	8.19	8.13	8.23	−0.10	.714
STAR reading June 14/15	398.18	438.30	376.67	61.63	.001
STAR math June 14/15	563.17	572.85	557.99	14.86	.175
Age	7.87	7.74	7.94	−0.2	.042
Female	50.5	50	50.7	−0.7	.854
Asian	3.5	3.4	3.5	−0.1	.931
Black	12	11.6	12.2	−0.6	.572
Hispanic	44	32.3	50.9	−18.6	.000
White, not Hispanic	39.9	52.2	32.7	19.5	.001
Native American	0.6	0.4	0.8	−0.4	.888
Free or reduced price lunch	68.8	53.4	77.2	−23.8	.000
English as a second language	9.4	3.4	12.7	−9.3	.000
Special education	9.9	6.9	11.5	−4.6	.078
Rising 1st grade	24.5	28.1	22.6	5.5	.137
Rising 2nd grade	25.1	25.1	25.1	0.0	.976
Rising 3rd grade	24.8	23.8	25.3	−1.5	.639
Rising 4th grade	25.4	22.5	26.9	−4.4	.245
Elementary school 1	50.1	53	48.6	4.4	.414
Elementary school 2	49.6	47	50.9	−3.9	.414
CF Sending district	26.1	15.1	32.2	−17.1	.001
CU Sending district	26.9	32.3	23.9	8.4	.101
LN Sending district	15	22.4	11	11.4	.000
PA Sending district	31.3	29.3	32.4	−3.1	.195
N (students)	670	232	438		

NOTE: Sample sizes for baseline test scores are not constant across variables (Strategic Teaching and Evaluation of Progress [STEP]: 232 students in study and 390 students not in study; STAR: 163 students in study and 305 students not in study). Rising first graders do not have STAR baseline scores as the test is not assessed in kindergarten. Age is as of 07/01/2015. P-values of the difference estimated from models where a given characteristic is regressed on an indicator for opting into the study and household random effects. CF = Central Falls, CU = Cumberland, LN = Lincoln, and PA = Pawtucket.

The text messages were framed as "Pro-tips" about specific literacy and enrichment activities that parents and children could engage in over the summer. The messages emphasized the importance of reading and the role of parents in encouraging reading at home during the summer months. The texts also provided information on resources and ideas for summer learning activities. The content of the messages was organized under three distinct categories:

- **Resources:** messages that provided information about accessible and affordable educational resources that parents and students could utilize.

These messages about local summer resources were intended to reduce barriers to learning for all families, with a particular emphasis on those with less access to educational activities and familiarity with relevant resources.

e.g. "Pro-tip: RI public libraries have built suggested kid (and adult) summer reading lists full of great reads. Learn more at www.askri.org"

- **Ideas:** messages that contained suggestions for creative and effective practices and activities for parents to support their children's literacy development. These messages were intended to expand parents' tool-kit of educational activities that could be flexibly and easily integrated into summer schedules.

e.g. "Pro-tip: Take turns reading OUT LOUD with your scholar. You read a page then your child reads a page, and so on (great at any age)!"

- **Signals:** messages that conveyed information about summer learning loss and reinforced the positive effects of reading and learning outside of classroom time. These messages served to increase the saliency of summer reading and nudge parents whom, for many reasons, might not be consistently helping their children engage in educational activities.

e.g. "Did you know? Kids who read 4+ books over the summer fare MUCH better on tests in the fall than their peers who read 0–1 books?"

Research Design

Data

Reading achievement. Our primary outcome of interest is student reading achievement captured by two widely used literacy and reading comprehension tests, the Standardized Test for the Assessment of Reading (STAR) and the Strategic Teaching and Evaluation of Progress (STEP). Both assessments are vertically equated, which allows us to document how students' literacy skills changed over time and to pool students' scores across grade levels. The STAR test, developed by Renaissance Learning, is a computer adaptive test that assesses reading comprehension in 10 minutes or less through twenty-five multiple-choice items that test vocabulary in-context. The test is administered to students starting in first grade and is scored on a scale ranging from 0 to 1,400.

The STEP test, developed by the University of Chicago Consortium on School Research, is administered by teachers working one-on-one with students to assess a range of reading comprehension skills. Beyond measuring word recognition, reading speed and accuracy, STEP also evaluates comprehension and critical thinking. The assessment is divided into thirteen steps or scale points, which in turn are subdivided into three shorter levels, and is administered to students in kindergarten through third grade. The STEP assessment is generally scored on a scale ranging from –1 (pre-literacy) to 12 (third-grade literacy level). Teachers in one of the BVP elementary schools also used the Fountas and Pinnell Benchmark Assessment Systems (BAS) to extend the STEP scoring range up to 27 for students who had reached a third-grade literacy level. This reading ability and comprehension assessment, like the STEP, is conducted one-on-one between teachers and students and is graded on a 15-point scale. In the other elementary school, scores were capped at 12 on the STEP assessment, which limited our ability to capture growth in reading skills among students reading above a third-grade level. Both the STAR and STEP assessments were administered in September, November, February, and June of the 2015/16 academic year, except in one of the schools where teachers did not administer the STEP assessment in September. Examining how student achievement in reading is affected over the course of the following year allows us to test a common hypothesis in sociology and social psychology that small interventions such as ours can trigger recursive processes that, when sustained, result in a cumulative advantage over time (DiPrete and Eirich 2006; Yeager and Walton 2011).

Parent engagement. We were also interested in analyzing whether parents who received text messages from BVP about how to support their child's literacy development would be motivated to become more engaged in school activities both during the summer and after the start of the new school year. To examine this question, we worked with BVP to collect several measures of parent engagement by recording whether parents participated in the following chronologically ordered events and activities: a back-to-school ice cream social for teachers, parents, and students; visits where teachers meet with parents at home or another designated location outside of school; and fall semester parent-teacher conferences. At the conclusion of the pilot program we invited all parents in the study to sign up to receive text messages during the school year about how they could support student learning outside of school time.

Parent survey. We administered surveys to parents after the conclusion of the summer text messaging program to confirm the delivery of the text messages and collect data on potential mechanisms through which the text messages might have affected student outcomes. The survey asked about student reading habits, parent involvement in student learning, and reasons for increased (decreased) reading over summer. The survey included questions about the frequency with which parents and students engaged in the different activities over the summer suggested in the series of text messages (text messages were not mentioned in these questions). Parents responded to each item on a 5-point Likert scale ranging from *never (0 times)* to *more than once a week (~30 times)*.

The poststudy survey was administered online during early October. Recruitment was done via text, email, school newsletters, and flyers sent home with students. Raffle tickets for a $100 Amazon gift card were offered for participation. These efforts resulted in a 69 percent household response rate among study participants. However, families in the treatment group were 11 percentage points less likely to complete the survey than those from the control group (63 percent treatment vs. 74 percent control). In appendix Table A1, we report the student characteristics of parents who did and did not respond to the survey. Nonrespondents were significantly more likely to be Hispanic, low income, and to have students who were lower achieving in reading.

Given the differential survey response rate across treatment status and select student characteristics, we interpret our analyses of potential mechanisms based on parent responses as exploratory rather than causal evidence.

Randomization

We evaluate the causal effect of our pilot text-messaging program to promote literacy skills development by conducting a cluster randomized trial at the household level. Our research design and analyses described below were preregistered with the Institute for Education Sciences What Works Clearinghouse Randomized Control Trial Registry (ID #489). We randomly assigned students and their parents to receive texts or to a control condition in which households only received standard school announcements via text-messages. We chose to assign treatment at the household level to reduce potential spillovers between siblings. If the text messages had an effect on parents' behavior, it would likely change parents' involvement with all their elementary-age children. While this design approach reduces the potential for spillover effects, it does not eliminate the possibility that parents or students in the treatment group could communicate and share information provided in the text messages with parents or students in the control group over the summer or the following school year. We examine the potential threat posed by spillovers in detail below based on self-reported data from the parent survey.

We examine the validity of the randomization process by testing for mean differences across students in the treatment and control groups. As shown in Table 2, there were no statistically significant differences between the two groups across twenty-three observable characteristics, affirming the validity of the randomization process.

Analytic Approach

We begin by estimating the effect of being a student in a household randomly assigned to receive summer learning text messages, TREAT (treatment), using a multilevel model as follows:

$$Y_{ij} = \alpha + \beta_1 TREAT_j + \delta X_{ij} + \left(v_j + \varepsilon_{ij} \right). \tag{1}$$

Here Yij represents a given outcome of interest for student i from family j, Xij is a vector of both household-level controls (sending district and FRPL status) and student-level controls (age, ELL, race, disability, and grade). The coefficient on TREAT, β_1, captures our estimate of the intent-to-treat (ITT) effect of summer learning text messages given that we cannot confirm with certainty that all the text messages were received or read by participating parents. A positive and statistically significant estimate of β_1 will suggest that assigning households to receive summer learning text messages improved student achievement in reading. We specify an error structure where individual students are nested within households by fitting models with household random effects, which are orthogonal to *TREAT* by construction.

In a second specification of our model, we include 2014/15 end-of-year STEP test scores to control for baseline literacy levels.

$$Y_{ij} = \alpha + \beta_1 TREAT_j + \lambda STEP_i^{June\ '15} + \delta X_i + \left(v_j + \varepsilon_{ij} \right). \tag{2}$$

The addition of STEP scores serves to further test the robustness and increase the precision of our estimates. We are unable to fit corresponding models in our full sample using prior scores on the STAR exam given that baseline STAR scores are not available for incoming first graders as the test is not administered in kindergarten.

Next, we leverage the repeated outcome measures of reading achievement by estimating pooled effects in a student-by-test-period dataset. These stacked models provide a single estimated treatment effect that averages across the four test administrations in 2015/16 and increases the precision of our estimates (McKenzie 2012).

$$Y_{ijt} = \alpha + \beta_1 TREAT_j + \lambda STEP_i^{June\ '15} + \delta X_{ij} + \left(v_j + \varepsilon_i + \eta_{ijt} \right). \tag{3}$$

Here we model STAR or STEP test scores for student i in family j in time t where t captures the four time periods when students are assessed. Our covariates remain the same as in equation (2), while we expand our multilevel error structure to include both random effects for households (v_j) and students (ε).

We then explore whether the treatment had a differential effect on subgroups of students as specified in the preregistration plan. We do this by refitting equation (2) to include the main effect of a given student characteristic and its interaction effect with the treatment indicator. The subgroups we examine are eligibility for FRPL, race (African American and Hispanic), and grade level (first and second; third and fourth).

We fit parallel logistic regression models using the same structural components from equation (2) when examining parents' school engagement outcomes. We present parameter estimates from these models as odds ratios as well as marginal effects to facilitate a direct comparison with our achievement results. Finally, we fit corresponding ordered logistic regression models with the same structural components of equation (2) when analyzing responses to survey items, and report the results as proportional odds ratios. For both of these models we account for the multilevel nature of the data by clustering our standard errors at the household level. This approach, which is necessary given the lack of convergence for models with random effects, produces consistent estimates of our parameters but less efficient estimates of our standard errors.

TABLE 2
Student Baseline Characteristics, by Treatment Status

	Students in Treatment Group	Students in Control Group	Difference	P-Value
STEP June 14/15	7.96	8.30	−0.34	.428
STAR reading June 14/15	446.92	430.19	16.73	.539
STAR math June 14/15	567.63	577.76	−10.13	.558
Age	7.69	7.79	−0.10	.530
Female	51.7	48.2	3.5	.601
Asian	2.5	4.4	−1.9	.443
Black	12.7	10.5	2.2	.449
Hispanic	28.0	36.8	−8.8	.150
White, not Hispanic	55.9	48.2	7.7	.548
Native American	0.8	0.0	0.8	.326
Free or reduced price lunch	55.9	50.9	5.0	.379
English as a second language	2.5	4.4	−1.9	.440
Enrolled in special education	7.6	6.1	1.5	.656
Rising 1st grade	31.4	24.8	6.6	.267
Rising 2nd grade	23.7	26.5	−2.8	.623
Rising 3rd grade	23.7	23.9	−0.2	.973
Rising 4th grade	21.2	23.9	−2.7	.624
Elementary school 1	50.0	56.1	−6.1	.182
Elementary school 2	50.0	43.9	6.1	.182
CF sending district	14.4	15.8	−1.4	.567
CU sending district	33.9	30.7	3.2	.604
LN sending district	23.7	21.1	2.6	.627
PA sending district	27.1	31.6	−4.5	.912
N (students)	118	114		
N (parents)	91	92		

NOTE: Sample sizes for baseline test scores are not constant across variables (STEP: 118 students in treatment group and 112 students in control group; STAR: 79 students in treatment group and 84 students in control group). Rising first graders do not have STAR baseline scores as the test is not assessed in kindergarten. Age is as of 07/01/2015. P-values calculated by regressing the indicator for treatment on each variable with household random effects. CF = Central Falls, CU = Cumberland, LN = Lincoln, and PA = Pawtucket.

Findings

Take-up

BVP's communication management system allowed us to track the distribution of text messages to parents in the treatment group. These records reveal that 97.3 percent of messages were sent and delivered. To confirm the effective reception of messages, we included questions in the poststudy survey on whether

TABLE 3
Confirmation of Treatment Delivery

	Did Parent Receive Texts	Number of Texts Received	Number of Summer Learning Texts Received
Treat	0.311***	8.131***	6.067***
	(0.078)	(1.364)	(1.352)
Constant	0.515***	3.249***	2.666***
	(0.053)	(0.927)	(0.944)
N (students)	161	159	136

NOTE: Ordinary least squares (OLS) regressions are unconditional but include a random effect for households. Standard errors are shown in parenthesis.
***p < .01.

households had received text messages from BVP, if they had received text messages about learning and literacy skills specifically, and if so, how many they had received. As shown in Table 3, households in the treatment group were 31 percentage points more likely to report having received text messages over the summer than households in the control group. On average, households in the treatment group reported receiving an average of eight more text messages from BVP over the summer than parents in the control group and six more text messages specifically about summer learning and literacy skills. These findings confirm that the delivery of the treatment was largely successful given that recall bias when answering survey questions about past behavior likely contributed to differences in the reported and actual number of texts received.

Effect on literacy skills

We report estimates from our model of the treatment effect on reading achievement scores in Table 4. We include treatment effects for STAR and STEP tests taken in September, November, February, and June of the 2015/16 school year as well as an estimate that pools scores from across these test administrations. Estimates across models, tests, and time periods are uniformly positive, and for STEP, significant at the .1 level. Estimates remain largely unchanged when we control for baseline literacy levels with the inclusion of STEP test scores from June of the prior academic year, while the corresponding standard errors become meaningfully smaller due to the reduction in residual variance.

Focusing on models that include STEP baselines scores, we find point estimates ranging from 5.9 to 20.8 scaled score points on the STAR assessments, with a pooled estimate of 13.9 scaled score points (p = .35) although none of these estimates is statistically significant. The magnitude of the pooled estimate, while indistinguishable from zero, is almost one and half times the average rate of summer learning loss in the school. Given that the standard deviation of STAR test scores among first through fourth graders is 215.8, these estimates correspond to

TABLE 4
Effects of Summer Learning Texting Intervention on Reading Achievement

	Sept 15/16		Nov 15/16		Feb 15/16		June 15/16		Stacked periods	
				Panel A: STAR						
Treat	6.26	5.89	20.44	20.75	15.02	16.08	18.05	18.37	12.39	13.92
	(20.40)	(15.82)	(20.96)	(15.42)	(21.00)	(16.54)	(23.86)	(19.39)	(20.19)	(15.17)
STEP June 14/15		y		y		y		y		y
N (students)	224	224	225	225	223	223	224	224	896	896
Effect size	.03	.03	.09	.10	.07	.07	.08	.09	.06	.06
				Panel B: STEP						
Treat	0.543	0.246	0.333	0.301°	0.282	0.326	0.488	0.476°	0.330	0.361°
	(0.447)	(0.210)	(0.284)	(0.171)	(0.294)	(0.214)	(0.323)	(0.263)	(0.279)	(0.193)
STEP June 14/15		y		y		y		y		y
N (students)	112	112	223	223	227	227	217	217	779	779
Effect size	.22	.10	.13	.12	.11	.13	.20	.19	.13	.15

NOTE: Columns show treatment estimates from OLS models that include as covariates student demographics, grade level, school, and sending district. The second column for each outcome includes scores on the STEP exam from June of 14/15 as a control for baseline achievement. All models include household random effects. In last column of Panel B for grade interactions, we fit the model via restricted maximum likelihood (REML) as the sample is not large enough to converge. Sample for Sept 15/16 is reduced because only one school tested in that period. Effect size shows the treatment estimate in standard deviation units based on a sample of all first to fourth graders in the study schools. Standard errors are shown in parenthesis.
°$p < .1$.

effect sizes ranging from .03 to .10 standard deviations (SDs) with a pooled estimate of .06 SD.

Treatment effects on student reading fluency as measured by the STEP exam range from .25 to .49 score levels with a pooled estimate of .36 score levels ($p = .06$). Estimates for the November, June, and pooled effect are all marginally significant at the .10 level. Converting these into effect sizes using the standard deviation of STEP tests among first through fourth graders of 2.47, these effects range from .10 to .19 SD with a pooled effect size of .15 SD ($p = .07$). Figures 2 and 3 display the time dynamics of the estimated standardized effects for STAR and STEP, respectively. The pattern of results over the course of the 2015/16 school year is suggestive of sustained effects on STAR and incrementally increasing effects on STEP although we do not have the power to distinguish these point estimates across time from each other.

We extend our primary test-score analyses to examine whether the summer learning text messages had a differential effect on students by grade level, socioeconomic status, and race. These analyses are exploratory in nature as they are

FIGURE 2
Effect Sizes on the STAR Reading Assessment across the School Year

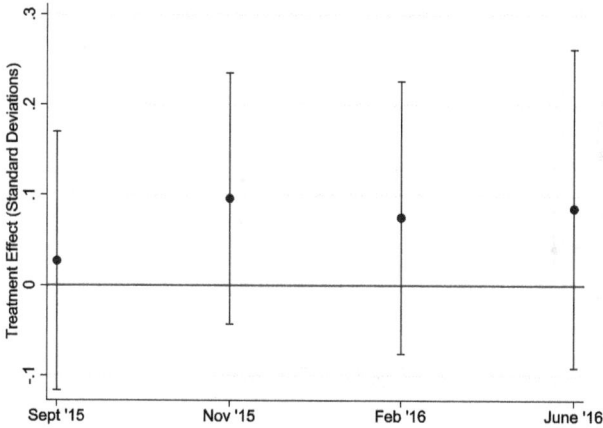

NOTE: STAR scaled scores are standardized in a sample of all first to fourth graders in the study schools. Model for treatment effects is estimated with household random effects and includes student demographics, grade level, school, sending district, and June 2014/15 STEP scores as covariates.

underpowered to detect small to moderate differences across subgroups. In Table 5, we report estimates from models where we interact the main effect of treatment with indicators for upper grade levels (third and fourth grade), FRPL eligibility, Hispanic, and African American.

We find compelling evidence that the positive effects of the text messaging intervention were concentrated among students in the upper elementary grade levels. Estimates for the coefficient associated with the *TREAT**(third and fourth graders) variable reported in Table 5 provide the difference in the magnitude of treatment effects between third and fourth graders relative to first and second graders, as well as the corresponding significance test of this difference. Focusing on our pooled effect estimates, we find that the treatment effect was 57.2 scale score points (p = .04) larger for upper-grade students relative to lower-grade student on the STAR exam and .65 score levels (p = .09) larger on the STEP exam. These estimates correspond with effect size *differences* of exactly .26 SD for both reading assessments.

We plot the subgroup effect sizes for first and second graders (the standardized coefficient on *TREAT*) and for third and fourth graders (the standardized linear combination of the coefficients on *TREAT* and *TREAT**[third and fourth graders]) in Figures 4 and 5, respectively.

As can be seen, point estimates for upper grades (third and fourth) for both STAR and STEP illustrate large effects that appear to increase over the course of the semester. Effect sizes for upper grade students ranged from .14 SD to .30 SD on STAR and .24 SD to .38 SD on STEP. Seven out of eight of these estimated effects are

FIGURE 3
Effect Sizes on the STEP Reading Assessment across the School Year

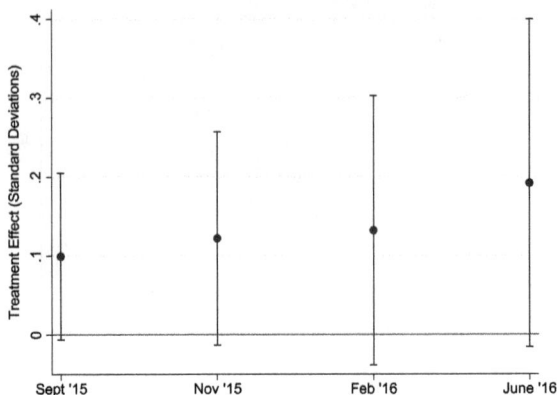

NOTE: STEP scaled scores are standardized in a sample of all first to fourth graders in the study schools. Model for treatment effects is estimated with household random effects and includes student demographics, grade level, school, sending district, and June 2014/15 STEP scores as covariates.

significant at the .05 level. For pooled effect estimates, effect sizes for upper grade students were 0.21 SD (p = .036) on the STAR exam and 0.29 SD (p = .008) on the STEP exam. In stark contrast, we find near zero and statistically insignificant effects on lower grade students. One possible explanation for this pattern is that older students, most of whom have mastered basic literacy skills, were more likely to benefit from a general literacy text-messaging initiative such as ours. Younger students might need to be exposed to specific pre- and emerging-literacy skill-building activities such as those provided by York and Loeb (2014).

We find little evidence of any differential effects on students based on socioeconomic status given estimates are both positively and negatively signed and never statistically significant. Our estimates do suggest that the text-messaging program was differentially more effective for African American students compared to non-Hispanic white students. Estimates for both tests in all four testing periods are positively signed while two for the STEP assessment—September (p = .05) and November (p = .04)—are significant at the .05 level. These estimates suggest that the text-messaging program may advance efforts to reduce educational disparities.

Effect on parent engagement

We next examine the effect of summer learning text messages sent to parents on their engagement in academic events that occurred at the end of the summer and throughout the fall semester. Although the summer learning text messages did not directly encourage parents to attend or participate in school-related activities, the text messages were intended to help parents become more engaged in the learning process of their children and thus, we theorized, more likely to participate in academic events in general. In Table 6, we report treatment effects, displayed as odd ratios, on attendance at an ice cream summer social event, a home visit with a teacher, and a parent-teacher conference in the fall; and on signing up to receive future messages about learning outside of school time. We find statistically significant effects on one out of the four measures of parent engagement—attending a fall semester parent-teacher conference. We estimate that receiving the summer learning text messages increased the probability that a parent would attend the meeting by a predicted marginal effect of 5.4 percentage points on top of a control group mean of 91 percent. The sign of the predicted marginal effect is negative for the ice cream social, near zero for home visits, and positive for text messages sign-ups. These mixed results suggest that parent engagement in their children's education can take multiple forms (e.g., with students at home, with teachers, with school-wide events) and that effects of interventions intended to promote engagement of one type may translate to additional but not all forms of engagement. Specific direct invitations and reminders might be required for different academic events and forms of engagement (Hoover-Dempsey et al. 2005).

Mechanisms

We explore the potential mechanism through which effects on reading achievement may operate by analyzing parent responses to a poststudy survey. The survey asked parents about the frequency with which they engaged in specific parent-student learning activities such as reading out loud, explaining new words, and going to a library. In Table 7, we report proportional odd ratios from ordered logistic regression models for responses to individual survey questions. We find no clear pattern of results or statistically significant effects on the frequency of parent's self-reported literacy activities. Estimates are both positive (above one) and negative (below one). Despite the exploratory and limited nature of these data, these estimates do not point toward any specific parent behavior that might have been a primary mechanism for how the summer learning text messages to parents increased students' achievement in reading.

Spillover

Our research design—clustered randomization at the household level— captures any spillover effects among siblings living in the same household. We could not, however, prevent parents in the treatment group from speaking to other parents in the control group about the content of the text messages they received. If parents shared the content of the messages (e.g., ideas about how to improve reading habits over the summer); with parents in the control group this could attenuate the treatment effect. We examine whether there is evidence of

TABLE 5

Tests for Differential Effects of Summer Learning Texting Intervention on Reading Achievement

	Sept 15/16			Nov 15/16			Feb 15/16			June 15/16			Stacked periods		
							Panel A: STAR								
Treat	-15.25 (21.53)	12.17 (24.13)	10.82 (21.37)	-1.20 (21.04)	27.907 (23.39)	21.74 (20.81)	8.50 (22.06)	6.69 (25.06)	-24.35 (21.95)	-15.16 (25.57)	21.96 (29.27)	18.23 (25.87)	-12.70 (19.95)	17.33 (22.89)	16.60 (20.42)
Treat × 3rd & 4th	45.01 (31.34)			46.73 (30.72)			87.47*** (32.00)			72.41** (36.70)			57.23** (28.42)		
Treat × FRPL		-11.81 (34.07)			-13.55 (33.14)			17.59 (35.27)			-6.76 (41.24)			-6.44 (32.35)	
Treat × Hispanic			-26.02 (35.76)			-15.17 (34.73)			13.10 (36.98)			-21.47 (43.30)			-18.35 (34.02)
Treat × Afri. Amer.			29.86 (50.59)			33.22 (49.45)			29.70 (53.89)			63.70 (62.90)			28.44 (48.57)
N (students)	224	224	224	225	225	225	223	223	223	224	224	224	896	896	896
							Panel B: STEP								
Treat	-0.168 (0.301)	0.212 (0.319)	0.107 (0.276)	0.098 (0.239)	0.247 (0.258)	0.080 (0.229)	-0.037 (0.292)	0.074 (0.325)	0.094 (0.284)	0.089 (0.352)	0.185 (0.393)	0.220 (0.346)	0.052 (0.265)	0.214 (0.279)	0.120 (0.245)
Treat × 3rd & 4th	0.763* (0.405)			0.417 (0.343)			0.773* (0.425)			0.843 (0.518)			0.651* (0.384)		
Treat × FRPL		0.064 (0.453)			0.104 (0.366)			0.475 (0.459)			0.554 (0.559)			0.280 (0.396)	
Treat × Hispanic			0.035 (0.485)			0.271 (0.379)			0.574 (0.477)			0.614 (0.583)			0.516 (0.411)
Treat × Afri. Amer.			1.330* (0.685)			1.083** (0.538)			0.440 (0.689)			0.518 (0.842)			0.662 (0.590)
N (students)	112	112	112	223	223	223	227	227	227	217	217	217	779	779	779

NOTE: Columns show treatment estimates and interaction effects for subgroups of interest from OLS regressions that include as covariates student demographics, grade level, school, sending district, and June STEP 14/15 scores. All models include household random effects. In the last column of Panel B for grade interactions we fit the model via restricted maximum likelihood (REML) as the sample is not large enough to converge. Sample for Sept 15/16 is reduced because only one school tested in that period. Standard errors are shown in parenthesis.

$^*p < .1.$ $^{**}p < .05.$ $^{***}p < .01.$

FIGURE 4

Effect Sizes by Grade Level on the STAR Reading Assessment across the School Year

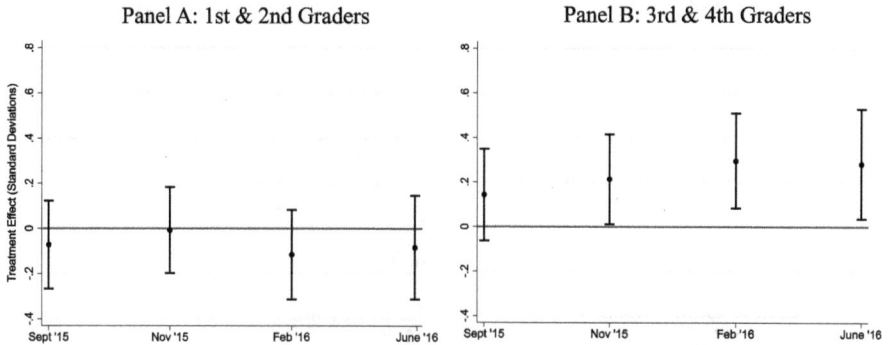

NOTE: Estimates from equation (2) where *TREAT* is replaced by two mutually exclusive treatment indicators, *TREAT*°(1st & 2nd Graders) and *TREAT*°(3rd & 4th Graders). See Figure 2 for further model details.

spillover by analyzing parents' responses to a question in the poststudy survey on whether they had shared any of the texts with other BVP parents. We find that 31 percent of parents from the treatment group who responded to the question in the survey ($n = 63$) indicated that they had shared texts with other BVP parents. We also were notified by BVP administrators that on two occasions a BVP parent posted a comment on the school Facebook page describing the general content of a text message they received. This anecdotal evidence suggests that, if anything, our findings are likely conservative estimates given the potential for the treatment-control contrast to be attenuated by parents in the treatment group influencing the summer reading practices of parents in the control group.

Attrition

Given that test score data are missing for up to 6.5 percent of our sample for some test-score administrations, we test for differential attrition from the study across treatment and control groups for each of our achievement outcomes. Specifically, we explore whether students in the treatment group were more likely than students in the control group to be absent for STAR or STEP assessments during the 2015/16 school year. We accomplish this by predicting the likelihood that a student is missing a score for a given assessment based on their treatment status. We report the estimated coefficients on *TREAT* in Table 8. Differences in missingness rates across the treatment and control groups are not statistically significant and never larger than 3.3 percentage points. These tests reveal no evidence to suggest differential attrition poses a threat to our test-score effect estimates.

FIGURE 5
Effect Sizes by Grade Level on the STEP Reading Assessment across the School Year

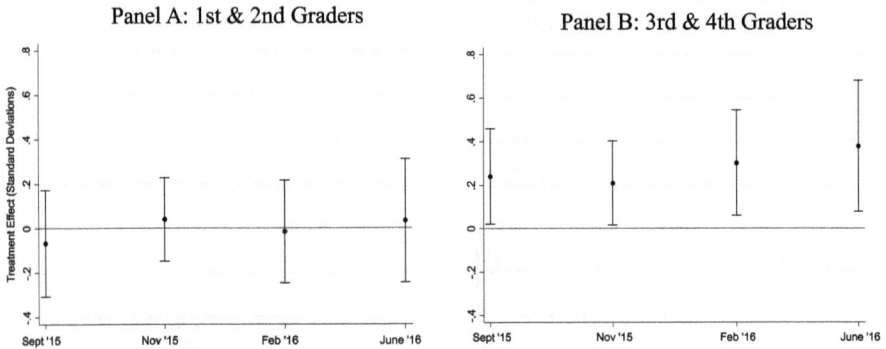

NOTE: Estimates from equation (2) where *TREAT* is replaced by two mutually exclusive treatment indicators, *TREAT*°(1st & 2nd Graders) and *TREAT*°(3rd & 4th Graders). See Figure 3 for further model details.

Lessons for Future Text-Messaging Programs for Parents

Our interpretation of the impact evaluation results described above suggest that summer literacy text-messaging programs for parents have potential but that design details and implementation strategies matter. The process of designing, implementing, and evaluating our pilot text-messaging intervention intended to support parents to engage in literacy enrichment activities with their children during the summer affords several lessons for program redesign and scale-up efforts. Parents' responses to questions about whether they faced any difficult challenges over the summer that limited the amount of reading they could do with their children suggest some parents faced substantial obstacles that were unaddressed by the text-messaging initiative. Across the treatment group, nearly 25 percent of respondents reported facing a unique or difficult challenge that acted as a barrier to engaging in reading activities with their children.

We coded parents' responses to an open-ended follow-up question into five broad categories to describe the general nature of these challenges and present the results in Table 9. The most common challenges reported by parents were vacation conflicts followed by health issues and work demands. For example, one parent wrote that "working all day shifts not coming home till 10 p.m. at night six days a week" presented a significant challenge to engaging in the suggested literacy activities. Another described her challenge as "[My] child's two younger brothers and myself have a lot of serious medical issues. We have a lot of doctor appointments, usually several a week. I am also on the phone a lot due to all these appointments."

Text-messaging interventions should be designed with careful attention paid to the content, frequency, and duration of the initiative, especially as they pertain

TABLE 6
Effects of Summer Learning Texting Intervention on Parent Engagement

	Attend Ice Cream Social	Host Home Visit or Meet Teacher Outside School	Attend Parent-Teacher Conference	Sign Up for Additional Text Messages
Treat	0.697	1.011	5.640°°	1.427
	[1.151]	[0.031]	[2.154]	[0.733]
N (students)	231	231	231	231
Marginal effect	−.082	.002	.054	.037
	(.071)	(.066)	(.027)	(.049)

NOTE: Odd ratios and marginal effects reported in table. Logistic regressions include as covariates student characteristics, indicators for grade level, school, and sending district, as well as June 14/15 STEP scores. FRPL not included in the vector of student covariates for Parent Conference Attendance as it predicts the outcome perfectly. ESL was not included in the vector of student covariates for "sign up for additional text messages" as it predicts failure perfectly. Standard errors clustered at the household level. T statistics are shown in brackets and standard errors shown in parentheses.
°°$p < .05$.

to helping specific groups of families and their children. Our program delivered messages that promoted literacy activities to students that ranged from slightly under six to just over ten years old. The effects that we found are largely concentrated among elementary school students in higher grades, suggesting our focus on reading activities may have been less appropriate for parents with younger children still developing preliteracy skills. A recent study by Doss et al. (2016) found evidence supporting this hypothesis. The authors found larger effects for an early literacy text-messaging program that was differentiated and personalized based on the child's developmental level compared to one that delivered more general literacy suggestions to parents of preschool students. Furthermore, several parents' open-ended survey responses expressed the desire for messages to be more relevant to their students' coursework in the prior and upcoming school years. Together, insights from these studies point to the importance of targeting grade-specific skills with text messaging literacy interventions. They also point to the potential to further individualize text-messaging interventions based on students' performance on interim reading assessments such as the STEP and STAR exams. The possibility of automating the targeting of more specific messages based on age, achievement, or other characteristics might allow similar interventions to increase their efficacy while remaining scalable and cost-effective.

Future text-messaging interventions could attempt to increase participation and impacts by refining several program implementation practices. Opt-in policies may cause programs to miss families whose children experience the largest summer learning loss even when opting in only requires replying to a text

TABLE 7
Effects of Summer Learning Texting Intervention on
Parent-Student Literacy Activities

	Treatment	T-Statistic	N (students)
Told a story to child	1.629	[1.339]	158
Read a book out loud to child	1.228	[0.560]	158
Gave a book to child to read	0.534	[1.625]	159
Asked child about books he/she read	0.685	[0.964]	158
Encouraged child to read on his/her own	1.224	[0.409]	161
Encouraged child to write on his/her own	0.619	[1.306]	160
Wrote with child	0.778	[0.640]	158
Explained new words to child	0.874	[0.365]	158
Took child to library	0.491°	[1.936]	160
Checked out books from library with child	0.581	[1.492]	160
Took child to a museum	1.575	[1.204]	159
Helped child with BVP homework packet	0.929	[0.178]	161

NOTE: Survey questions are about how often parents and children participated in a given activity. Parents answered questions about each student in a household using a 5-point Likert scale, ranging from *never* to *more than once a week*. Odd ratios shown in table. Ordered logistic regression include as covariates student demographics, grade level, school, sending district, and STEP June 14/15 scores. Standard errors clustered at the household level. T-statistics in brackets.
°$p < .1$.

message. Changing the default setting to be opt-out can dramatically increase participation rates for parent informational interventions delivered via text message (Bergman and Rogers 2017). Our study also illustrates the critical importance of updating cellphone records proactively throughout the summer and academic year. We found that approximately one out of every four phone numbers provided by parents did not work six months later.

Responses on the parent survey also reveal the importance of identifying which parent in a household should receive the texts. In our study, texts were sent to the primary phone number listed in parents' contact information. Parents reported that in some instances this was not the parent who was home most often or who was most likely to engage with his or her child in literacy development activities. Text-messaging programs might instead aim to send messages to all adult members of a household as well as to older siblings in certain cases. This would increase the likelihood that messages reach the adult most likely to interact with students. It might also generate momentum for a focus on literacy development at home by prompting adults to discuss the tips and activity suggestions that they receive. Finally, the enthusiasm of several parents who posted the literacy development techniques they practiced with their children on the schools' social media sites points to the potential of using social networks to amplify the impact of text-messaging interventions.

TABLE 8
Differential Attrition Tests for Reading Test Score Outcomes

	Treatment
STAR Sept 15/16	−.001
	(.024)
STAR Nov 15/16	−.013
	(.024)
STAR Feb 15/16	−.024
	(.027)
STAR June 15/16	−.001
	(.024)
STEP Sept 15/16	.033
	(.029)
STEP Nov 15/16	−.027
	(.026)
STEP Feb 15/16	−.001
	(.020)
STEP June 15/16	−.012
	(.033)
N (students)	232

NOTE: Attrition coefficients attained by regressing a binary indicator for missing data on an indicator for treatment status. Models include household random effects. Standard errors in parenthesis.

Conclusion

The Coleman Report first documented how students' experiences outside of school are the dominant influence on their success inside the classroom. This seminal finding and a large body of subsequent evidence affirming it (Goldhaber and Brewer 1997; Goldhaber, Brewer, and Anderson 1999; Nye, Konstantopoulos, and Hedges 2004; Altonji and Mansfield 2011) could be interpreted to mean that efforts to address inequitable educational outcomes need not directly involve schools at all. We posit, though, that schools can magnify their potential impacts by engaging parents and partnering with them to further support students' learning. This text-messaging study illustrates one of many potential ways in which schools can leverage their relationships with parents to help create better learning opportunities for students beyond the school walls and academic calendar.

The sustained and even increasing positive effects on the literacy skills of upper elementary students throughout the school year suggest the test-messaging intervention effects were the result of a process of cumulative advantage, cumulative exposure, or both (DiPrete and Eirich 2006). Scholars have posited that reading ability develops through a virtuous cycle where, for example, having a larger vocabulary

TABLE 9
Coded Responses to the Types of Challenges That Limited Parents'
Abilities to Read with Their Children during the Summer

	Treatment	Control	In Analysis
Health issues	3	2	5
Work demands	2	4	6
Summer plans	8	3	11
Family challenges	3	4	7
Student resistance	0	1	1
Undisclosed	0	2	2
N (parents w/unique challenge)	14	13	27
N (parents survey responders)	60	70	130

NOTE: Table shows response counts for a survey question asking whether parents faced any unique challenges that impeded their ability to read with their children over the summer months. Challenge types were determined by analyzing parents' short answer responses. Each response was coded for each of the types of challenges parents mentioned. Counts are at the household level.

improves reading comprehension, which in turn improves textual inferences and expands vocabulary (Stanovich 1986). It could be that improvements in students' literacy skills over the summer allowed them to access and benefit more from literacy instruction during the school year. It is also possible that the intervention had a lasting effect on the frequency and quality of literacy activities that parents engaged in with their children at home beyond the summer intervention. This cumulative benefit of the increase in the quality of learning opportunities outside of school could also explain the larger effects that we observed over time.

Text-messaging interventions such as the one that we studied are particularly attractive given evidence that they can be taken to scale with limited financial investments and have been shown to be effective across a range of contexts (Castleman 2015). Our intervention leveraged texts as a way to deliver encouragement, reminders, and suggestions for literacy activities. The feedback that we received from parents about this intervention suggests that future development and scaling-up efforts of text-messaging campaigns during the summer would benefit from efforts to address challenges that limited parents' ability to provide enriching literacy activities for their children. For example, schools could experiment with combining a text-messaging campaign with a program to provide summer reading materials or transportation to libraries, museums, and other learning activities. The results of this intervention coupled with feedback from parents suggest that similar interventions could be improved by individualizing the content of the messages based on students' specific learning abilities and needs.

Many of the inequitable educational outcomes documented in the Coleman Report remain more than 50 years later. Addressing these persistent inequities will require schools and educators to move beyond the traditional domain of the classroom. This study provides an example of how schools have the potential to extend their influence on students' educational opportunities by partnering with and enabling parents.

Appendix

TABLE A1

Baseline Characteristics of Students in Analysis, by Survey Respondents

	All Students in Study	Responded to Survey	Did Not Respond to Survey	Difference	*P-Value*
Received treatment	0.51	0.47	0.59	−0.12	.091
STEP June 14/15	8.13	8.29	7.76	0.52	.257
STAR reading June 14/15	438.30	465.32	380.62	84.71	.009
STAR math June 14/15	572.85	585.47	545.92	39.55	.025
Age	7.74	7.76	7.69	0.07	.703
Female	50.0	48.4	53.5	−5.1	.476
Asian	3.4	3.1	4.2	−1.1	.667
Black	11.6	11.2	12.7	−1.5	.971
Hispanic	32.3	26.7	45.1	−18.4	.005
White, not Hispanic	52.2	58.4	38.0	20.4	.145
Native American	0.4	0.6	0.0	0.6	.505
Free or reduced price lunch	53.4	42.9	77.5	−34.6	.008
English as a second language	3.4	3.1	4.2	−1.1	.664
Special education	6.9	4.3	12.7	−8.4	.02
Rising 1st grade	28.1	30.4	22.9	7.5	.238
Rising 2nd grade	25.1	22.4	31.4	−9.0	.142
Rising 3rd grade	23.8	21.1	30.0	−8.9	.143
Rising 4th grade	22.5	25.5	15.7	9.8	.101
Elementary school 1	53.0	53.4	52.1	1.3	.938
Elementary school 2	47.0	46.6	47.9	−1.3	.938
CF sending district	15.1	13.0	19.7	−6.7	.057
CU sending district	32.3	36.0	23.9	12.1	.069
LN sending district	22.4	23.0	21.1	1.9	.755
PA sending district	29.3	26.7	35.2	−8.5	.626
N (students)	232	161	71		

NOTE: Characteristics of students in households that responded and did not respond to the parent survey. *P*-values calculated by regressing the indicator for treatment on each variable with household random effects.

References

Alexander, Karl L., Doris R. Entwisle, and Linda S. Olson. 2001. Schools, achievement, and inequality: A seasonal perspective. *Educational Evaluation and Policy Analysis* 23 (2): 171–91.

Alexander, Karl L., Doris R. Entwisle, and Linda Steffel Olson. 2007. Lasting consequences of the summer learning gap. *American Sociological Review* 72 (2): 167–80.

Allington, Richard L., Anne McGill-Franzen, Gregory Camilli, Lunetta Williams, Jennifer Graff, Jacqueline Zeig, Courtney Zmach, and Rhonda Nowak. 2010. Addressing summer reading setback among economically disadvantaged elementary students. *Reading Psychology* 31 (5): 411–27.

Altonji, Joseph G., and Richard K. Mansfield. 2011. The role of family, school, and community characteristics in inequality in education and labor market outcomes. In *Whither opportunity: Rising inequality and the uncertain life chances of low-income children*, eds. Greg Duncan and Richard Murnane, 339–58. New York, NY: Russell Sage Foundation.

Anderson, Kellie J., and Kathleen M. Minke. 2007. Parent involvement in education: Toward an understanding of parents' decision making. *Journal of Educational Research* 100 (5): 311–23.

Atteberry, Allison, and McEachin, Andrew. 2016. School's out: Summer learning loss across grade levels and school contexts in the U.S. today. In *The summer slide: What we know and can do about summer learning loss*, eds. K. Alexander, S. Pitcock, and M. Boulay, 35–54. New York, NY: Teachers College Press.

Barnard, Wendy Miedel. 2004. Parent involvement in elementary school and educational attainment. *Children and Youth Services Review* 26 (1): 39–62.

Bergman, Peter. 2015. Parent-child information frictions and human capital investment: Evidence from a field experiment. CESifo Working Paper Series No. 5391. Available from http://www.columbia .edu/~psb2101/BergmanSubmission.pdf.

Bergman, Peter, and Eric W. Chan. 2017. Leveraging technology to engage parents at scale: Evidence from a randomized controlled trial. CESifo Working Paper Series No. 6493. Available from http://www .columbia.edu/~psb2101/ParentRCT.pdf.

Bergman, Peter, and Todd Rogers. 2017. Is this technology useless? How seemingly irrelevant factors affect adoption and efficacy. Teachers College Columbia University Working Paper, New York, NY.

Borman, Geoffrey D., and N. Maritza Dowling. 2006. Longitudinal achievement effects of multiyear summer school: Evidence from the Teach Baltimore randomized field trial. *Educational Evaluation and Policy Analysis* 28 (1): 25–48.

Borman, Geoffrey D., Michael E. Goetz, and N. Maritza Dowling. 2009. Halting the summer achievement slide: A randomized field trial of the KindergARTen Summer Camp. *Journal of Education for Students Placed at Risk* 14 (2): 133–47.

Burkam, David T., Douglas D. Ready, Valerie E. Lee, and Laura F. LoGerfo. 2004. Social-class differences in summer learning between kindergarten and first grade: Model specification and estimation. *Sociology of Education* 77 (1): 1–31.

Castleman, Benjamin L. 2015. *The 160-character solution: How text messaging and other behavioral strategies can improve education*. Baltimore, MD: JHU Press.

Chaplin, Duncan, and Jeffrey Capizzano. 2006. *Impacts of a summer learning program: A random assignment study of Building Educated Leaders for Life (BELL)*. Washington, DC: Urban Institute.

Cheung, Cecilia Sin-Sze, and Eva M. Pomerantz. 2012. Why does parents' involvement enhance children's achievement? The role of parent-oriented motivation. *Journal of Educational Psychology* 104 (3): 820–32.

Coleman, James Samuel, and the U.S. Department of Health. 1966. *Equality of educational opportunity*. Vol. 2. Washington, DC: US Department of Health, Education, and Welfare, Office of Education.

Cooper, Harris, Kelly Charlton, Jeff C. Valentine, Laura Muhlenbruck, and Geoffrey D. Borman. 2000. Making the most of summer school: A meta-analytic and narrative review. *Monographs of the Society for Research in Child Development* 65 (1): 1–127.

Cooper, H., B. Nye, K. Charlton, J. Lindsay, and S. Greathouse. 1996. The effects of summer vacation on achievement test scores: A narrative and meta-analytic review. *Review of Educational Research* 66 (3): 227–68.

Deming, David. 2009. Early childhood intervention and life-cycle skill development: Evidence from Head Start. *American Economic Journal: Applied Economics* 1 (3): 111–34.

DiPrete, Thomas A., and Gregory M. Eirich. 2006. Cumulative advantage as a mechanism for inequality: A review of theoretical and empirical developments. *Annual Review of Sociology* 32:271–97.

Doss, Christopher, Erin M. Fahle, Susanna Loeb, and Benjamin N. York. 2016. Supporting parenting through differentiated text messaging: Testing effects on learning during kindergarten. Stanford Working Paper. Available from https://cepa.stanford.edu/content/supporting-parenting-through-differ entiated-and-personalized-text-messaging-testing-effects-learning-during-kindergarten.

Downey, Douglas B., Paul T. von Hippel, and Beckett A. Broh. 2004. Are schools the great equalizer? Cognitive inequality during the summer months and the school year. *American Sociological Review* 69 (5): 613–35.

Downey, Douglas B., Paul T. von Hippel, and Melanie Hughes. 2008. Are "failing" schools really failing? Using seasonal comparison to evaluate school effectiveness. *Sociology of Education* 81 (3): 242–70.

Fan, Xitao, and Michael Chen. 2001. Parental involvement and students' academic achievement: A meta-analysis. *Educational Psychology Review* 13 (1): 1–22.

Fryer, Roland G., Jr. 2014. Injecting charter school best practices into traditional public schools: Evidence from field experiments. *Quarterly Journal of Economics* 129 (3): 1355–1407.

Fryer, Roland G., Jr., and Steven D. Levitt. 2004. Understanding the black-white test score gap in the first two years of school. *Review of Economics and Statistics* 86 (2): 447–64.

Goldhaber, Dan D., and Dominic J. Brewer. 1997. Why don't schools and teachers seem to matter? Assessing the impact of unobservables on educational productivity. *Journal of Human Resources* 32 (3): 505–23.

Goldhaber, Dan D., Dominic J. Brewer, and Deborah J. Anderson. 1999. A three-way error components analysis of educational productivity. *Education Economics* 7 (3): 199–208.

Henderson, Anne T. 1987. *The evidence continues to grow: Parent involvement improves student achievement. an annotated bibliography*. National Committee for Citizens in Education Special Report. Columbia, MD: National Committee for Citizens in Education.

Houtenville, Andrew J., and Karen Smith Conway. 2008. Parental effort, school resources, and student achievement. *Journal of Human Resources* 43 (2): 437–53.

Hoover-Dempsey, Kathleen V., Joan M. T. Walker, Howard M. Sandler, Darlene Whetsel, Christa L. Green, Andrew S. Wilkins, and Kristen Closson. 2005. Why do parents become involved? Research findings and implications. *Elementary School Journal* 106 (2): 105–30.

Hurwitz, Lisa B., Alexis R. Lauricella, Ann Hanson, Anthony Raden, and Ellen Wartella. 2015. Supporting Head Start parents: Impact of a text message intervention on parent–child activity engagement. *Early Child Development and Care* 185 (9): 1373–89.

Jackson, C. Kirabo, Rucker C. Johnson, and Claudia Persico. 2016. The effects of school spending on educational and economic outcomes: Evidence from school finance reforms. *Quarterly Journal of Economics* 131 (1): 157–218.

Jacob, Brian A., and Lars Lefgren. 2004. Remedial education and student achievement: A regression-discontinuity analysis. *Review of Economics and Statistics* 86 (1): 226–44.

Kim, James S. 2006. Effects of a voluntary summer reading intervention on reading achievement: Results from a randomized field trial. *Educational Evaluation and Policy Analysis* 28 (4): 335–55.

Kim, James S. 2007. The effects of a voluntary summer reading intervention on reading activities and reading achievement. *Journal of Educational Psychology* 99 (3): 505–15.

Kim, James S., and Jonathan Guryan. 2010. The efficacy of a voluntary summer book reading intervention for low-income Latino children from language minority families. *Journal of Educational Psychology* 102 (1): 20–31.

Kim, James S., and Thomas G. White. 2008. Scaffolding voluntary summer reading for children in grades 3 to 5: An experimental study. *Scientific Studies of Reading* 12 (1): 1–23.

Konstantopoulos, Spyros, and Geoffrey Borman. 2011. Family background and school effects on student achievement: A multilevel analysis of the Coleman data. *Teachers College Record* 113 (1): 97–132.

Kraft, Matthew A., and Shaun M. Dougherty. 2013. The effect of teacher–family communication on student engagement: Evidence from a randomized field experiment. *Journal of Research on Educational Effectiveness* 6 (3): 199–222.

Kraft, Matthew A., and Todd Rogers. 2015. The underutilized potential of teacher-to-parent communication: Evidence from a field experiment. *Economics of Education Review* 47:49–63.

Lafortune, Julien, Jesse Rothstein, and Diane Whitmore Schanzenbach. 2016. School finance reform and the distribution of student achievement. National Bureau of Economic Research Working Paper No. w2201, Cambridge, MA.

Mapp, Karen L., and P. J. Kuttner. 2013. *Partners in education: A dual capacity-building framework for family–school partnerships.* Austin, TX: SEDL and U.S. Department of Education.

Matsudaira, Jordan D. 2008. Mandatory summer school and student achievement *Journal of Econometrics* 142 (2): 829–50.

McKenzie, David. 2012. Beyond baseline and follow-up: The case for more T in experiments. *Journal of Development Economics* 99 (2): 210–21.

Nye, Barbara, Spyros Konstantopoulos, and Larry V. Hedges. 2004. How large are teacher effects? *Educational Evaluation and Policy Analysis* 26 (3): 237–57.

Quinn, David M. 2015. Kindergarten black–white test score gaps: Re-examining the roles of socioeconomic status and school quality with new data. *Sociology of Education* 88 (2): 120–39.

Quinn, David M., North Cooc, Joe McIntyre, and Celia J. Gomez. 2016. Seasonal dynamics of academic achievement inequality by socioeconomic status and race/ethnicity: Updating and extending past research with new national data. *Educational Researcher* 45 (8): 443–53.

Schacter, John, and Booil Jo. 2005. Learning when school is not in session: A reading summer day-camp intervention to improve the achievement of exiting first-grade students who are economically disadvantaged. *Journal of Research in Reading* 28 (2): 158–69.

Sénéchal, Monique, and Laura Young. 2008. The effect of family literacy interventions on children's acquisition of reading from kindergarten to grade 3: A meta-analytic review. *Review of Educational Research* 78 (4): 880–907.

Stanovich, Keith E. 1986. Matthew effects in reading: Some consequences of individual differences in the acquisition of literacy. *Reading Research Quarterly* 21 (4): 360–407.

Steffes, Tracy L. 2012. *School, society, and state: A new education to govern modern America, 1890–1940.* Chicago, IL: University of Chicago Press.

Thaler, Richard H., and Cass R. Sunstein. 2008. *Nudge: Improving decisions about health, wealth, and happiness.* New York, NY: Penguin Books.

Todd, Petra E., and Kenneth I. Wolpin. 2007. The production of cognitive achievement in children: Home, school, and racial test score gaps. *Journal of Human Capital* 1 (1): 91–136.

White, Thomas G., James S. Kim, Helen Chen Kingston, and Lisa Foster. 2014. Replicating the effects of a teacher-scaffolded voluntary summer reading program: The role of poverty. *Reading Research Quarterly* 49 (1): 5–30.

Yeager, David S., and Gregory M. Walton. 2011. Social-psychological interventions in education: They're not magic. *Review of Educational Research* 81 (2): 267–301.

York, Benjamin N., and Susanna Loeb. 2014. One step at a time: The effects of an early literacy text messaging program for parents of preschoolers. National Bureau of Economic Research Working Paper, Cambridge, MA.

New Tools for Old Problems: Inequality and Educational Opportunity for Ethnic Minority Youth and Parents

By
NANCY E. HILL,
JULIA R. JEFFRIES,
and
KATHLEEN P. MURRAY

Fifty years after the Coleman Report delineated deep inequities across race and ethnicity in school contexts and outcomes, American families still navigate largely inequitable educational systems. The Coleman Report—with only slightly veiled surprise—also revealed the deep value African Americans place on education, their strong motivation to succeed, and the high expectations that they have for academic success. This article provides a critical analysis of the policies designed to increase equity in and access to high-quality education. With a special focus on adolescents, we show how these policies are experienced differently by families in ways that sustain inequities across ethnicity, race, and socioeconomic background. We also review research on the experiences of students in schools, arguing that policy attempts to mitigate disparities in educational experiences across race and socioeconomic condition have had little if any effect.

Keywords: educational inequities; school choice; Coleman Report; parenting; school context; race

The Coleman Report's (1966) findings on the racial stratification and educational inequality in the United States was a wake-up

Nancy E. Hill is a developmental psychologist and the Charles Bigelow Professor of Education at Harvard University. Professor Hill's research focuses on ethnicity, socioeconomic status, and culture as they influence parenting beliefs and practices, especially as they relate to children and adolescents' academic adjustment and preparations for postsecondary school transitions.

Julia R. Jeffries is a doctoral student at the Harvard Graduate School of Education. Her research interests lie in the study of racial and ethnic identity development in students and teachers, as well as openness to conversations about race and racism in the classroom.

Kathleen P. Murray earned her master's degree in education in prevention science and practice from Harvard Graduate School of Education in 2017. Prior to that, she was a teacher and administrator at a charter school serving low-income, ethnic minority youth. Currently, she is a law student at Northwestern Pritzker School of Law.

Correspondence: Nancy_hill@gse.harvard.edu

DOI: 10.1177/0002716217730618

call to many at the time of its release—a decade after court rulings on desegregation (e.g., *Brown v. Topeka Board of Education*) (Coleman et al. 1966). According to the report, 80 percent of all Euro-American/white students attended schools that were 80 to 100 percent Euro-American. African Americans were the most segregated, with nearly 100 percent segregation in the South. In 1966, the average African American attended schools where 65 percent of the teachers were African American, with racially matched teachers nearly 100 percent in the South. Further, African Americans had less access to facilities that promoted achievement (e.g., science labs, gymnasium) and weaker curricula in 1966. This was especially true in the South. Not surprisingly, African Americans scored lower than Euro-Americans on standardized tests, and Asian Americans scored higher than both groups.

Within the schools and classrooms in 1966, African American children were more likely to be in classes with peers whose parents had less educational attainment than were their Euro-American counterparts. African American students were exposed to schools with greater turmoil and academic issues than the average Euro-American student. For example, African Americans were more likely to attend schools with high dropout rates and lower attendance rates than their Euro-American counterparts. One in four African American students was likely to be exposed to schools with high dropout rates, while this was true for only one out of every ten Euro-American students. Further, African Americans were more likely to attend schools with less experienced teachers. These characteristics of the school context (e.g., peers, teachers, curriculum) were more strongly related to academic outcomes for African Americans, compared to Euro-Americans.

Similar disparities and inequities remain today—more than 50 years later. Indeed, segregation is deepening, rather than declining (Ayscue and Orfield 2015; Orfield and Frankenberg 2013). As was the case in 1966, Euro-American students today attend schools with a majority of other Euro-Americans (81.9 percent; Walsemann, Bell, and Maitra 2011). In contrast, African Americans attend schools comprising an average of 35 percent Euro-Americans. Latinos attend the most segregated schools in the nation (Hill and Torres 2010). Further, African American and Latino youth are much more likely to attend schools that have fewer resources, less experienced teachers, high rates of behavioral problems among students, fewer advanced courses, and fewer guidance and career counselors than are Euro-American youth (Hill and Torres 2010; Hill 2011; Reardon and Bischoff 2011). There are disparities in the quality of the curriculum. African Americans and Latinos are also less likely to have teachers who match their racial/ethnic background today than in 1966.

One clear difference today, compared to 50 years ago, is the significant increase in Latino students in U.S. schools. Although the Coleman Report included Latinos, especially Puerto Rican youth, in its figures, the emphasis was on disparities between African Americans and Euro-Americans. In 2017, the demographics of the American school population reflect diversity that has increased substantially. Even between 2003 and 2014, the Euro-American student population in the United States decreased from 59 percent to 49 percent, whereas the Latino population increased from 19 percent to 25 percent and the

African American population remained relatively flat (U.S. Department of Education National Center for Education Statistics 2015). With inequities in access to high-quality education persisting and ethnic and racial gaps in achievement pernicious and resistant to improvement after more than 50 years, both market-based and empowerment strategies to reduce inequality of access and achievement gaps have been employed.

In this article, we analyze policy attempts to mitigate educational inequality, and how those policies have been experienced by parents and families and by youth in American schools. We pay particular attention to adolescents as they prepare for postsecondary transitions into college and the labor market.

A range of policy approaches have aimed to redress inequalities and inequities. These include school finance policies (see Rebell, this volume), cross-sector collaborations (see Riehl and Lyon, this volume), market forces and privatization such as school voucher programs (see Mizala and Torche, this volume), and standards-based reforms, among other policies. This article focuses on student assignment policies aimed at improving school equity, including empowerment strategies such as choice and voucher policies. Legal means to reduce inequalities, and demand desegregation and equitable funding across schools have not been effective—it has instead resulted in "white flight" from urban districts (Ryan 2010; Edsall and Edsall 1992; Orfield 2001). Indeed, the Coleman Report described the ways that Euro-American families exercised "choice" in 1966: moving their children to predominantly white suburbs or enrolling them in private schools. A report commissioned in 1970 to document the progress of desegregation reported the significant increase in the establishment of segregated private schools to receive the "white flight" from integration (Fancher 1970). Providing parents with market-based strategies, such as school choice, charter schools, and vouchers, arose as a means for reducing inequality, by providing low-income and families of color with choices that are not tied to economic means. That is, they address inequalities and inequities through parental empowerment. These strategies serve the dual goal of allowing middle-class and Euro-Americans more options to stay in an urban district while navigating racially diverse schools and providing low-income parents the options to leave low-performing schools in their neighborhoods—thereby attempting to create equity and equality by putting parents "in control." Such policies shift the responsibility from schools to parents—parents can select their desired school. Thus, equity in school means giving parents sufficient choice to obtain the education they want for their children (Scott 2013).

Assignment Policy Tools to Address Inequality

Around the same time as the *Brown v. Board of Education* decision, Friedman (1955) envisioned vouchers that parents could take to any school of their choosing—taking their public school per capita budgeted expenditure with them. Vouchers would allow parents to exercise choice and signal high- and low-quality schools without moving neighborhoods. Friedman predicted that market pressures would entice low-quality schools to improve or close. And the significant reduction in budget due to voucher transfers would almost ensure that schools not chosen by parents would become worse. It also was assumed that high-quality schools would be replicated, merely because of demand. Friedman imagined that schools would have children from many different neighborhoods, enhancing the demographic diversity of the school. However, his primary goal was the creation of competition among schools, not diversity (Friedman 1955).

Within market-based systems, consumer choice provides the key mechanism by which forces are applied to producers to incentivize quality goods. In the education marketplace, parents are these consumers (Friedman 1955). Consumers make decisions in their individual best interest or, in the case of the education market, in their child's best interest. Therefore, if a goal of school choice policies is to increase equitable access to high-quality education or racial/ethnic/economic integration, they will require individual parents to support this goal by *simultaneously* considering the needs of their own child and the impact of their choice on the needs of all students in the system. That is, such policies rely on the outcome of a collective movement and assume that individual family decisions in the best interests of one's own child will also benefit other students in the school district. In reality, families are making individual decisions based on the best interest of their children and these individual choices have not resulted in a collective movement that reduces educational inequality in the way that policy-makers often say or hope that they do (Jonathan 1989; Ryan 2010). An analysis of parents' decision-making preferences, sources of information, and selection processes provides evidence of how well equipped school choice policies are to achieve these goals.

In the 1990s, Chubb and Moe revitalized Friedman's idea that parents, behaving like consumers in an education market, could motivate competition and thus innovation in schools. They argued that empowering parents to choose would allow the specific needs of individual students to be central to the process (Chubb and Moe 1990). However, even early on, they understood the potential limitations that would need remediation to ensure efficiency and equity in the market. Specifically, they understood that varying access to information could result in parents making choices that are not in their child's best interest (Chubb and Moe 1990). Because public education serves both the individual and society, choices that are not in the best interest of the individual child are also not in the best interest of society. When some parents are able to make decisions in their children's best interest and others are not, if the empowered parents do not then consider the interests of less advantaged children, the market creates winners and losers. And those winners and losers are children and society.

As such, economists, political scientists, sociologists, psychologists, conservative and liberal policy-makers, and advocates disagree about how those imperfections affect the merit of parent choice as a policy, with concerns about equity at the forefront of the debate. Researchers theorize that truly free, rational choice in the education market is compromised because Euro-American middle-class and wealthy parents have greater resources and information and have fewer "market constraints." Some argue that minority parents do not consider the most academically rigorous schools, which are predominantly Euro-American, in part, due to a lack of trust in majority-dominant institutions (Wells and Crain 1992) and because of their desire for culturally inclusive environments. In contrast, other theorists prefer policies focused on parental choices over government driven reallocation of educational resources, suggesting that parents evaluate schools as effectively as experts and know their children's needs best (Bast and Walberg 2004). However, parents are not always able to effectively judge the quality of schools. Parents often misidentify the reading proficiency rates, racial composition and discipline incidences at the schools that they choose (Schneider et al. 1998; Van Dunk and Dickman 2002) and may move their children into failing schools (Stein, Goldring, and Cravens 2011). Even as parents' choice processes are similar across ethnicity, actual choices differ in academic quality (Bell 2009).

Regardless of whether parents are equipped to make individual choices that benefit all children, there has been a significant increase in school choice policies since the 1990s that requires parents to make such choices. From a combination of parents' self-reports and inferences based on actual choices, parent preferences for school characteristics vary considerably based on urbanicity and the structure of the school choice system studied. For example, parents consistently show a preference for school proximity, but their willingness to trade location for academic achievement varies based on context and, presumably, the availability of free public transportation (Hastings, Kane, and Staiger 2005; Glazerman 1998; Goyette 2008; Fuller and Elmore 1996). Indeed, Coleman's analysis in 1966 anticipated this finding, reporting that African American parents preferred enrolling their children in schools closer to home because of the high cost of transportation (cf. Coleman et al. 1966, 472).

Another consistent finding that is at odds with the goals of integration and equity is that parents seek schools comprising mostly their own race (Hastings, Kane, and Staiger 2005; Glazerman 1998; Goyette 2008; Fuller and Elmore 1996; Saporito and Lareau 1999). Further, parents choose schools where the average achievement score or academic reputation matches their child's achievement (Glazerman 1998; Bell 2009).

While, on average, parents of all races prefer schools where their race is in the majority, Euro-American parents demonstrate an active avoidance of majority African American schools (Saporito and Lareau 1999). Indeed, an analysis of the characteristics of schools selected as parents' first choice in a diverse urban district (i.e., 31 percent African American, 42 percent Latino, and 14 percent Euro-American) showed that parents seem to prefer ethnic and racial diversity, but only when there is a critical mass of "same race" students in the school (Johnston 2015). While racial composition is less likely to cause African American parents to eliminate a school, they do show a slight avoidance of high-poverty schools (Saporito and Lareau 1999). Coleman anticipated that alternative assignment plans might impact racial/ethnic compositions of schools and, in fact, they do. Coleman quotes a superintendent who did not want to publish data of school demographics because he feared that white parents would avoid schools with "too much of a minority group in it" (Coleman et al. 1966, 463). In terms of socioeconomic status (SES), high-SES parents are more likely to choose schools with high test scores (Hastings, Kane, and Staiger 2005), whereas low-SES parents are more likely to choose schools for reasons other than academics and in balancing competing demands often choose failing schools (Bell 2009). Not surprisingly, these preferences suggest that parents are unlikely to consider the needs of society as a whole, or broader equity goals, when making school decisions for their child.

Despite indicating preferences for certain school characteristics over others, parents' decision-making does not always result in the selection of a school that matches their own preferences; nor does it always lead to a choice that will create equity for all students (Bell 2009; Stein, Goldring, and Cravens 2011). Given that there are often more options than parents can deeply evaluate, they often narrow their set of choices early on based on broad criteria. Bounded rational choice models suggest that humans cannot take into account all factors and information when making choices (Simon 1986). They use strategies to limit the options before digging into the deep analysis of options (Simon 1990). As part of this process, parents narrow their choice set based on information and beliefs about schools shared in their social networks (Holme 2002; Bell 2009; Horvat, Weininger, and Lareau 2003). While some ascribe the creation of narrowed choice sets to only the best-informed consumers, others find that most families engage in a two-step elimination and evaluation process (Bell 2009; Saporito and Lareau 1999; Buckley and Schneider 2003; Schneider et al. 1998).

While this two-step process of first eliminating and then evaluating exists among all racial groups, Euro-American families tend to eliminate schools in the first step based on race, whereas African American families tend to eliminate schools in the first step based on concentration of poverty (Saporito and Lareau 1999). Additionally, ethnic minority parents are more likely to choose programs with which they are familiar, but are less likely to be familiar with magnet schools and other choice options (Henig 1996). However, in an urban district with a range of SES among the African American and Euro-American populations (i.e., ethnicity and SES are less confounded), African Americans were not significantly less familiar with schools in the district (Hill 2017). While all parents appear to use information from social networks to make school choices, high-SES parents are more likely to rely on parents of their student's school peers, while low-SES parents depend on information from family members (Horvat, Weininger, and Lareau 2003). In the end, even if their full set of choices are similar, differences in making the first cut results in inequitable choice sets (Bell 2009).

In addition to preferences about school characteristics and decision-making processes, an understanding of the sources of information used by parents to evaluate these factors is essential to assessing their effectiveness as choosers and, therefore, the effectiveness of school choice policies. In fact, the most relevant question when considering school choice effectiveness might not be an evaluation of parents' capacity for rigorous decision-making, but an evaluation of the availability and quality of the information with which they can make those decisions (Lubienski 2008). As use of choice programs has increased, so have the number of choices available for parents to consider, as has the amount of information about those choices. With the Internet and the enormous amount of information of varying quality and accuracy available, there may be too much for parents to assess (Schneider, Teske, and Marschall 2000). Through an analysis of parent Internet behavior, researchers found that few school websites offer information on programming or themes, instead focusing on objective input (i.e. student-to-teacher ratio) and output (i.e. achievement data) statistics. However, determining a school's effectiveness, the value added to a student by attending, requires a sophisticated analysis of complex factors, not simple statistics, especially if it is based on students' interests and learning styles (Lubienski 2008).

The limitations of formal school websites, however, may be less relevant for some parents. Based on a survey of what parents find useful, the perceived helpfulness of school-based and formal information sources decreases with parents' education level, while the perceived value of information from their child's peers' parents and other social networks increases (Schneider, Teske, and Marschall 2000). Additionally, Euro-American parents also find fewer school-based and formal sources useful, while finding information from social networks more useful than do ethnic minority parents. In fact, Euro-American and highly educated parents find fewer sources of information useful overall (Schneider, Teske, and Marschall 2000). While parents of all races and backgrounds value information from their social networks (Holme 2002; Bell 2009; Horvat, Weininger, and Lareau 2003; Jonathan 1989), on average, urban minority parents talk with only one or two people about school options (Schneider et al. 1998). Therefore, for poor, minority parents, social networks may contain far fewer sources of information about schools and those sources are likely to be equally as disconnected as the parents themselves (Schneider et al. 1998).

As the original market-based school intervention, voucher programs aspire to grant low-income students access to formerly cost-prohibitive private schools. However, analyses of voucher programs' impact on student achievement are mixed (Rouse 1998; Metcalf et al. 2002; Krueger and Zhu 2004; Howell et al. 2002; Greene 2000, Belfield 2006). If voucher-provided access to private schools does impact the achievement of individual students, especially students of color, as some of these studies suggest, an assessment of who uses voucher programs is essential. For vouchers to have a broad social impact, they must ensure equity as much as they ensure individual access. Unfortunately, voucher users are not representative of all public school students. Voucher users are more likely to have attended private schools before being offered a voucher, begging the question of whether they are subsidizing the status quo, instead of increasing social mobility (Belfield 2006; Paul, Legan, and Metcalf 2007). Further, admission procedures at schools accepting vouchers can lead to increased sorting by both income and ability (Chakrabarti 2013). Voucher recipients are disproportionately Euro-American or Hispanic, with African Americans underrepresented (Metcalf et al. 2002). In fact, after applying for and being awarded a voucher, low-income and minority students are less likely to use it (Paul, Legan, and Metcalf 2007). As the Coleman Report found, voucher and "freedom of choice" programs have resulted in the "token enrollment" of a few African American students in predominantly Euro-American schools (Coleman et al. 1966, 467). Thus, while voucher programs might allow a number of students access to private schools, questions remain about who these programs benefit and if they serve the goal of achieving equity.

Contrary to the goal of desegregation and increased equity, school choice policies have enabled parents of all races to self-segregate in a way that reifies and continues to perpetuate institutional inequality. In fact, the effect of school choice on segregation has been one of the most well-documented and researched phenomena regarding the effects of school choice policies after *Brown v. Board of Education* (cf. Orfield and Frankenberg 2013). These policies have been implemented with the goal of giving parents more options to secure high-quality education for their children and, in the process, reduce inequities across racial and ethnic background. However, they have fallen short in part because true market pressures are not applied. That is, failing schools are not systematically closed or improved and parents do not systematically receive their top choice. Further, to reduce inequalities, such policies rely on parents' choices to serve the needs of their own children while also serving the collective needs of society. Given the implicit individualism and competition in American culture, it is unreasonable to expect parents to make choices in the best interest of society rather than that of their own children. Even the language around having schools "compete" signals and triggers competition among families. Only some students will "win the lottery" for a seat in the best schools. This framing elicits a competitive, individualist mindset, rather than a collaborative one. Parents across race and ethnicity, then, experience these policies differently.

Parents' Experiences with Choice across Ethnicity

Ethnic minority and low-income parents experience higher stakes when making school-choice decisions for their children. Often, these parents are not experiencing "choice" as opportunity but, rather, as navigating a set of unsatisfactory options and constraints. There are greater constraints on the options for African American, Latino, and low-income families, compared to middle-class and wealthy Euro-American families. Middle-class and wealthy Euro-Americans can use social capital and resources to increase their choices to include private schools outside their district and options to move out of a district to access schools that match their priorities. This means they can be more flexible in choice options and more "risky" in their choice of urban schools (Kimelberg 2014). Many such parents see themselves as taking a chance on urban schools, knowing they can move or consider private schools should it not work out. This flexibility is less true for African Americans, Latinos, and low-income families (Kimelberg 2014).

Further, ethnic minority parents often find that they must make trade-offs between academic excellence and affirming their child's ethnic and cultural identity. Such trade-offs are often required for ethnic minority parents who send their children out of district to academically rigorous suburban schools or to predominately Euro-American private schools (Hill 2009). These are schools where youth find themselves as cultural minorities and where they are likely to experience discrimination (Carter Andrews 2012) and diminished expectations (Tenenbaum and Ruck 2007). However, many endure the misfit and the discrimination and marginalization to gain access to academically rigorous schools—an inequitable cost.

Similarly, ethnic minority parents are often required to trade quality for safety. Like most parents, African American parents highly value academic achievement. However, when living in neighborhoods with concentrated poverty and crime, they must prioritize safety and often look for schools that have both strong academic standards and high levels of structure and discipline (Rhodes and DeLuca 2014; DeLuca and Rosenblatt 2010). Many of these parents have concerns about sending their children to schools that are predominantly Euro-American. At the same time, they may find that their local school and its neighborhood are unsafe. Therefore, they often opt into charter schools that are more heavily concentrated with students of their own racial and ethnic backgrounds to allow their children to feel safe and comfortable in their school environments (Lewis and Danzig 2010). This increases racial segregation and often exposes African American youth to schools with no-nonsense disciplinary policies and strict expectations for conformity. Some research shows that strict monitoring and discipline does not facilitate the development of aspirations, creativity, and self-expression that is encouraged in higher-income private school and suburban settings (cf. Hill and Wang 2015). Similarly, low-income parents might choose a school that is farther away—not because it is academically better, but because doing so removes youth from neighborhoods or schools where there are gangs or where they find it too dangerous for their children to walk. Whereas the Coleman Report, in 1966, documented "token enrollment" of a few African American students in predominantly Euro-American schools as a result of choice plans; in 2017, choice plans experience far greater minority student and parent participation, but this results in enrollment in predominantly African American and Latino charter schools, rather than increasing integration.

African American, Latino, and low-income families more often find themselves juggling the high costs of the logistics of family life. Even while highly valuing academic achievement in selecting schools, the realities of balancing before-school and afterschool care, transportation, and navigating dangerous neighborhoods around neighborhood schools eclipse these parents' ability to choose schools for academic rigor (Rhodes and DeLuca 2014; Kimelberg 2014; Condliffe, Boyd, and DeLuca 2015). For most low-income families, the best schools based on academics are far from where they live. Parents should be able to match their children to schools that fit their interests and learning styles. Low-income, urban parents are less able to actualize these goals than are middle-class parents; their choices often dissolve into choosing a school that is "not bad," rather than a school that is great (Rhodes and DeLuca 2014).

African American and low-income students often find that their options for high school enrollment and school choice are diminished, and they often have fewer knowledgeable adults available to guide them through the school selection process (Condliffe, Boyd, and DeLuca 2015) compared to middle-class students (Kimelberg 2014), even if they remain in the same urban district. In selecting high schools through school choice policies in an urban district, middle-class parents were more hypervigilant about the high school options than they were for elementary school options (Kimelberg 2014). If unable to get into the charter, exam school, or another academically rigorous high school, these parents had more options for accessing out-of-district schools including private school and moving out of the district. In contrast, African American and low-income students' options were more restricted for high school. In the opposite pattern of middle-class families, the low-income African American students were often making the decision about high school enrollment on their own, with little parental involvement (Condliffe, Boyd, and DeLuca 2015). Further, because of the inadequacies of their elementary and middle school academic record, many low-income African American students are ineligible for academically rigorous exam schools and charter schools. These youth are penalized and have their academic and future opportunities foreclosed because of academic mistakes and poor schooling options at the elementary and middle school levels. Indeed, attending a predominantly African American elementary school was found to have a negative effect on high school grades even after controlling for individual- and school-level characteristics (Mickelson and Heath 1999).

Even after parents navigate their options and make their choices, there are different ethnic implications based on the ultimate school assignment. When engaging school choice policies, the risk is that youth may not get their first choice. Whereas most district websites indicate that there are no demographic differences in those who get their first choice and those who do not, at least one study has found that getting one's first choice school was associated with the amount of information that parents reported they received and used in making choices (Yettick 2016), and there are ethnic and SES differences in amount and quality of information that parents receive (Horvat, Weininger, and Lareau 2003). Gaining access to one's first choice school is related not only to improvements in academic achievement but in reductions in problem behavior, including involvement in crime and increased chances of attending college (Deming 2012). The positive benefits of gaining access to one's first choice school were stronger for African Americans, compared to other ethnic groups. Further, after enrollment, African American and Latino families were less likely than Euro-American and Asian families to leave a school when they are unsatisfied with it (James 2014). Euro-American and wealthier families have more contingency options when they do not get their first choice (Kimmelberg 2014). This means that African American and Latino families are likely to remain in underperforming and failing schools, compounding their negative effects. This affirms that, in the context of school choice policies, the stakes are higher for low-income and African American families than for Euro-American and middle-class families.

The school choice and enrollment process is riskier for African American, Latino, and low-income families. The schools that comprise the default options for African Americans and Latinos are worse and more limited than they are for middle-class and Euro-American families, even when they are in the same districts. This means that the burdens and costs of inequality are more strongly felt by students of color and low-income students. Ultimately, these policies are called "choice," but in reality, parents are not guaranteed their first choice. If their preferred school lacks sufficient seats, families lose control of where their child will attend school. Given that it is politically difficult to close or improve low-performing schools and that there are insufficient seats in higher-performing schools, certain students are relegated to failing or underperforming schools. Perhaps unsurprisingly, the students who end up at these schools tend to be ethnic minority and low-income students. Again, this is the same conclusion that Coleman made in 1966. He stated, "Voluntary transfer plans have been widely criticized as ineffective and even deceptive. It is argued that they place all of the burden—including the burden of expense and initiative—on the [African American] child and his parent, that the [African American] is least able to bear these burdens" (Coleman et al. 1966, 472).

Policy Reinforcing Inequality: The Student Experience

As Coleman found in 1966, there are significant racial and ethnic disparities in students' experiences at school today. Despite school choice, open enrollment, vouchers, and other policy mechanisms, the vast majority (about 70 percent) of students attend the school where they are assigned based on their residence (Rhodes and DeLuca 2014). This results in differential school experiences. African American students' experiences at school often work against their ability to achieve. There are disparities in the quality of the curriculum. Only 57 percent of African American students attend schools that provide access to a full range of math and science classes (U.S. Department of Education Office of Civil Rights 2014). The same report shows that only 66 percent of schools with high African American and Latino enrollment offer a course in Chemistry and only 74 percent offer Algebra II, gateway courses for college. Even with equivalent ability levels, African American and Latino high school students are more likely to be tracked into courses that are less rigorous academically than are Euro-American students (Darling-Hammond 2004; Mickelson and Everett 2008). High-ability African American students are less likely to be placed in gifted or advanced classes than are Euro-American students with average ability levels (Mickelson and Heath 1999).

Apart from differential curricula and schools, desegregation does not ensure equality and the reduction of inequities. Within schools, African American and Latino students have more negative experiences with teachers and other adults in the building than their white peers. The evidence of differential expectations for achievement by teachers and treatment in the classroom is well established (Tenenbaum and Ruck 2007). Based on a meta-analysis of thirty-nine studies (Tenenbaum and Ruck 2007), African American students were less likely to experience teachers who made positive referrals for them, engaged them with positive speech, or encouraged them. Further, teachers held lower expectations for their achievement. In a separate study, lower-achieving African American students were most vulnerable to unsupportive teachers, with significant negative impacts on achievement (Midgley, Feldlaufer, and Eccles 1989) and lower levels of school satisfaction and engagement (Buehler et al. 2015). There are similar challenges in interactions with school guidance counselors.

African American youth are challenged by the inability to develop effective relationships with school counselors (Bryant 2015). Schools with the largest African American and Latino enrollments have an average of 332 students per counselor (Bryant 2015), making it nearly impossible for students to develop the kind of high-quality relationships needed to assist them with college and career readiness. In our own research with an ethnically diverse high school with 59 percent Euro-American and 41 percent students of color (*n* ~ 1,100), we found that African American students were *more* likely to meet with guidance counselors than were Euro-American students. Further, African American students reported that these meetings were more valuable to them than did Euro-American students (Hill et al. 2016). While there is a shortage of school counselors in most high schools that African American students attend, these findings suggest that when counselors are available, African American students both seek out and value relationships with them. Indeed, the beneficial associations between positive adult relations at school and envisioning a meaningful future and beliefs about the job market were stronger for African American youth compared to Euro-American youth (Hill et al. 2016). However, most African American and Latino students attend schools with few counselors. Adolescents need an adult at school who knows them and supports them (Eccles 2004), whether a teacher or a counselor. When adolescents are unable to develop a close relationship and instead feel as though they do not belong at school, they are more likely to engage in problematic behaviors such as substance use and report higher levels of depressive symptoms (Barber and Olsen 2004).

There is strong and consistent evidence that African Americans are more likely than Euro-Americans to be suspended and receive in-school detentions that exclude them from school (Fabelo et al. 2011; Losen and Gillespie 2012), although there is little evidence that African Americans have higher rates of problem behavior (Losen and Skiba 2010; Skiba et al. 2015). Indeed, between 2000 and 2014, the disparities in disciplinary practices between African Americans and Euro-Americans increased. Whereas the suspension rates for Euro-American students decreased, the rates increased for African American students (Losen and Skiba 2010). Although these studies focused mostly on adolescents, disparities in suspensions and expulsions have been found as early as the preschool years (Meek and Gilliam 2016). Suggesting teacher bias, the disparities are greatest for infractions that can be interpreted subjectively, such as defiance or disruption, compared to explicit rule violations such as truancy or cigarette smoking (Fabelo et al. 2011). Further, disparities are most prominent among teachers with less experience. Given that African American youth are more likely to attend schools with novice teachers, the risk of receiving discipline that is harsh and it resulting in separation from school is even greater.

African American students experience broader discrimination at school through differential treatment by teachers, both regarding their academics and behavior. The negative impact of discrimination on mental health and academic achievement is well documented (Hughes et al. 2006; Umana-Taylor et al. 2014). African American boys and girls report experiencing both racial and gender discrimination. Contrary to what one might expect, African American boys reported greater amounts of gender discrimination than did African American girls (Cogburn, Chavous, and Griffin 2011). In the Cogburn, Chavous, and Griffin (2011) study, there were no differences across genders in levels of reported racial discrimination. Cogburn, Chavous, and Griffin interpreted these findings through the lens of social dominance theory (Sidanius et al. 2004), whereby, in hierarchical societies, discrimination is more acutely targeted toward males because they are viewed as greater threats to the power structures.

Discrimination is experienced in a variety of ways, is more likely to be experienced in integrated schools, and is negatively associated with well-being and mental health. Among more subtle types of discrimination, students describe being expected to speak as if they represented the entire race, being stared at by Euro-American students when curricular material focused on race or African Americans, having one's thoughts ignored or devalued in class or when working in small groups, and being wrongly accused of behavior infractions due to race (Carter Andrews 2012). The subtle and not-so-subtle micro- (and macro-) aggressions weaken African American students' connections to school. Further, there is a positive relation between the size of the Euro-American school population and African American students' depressive and somatic symptoms (Walsemann, Bell, and Maitra 2011). This association was explained by experiences of discrimination. Thus, African American students' achievement often occurs despite feeling unsupported and marginalized at school. This marginalization occurs at the hands of school personnel and fellow students.

In addition to navigating relationships with teachers and counselors, and the broader classroom context, African American youth must navigate the peer context. The ubiquitous notion of high-achieving African American students being accused of "acting white" and developing oppositional stances toward school, first identified by Fordham and Ogbu (1986), has been well studied and widely reported in the scientific and popular literature. African American youth are discouraged from achieving, hide their achievement, and experience sanctions from their African American peers for focusing on schoolwork, diminishing their academic performance. The premise of "acting white" fits the stereotypes of African American youth as less intelligent, unmotivated, and underachieving and explains African American youths' feeling that they do not belong at school in a way that preserves their self-esteem. Further, by separating academic achievement from its long-standing, deep-seated place within African American history and culture, it has the pernicious effect of becoming a litmus test of "blackness" among African American youth at a time when they are exploring and developing their African American identities. As African American youth develop their African American identity (i.e., becoming black, experience nigressence; Cross 1991), they try on, explore, and endorse aspects of African American culture and identity. During this phase, they may eschew characteristics and activities that are not deemed "African American" or "black." If their experiences at school do not feel inclusive or provide models and examples of African American achievement, achievement may be wrongly deemed as "not African American." That is, African American students' academic performance will not be affirmed as part of their identity. This can occur especially when the curriculum does not reflect their culture and when peer groups or teachers are not available to help connect achievement with African American culture.

The complexities of navigating African American peer groups and achievement have been documented as they relate to identity exploration and affirmation, and aspects of African American culture. African Americans are accused of "acting white" because their academic achievement itself. However, Sankofa et al. (2005) distinguished high-achieving African American students who achieve through values that are consistent with African American culture (e.g., interdependent, communal mindsets) from those who achieve through Euro-American cultural values (e.g., competition, independence). They discovered that it was not academic achievement but the misalignment of cultural values that resulted in being accused of "acting white." Only those who were perceived as achieving through Euro-American values and practices were deemed as "acting white" by their peers. Those who achieved at similar levels but were viewed as maintaining their cultural values were not accused of acting white. The challenge for schools and for African American youth is that the "hidden curriculum" undergirding many classes and especially advanced classes requires and highlights competition and individualism (Giroux 1981). Indeed, these students may be "acting white," as one of the only *means* of achieving, even as their achievement itself is wholly valued as African American.

Similarly, research on ethnic and racial identity development demonstrates the complexities of the relations between achievement and "acting white." Distinguishing between "reactionary" and authentic identities, Spencer and Harpalani (2008) demonstrated that youth who have erected shallow and oppositional identities, in response to discrimination and marginalization, are more likely to devalue achievement. In contrast, African American youth who have developed an authentic and deep ethnic identity have high self-esteem, achievement goals, and achievement that is positively related to their Afrocentricity (Spencer et al. 2001). It is not achievement itself that reflects "acting white" but the interactions of African American students' understanding of the centrality of education within African American culture and history. The school context that does not affirm African American identities in its curriculum or in its interactions with African American youth, and the ways in which African American youth must engage in school to succeed, create an unnecessary conflict between achievement and African American identity (Cross 2003, 2011; Spencer et al. 2003).

Indeed, the peer context is among the most challenging for achievement for African American and Latino youth. In a study of sixty-five African American and Latino youth and their parents participating in eighteen focus groups about resources that support and impede achievement, a consistent theme that emerged centered upon significant concerns about the negative influence of peers and the need to manage them to succeed (Hill 2012). They stressed the importance of staying away from negative influences and making sure that they were not near misbehavior (lest they be deemed guilty by association). As one mother described, her teen needed "internal strength" to deal with the peer context. Many parents stressed the importance of identifying the "right" crowd. As another teen expressed: "My mom always tells me that I'm judged by the company that I keep. So she tells me to choose who I hang out with, don't mix with the wrong crowd" (Hill 2012, 117). When African American youth are unable to effectively navigate toward peer groups that support their own achievement, African American parents will move their youth to different schools. As one mother said, "I had to get them out, I am glad I got them away from that environment. It took me a long time, but we did get away from [the gangs]" (Hill 2012, 120). This is consistent with the work of others who document the role of navigating peer groups through school choice (Kimelberg 2014).

This raises the question of how youth navigate the peer context in relation to their personal achievement. Social networks and cliques within middle and high schools vary in the extent to which they value and affirm academic achievement (Hamm et al. 2013). Affiliating with a friendship group that values and promotes achievement can buffer youth from the social costs of achieving within the broader peer group (Horvat and Lewis 2003; Tyson, Darity, and Castellino 2005). Whereas African American peer groups have been cast as monolithic and devaluing academic pursuits, these groups vary in their promotion of effort and academic achievement among African American youth (Hamm et al. 2013). In the predominantly African American schools in their study, the peer groups that promoted academic achievement were central to the social network structure. African American boys who affiliated with peer groups that promoted academic achievement, not only had better achievement, they were more liked by others and had similar popularity, compared to boys in other peer groups. Twenty-four percent of boys remained in a peer group that affirmed academic achievement across the entire academic year. African American peer groups that support achievement are present even in schools with high levels of underachievement. Youth who value achievement navigate the peer contexts to find these groups. Within these groups, there is no social cost to achievement, and youth are able to develop the positive association between their African American identity and academic excellence. However, without a critical mass of African American students, it is more difficult to identify this need for social support. Indeed, in schools where African American youth are in the minority, the negative association between African Americans' perceived acceptance within their peer group and their achievement orientation is strongest (Fuller-Rowell and Doan 2010).

Since the time of the Coleman Report (1966), much has changed in the United States' educational landscape, while much has remained the same. School assignment policies have been the target for solving inequities in access to high-quality schools and have been attempted across the decades with only modest progress. Today, just as in 1966, schools are highly segregated. Differences today include that African American youth are less likely to have African American teachers; African American parents feel less welcome in the school building (Hill 2009); and the school climate, including interactions with teachers and peers, often does not affirm African American identities. Integration policies in the decade post the *Brown v. Board of Education* decision often led to wide-scale dismissal of African American teachers from public schools (Fancher 1970). However, having teachers who affirm and support youths' emerging ethnic identities is essential for healthy development and academic achievement.

Nevertheless, because of decades of modest attempts at integration, a small number of African American students attend high-quality schools that are predominantly Euro-American. Given the knowledge and resources required of ethnic minority and low-income families to navigate school choice policies and send their children out of district or to schools that are far from their homes, only a select few are able to take advantage of these opportunities. These families tend to be the most advantaged. This has resulted in a within–ethnic group segregation of the most advantaged African Americans from the most disadvantaged, resulting in even higher concentrations of poverty and low academic performance among urban schools today compared to 1966. The connection between individual families' interests and the interests of the greater good is even more strained for African Americans than it is for their white counterparts. African American students whose parents have the social and financial capital and knowledge to effectively navigate the school choice system or access private schools often leave behind their local schools and communities. What is good for the community is not necessarily what is in the best interests of individual African American families. This paradox is acute and pernicious for African Americans and the African American community. In 1966, all African Americans—lower, working, and professional classes—were in the same situation. Indeed, the youth interviewed by Fancher (1970) foretold this possible outcome, and many at that time were dubious of the "integration" and "free choice" policies as solutions. Many youth reported wanting financial and curricular control of their schools and saw the real costs of moving from their neighborhood schools that were connected to their communities and employed teachers who resided in their neighborhoods to schools that were far away and controlled by whites. Their concerns ring true today.

Conclusion

There have been many policies to address and much discussion about the importance of educational equity in the United States, but there has been little success in improving the disparities in educational experiences across racial classifications and socioeconomic status. School choice and other market-based policies, as drivers for equity, imply scarcity and competition and rely on parents to undergo market-based analyses of schools and make informed decisions with similar conditions and constraints. Market-based policies also create "winning" and "losing" schools and, ultimately, "winning" and "losing" children. In our view, this should not be the goal of an educational system.

Reliance on a market-based system to reduce educational inequality implicitly accepts that certain students will be relegated to, or forced to attend, schools that are failing. Often the students who are relegated to these schools are low-income students of color, whose families have fewer resources, lack of information, and less comprehensive choice sets. They create a false and unfair choice for low-income minority families, who face the choice among academically weak schools; highly segregated no-nonsense schools; culturally isolating private schools, accessed by vouchers; or out-of-district, suburban, predominately Euro-American schools. School enrollment policies, regardless of whether they include partial or full choice, will work only if there are enough schools (and seats in schools) that provide high-quality education so that all students can achieve regardless of where they go to school. Choices should be relegated to differences in extracurricular activities, curricular emphasis, and schedules and not on differences in academic excellence or college and career preparedness.

References

Ayscue, Jennifer B., and Gary Orfield. 2015. School district lines stratify educational opportunity by race and poverty. *Race and Social Problems* 7 (1): 5–20.

Barber, B. K., and J. A. Olsen. 2004. Assessing the transitions to middle and high school. *Journal of Adolescent Research* 19:3–30.

Bast, Joseph L., and Herbert J. Walberg. 2004. Can parents choose the best schools for their children? *Economics of Education Review* 23 (4): 431–40.

Belfield, Clive. 2006. *Vouchers and the Cleveland Scholarship Program: Little progress so far*. Economic Commentary. Cleveland, OH: Federal Reserve Bank of Cleveland.

Bell, Courtney A. 2009. All choices created equal? The role of choice sets in the selection of schools. *Peabody Journal of Education* 84 (2): 191–208.

Bryant, Rhonda Tsoi-A-Fatt. 2015. *College preparation for African American students: Gaps in the high school educational experience*. Washington, DC: Center for Law and Social Policy (CLASP).

Buckley, Jack, and Mark Schneider. 2003. Shopping for schools: How do marginal consumers gather information about schools? *Policy Studies Journal* 31 (2): 121–45.

Buehler, Cheryl, Anne C. Fletcher, Carol Johnston, and Bridget B. Weymouth. 2015. Perceptions of school experiences during the first semester of middle school. *School Community Journal* 25 (2): 55–83.

Carter Andrews, Dorinda J. 2012. Black achievers' experiences with racial spotlighting and ignoring in a predominantly white high school. *Teachers College Record* 114 (10): 1–46.

Chakrabarti, Rajashri. 2013. Do vouchers lead to sorting under random private school selection? Evidence from the Milwaukee voucher program. *Economics of Education Review* 34:191–218.

Chubb, John E., and Terry M. Moe. 1990. *Politics, markets, and America's schools*. Washington, DC: Brookings Institution Press.

Cogburn, Courtney D., Tabbye M. Chavous, and Tiffany M. Griffin. 2011. School-based racial and gender discrimination among African American adolescents: Exploring gender variation in frequency and implications for adjustment. *Race and Social Problems* 3 (1): 25–37.

Coleman, James, Ernest Campbell, Carol Hobson, James McPartland, Alexander Mood, Frederick Weinfield, and Robert York. 1966. *Equality of educational opportunity* (OE-36001). Washington, DC: U.S. Department of Health, Education, and Welfare, Office of Education.

Condliffe, Barbara F., Melody L. Boyd, and Stefanie DeLuca. 2015. Stuck in school: How social context shapes school choice for inner-city students. *Teachers College Record* 117 (3): 1–36.

Cross, William E. 1991. *Shades of black: Diversity in African American identity*. Philadelphia, PA: Temple University Press.

Cross, William E. 2003. Tracing the historical origins of youth delinquency & violence: Myths & realities about black culture. *Journal of Social Issues* 59 (1): 67–82.

Cross, William E. 2011. The historical relationship between black identity and black achievement motivation. In *African American children's mental health: Development in context*, eds. Nancy E. Hill, Tammy L. Mann, and Hiram E. Fitzgerald, 1–27. New York, NY: Praeger.

Darling-Hammond, L. 2004. Inequality and the right to learn: Access to qualified teachers in California's public schools. *Teachers College Record* 106 (10): 1936–66.

DeLuca, Stefanie, and P. Rosenblatt. 2010. Does moving to better neighborhoods lead to better schooling opportunities? Parental school choice in an experimental housing voucher program. *Teachers College Record* 112 (5): 7–8.

Deming, David J. 2012. Does school choice reduce crime? Evidence from North Carolina. *Education Next* 12 (2): 70–76.

Eccles, Jacquelynne S. 2004. School, academic motivation, and stage environment fit. In *Handbook of adolescent psychology*, eds. Richard M. Lerner and Lawrence D. Steinberg, 125–53. Hoboken, NJ: Wiley.

Edsall, T., and M. Edsall. 1992. *Chain reaction: The impact of race, rights, taxes on American politics*. New York, NY: Norton.

Fabelo, Tony, Michael D. Thompson, Martha Plotkin, Dottie Carmichael, Miner P. Marchbanks III, and Eric A. Booth. 2011. *Breaking schools' rules: A statewide study of how school discipline relates to students' success and juvenile justice involvement*. New York, NY: Council of State Governments Justice Center and The Public Policy Research Institute, Texas A&M University.

Fancher, Betsy. 1970. *Voices from the South: Black students talk about their experiences in desegregated schools*. Atlanta, GA: Southern Regional Council.

Fordham, Signithia, and John U. Ogbu. 1986. Black students' school success: Coping with the "burden of acting white." *Urban Review* 18 (3): 176–206.

Friedman, Milton. 1955. The role of government in education. In *Economics and the public interest*, ed. Robert A. Solo, 123–44. New Brunswick, NJ: Rutgers University Press.

Fuller-Rowell, T. E., and S. Doan. 2010. The social costs of academic success across ethnic groups. *Child Development* 81:1696–1713.

Fuller, Bruce F., and Richard F. Elmore. 1996. *Who chooses? Who loses? Culture, institutions and the unequal effects of school choice*. New York, NY: Teachers College Press.

Giroux, Henry A. 1981. *Ideology, culture, and the process of schooling*. Philadelphia, PA: Temple University.

Glazerman, Steven M. 1998. School quality and social stratification: The determinants and consequences of parental school choice. Paper presented at the Annual Meeting of the American Educational Research Association, April 1998, San Diego, CA.

Goyette, Kimberly A. 2008. Race, social background, and school choice options 1. *Equity & Excellence in Education* 41 (1): 114–29.

Greene, Jay, ed. 2000. The effect of school choice: An evaluation of the Charlotte Children's Scholarship Fund. *Education Next*, 1–26. Available from http://media.hoover.org/sites/default/files/documents/ednext20012unabridged_greene.pdf.

Hamm, Jill V., Kerrylin Lambert, Charlotte A. Agger, and Thomas W. Farmer. 2013. Promotive peer contexts of academic and social adjustment among rural African American early adolescent boys. *American Journal of Orthopsychiatry* 83 (2–3): 278–88.

Hastings, Justine, Thomas Kane, and Douglas Staiger. 2005. Parental preferences and school competition: Evidence from a public school choice program. NBER Working Paper 11805, National Bureau of Economic Research, Cambridge, MA.

Henig, Jeffrey. 1996. The local dynamics of choice: Ethnic preferences and institutional responses. In *Who chooses, who loses? Culture, institutions, and the unequal effects of school choice*, eds. Bruce F. Fuller and Richard Elmore, with Gary Orfield. New York, NY: Teachers College Press.

Hill, Nancy E. 2009. Culturally-based world views, family processes, and family school interactions. In *The handbook on school-family partnerships for promoting student competence*, eds. S. L. Christenson and Amy Reschly, 101–27. New York, NY: Routledge.

Hill, Nancy E. 2011. Undermining partnerships between African-American families and schools: Legacies of discrimination and inequalities. In *African American children's mental health*, eds. Nancy E. Hill, Tammy L. Mann, and Hiram E. Fitzgerald, 199–230. Santa Barbara, CA: Praeger.

Hill, Nancy E. 2012. Parent-child and child-peer close relationships: Understanding parental influences on peer relations from a cultural context. In *Interdisciplinary research on close relationships: The case for integration*, eds. Timothy J. Loving and Lorne Cambell, 109–34. Washington, DC: APA.

Hill, Nancy E. 2017. Data analyses from Project PASS: Promoting academic success for students. Working paper, Cambridge, MA.

Hill, Nancy E., Mandy Savitz-Romer, Belle Liang, and John Perella. 2016. Access to and value of adult relations in high school and other effective policies. SRCD Special Topics Meeting on Babies Boys and Men of Color, Tampa, FL.

Hill, Nancy E., and K. Torres. 2010. Negotiating the American dream: The paradox of Latino students' goals and achievement and engagement between families and schools. *Journal of Social Issues* 66 (1): 95–112.

Hill, Nancy E., and Ming-Te Wang. 2015. From middle school to college: Promoting engagement, developing aspirations and the mediated pathways from parenting to post high school college enrollment. *Developmental Psychology* 51 (2): 224–35.

Holme, Jennifer Jellison. 2002. Buying homes, buying schools: School choice and the social construction of school quality. *Harvard Educational Review* 72 (2): 177–205.

Horvat, Erin McNamara, and K. S. Lewis. 2003. Reassessing the "burden of acting white": The importance of peer groups in managing academic success. *Sociology of Education* 76:265–80.

Horvat, Erin McNamara, Elliot B. Weininger, and Annette Lareau. 2003. From social ties to social capital: Class differences in the relations between schools and parent networks. *American Educational Research Journal* 40 (2): 319–51.

Howell, William G., Patrick J. Wolf, David E. Campbell, and Paul E. Peterson. 2002. School vouchers and academic performance: Results from three randomized field trials. *Journal of Policy Analysis and Management* 21 (2): 191–217.

Hughes, Diane, James Rodriguez, Emilie Philips Smith, Deborah J. Johnson, Howard C. Stevenson, and Paul Spicer. 2006. Parents' ethnic-racial socialization practices: A review of the research and directions for future study. *Developmental Psychology* 42:747–70.

James, Osamudia R. 2014. Opt-out education: School choice as racial subordination. *Iowa Law Review* 99:1083–1135.

Johnston, William R. 2015. The roots of opting out: Family, school, and neighborhood characteristics associated with non-local school choices. PhD diss., Harvard University, Cambridge, MA.

Jonathan, Ruth. 1989. Choice and control in education: Parental rights, individual liberties and social justice. *British Journal of Educational Studies* 37 (4): 321–38.

Kimelberg, S. M. 2014. Middle-class parents, risk and urban public schools. In *Choosing homes, choosing schools*, eds. Annette Lareau and Kimberly A. Goyette, 207–36. New York, NY: Russell Sage Foundation.

Krueger, Alan, and Pei Zhu. 2004. Another look at the New York City school voucher experiment. *American Behavioral Scientist* 47 (5): 658–98.

Lewis, Wayne D., and Arnold Danzig. 2010. Seeing color in school choice. *Journal of School Public Relations* 31:205–23.

Losen, D. J., and J. Gillespie. 2012. *Opportunities suspended: The disparate impact of disciplinary exclusion from school*. Los Angeles, CA: Center for Civil Rights Remedies at the Civil Rights Project at UCLA.

Losen, D. J., and R. J. Skiba. 2010. *Suspended education: Urban middle schools in crisis*. Montgomery, AL: Southern Poverty Law Center.

Lubienski, Christopher. 2008. The politics of school choice: Theory and evidence on quality of information. In *School choice policies and outcomes: Empirical and philosophical perspectives*, eds. Walter Feinberg and Christopher Lubienski, 99–120. Albany, NY: State University of New York Press.

Meek, Shantel E., and Walter S. Gilliam. 2016. Expulsion and suspension in early education as matters of social justice. Discussion paper. National Academy of Medicine Perspective. Washington, DC: National Academy of Medicine.

Metcalf, Kim K., Stephen D. West, Natalie Legan, Kelli Paul, and William J. Boone. 2002. *Evaluation of the Cleveland Scholarship and Tutoring Program, 1998–2001*. Summary Report [and] Technical Report. Bloomington, IN: Indiana Center for Evaluation.

Mickelson, Roslyn Arlin, and B. J. Everett. 2008. Neotracking in North Carolina: How high school courses of study reproduce race and class-based stratification. *Teachers College Record* 110 (3): 535–70.

Mickelson, Roslyn Arlin, and Damien Heath. 1999. The effects of segregation and tracking on African American high school seniors' academic achievement. *Journal of Negro Education* 68 (4): 566–86.

Midgley, Carol, H. Feldlaufer, and J. S. Eccles. 1989. Student/teacher relations and attitudes toward mathematics before and after the transition to junior high school. *Child Development* 60:981–92.

Mizala, Alejandra, and Florencia Torche. 2017. The effect of making a school voucher means-tested on test scores: Evidence from Chile's universal voucher system. *The ANNALS of the American Academy of Political and Social Science* (this volume).

Orfield, G. 2001. *Schools more separate: Consequences of a decade of resegregation*. Cambridge, MA: Harvard University, Civil Rights Project.

Orfield, Gary, and Erika Frankenberg. 2013. *Educational delusions: Why choice can deepen inequality and how to make schools fair*. Berkeley, CA: University of California Press.

Paul, Kelli M., Natalie A. Legan, and Kim K. Metcalf. 2007. Differential entry into a voucher program: A longitudinal examination of families who apply to and enroll in the Cleveland Scholarship and Tutoring Program. *Education and Urban Society* 39 (2): 223–43.

Reardon, Shaun, and K. Bischoff. 2011. *More unequal and more separate: Growth in the residential segregation of families by income 1970–2009*. New York, NY: Russell Sage Foundation.

Rebell, Michael A. 2017. The courts' consensus: Money does matter for educational opportunity. *The ANNALS of the American Academy of Political and Social Science* (this volume).

Rhodes, A., and Stefanie DeLuca. 2014. Residential mobility and school choice among poor families. In *Choosing homes, choosing schools: Residential segregation and the search for a good school*, eds. Annette Lareau and Kimberly A. Goyette, 137–66. New York, NY: Russell Sage Foundation.

Riehl, Carolyn, and Melissa A. Lyon. 2017. Counting on context: Cross-sector collaborations for education and the legacy of James Coleman's sociological vision. *The ANNALS of the American Academy of Political and Social Science* (this volume).

Rouse, Cecilia Elena. 1998. Private school vouchers and student achievement: An evaluation of the Milwaukee Parental Choice Program. *Quarterly Journal of Economics* 113 (2): 553–602.

Ryan, James E. 2010. *Five miles away: A world apart*. New York, NY: Oxford University Press.

Sankofa, Biko Martin, Eric A. Hurley, Brenda A. Allen, and A. Wade Boykin. 2005. Cultural expression and black students' attitudes toward high achievers. *Journal of Psychology* 139 (3): 247–59.

Saporito, Salvatore, and Annette Lareau. 1999. School selection as a process: The multiple dimensions of race in framing educational choice. *Social Problems* 46 (3): 418–39.

Schneider, Mark, Paul Teske, and Melissa Marschall. 2000. *Choosing schools: Consumer choice and the quality of American schools*. Princeton, NJ: Princeton University Press.

Schneider, Mark, Paul Teske, Melissa Marschall, and Christine Roch. 1998. Shopping for schools: In the land of the blind, the one-eyed parent may be enough. *American Journal of Political Science* 42 (3): 769–93.

Scott, Janelle. 2013. School choice and the empowerment imperative. *Peabody Journal of Education* 88 (1): 60–73.

Sidanius, J., F. Pratto, C. van Laar, and S. Levin. 2004. Social dominance theory: Its agenda and method. *Political Psychology* 25:845–80.

Simon, H. 1986. Rationality in psychology and economics. *Journal of Business* 59 (4, part 2): s209–s224.

Simon, H. 1990. Invariants in human behavior. *Annual Review of Psychology* 41:1–19.

Skiba, R. J., C. G. Chung, M. Trachok, T. Baker, A Sheya, and R. L. Hughes. 2015. Where should we intervene? How infractions, students, and schools all contribute to out-of-school suspension. In *Closing the school discipline gap: Research for policymaker*, ed. D. J. Losen, 132–46. New York, NY: Teachers College Press.

Spencer, Margaret Beale, William E. Cross, V. Harpalani, and T. N. Goss. 2003. Historical and developmental perspectives on black academic achievement: Debunking the "acting white" myth and posing new directions for research. In *Surmounting all odds: Education, opportunity, and society in the new millennium*, eds. Carol Camp Yeakey and Ronald D. Henderson, 273–303. Greenwich, CT: Information Age.

Spencer, Margaret Beale, and V. Harpalani. 2008. What does "acting white" actually mean? Racial identity, adolescent development, and academic achievement among African American youth. In *Minority status, oppositional culture and schooling*, ed. John U. Ogbu, 222–39. New York, NY: Routledge.

Spencer, Margaret Beale, Elizabeth Noll, Jill Stoltzfus, and Vinay Harpalani. 2001. Identity and school adjustment: Revisiting the "acting white" assumption. *Educational Psychologist* 36 (1): 21–30.

Stein, M., E. Goldring, and X. Cravens. 2011. Do parents do as they say? In *School choice and school improvement*, eds. M. Berends, M. Cannata, and M. Goldring, 103–14. Cambridge, MA: Harvard Education Press.

Tenenbaum, Harriet R., and Martin D. Ruck. 2007. Are teachers' expectations different for racial minority than for European American students? A meta-analysis. *Journal of Educational Psychology* 99 (2): 253–73.

Tyson, Karolyn, William Darity, and Domini R. Castellino. 2005. It's not "a black thing": Understanding the burden of acting white and other dilemmas of high achievement. *American Sociological Review* 7:582–605.

Umana-Taylor, Adriana, Stephen M. Quintana, Richard Lee, M., William E. Cross, Deborah Rivas-Drake, Seth J. Schwart, Moin Syed, Tiffany Yip, Eleanor Seaton, and Ethnic and Racial Identity in the 21st Century Study Group. 2014. Ethnic and racial identity during adolescence and into young adulthood: An integrated conceptualization. *Child Development* 85 (1): 21–39.

U.S. Department of Education, National Center for Education Statistics. 2015. *State nonfiscal survey of public elementary and secondary education, 2003–04 and 2013–14*. Washington, DC: U.S. Department of Education, National Center for Education Statistics.

U.S. Department of Education, Office of Civil Rights. 2014. *Civil rights data collection data snapshot: College and career readiness*. Washington, DC: U.S. Department of Education, Office of Civil Rights.

Van Dunk, Emily, and Anneliese Dickman. 2002. School choice accountability: An examination of informed consumers in different choice programs. *Urban Affairs Review* 37 (6): 844–56.

Walsemann, Katrina M., Bethany A. Bell, and Debeshi Maitra. 2011. The intersection of school racial composition and student race/ethnicity on adolescent depressive and somatic symptoms. *Social Science & Medicine* 72 (11): 1873–83.

Wells, A. S., and R. L. Crain. 1992. Do parents choose school quality or school status? A sociological theory of free market education. In *The choice controversy*, ed. Peter W. Cookson, 65–82. Newbury Park, CA: Corwin.

Yettick, Holly. 2016. Information is bliss. *Urban Education* 51:859–90.

Paternal Incarceration and Children's Schooling Contexts: Intersecting Inequalities of Educational Opportunity

By
ANNA R. HASKINS

Research on the collateral consequences of mass imprisonment has focused on the interactions that families and communities have with the criminal justice system. Less attention is paid to interactions that children of the incarcerated have with another important social institution: schools. This article describes the types of schools that children with incarcerated fathers attend. Using newly available data on children's early elementary environments from a longitudinal birth-cohort sample of urban families, the analyses show that children of the incarcerated are more often in disadvantaged schools and in schools with climates worse than the schools of same-age peers with no histories of paternal incarceration. I offer a first exploratory step toward understanding the interplay among three of America's most powerful social institutions—families, schools, and the criminal justice system—and the ways that they interact to structure the educational trajectories of what scholars are calling "children of the prison boom."

Keywords: parental incarceration; educational inequality; school contexts

The family, the criminal justice system, and schools are three of America's most powerful social institutions, all of which play significant roles in the intra- and intergenerational

Anna R. Haskins is an assistant professor of sociology at Cornell University and an affiliate of the Cornell Prison Education Program, the Center for the Study of Inequality, and the Cornell Population Center. Her scholarly interests are in educational inequality, social stratification, race and ethnicity, and the intergenerational social consequences of mass incarceration. Currently her work assesses the effects of paternal incarceration on school-aged children's educational outcomes and engagement in schooling.

NOTE: The Fragile Families and Child Wellbeing Study is supported by the Eunice Kennedy Shriver National Institute of Child Health and Human Development through grants R01HD36916, R01HD39135, and R01HD40421, as well as a consortium of private foundations. See http://www.fragilefamilies.princeton .edu/funders.asp.

Correspondence: arh96@cornell.edu

DOI: 10.1177/0002716217732011

transmission of (dis)advantage in the United States. Families transmit socioeconomic standing through educational and occupational background, parental resources, and family structure characteristics, all of which have important implications for a child's short- and long-term position in the stratification structure (Blau and Duncan 1967). For decades, school effects research has drawn attention to the various ways that schools shape student learning and achievement, demonstrating (net of individual student or family-level characteristics) that schools have the ability to both exacerbate and attenuate students' social mobility trajectories (Borman and Dowling 2010; Coleman et al. 1966; Downey and Condron 2016). And finally, alongside families and schools, the criminal justice system as a social sorting mechanism has recently increased in importance, with scholars of mass incarceration suggesting that its sizable and enduring negative effects deepen disadvantage and nearly eliminate traditional pathways of upward social mobility (Wakefield and Uggen 2010; Western and Pettit 2010).

Drawing attention to the intersection between families, schools, and the criminal justice system—as important players in the promotion or reduction of educational opportunity—is in many ways at the heart of much of James Coleman's research. Currently, schools serve as important conduits of resources and opportunities for American children, having increasingly become integral sites of social mobility or exclusion. Thus, given the growing number of children with incarcerated and formerly incarcerated parents, the long-term prospects of "children of the prison boom" are likely tightly linked to these children's success in schools.

This article highlights the ways in which mass incarceration has shaped schooling in the United States and, in doing so, updates the conversation around (in)equality of educational opportunity. Using data from the Fragile Families and Child Wellbeing Study and focusing on elementary school–aged children, this article first describes the types of schools that children with incarcerated fathers attend and who teaches them in those schools, comparing those learning conditions to the learning conditions of children whose fathers are not incarcerated. Compositional, structural, and climatic characteristics of school contexts are emphasized, with results suggesting that children impacted by paternal incarceration attend more compositionally disadvantaged schools (e.g., higher percentages of the student body are eligible for free or reduced lunch, larger concentrations of minority students) and schools with worse climatic environments (e.g., more neighborhood disorder, harsher disciplinary climates, lower teacher-reported positive school climate). Second, I explore whether the association between paternal incarceration and child cognitive outcomes is modified by schools. Findings suggest that school contexts should indeed be considered in the broader stratification implications of mass incarceration for children.

Mass Imprisonment and the Growth of Parental Incarceration: Implications for Children

The number of school-aged children in the United States with currently or formerly incarcerated parents is at record levels (Murphey and Cooper 2015; Sykes and Pettit 2014), fueling growing interest in developing a multifaceted and interactional understanding of the ways that mass incarceration facilitates intergenerational social inequality and exclusion (for a review, see Foster and Hagan 2015). Estimates suggest that parental incarceration has now touched at least five million, and possibly upwards of eight million, children nationwide, indicating that around one in every fourteen minors has had a parent at some point in their lives under some form of correctional supervision (Murphey and Cooper 2015; Sykes and Pettit 2014; Travis, McBride, and Solomon 2005).[1]

While rich, poor, minority, and majority children all can experience parental incarceration, the cumulative risk of exposure is greatest for low–socioeconomic status (SES) and minority children. Racial disproportionality is one of the defining characteristics of mass incarceration in the United States, and children of color represent the population most at risk of experiencing parental incarceration. Nationally one in every four African American and one in every ten Latino children can expect to have a parent incarcerated during their early lives, compared to one in twenty-five white children (Sykes and Pettit 2014; Wildeman 2009). Moreover, children living in poverty are three times more likely to experience the incarceration of a residential parent than their economically advantaged peers (Murphey and Cooper 2015). Thus, demographically, children of the incarcerated are disproportionally minority and low-income—characteristics that to this day continue to have implications for equality of educational opportunity.

Parental incarceration and children's early educational outcomes

Studies exploring the effects of a parent's incarceration on their children have shown that, independent of preexisting social inequalities, having an incarcerated parent places children at risk for disadvantage across a range of social, economic, behavioral, and health outcomes (Travis, Western, and Redburn 2014; Wakefield and Wildeman 2014). Parental incarceration for school-aged children produces unique risk factors related to the stable development of strong academic abilities and healthy school ties. Reductions in behavioral school readiness set children with incarcerated fathers apart from their peers early on (Geller et al. 2012; Haskins 2014). And recent work has found that paternal incarceration contributes to decreases in elementary-aged children's assessed cognitive skills (Haskins 2016); behavioral functioning (Haskins 2015); and their parents' involvment in schooling (Haskins and Jacobsen 2017); alongside increases in their likelihood of special education placement (Haskins 2014), grade retention (Turney and Haskins 2014), and school disciplinary action (Jacobsen 2015; Johnson 2009). Early educational experiences can profoundly shape later-life trajectories and together this work suggests that children who experience parental incarceration are at a clear disadvantage.

Equality of Educational Opportunity, School Effects, and Schooling Contexts

However, what remains unknown is the influence that schools could have on the educational development of children with incarcerated parents. From the onset of nation-wide compulsory education over a century ago, schools have become an important institution for social mobility and stratification in the United States. Historically, the American "common school" has been idealized as a place where academic access and achievement should not be dependent on family background or personal circumstances and a common educational experience is provided for all American children. Outside of the family, schools are often the primary institution with which young children regularly interact, and understanding the role that schools and their contexts play in structuring the educational trajectories of children with incarcerated parents can help scholars and policymakers to develop a more careful accounting of the ways in which mass incarceration's collateral costs interact with other important social institutions to influence inequality and social mobility.

School effects research has evolved over several decades to cover an array of components of schooling that have deepened our understanding of the influence of schools on students. Components studied have included teacher characteristics (e.g., Goldhaber and Brewer 2000; Greenwald, Hedges, and Laine 1996), school expenditures, resources and composition (e.g., Condron 2009; Condron and Roscigno 2003; Murnane 1975), and peer characteristics (e.g., Hanushek et al. 2003). While diverse in range, the exploration of these components has produced a wide body of work that indicates that schools and their contextual characteristics have the ability both to promote and constrain students' academic outcomes, educational attainment, and social mobility trajectories.

Compositional, structural, and climatic school context factors

Schools in the United States are still highly segregated (Logan, Minca, and Adar 2012), and a school's racial and socioeconomic compositions remain two of the strongest contextual correlates of poor educational outcomes, mainly to the detriment of minority children (Berends, Lucas, and Penaloza 2008; Coleman et al. 1966; Condron 2009). In addition to student body composition, schools can also differ by sector (e.g. public, private, charter), size of student body, and the attributes of the teachers—or what can be suggested as school structural factors. Students in private schools achieve at higher levels than those in public schools (Braun, Jenkins, and Grigg 2006), predominantly minority schools tend to have larger class sizes than majority white schools (Phillips and Chin 2004), and recent work has demonstrated that schools serving predominantly low-income and minority families disproportionately employ teachers with lower levels of education, nonstandard certification, and fewer years of teaching experience to the academic detriment of their students (Clotfelter, Ladd, and Vigdor 2005, 2007; Condron 2009).

Characteristics of a school's disciplinary climate, surrounding neighborhood, and student learning environments also play a role in contributing to a school climate that may help or hinder a child's educational development. The "prisonization" of the American schooling system has recently received a lot of attention, with scholars suggesting that strict discipline and policing within schools fosters a culture of fear and coercion that disrupts learning, and creates feelings of mistrust (Gregory, Skiba, and Noguera 2010; Sander 2010; Wildhagen 2012). Schools with strict or negative disciplinary climates—including metal detectors, security guards, or high suspension/expulsion rates—often found in urban areas, are likely to be detrimental to student learning and may even increase student misbehavior and racial achievement gaps (Gregory, Skiba, and Noguera 2010).

Alternatively, strong school climates that support academic growth and positive sociobehavioral skill development have the potential to positively impact children's skill development (Bodovski, Nahum-Shani, and Walsh 2013). Disorder in the neighborhood directly surrounding the school is also likely linked to lower student achievement. Minority and impoverished children are most likely to attend schools in neighborhoods characterized by problem conditions such as crime, violence, drugs, loitering, and litter (Lee and Burkam 2002). These poor environmental conditions outside of the school introduce an added component of contextual disorder that likely compounds with other school context characteristics to negatively impact student well-being and development.

Parental incarceration and children's schooling contexts

While differences in school context have been one of the main ways that researchers have suggested schools might serve as moderators of the effects of preexisting social inequalities on educational outcomes, very little scholarly attention has been paid to the proximal contextual schooling environments with which children with incarcerated parents interface daily. Schools and the conditions of their context have the potential to really matter for these "children of the prison boom," particularly because education is still viewed as one of the primary means for upward mobility, and it is during their elementary to middle school years that the majority of children first experience parental incarceration (Murphey and Cooper 2015).

For school-aged children, parental incarceration can be a complex and multifaceted stressor. While other forms of parental absence (e.g. family dissolution, divorce, military deployment, or death) can be traumatic and stressful, parental incarceration is additionally stigmatizing and shameful. Seminal sociological research discusses the stigma experienced by individuals with a criminal record (Goffman 1963; Pager 2003), and such stigma likely spills over to connected families and children (Braman 2004; Murray and Farrington 2008), hampering children's learning and shaping teacher expectations (Dallaire, Ciccone, and Wilson 2010; McKown and Weinstein 2003). Dallaire and Aaron (2010) write, "children in this age range with incarcerated parents may be exposed to more proximal risk factors in key microsystem contexts, including more harsh, unresponsive parenting practices in the familial context, teacher stigmatization in the academic context, and risk for association with delinquent peers in the peer context" (p. 102). Moreover, with increases in security and direct connections to public agencies (including the police), schools may be perceived as "surveilling institutions," making parents with incarceration histories reluctant to engage fully in school-based components of their child's education (Haskins and Jacobsen 2017). Not only do children of the incarcerated enter formal schooling at a disadvantage compared to peers, but they may also face additional risks due to interactions within, and the quality of, their school environments.

From qualitative work by Nesmith and Ruhland (2008) emphasizing the impact of parental incarceration from the child's perspective, there is evidence of the dual ways in which children see interactions with schools as both stigmatizing and supportive. School counselors, social workers, psychologists, teachers, and classmates can provide valuable social support systems for children experiencing parental incarceration. However, these same actors can also negatively impact children through stigmatization, further hampering the development of their socioemotional and cognitive competencies. Additionally, recent work has also helped to bring attention to schools by assessing the potential school-level spillover implications of mass incarceration for adolescents (Hagan and Foster 2012a, 2012b). By aggregating individual reports of parental incarceration experiences from National Longitudinal Study of Adolescent Health data to the school-level, Hagan and Foster (2012a, 2012b) find that students who attended high schools with high rates of either maternal or paternal incarceration had lower grades and educational attainment than peers attending low parental incarceration (but otherwise similar) schools, regardless of if they themselves had an incarcerated parent.

These studies, while illustrative, present only the beginning of what is needed to fully understand the social implications of the interplay among families, schools, and the criminal justice system for young American children. With education in the United States being viewed as one of the primary means to upward social mobility, schools (and the conditions of their context) can be important agents in mitigating or exacerbating the unintended consequences of mass parental incarceration on the educational experiences and academic trajectories of American children.

Research Questions and Study Contributions

Surprisingly little is known about the types of schools that children with incarcerated parents attend. Given the importance of middle childhood (ages 6–12) for the building of academic and peer competencies (Dallaire and Aaron 2010), the elementary school contexts of children of the incarcerated may indeed be consequential in shaping their educational development. Using newly available data on children's elementary environments from a longitudinal birth-cohort of urban families—the Fragile Families and Child Wellbeing Study—this article focuses on school contexts, in an effort to understand what role, if any, schools and their contextual characteristics play in shaping educational opportunities for children of the incarcerated.

This article proceeds by first descriptively asking, What types of schools and teachers do children with incarcerated fathers attend and have, compared to similar children who do not experience paternal incarceration? This question assesses school contextual environments along the lines of compositional, structural, and climatic characteristics that are widely considered to tap contextual dis/advantage. Second, I ask whether the association between paternal incarceration and child cognitive outcomes is modified by school context, and whether school characteristics compound or attenuate educational inequality. Research has shown that paternal incarceration has independent negative effects on children's educational outcomes (e.g., Haskins 2015, 2016), and given that schools are the primary institution with which young children regularly interact, identifying particular characteristics of schools that may moderate this negative impact is worthwhile. In a recent review piece by Foster and Hagan (2015), which outlines a multilevel theoretical framework for the ways in which parental incarceration impacts child inequality, schools are prominently featured as an important mesolevel social institution. This work takes a descriptive step forward, suggesting that schools should indeed be considered prominently in the broader stratification implications of mass incarceration for children.

Data, Measures, and Analysis

Data

The Fragile Families Study (FFS) is a longitudinal birth-cohort study that follows 4,898 focal children and their parents. Collected from twenty large U.S. cities between 1998 and 2000, marital and nonmarital births were randomly sampled within hospitals across cities that were stratified by labor-market conditions and policy environments (Reichman et al. 2001).[2] When appropriately weighted, the dataset is nationally representative of births to parents in large urban areas during those years. For mothers, baseline interviews took place in hospitals within 48 hours after the birth of the focal child, and for fathers, soon thereafter. Since the baseline wave, five additional follow-up waves of phone interviews have occurred, taking place when the child is approximately 1, 3, 5, 9, and 15 years old. Waves include interviews of parents, in-home assessments of the child and their home environment (starting at wave 3); and for wave 4 when the child was 9 years old and had entered formal schooling, a teacher survey, a large range of educational assessments, and administrative data on the child's elementary school were collected. The baseline response rate for the nationally representative sample of mothers is 86 percent while for fathers it is slightly lower at 79 percent. Follow-up interview response rates for both parents across waves can be found in the appendix.

The FFS is ideally situated to explore questions related to paternal incarceration and child outcomes and is significantly underused by researchers interested in schools, schooling, and educational outcomes. Not only does it follow both parents over time as their child grows, but it has good response rates (given the focal population) and sizable variation by race and paternal incarceration experiences. Moreover, the restricted data, in particular, contain a wealth of background, demographic, environmental, household, health, neighborhood, and economic information to include as controls in analyses.

Analyses for this article take advantage of information from the first four waves of available data, covering the first nine years of the focal child's life and relying heavily on information collected on the focal child's elementary experiences and environments from teacher surveys and linked school administrative data. I used multiple imputation (MI) procedures to preserve as many observations of relevant variables as possible. Imputed values were derived in Stata 12 using the ICE (Imputation by Chained Equations) procedure, which produced five datasets.[3] Statistical analysis was then done on each individual dataset and averaged to yield a final single set of results (Royston 2005a, 2005b; Rubin 1987). The descriptive analyses of school context indicators include the full FFS sample (N = 4,898); however, any children with missing information on the four cognitive outcomes explored in moderating analyses are dropped, producing, on average, an analytic sample of N = 3,347. Table 2 provides a descriptive snapshot of this analytical sample by paternal incarceration status.

Measures

School context indicators. Table 1 includes a list of the fifteen variables that I use to explore the compositional, structural, and climatic indicators of school context. These measures comprise teacher, classroom, and school characteristics drawn from two sources: teacher reports (TRs) from the teacher survey and school administrative reports (ARs) provided in the school supplement collected from the National Center for Education Statistics' 2008–2009 Common Core of Data's Public Elementary/Secondary School Universe Survey Data and the 2007–2008 Private School Universe Survey. From TRs, the following ten school context variables are used: (1) number of students in class repeating current grade, (2) teacher age, (3) highest level of education, (4) elementary certified, (5) race white, (6) years of experience as a teacher, (7) teacher's current class size, (8) teacher reports of school neighborhood disorder (9) positive school climate, and (10) harsh disciplinary climate. School ARs add the remaining five indicators: (11) school receipt of Title I funding, (12) whether the school is public, (13) school-wide student/teacher ratio, and percent of the student body that is (14) free or reduced price lunch eligible and (15) minority.

Compositional indicators that represent proxies for the school racial and socio-economic composition include ARs of the *percent of the school's student body receiving free or reduced-price lunch* (range 0–100), *percent of student body that is minority* (black and Hispanic combined; range 0–100), *school-wide Title I funding receipt* (yes/no), and TRs of the *number of students in their classroom repeating current grade* (range 0–17). The school context indicators that tap the structural factors of teacher attributes, school sector, and size are teacher reported *age* (range 22–73), *race as white* (yes/no), *highest level of education completed* (range 1–3; 1 = HS/associate's degree, 2 = BA/BA+; 3 = MA/MA+), *certified in elementary education* (yes/no), *years of teaching experience* (range 0–52), *class size* (range 0–50), ARs of *school's student/teacher ratio* (range 1–44), and if a *public school* (yes/no). Last, TRs to a number of items are scaled to create three constructs that tap a school's poor or good climatic contexts: *positive school*

TABLE 1
Descriptive Statistics for School Context Variables by Paternal Incarceration Status

			Father Never Incarcerated (G1)		Father Incarcerated								Overall			
					Ever (G2)		Before or by YR1 (G3)		Btw YR1 & YR9 (G4)							
School Context Variables	Range	TR/AR	Mean	SD	Mean	SD	Mean	SD	Mean	SD	G1 vs. G2 t test sig.	G1 vs. G3 t test sig.	G1 vs. G4 t test sig.	G3 vs. G4 t test sig.
			n = 2,454		n = 2,444		n = 1,623		n = 821					
Compositional														
% Free/Reduced Lunch	(0–100)	AR	34.44	(36.80)	46.23	(38.54)	47.29	(38.53)	44.12	(38.49)	***	***	***	NS
% Minority (black&Hispanic)	(0–100)	AR	57.09	(36.91)	65.22	(35.09)	65.37	(34.81)	64.93	(35.67)	***	***	***	NS
# of students in class repeating grade	(0–17)	TR	0.86	(1.29)	1.1	(1.49)	1.11	(1.48)	1.09	(1.51)	***	***	***	NS
School-wide title I funding		AR	0.92	(0.28)	0.94	(0.23)	0.95	(0.22)	0.93	(0.26)	***	***	NS	NS
Structural														
Teacher age	(22–73)	TR	41.7	(12.23)	41.51	(12.42)	41.28	(12.36)	41.98	(12.54)	NS	NS	NS	NS
Teacher's highest level of education	(1–3)	TR	2.41	(0.57)	2.42	(0.57)	2.42	(0.57)	2.43	(0.57)	NS	NS	NS	NS
Teacher is elem. ed. certified		TR	0.87	(0.33)	0.86	(0.34)	0.87	(0.34)	0.86	(0.35)	NS	NS	NS	NS
Teacher white		TR	0.70	(0.46)	0.64	(0.48)	0.64	(0.48)	0.64	(0.48)	***	***	**	NS
Years as a teacher	(0–52)	TR	12.43	(9.85)	12.68	(9.79)	12.72	(9.87)	12.59	(9.65)	NS	NS	NS	NS
Class size, # of students	(0–50)	TR	19.49	(6.49)	19.5	(6.55)	19.45	(6.62)	19.61	(6.40)	NS	NS	NS	NS
Public school		AR	0.59	(0.49)	0.66	(0.47)	0.67	(0.47)	0.64	(0.48)	***	***	**	NS
Student/teacher ratio	(1–44)	AR	14.91	(4.67)	14.81	(4.51)	14.74	(4.39)	14.94	(4.74)	NS	NS	NS	NS
Climatic														
Neighborhood disorder (α = 89)	(1–3)	TR	1.72	(0.66)	1.87	(0.67)	1.86	(0.67)	1.89	(0.67)	***	***	***	NS
Positive school climate (α = .81)	(1–5)	TR	3.75	(0.81)	3.61	(0.83)	3.61	(0.84)	3.63	(0.83)	***	***	***	NS
Harsh disciplinary environment	(0–7)	TR	3.68	(1.43)	3.85	(1.42)	3.84	(1.42)	3.87	(1.43)	***	***	**	NS

NOTE: TR = teacher reports; AR = administrative reports; overall N = 4,898.
$**p < .01$, $***p < .001$.

climate (α = .802), *neighborhood disorder* (α = .898), and *harsh disciplinary climate* (a count). The appendix lists the individual survey items used to create these respective measures. For positive school climate and neighborhood disorder, responses for each of the items were summed and then averaged, with higher numbers indicating a more positive school climate or lower numbers, more school neighborhood disorder. For harsh disciplinary climate, a count of whether seven security measures were present at the school was summed, with higher numbers indicating a harsher disciplinary environment.

Child educational outcomes. A total of four cognitive skills are used in the exploration of the impact of school context on the association between paternal incarceration and child educational outcomes. These represent the child's (1) verbal ability (Peabody Picture Vocabulary Test-III; PPVT), (2) reading comprehension (Passage Comprehension Subtest 9 of the Woodcock-Johnson III Tests of Achievement; WJ Reading), (3) math problem-solving skills (Applied Problems Subtest 10 of the Woodcock-Johnson III Tests of Achievement; WJ Math), and (4) working memory (the Forward and Backward Digit Span Tests of the Wechsler Intelligence Scale for Children IV; Digit Span). Each of these outcomes is administered as standardized assessments, measured at the nine-year follow-up wave to the subset of focal children whose parents agreed to participate in the "in-home" portion of survey.[4] See the appendix for detailed descriptions of the specific skills that each assessment measures and their associated source documentation. For ease of interpretation, the scores for each of these outcomes are standardized with coefficients reported in standard deviation units. Higher numbers indicate children's higher cognitive capacities in the tested area.

Paternal incarceration. This key explanatory variable is based on a combination of mother and father reports of father's current or previous incarceration status across study waves (baseline/child's birth, wave 1/age 1, wave 2/age 3, wave 3/age 5 and wave 4/age 9). This measure combines reports of whether the father was "currently incarcerated" at the time of the interview and whether the father was "ever incarcerated" at any point prior to the interview wave. Mothers are asked, through a variety of interview questions, if their child's father ever spent time in jail or prison, and fathers are asked if they have ever been imprisoned. If either mother or father answer yes to any question related to paternal incarceration, the father is indicated as "ever" incarcerated for that and subsequent waves.

Accordingly, paternal incarceration at age nine is indicated in one of two ways throughout this article. For ease of descriptive comparisons, at times, a binary measure of children with "ever" and "never" incarcerated fathers is used. For this ever/never measure, children with fathers who have any history of incarceration (whether past or present) by the year nine follow-up interview are grouped as having "ever" incarcerated fathers. Children with fathers who have no discernible incarceration histories or experiences (as reported by either mother or father consistently across all five waves) are then reported as having "never" incarcerated fathers.

For multivariate analyses, a second measure of paternal incarceration is used to best address issues of timing and selection into incarceration without losing pertinent data. For this measure, a three-category indicator of paternal incarceration is created where a child either has a father who was (1) incarcerated sometime before/by age one, (2) incarcerated for the first time between age one and nine, or (3) never incarcerated. These specific groupings are made to ensure appropriate time ordering of control variables. The first group of children's fathers experienced incarceration *before or by year one*. Fathers in this group could have experienced incarceration *at any point* before the birth of the focal child up until the year one follow-up interview when paternal incarceration was first measured. This group is the largest in the data, but also introduces bias because incarceration potentially occurred before the measurement of important baseline covariates.

Acknowledging this concern, I created a second group of children whose fathers experienced *first-time* incarceration sometime between the year one and year nine follow-up interviews, and not earlier. This group excludes any father with previously indicated incarceration experience at year one. Fathers in the *between years one and nine* group account for a smaller number of the proportion of incarcerated fathers but are more reliable for estimating effects since their first-time incarceration occurred after the collection of relevant baseline and year one covariates. Last, I use children with *never* incarcerated fathers as the comparison group for all analyses. Unfortunately, the FFS does not offer any information on duration or frequency of the father's incarceration, nor can it distinguish between stays in prison as opposed to jail, or levels of severity of the crime committed.

Controls. Incarceration does not happen at random, nor is selection into schools a random occurrence. The incarcerated are disproportionately poor, African American, and poorly educated (Uggen, Wakefield, and Western 2005), and since children of the incarcerated are more likely to suffer from forms of sociostructural disadvantage prior, or in addition, to their parent's incarceration, researchers must contend with the possibility that these preexisting differences account for much of the disadvantages that these children face. Controlling for as many observed characteristics of families and their children likely to be associated with paternal incarceration, child educational outcomes, and selection into schools can help to better identify the relationship between paternal incarceration, school context, and educational outcomes.

Because the FFS data are so robust, they allow for the control of a host of characteristics of mothers, fathers, and their children, including basic demographic and household characteristics, measures of health and economic well-being, an indicator for interview city, a number of census-tract characteristics, and specific measures of paternal and maternal psycho-social and deviant behaviors. All controls included in the analyses are measured at either the baseline or year one follow-up interviews or are assumed fixed traits.[5] A list of all included variables, fifty-seven in total, along with descriptive statistics by paternal incarceration status are provided in Table 2.

(text continues on p. 149)

TABLE 2

Descriptive Statistics for Outcome and Control Variables by Paternal Incarceration Status

| | | Father Never Incarcerated | | Father Incarcerated | | | | G1 vs. G2 t test | G1 vs. G3 t test | G2 vs. G3 t test | Ns | | | |
| | | (G1) | | Before or by YR1 (G2) | | Btw YR1 & YR9 (G3) | | | | | | | | |
Variable Names		Mean	SD	Mean	SD	Mean	SD	sig.	sig.	sig.	G1	G2	G3	Total
Outcome Variables														
Cognitive (standardized)														
PPVT	A	0.2	(1.04)	-0.11	(0.88)	-0.11	(0.93)	***	***	NS	1629	1155	562	3346
WJ Reading	A	0.17	(0.96)	-0.05	(1.01)	-0.12	(0.97)	***	***	NS	1621	1149	563	3333
WJ Math	A	0.18	(1.01)	-0.08	(0.94)	-0.14	(0.95)	***	**	NS	1623	1156	564	3343
Digit Span	A	0.07	(0.97)	-0.05	(0.98)	-0.17	(1.00)	**	***	°	1639	1160	568	3367
Demographic and Household Characteristics														
Child race black		0.45		0.67		0.64		***	***	NS				
Child race white		0.25		0.11		0.13		***	***	NS				
Child race Hispanic		0.29		0.22		0.23		***	**	NS				
Child gender male		0.53		0.52		0.53		NS	NS	NS				
Low birth weight		0.08		0.12		0.1		***	NS	NS				
Child healthy		0.98		0.96		0.96		**	**	NS				
Maternal cognitive (0–15)		6.93	(2.77)	6.56	(2.64)	6.7	(2.43)	***	+	NS				
Maternal self-control (6–24)		18.22	(3.56)	17.19	(3.71)	17.81	(3.73)	***	°	**				
Maternal age at 1st birth (13–45)		23.12	(5.68)	19.72	(3.81)	20.1	(4.11)	***	***	+				
Maternal education (1–4)		2.42	(1.05)	1.82	(0.81)	1.89	(0.84)	***	***	+				
Mother cohabiting with father		0.33		0.4		0.4		***	**	NS				
Mother married to father		0.38		0.07		0.12		***	***	***				
Grandparent in HH		0.21		0.33		0.32		***	***	NS				
# of children in HH (0–8)		1.17	(1.25)	1.42	(1.38)	1.32	(1.28)	***	**	NS				
Economic Indicators														
Poverty Status (1–5)		2.53	(1.39)	3.4	(1.28)	3.25	(1.30)	***	***	°				

(continued)

145

TABLE 2 (CONTINUED)

Variable Names	Father Never Incarcerated (G1)		Father Incarcerated Before or by YR1 (G2)		Father Incarcerated Btw YR1 & YR9 (G3)		G1 vs. G2 t test sig.	G1 vs. G3 t test sig.	G2 vs. G3 t test sig.	Ns G1	G2	G3	Total
	Mean	SD	Mean	SD	Mean	SD							
Child Living in Public Housing	0.07		0.15		0.15		***	***	NS				
Neighborhood Unsafe	0.13		0.18		0.21		***	***	NS				
Census Tract Characteristics													
% of population white	0.36	(0.33)	0.27	(0.29)	0.28	(0.29)	***	***	NS				
% of population black	0.36	(0.36)	0.47	(0.37)	0.48	(0.38)	***	***	NS				
% of female pop. of childbearing age	0.52	(0.07)	0.52	(0.06)	0.52	(0.07)	NS	NS	NS				
% of HHs female-headed w/ children <18	0.19	(0.12)	0.24	(0.13)	0.24	(0.14)	***	***	NS				
mean # of persons per HH	2.78	(0.59)	2.82	(0.55)	2.74	(0.52)	+	NS	°°				
% of 25+ population with HS+ education	0.72	(0.15)	0.67	(0.14)	0.68	(0.14)	***	°°°	NS				
% of 25+ population with BA+ education	0.2	(0.17)	0.14	(0.12)	0.14	(0.12)	***	***	NS				
% of civilian labor force unemployed	0.1	(0.07)	0.12	(0.08)	0.12	(0.08)	***	***	NS				
% of housing units vacant	0.07	(0.06)	0.09	(0.08)	0.1	(0.08)	***	***	+				
% of occupied housing units renter-occ	0.5	(0.25)	0.52	(0.22)	0.53	(0.22)	°°	°°	NS				
median housing value in dollars in 1999	121960	(104477)	101392	(98884)	93612	(98875)	***	***	NS				
% of HH on public assistance	0.07	(0.07)	0.09	(0.07)	0.09	(0.08)	***	***	NS				

(continued)

146

TABLE 2 (CONTINUED)

| | Father Never Incarcerated | | Father Incarcerated | | | | G1 vs. G2 t test sig. | G1 vs. G3 t test sig. | G2 vs. G3 t test sig. | Ns | | | |
| | (G1) | | Before or by YR1 (G2) | | Btw YR1 & YR9 (G3) | | | | | G1 | G2 | G3 | Total |
Variable Names	Mean	SD	Mean	SD	Mean	SD							
% of families below poverty level in 1999	0.17	(0.13)	0.21	(0.14)	0.22	(0.15)	***	***	NS				
% of families w/ 1999 income <$10K	0.11	(0.09)	0.14	(0.11)	0.15	(0.12)	***	***	NS				
% of families w/ 1999 income $10-14,999K	0.06	(0.05)	0.07	(0.04)	0.08	(0.05)	***	***	NS				
% of families w/ 1999 income $15-24,999K	0.13	(0.06)	0.15	(0.06)	0.15	(0.06)	***	***	NS				
% of families w/ 1999 income $25-34,999K	0.13	(0.05)	0.14	(0.05)	0.14	(0.05)	***	***	NS				
% of families w/ 1999 income $35-49,999K	0.16	(0.05)	0.16	(0.05)	0.16	(0.05)	NS	NS	NS				
% of families w/ 1999 income $50-74,999K	0.19	(0.07)	0.17	(0.07)	0.17	(0.08)	***	***	NS				
% of families w/ 1999 income $75-99,999K	0.1	(0.06)	0.08	(0.06)	0.08	(0.06)	***	***	NS				
% of families w/ 1999 income $100-149,999K	0.07	(0.07)	0.05	(0.05)	0.05	(0.05)	***	***	NS				
Interview city (20 indicator variables)													
Paternal Demographic and Psycho-Social Characteristics													
Paternal age (15-53)	29.43	(7.50)	26.23	(6.48)	25.43	(6.63)	***	***	**				
Father employed	0.89		0.65		0.81		***	***	***				

(continued)

147

TABLE 2 (CONTINUED)

Variable Names	Father Never Incarcerated (G1) Mean	SD	Father Incarcerated Before or by YR1 (G2) Mean	SD	Btw YR1 & YR9 (G3) Mean	SD	G1 vs. G2 t test sig.	G1 vs. G3 t test sig.	G2 vs. G3 t test sig.	Ns G1	G2	G3	Total
Father U.S. citizen	0.78		0.93		0.89		***	***	°°				
Paternal cognitive (0-15)	6.57	(2.91)	6.42	(2.58)	6.23	(2.60)	NS	°°	NS				
Paternal education (1-4)	2.37	(1.03)	1.74	(0.73)	1.86	(0.78)	°°°	°°°	°°				
Paternal self-control (6-24)	18.55	(3.73)	16.48	(4.21)	17.62	(3.90)	°°°	°°°	°°°				
Paternal drug and alcohol problems	0.06		0.24		0.13		°°°	°°°	°°°				
Paternal domestic violence	0.07		0.22		0.11		°°°	°°°	°°				
Father had two bio-parent HH at 15	0.51		0.3		0.36		°°°	°°°	°°				
Father's bio father involved	0.73		0.59		0.66		°°°	°°°	°°				
Post-baseline													
Paternal multi-partner fertility at YR1	0.29		0.54		0.4		°°°	°°°	°°°				
Paternal anxiety at YR1	0.03		0.07		0.07		°°°	°°	NS				
Paternal depression at YR1	0.09		0.14		0.13		°°°	°°	NS				
Paternal contact with child at YR1 (0-30)	24.41	(10.58)	16.69	(13.58)	21.42	(11.88)	°°°	°°°	°°°				
Maternal parenting stress at YR1 (0-12)	4.63	(2.67)	4.87	(2.70)	4.62	(2.60)	°	NS	+				
Maternal anxiety at YR1	0.02		0.06		0.04		°°°	NS	+				
Maternal depression at YR1	0.12		0.19		0.12		°°°	NS	°°°				
# of maternal bio kids at YR1 (1-16)	2.06	(1.24)	2.29	(1.40)	2.12	(1.24)	°°°	NS	°°				
	n = 1,639		n = 1,160		n = 568								

N = 3,367

°p < .05. °°p < .01. °°°p < .001.

148

Analysis

This article is exploratory and contains a two-stage analysis. The first paints a basic but much needed descriptive picture of the types of elementary schools that children with and without incarcerated fathers by age nine attend to determine if there are any contextual differences in schooling experiences. Unadjusted means for children with paternal incarceration experiences on each of the fifteen school context measures are compared to the means of children with no paternal incarceration by year nine to determine if significant differences in school context exist. Mean *t*-test comparisons of school context indicators across paternal incarceration groups are done for the full FFS sample.

Building off the descriptive differences identified in stage one, the second stage relies on multivariate regression models to explore the relationship among paternal incarceration, school context, and child cognitive outcomes, while controlling for important characteristics of children and families.[6] These analyses assess the moderating relationship of six (of the original fifteen) school context indicators in the association between paternal incarceration and four child cognitive outcomes. In each analysis, model 1 first establishes the relationship between paternal incarceration at the two time points (*before or by year one* and first time *between year one and year nine*) and the specific child cognitive outcome explored, controlling for all fifty-seven covariates found in Table 2. Model 2 then individually introduces six school context variables (one at a time) along with their interactions with the two paternal incarceration categories into the analysis. Significant interactions would suggest differences in the impact of school context characteristics for the outcome explored based on having an incarcerated father either before/by year one compared to never, or between year one and year nine versus never. These analyses allow me to see if school context characteristics modify the negative association between paternal incarceration and child educational outcomes in ways that reproduce, attenuate, or do not impact the educational outcomes of impacted children.

Results

Many of the children in the FFS experience paternal incarceration. Figure 1 shows this prevalence over waves within the nonimputed data, with just over 45 percent of children having a father incarcerated by the fourth wave—when the child is approximately age nine. The racial breakdown of paternal incarceration status across blacks, whites, and Hispanics by year nine can be seen in Figure 2. Nonimputed data show that black and Hispanic children in the FFS are more likely than whites to experience paternal incarceration. For blacks this reaches 57 percent by year nine, with Hispanics at around 40 percent and whites at nearly 30 percent. These are all high percentages compared to population-level estimates of exposure to paternal incarceration for these respective racial groups. Nevertheless, white children in the sample are still more likely to have never experienced paternal incarceration (71 percent), while nearly two-thirds of the

FIGURE 1
Prevalence of Paternal Incarceration in the FFS over Waves

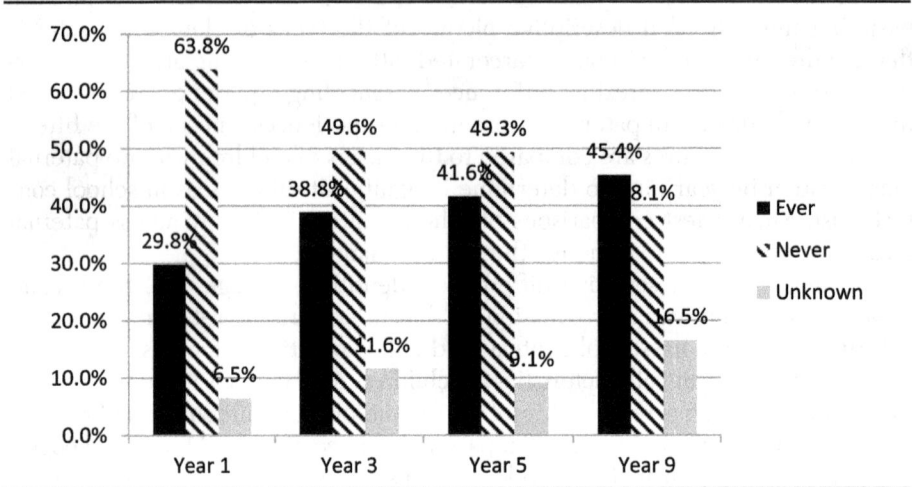

FIGURE 2
Exposure to Paternal Incarceration in the FFS by Year Nine and Race

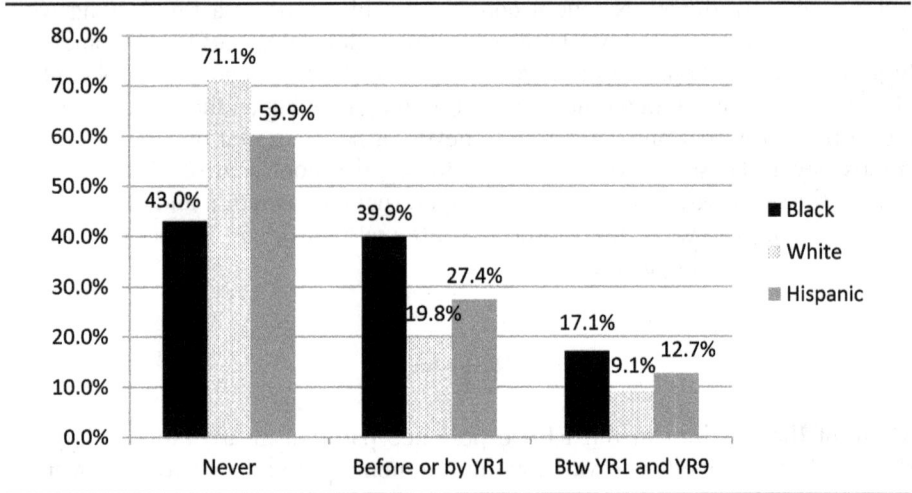

black children in the sample have had a father incarcerated at some point by the time they are only nine years old.

Basic profile of schools attended by children with and without incarcerated fathers

The first question descriptively assessed if children with incarcerated fathers attend qualitatively different elementary schools than urban peers with no paternal incarceration experience. For this analysis, four mean comparisons across each school context measure are made: (1) children with no paternal incarceration (G1) are compared to children with ever incarcerated fathers (G2), (2) children with no paternal incarceration (G1) are compared to children with a father incarcerated before or by year one (G3), (3) children with no paternal incarceration (G1) are compared to children experiencing first-time paternal incarceration between years one and nine (G4), and finally, (4) children with a father incarcerated before or by year one (G3) are compared to children experiencing first-time paternal incarceration between years one and nine (G4).

To begin, children in wave 4 of the FFS data are on average almost 9.5 years old, with an age range from between 8.75 to 11 years. The majority of these children are in third grade, and there are no significant differences in age or grade by race, gender, or paternal incarceration status. Descriptive (unadjusted) mean t-test analyses in Table 1 show that there are indeed significant differences in the types of schools and teachers children with incarceration fathers attend and have compared to their never peers. Overall, children in the FFS with incarcerated fathers differ significantly from their never peers along nine of the fifteen school context variables, with differences falling primarily along compositional and climatic school context lines.

In terms of the compositional context indicators, children with incarcerated fathers by age nine (in either of the two timing groups) are significantly more likely to attend a school that receives Title I funding, has higher percentages of the student body eligible for free or reduced-priced lunch, larger concentrations of minority students, and more students in their classroom repeating the current grade. Each of these measures is an indicator of poor school quality and together they paint a picture showing that, even within an urban population, children without incarcerated fathers attend higher quality schools than their peers who experience paternal incarceration.

Differences between indicators of a school's structural context, however, do not seem to vary much between children with and without incarcerated fathers. In fact, out of the eight measures included in this general category, only two are significantly different. Children with incarcerated fathers (again, in either of the two timing groups) are significantly more likely to be in a public school, but less likely to have white teachers. Interestingly, none of the teacher quality indicators, such as years of teaching experience, highest level of education, or elementary certification, differed between the paternal incarceration groups, nor did class size or school reports of student-teacher ratios.

Climatic measures of school context also present strong descriptive evidence that children experiencing paternal incarceration attend schools in neighborhoods with more disorder, harsher disciplinary climates, and lower teacher reported positive school climate. Across the board, urban children without incarcerated fathers are in schools with higher quality climates compared to peers in either of the two paternal incarceration groups. Together these aggregate mean descriptive differences demonstrate that urban children with incarcerated fathers do attend qualitatively different schools compared to same-age peers without incarcerated fathers, and particularly in terms of poorer compositional and climatic school environments.

In summary, unadjusted mean t-tests across a range of school context measures indicate that children with incarcerated fathers do indeed attend qualitatively different schools, with aggregate patterns primarily showing that those who experience paternal incarceration attend more disadvantaged schools (e.g., public schools, schools that receive Title I funding, and those with higher percentages of minority students, students eligible for free or reduced-priced lunch, and teacher reports of neighborhood disorder and harsh disciplinary environments). Structural factors such as teacher attributes and class size generally do not seem to differ for FFS children with and without paternal incarceration experiences, potentially because students are predominantly in urban public schools with federal class size caps and that pull from similar teacher pools.

Moderating influence of school context on cognitive outcomes for children with incarcerated fathers

Table 2 presents descriptive statistics (unadjusted means and *SD*s) for the analytic sample used to explore the second research question: Is the effect of paternal incarceration on child cognitive outcomes modified by school context characteristics, and do these characteristics reproduce or attenuate educational inequality? Four outcomes are explored and across all of them, children with incarcerated fathers in either of the two timing groups score lower on these cognitive outcomes than those without incarcerated fathers. Mean comparisons between the never and the two paternal incarceration groups ("before or by year one" and "first-time between year one and year nine") show that mean differences for all outcomes are statistically different and in the expected direction.

Descriptively, children experiencing paternal incarceration are more likely to be black; experience higher levels of poverty; live in multigenerational households, reside in neighborhoods perceived to be unsafe; and with higher percentages of female-headed households, unemployment, families below the poverty line, and concentrations of racial minorities. Parents of children who experience paternal incarceration have lower levels of education and cognitive ability, are less likely to be married at the time of the child's birth and are younger, with lower levels of self-control (more impulsive behaviors). Fathers of these children have more problems with drugs, alcohol, and domestic violence; and report lower levels of either being raised in a two-biological parent household or having their biological father involved in their upbringing.

The following four tables (Tables 3–6) show the impact of school context variables on the association between paternal incarceration and the four cognitive outcomes explored: the PPVT, the WJ Reading, the WJ Math, and the Digit Span. Model 1 in each table establishes the relationship between paternal incarceration and the outcome explored, incorporating all fifty-seven controls (and twenty city indicators) listed in Table 2 into the analyses. Model 2 then introduces six school context variables along with their interactions with the two paternal incarceration categories into the model, individually, to see whether the relationship between parental incarceration and child educational outcomes is modified.[7]

TABLE 3
Ordinary Least Squares (OLS) Models for Moderating Effect of School Context Variables on PPVT Outcome

	PPVT						
	Model 1	Model 2					
	Full	+School Context Interactions (one at a time)					
Paternal Incarceration		%FRL	Disorder	Pos. Climate	Disciplinary	% Minority	#Repeat
Before/By YR1 (PI1)	.06	.09	−.05	.11	−.01	.07	.07
	(.04)	(.08)	(.12)	(.19)	(.10)	(.08)	(.05)
Btw YR1 & YR9 (PI2)	.00	.03	.09	.00	−.06	.13	.01
	(.05)	(.12)	(.14)	(.23)	(.12)	(.10)	(.05)
School context		**−.004**°	**−.10+**	.06	−.01	**−.003+**	**−.05+**
		(.00)	(.05)	(.04)	(.02)	(.00)	(.02)
PI1°school context		.00	.06	−.01	.02	.00	.00
		(.00)	(.06)	(.05)	(.03)	(.00)	(.03)
PI2°school context		.00	−.04	.00	.02	.00	.00
		(.00)	(.07)	(.06)	(.03)	(.00)	(.03)
Constant	−1.31+	−1.19+	−1.18+	−1.55°	−1.26+	−1.17+	−1.19+
	(0.61)	(0.61)	(0.62)	(0.62)	(0.62)	(0.62)	(0.62)
N = 3,346							
Individual-level controls	x	x	x	x	x	x	x

°$p < .05$. +$p < .1$. Boldface coefficients indicate statistical significance.

Starting with Table 3 and the PPVT, we see that four school context variables—%FRL, neighborhood disorder, %minority, and number of children in classroom repeating current grade—have statistically significant (albeit mostly marginal) main effects and are in the expected direction. Attending schools with higher free or reduced-priced lunch or minority populations, more children in the classroom who are educationally behind and in schools surrounded by more neighborhood disorder reduces a child's receptive vocabulary (PPVT). However, there seem to be no significant impacts for the interaction between any of the school context variables and the two paternal incarceration measures.

Table 4 presents results for the WJ Reading assessment. Here we see again three school context variables—%FRL, %minority, and number of children in classroom repeating current grade—have statistically significant (again, albeit

TABLE 4
OLS Models for Moderating Effect of School Context Variables on WJ
Reading Outcome

Paternal Incarceration	WJ Reading						
	Model 1	Model 2					
	Full	+School Context Interactions (one at a time)					
		% FRL	Disorder	Pos. Climate	Disciplinary	% Minority	#Repeat
Before/By YR1 (PI1)	.03	.07	−.05	.23	−.02	.02	.04
	(.04)	(.09)	(.12)	(.19)	(.11)	(.09)	(.06)
Btw YR1 & YR9 (PI2)	−.10+	−.16	−.19	.13	−.16	−.23+	−.09
	(.05)	(.10)	(.14)	(.24)	(.18)	(.11)	(.06)
School context		**−.003+**	−.06	.04	−.03	**−.004°**	**−.05+**
		(.00)	(.04)	(.04)	(.02)	(.00)	(.03)
PI1°school context		.00	.05	−.05	.01	.00	−.01
		(.00)	(.06)	(.05)	(.03)	(.00)	(.03)
PI2°school context		.00	.05	−.06	.02	.00	.00
		(.00)	(.07)	(.06)	(.04)	(.00)	(.04)
Constant	−1.16	−1.01	−1.06	−1.36+	−1.04	−1.01	−1.08
	(0.70)	(0.71)	(0.71)	(0.72)	(0.71)	(0.72)	(0.71)
N = 3,333							
Individual-level controls	x	x	x	x	x	x	x

°$p < .05$. +$p < .1$. Boldface coefficients indicate statistical significance.

mostly marginal) main effects and are in the expected direction. Attending schools with a larger concentration of minorities and a more socioeconomically disadvantaged population reduces a child's reading skills. However, there seem to be no significant impacts for the interaction between any of the school context variables and the two paternal incarceration measures.

Results for the WJ Math assessment are reported in Table 5. Unlike the previous cognitive outcomes, there seem to be no significant main effects for any of the school context indicators. Table 6 presents results for the Digit Span memory test. Only the number of children in the class that are repeating the current grade appears to have a meaningful impact on this outcome. FFS children in classrooms with higher counts of retained children have lower attentional capacity and working memory skills.

TABLE 5
OLS Models for Moderating Effect of School Context Variables on WJ Math Outcome

				WJ Math			
	Model 1	Model 2					
	Full	+School Context Interactions (one at a time)					
Paternal Incarceration		%FRL	Disorder	Pos. Climate	Disciplinary	% Minority	#Repeat
Before/By YR1 (PI1)	.02	.00	−.09	.21	−.02	.03	.05
	(.04)	(.09)	(.13)	(.22)	(.11)	(.09)	(.06)
Btw YR1 & YR9 (PI2)	−.09	−.11	.09	−.07	−.05	−.11	−.05
	(.05)	(.12)	(.14)	(.29)	(.14)	(.11)	(.06)
School context		.00	.01	.02	−.02	.00	−.04
		(.00)	(.05)	(.05)	(.02)	(.00)	(.03)
PI1°school context		.00	.06	−.05	.01	.00	−.03
		(.00)	(.07)	(.06)	(.03)	(.00)	(.03)
PI2°school context		.00	−.09	.00	−.01	.00	−.03
		(.00)	(.07)	(.08)	(.03)	(.00)	(.04)
Constant	−0.95	−0.86	−0.98	−1.03	−0.86	−0.87	−0.87
	(0.71)	(0.72)	(0.73)	(0.74)	(0.72)	(0.73)	(0.72)
N = 3,343							
Individual-level controls	x	x	x	x	x	x	x

In sum, when looking at the results, we see some evidence that even after controlling for individual-level covariates, poorer school contexts hinder the cognitive skill development of children, but we see very little evidence for the hypothesis that impacts of compositional, structural, and climatic school context characteristics differ between children with and without paternal incarceration. Of the moderating effects that were found across these four cognitive measures, most were only marginally significant.

Discussion

The purpose of this study was to offer a first step toward identifying differences in elementary school contexts between children experiencing paternal

TABLE 6
OLS Models for Moderating Effect of School Context Variables on Digit Span Outcome

	Digit Span						
	Model 1	Model 2					
	Full	+School Context Indicators (one at a time)					
Paternal Incarceration		%FRL	Disorder	Pos. Climate	Disciplinary	% Minority	#Repeat
Before/By YR1 (PI1)	.03	.08	−.07	.27	.05	.09	.04
	(.04)	(.09)	(.13)	(.21)	(.12)	(.09)	(.05)
Btw YR1 & YR9 (PI2)	−.11+	−.24+	−.09	−.16	−.11	−.15	−.08
	(.05)	(.12)	(.16)	(.26)	(.17)	(.11)	(.06)
School context		.00	−.06	.04	.00	.00	**−.05***
		(.00)	(.05)	(.03)	(.02)	(.00)	(.02)
PI1*school context		.00	.06	−.06	.00	.00	.00
		(.00)	(.07)	(.06)	(.03)	(.00)	(.03)
PI2*school context		.00	−.01	.02	.00	.00	−.02
		(.00)	(.08)	(.07)	(.04)	(.00)	(.03)
Constant	−0.77	−0.64	−0.69	−0.94	−0.76	−0.69	−0.71
	(0.72)	(0.72)	(0.72)	(0.73)	(0.72)	(0.73)	(0.71)
N = 3,367							
Individual-level controls	x	x	x	x	x	x	x

$*p < .05$. $+p < .1$. Boldface coefficients indicate statistical significance.

incarceration and their peers without incarcerated fathers. Analyses were then conducted to see if identified differences in school contexts had the potential to be either protective or additionally harmful to the educational development of children impacted by paternal incarceration. Results suggest that indeed there are strong descriptive differences between the school contexts of children with and without incarcerated fathers, consistently to the detriment of children experiencing paternal incarceration.

There was also some evidence that, even after controlling for a large number of demographic and sociostructural disadvantage characteristics, school environments matter for cognitive development of the children in the FFS sample.

However, there was weak to no evidence of moderating effects of school contexts on the relationship between paternal incarceration and children's cognitive outcomes. In other words, poor school contexts have similar negative or at least nonbeneficial impacts for all children in the FFS. While the null effects found for the outcomes explored suggest that the elementary schools attended by these students may not be adding to the larger problem created by mass parental incarceration, they currently are not an active part of the solution either.

Given that schools have historically been more amenable to policy reform than other institutions (the criminal justice system, in particular), we had hoped to find that schools and school contexts may have an ameliorating effect on the cognitive disadvantage experienced by young children due to paternal incarceration. The lack of evidence for this hypothesis could be because of a number of reasons. The data used are not the most representative of American children. The FFS is one of the better datasets with which to study paternal incarceration experiences, but it is representative only of children born in urban centers to predominantly unmarried "fragile" families, increasing the likelihood that there would not be enough variation in the sample of schools attended by these children (regardless of parental incarceration status) to determine meaningful school context difference.

Second, there may be meaningful differences *within* schools in the teacher quality, classroom contexts, and teacher-student interactions for children with and without incarcerated fathers. In fact, work by Dallaire, Ciccone, and Wilson (2010) has highlighted how teacher stigmatization and lowered expectations within schools further harm the educational success of children who have experienced parental incarceration. Unfortunately, given limitations of the data, I was unable to assess quality differences within schools as there are not enough children nested within the same schools in the FFS sample to run multilevel models across the teacher context characteristics available.

Conclusion

This article presents a rough first sketch of the school contexts for children with incarcerated fathers. From these exploratory analyses, there seems to be need for future work and better data to aid in answering the question of whether schools can either promote or constrain the academic outcomes of children of the incarcerated. Incarceration has proven to be a barrier to social mobility for imprisoned parents, as well as a formative obstacle in the well-being of their children's healthy development of cognitive and socioemotional skills. With education in the United States being viewed as one of the primary means to upward social mobility, the broader goal for this study was to identify ways in which school contexts could be leveraged to address the needs of the growing number of children experiencing parental incarceration. For children with incarcerated or formerly incarcerated fathers, their long-term prospects are likely tightly linked to their success in schools, and the school context could be central in fostering or inhibiting their educational growth.

Appendix A

Teacher Reported Climatic School Context Scales

Scale	Items	Alpha	Scale Items/Questions	Range	Response Options
Neighborhood Disorder	4	.898	How much of a problem is... CRIME in the neighborhood GARBAGE/LITTER/BROKEN GLASS in the neighborhood SELLING/USING DRUGS or DRINKING in the neighborhood GUNSHOT NOISE in the neighborhood	1–3	1 = no problem, 2 = somewhat of a problem, 3 = big problem
Positive School Climate	8	.802	The level of child misbehavior in this school interferes with my teaching Many of the children are not capable of learning the material I teach Routine administrative duties and paperwork interfere with my teaching	1–5	1 = strongly agree, 2 = agree, 3 = neither, 4 = disagree, 5 = strongly disagree
			I really enjoy my present teaching job I am certain I am making a difference in the lives of the children I teach If I could start over, I would choose teaching again as my career		1 = strongly disagree, 2 = disagree, 3 = neither, 4 = agree, 5 = strongly agree
			The amount of control you feel you have in your classroom		1 = no control, 2 = slight, 3 = some, 4 = moderate, 5 = a great deal of control
			Rate the behavior of the children in the child's classroom		1 = misbehaved very frequently, 2 = misbehaved often, 3 = misbehaved occasionally, 4 = behaved well, 5 = behaved exceptionally well
Harsh Disciplinary Climate	7	—	A count of the following items: School has... Security guards Metal detectors Locked exterior doors during the day Requirement that visitors sign in Limits on going to the restroom Teachers assigned to supervise hallways Hall passes required to leave class	0–7	0 = no, 1 = yes

Appendix B

Response Rates for Fragile Families and Child Wellbeing Study

	Mothers			Fathers		
	Overall	Married	Unmarried	Overall	Married	Unmarried
Baseline	86%	82%	87%	79%	89%	77%
Year 1	91%	91%	91%	74%	83%	71%
Year 3	88%	90%	88%	72%	83%	68%
Year 5	87%	88%	87%	70%	79%	67%
Year 9	76%	—	—	59%	—	—

SOURCE: Fragile Families and Child Wellbeing Study (Bendheim-Thoman Center for Research on Child Wellbeing 2008).
NOTES: See Reichman et al. (2001) for more details; fathers and mothers numbers for years 1, 3, 5 and 9 are percentages of eligible baseline mothers; national sample response rates used.

Appendix C

Detailed Description of Cognitive Outcome Measures

Verbal Ability: The Peabody Picture Vocabulary Test-III (PPVT) is used to evaluate Standard American English language development (Dunn and Dunn 1997). It specifically measures receptive vocabulary, an individual's listening comprehension of spoken words, and is a frequently used indicator of verbal intelligence and general scholastic aptitude (Tenenbaum et al. 2007).

Reading Comprehension: The Passage Comprehension Subtest 9 of the Woodcock-Johnson III Tests of Achievement (WJ Reading) evaluates reading comprehension. The WJ Reading specifically measures pictographic comprehension of words, phrases, and cloze skills, which are one's ability to identify and orally supply the correct deleted word that belongs in a sentence or passage of text (Woodcock, McGrew, and Mather 2001).

Math Problem Solving: The Applied Problems Subtest 10 of the Woodcock-Johnson III Tests of Achievement (WJ Math) evaluates children's quantitative reasoning, math knowledge, and ability to analyze and solve math word problems (Woodcock, McGrew, and Mather 2001). In this assessment, math problems are given orally and children must use language comprehension, math knowledge, and computational skills to perform simple calculations.

Working Memory: The Forward and Backward Digit Span Tests of the Wechsler Intelligence Scale for Children IV (Digit Span) indicates working memory. The Digit Span evaluates a child's attentional capacity (Wechsler 2003). It specifically measures the auditory short-term memory, sequencing, attention, and concentration skills, which are all closely related to achievement and learning due to their role as important components of higher order cognitive processes.

Notes

1. Calculating up-to-date and precise estimates of the reach of parental incarceration is quite difficult given the complexity, depth, and constant churning within our criminal justice system. Parents, at various points in time, can be confined in local jails, state and federal prisons, juvenile facilities or immigration detention centers, however national counts, often drawn from the Bureau of Justice Statistics or other correctional surveys, can only accurately account for parents in state and federal prisons who are currently incarcerated at the time of survey administration. These limited, point-in-time reports undoubtedly produce underestimates of the full extent of parental incarceration in the United States.

2. The FFS data, when weighted, are nationally representative of both marital and nonmarital births to parents residing in large cities with populations of 200,000 or more. However, nonmarital births were oversampled, thus nearly three-quarters of the parents in the study are unmarried (n= 3,712) at the initial baseline wave, while 1,186 are married.

3. Although one could further restrict the analytical sample to cases that were also not missing information on paternal incarceration at year nine prior to imputation, I drop only cases that have imputed values for the outcome. Differences in descriptive characteristics across the imputed and nonimputed datasets for the covariates included in the analytic models were negligible.

4. All families eligible for interview at year nine were contacted and invited to participate in the "in-home" survey. Among families contacted, about 72 percent completed this portion of the study (n = 3,391). Children with missing observations on the cognitive outcomes are those where a home visit could not be conducted or whose parent/caregiver only completed the parent portion of the in-home interview by telephone (Bendheim-Thoman Center for Research on Child Wellbeing 2011).

5. Cognitive ability is measured at the year 3 follow-up wave using the Wechsler Adult Intelligence test. It is considered to be a fixed trait of parents and therefore I feel comfortable including it as a pre-treatment control. Additionally, I make the assumption that paternal self-control, measured at the year one follow-up, is a fixed trait and treat it as a pre-treatment control.

6. Multilevel models are not used because very few children are actually in the same elementary schools. Over half of the FFS sample attended completely different schools, while remaining children are dispersed between schools that have between a minimum of 2 and a maximum of 8 shared students, with 4 to 8 shared children only occurring for 14 of the 3,374 schools in the data.

7. To better isolate the independent moderating effect of each school context variable, I do not simultaneously include the other school-level characteristics in this OLS models. In earlier analyses, however, these variables were included as controls and results did not change substantively.

References

Bendheim-Thoman Center for Research on Child Wellbeing. 2008. *Introduction to the Fragile Families public-use data: Baseline, one-year, three-year, and five-year telephone data*. Princeton, NJ: Office of Population Research, Princeton University.

Bendheim-Thoman Center for Research on Child Wellbeing. 2011. *Introduction to the Fragile Families public-use data: Baseline, one-year, three-year, five-year, and nine-year telephone data*. Princeton, NJ: Office of Population Research, Princeton University.

Berends, Mark, Samuel R. Lucas, and Roberto V. Penaloza. 2008. How changes in families and schools are related to trends in black-white test scores. *Sociology of Education* 81 (4): 313–44.

Blau, Peter M., and Otis Dudley Duncan. 1967. *The American occupational structure*. New York, NY: John Wiley & Sons, Inc.

Bodovski, K., I. Nahum-Shani, and R. Walsh. 2013. School climate and students' early mathematics learning: Another search for contextual effects. *American Journal of Education* 119 (2): 209–34.

Borman, G. D., and M. Dowling. 2010. Schools and inequality: A multilevel analysis of Coleman's equality of educational opportunity data. *Teachers College Record* 112 (5): 1201–46.

Braman, Donald. 2004. *Doing time on the outside: Incarceration and family life in urban America*. Ann Arbor, MI: University of Michigan Press.

Braun, Henry, Frank Jenkins, and Wendy Grigg. 2006. *Comparing private schools and public schools using hierarchical linear modeling.* NCES 2006-461. Washington, DC: NCES.

Clotfelter, Charles T., Helen F. Ladd, and Jacob L. Vigdor. 2005. Who teaches whom? Race and the distribution of novice teachers. *Economics of Education Review* 24 (4): 377–92.

Clotfelter, Charles T., Helen F. Ladd, and Jacob L. Vigdor. 2007. Teacher credentials and student achievement: Longitudinal analysis with student fixed effects. *Economics of Education Review* 26 (6): 673–82.

Coleman, James S., E. Q. Campbell, C. J. Hobson, James McPartland, A. M. Mood, F. D. Weinfeld, and R. L. York. 1966. *Equality of educational opportunity: Summary report.* Washington, DC: U.S. Department of Education.

Condron, Dennis J. 2009. Social class, school and non-school environments, and black/white inequalities in children's learning. *American Sociological Review* 74 (5): 683–708.

Condron, Dennis J., and Vincent J. Roscigno. 2003. Disparities within: Unequal spending and achievement in an urban school district. *Sociology of Education* 76 (1): 18–36.

Dallaire, Danielle H., and Lauren Aaron. 2010. Middle childhood: Family, school and peer contexts for children affected by parental incarceration. In *Children of incarcerated parents: A handbook for researchers and practitioners*, eds. J. M. Eddy and J. Poehlmann, 101–19. Washington, DC: The Urban Institute Press.

Dallaire, Danielle H., A. Ciccone, and L. C. Wilson. 2010. Teachers' experiences with and expectations of children with incarcerated parents. *Journal of Applied Developmental Psychology* 31 (4): 281–90.

Downey, Douglas B., and Dennis J. Condron. 2016. Fifty years since the Coleman Report. *Sociology of Education* 89 (3): 207–20.

Dunn, Lloyd M., and Leota M. Dunn. 1997. *Peabody picture vocabulary test.* 3rd ed. Circle Pines, MN: American Guidance Service.

Foster, Holly, and John Hagan. 2015. Punishment regimes and the multilevel effects of parental incarceration: Intergenerational, intersectional, and interinstitutional models of social inequality and systemic exclusion. *Annual Review of Sociology* 41:135–58.

Geller, Amanda, Carey E. Cooper, Irwin Garfinkel, Ofira Schwartz-Soicher, and Ronald B. Mincy. 2012. Beyond absenteeism: Father incarceration and child development. *Demography* 49 (1): 49–76.

Goffman, Erving. 1963. *Stigma: Notes on the management of spoiled identity.* Englewood Cliffs, NJ: Prentice-Hall.

Goldhaber, Dan D., and Dominic J. Brewer. 2000. Does teacher certification matter? High school teacher certification status and student achievement. *Educational Evaluation and Policy Analysis* 22 (2): 129–45.

Greenwald, R., L. V. Hedges, and R. D. Laine. 1996. The effect of school resources on student achievement. *Review of Educational Research* 66 (3): 361–96.

Gregory, Anne, Russell J. Skiba, and Pedro A. Noguera. 2010. The achievement gap and the discipline gap two sides of the same coin? *Educational Researcher* 39 (1): 59–68.

Hagan, John, and Holly Foster. 2012a. Children of the American prison generation: Student and school spillover effects of incarcerating mothers. *Law & Society Review* 46 (1): 37–69.

Hagan, John, and Holly Foster. 2012b. Intergenerational educational effects of mass imprisonment in America. *Sociology of Education* 85 (3): 259–86.

Hanushek, Eric A., John F. Kain, Jacob M. Markman, and Steven G. Rivkin. 2003. Does peer ability affect student achievement? *Journal of Applied Econometrics* 18 (5): 527–44.

Haskins, Anna R. 2014. Unintended consequences: Effects of paternal incarceration on child school readiness and later special education placement. *Sociological Science* 1:141–58.

Haskins, Anna R. 2015. Paternal incarceration and child-reported behavioral functioning at age 9. *Social Science Research* 52:18–33.

Haskins, Anna R. 2016. Beyond boys' bad behavior: Paternal incarceration and cognitive development in middle childhood. *Social Forces* 95 (2): 861–92.

Haskins, Anna R., and Wade Jacobsen. 2017. Schools as surveilling institutions? Paternal incarceration, system avoidance and parental involvement in schooling. *American Sociological Review* 82 (4): 657–84.

Jacobsen, Wade. 2015. Punished for their fathers? School discipline among children of the prison boom. Fragile Families Working Paper 14-08.

Johnson, Rucker C. 2009. Ever-increasing levels of parental incarceration and the consequences for children. In *Do prisons make us safer?*, eds. S. Raphael and M. Stoll, 177–206. New York, NY: Russell Sage Foundation.

Lee, Valerie E., and David Burkam. 2002. *Inequality at the starting gate: Social background differences in achievement as children begin school*. Washington, DC: Economic Policy Institute.

Logan, John R., Elisabeta Minca, and Sinem Adar. 2012. The geography of inequality: Why separate means unequal in American public schools. *Sociology of Education* 85 (3): 287–301.

McKown, C., and R. Weinstein. 2003. The development and consequences of stereotype consciousness in middle childhood. *Child Development* 74 (2): 498–515.

Murnane, Richard J. 1975. *The impact of school resources on the learning of inner city children*. Cambridge, MA: Ballinger.

Murphey, David, and P. Mae Cooper. 2015. *Parents behind bars: What happens to their children?* Bethesda, MD: Child Trends.

Murray, Joseph, and David P. Farrington. 2008. The effects of parental imprisonment on children. *Crime and Justice* 37:133–206.

Nesmith, Ande and Ebony Ruhland. 2008. Children of incarcerated parents: Challenges and resiliency, in their own words. *Children and Youth Services Review* 30 (10): 1119–30.

Pager, Devah. 2003. The mark of a criminal record. *American Journal of Sociology* 108 (5): 937–75.

Phillips, Meredith, and Tiffani Chin. 2004. School inequality: What do we know. In *Social inequality*, ed. K. M. Neckerman, 467–519. New York, NY: Russell Sage Foundation.

Reichman, Nancy E., Julian O. Teitler, Irwin Garfinkel, and Sara S. McLanahan. 2001. Fragile families: Sample and design. *Children and Youth Services Review* 23:303–26.

Royston, Paul. 2005a. Multiple imputation of missing values: Update. *Stata Journal* 5 (2): 188–201.

Royston, Paul. 2005b. Multiple imputation of missing values: Update of ICE. *Stata Journal* 5:527–36.

Rubin, Donald B. 1987. *Multiple imputation for non-response in surveys*. New York, NY: Wiley.

Sander, Janay. 2010. School psychology, juvenile justice, and the school to prison pipeline. *Communique* 39:4–5.

Sykes, Bryan L., and Becky Pettit. 2014. Mass incarceration, family complexity, and the reproduction of childhood disadvantage. *The ANNALS of the American Academy of Political and Social Science* 654 (1): 127–49.

Tenenbaum, Harriet R., Michelle V. Porche, Catherine E. Snow, Patton Tabors, and Stephanie Ross. 2007. Maternal and child predictors of low-income children's educational attainment. *Journal of Applied Developmental Psychology* 28 (3): 227–38.

Travis, Jeremy, Elizabeth C. McBride, and Amy L. Solomon. 2005. *Families left behind: The hidden costs of incarceration and reentry*. Washington, DC: Urban Institute Justice Policy Center.

Travis, Jeremy, Bruce Western, and S. Redburn, eds. 2014. *The growth of incarceration in the United States: Exploring causes and consequences*. Washington, DC: The National Academies Press.

Turney, Kristin, and Anna R. Haskins. 2014. Falling behind? Children's early grade retention after paternal incarceration. *Sociology of Education* 87 (4): 241–58.

Uggen, Christopher, Sara Wakefield, and Bruce Western. 2005. *Work and family perspectives on reentry*, eds. J. Travis and C. Visher, 209–43. New York, NY: Cambridge University Press.

Wakefield, Sara, and Christopher Uggen. 2010. Incarceration and stratification. *Annual Review of Sociology* 36:387–406.

Wakefield, Sara, and Christopher Wildeman. 2014. *Children of the prison boom: Mass incarceration and the future of American inequality*. Oxford: Oxford University Press.

Wechsler, David. 2003. *Wechsler Intelligence Scale for Children: WISC-IV*. San Antonio, TX: Psychological Corporation.

Western, Bruce, and Becky Pettit. 2010. Incarceration and social inequality. *Daedalus* 139 (3): 8–19.

Wildeman, Christopher. 2009. Parental imprisonment, the prison boom, and the concentration of childhood disadvantage. *Demography* 46 (2): 265–80.

Wildhagen, Tina. 2012. How teachers and schools contribute to racial differences in the realization of academic potential. *Teachers College Record* 114 (7): 1–27.

Woodcock, Richard W., K. S. McGrew, and N. Mather. 2001. *Woodcock-Johnson Tests of Achievement*. Itasca, IL: Riverside Publishing.

Means-Tested School Vouchers and Educational Achievement: Evidence from Chile's Universal Voucher System

By
ALEJANDRA MIZALA
and
FLORENCIA TORCHE

Chile features a universal school choice system, in which a government voucher provides families an opportunity to send students to public or private schools of their choosing. Since its implementation in 1981, the amount of the voucher was flat without adjustments for family income, creating incentives for schools to enroll students from economically advantaged families. In 2008, a policy change adjusted voucher values by the poverty level of students and the proportion of poor students attending each school. We evaluate the effect of this policy on primary school students' standardized test scores, using time-distributed fixed effects models. We find a positive and significant effect of the means-tested voucher policy on Math and Language achievement. The effect is much larger among private-voucher schools serving poor children, and it increased over the years after the policy change, suggesting that schools require some time to realize the benefits of the policy. Our findings show that moving from a flat to a means-tested voucher improves achievement and equality.

Keywords: school choice; voucher schools; educational inequality; academic achievement

The Coleman Report (Coleman et al. 1966) was a vast and path-breaking empirical research project that changed the ways in which researchers and policy-makers evaluated

Alejandra Mizala is director of the Center for Advanced Research in Education (CIAE) and a professor with the Center of Applied Economics, Department of Industrial Engineering at the University of Chile. Her research interests include the impact of the Chilean school choice system on educational outcomes, schools' and teachers' evaluation, and gender equality in education.

Florencia Torche is a professor of sociology at Stanford University. Her research interests include inequality and mobility, social demography, and sociology of education.

NOTE: We are grateful to Catalina Canals for excellent research assistance and to Margot Jackson and Susan Moffitt for their thoughtful suggestions. The first author acknowledges financial support from PIA-CONICYT FB0003.

Correspondence: amizala@dii.uchile.cl

DOI: 10.1177/0002716217732033

the role of schools in educational opportunity and inequality. Before the report, schools were mainly evaluated according to the resources allocated to students' education. After it, the evaluation of a school depended on its outcomes, i.e., the gains in students learning, the rate of student graduation, and the students' later performance in the labor market. In fact, the study pioneered the assessment of students through tests (Hanushek 2016; Alexander and Morgan 2016).

The Coleman Report fueled intense attention to school effects on student learning that remains relevant today. The report was commonly presented as evidence that between-school variation in resources—teacher characteristics, class size, infrastructure, per pupil expenditure, and so forth—has a relatively weak correlation with student achievement, and that families were the most important determinant of student outcomes. Still today, there is debate over the relevance of schools and families to students' outcomes and, more generally, the factors that shape students' results. Early studies motivated by the pioneering work of Coleman involved estimations of schools' educational productivity that linked output—educational achievement—with educational inputs and family and student characteristics (see for example Hanushek 1997).

Research also suggested that the relevance of school and family resources may vary across countries depending on the level of economic development. Heyneman and Loxley (1983) were the first to posit that, in low- and middle-income countries, variation in the quality of school resources and teachers could matter more than family inputs for academic achievement in primary school and that relevance of school and teacher quality increased as the income level of the country decreased. Reviews of the so-called school effects in low- and middle-income countries suggest that several factors are significant in less-developed contexts, including basic items such as instruction time, textbook availability, teacher absence, and specific teaching methods (Fuller and Clarke 1994; Hanushek 1995; Glewwe et al. 2013).

In addition to drawing attention to the relative importance of school and family inputs, the Coleman Report brought to the fore wide inequalities in achievement between groups defined by race and ethnicity, socioeconomic background, and region. In the early twenty-first century, the racial and socioeconomic achievement gaps remain substantial and vast socioeconomic and racial and ethnic inequalities persists in educational attainment (Belley and Lochner 2007; Fryer and Levitt 2006).

This article is motivated by the two main issues underlined by the Coleman Report: on one hand, the relevance of school-level factors on students' achievement, including the potentially strong role that school resources may play in low- and middle-income countries; on the other hand, the substantial achievement gaps between advantaged and disadvantaged groups in a given society. We address these issues with analysis of a major policy change in school financing aimed at improving equality of educational opportunity in Chile. We investigate whether focusing resources on schools serving disadvantaged students improves their educational outcomes and overall equality of educational achievement.

The Chilean Voucher System

Chile offers a unique setting to address these questions. In the early 1980s a military regime undertook sweeping reforms in many Chilean markets. The educational system was not an exception. A country-wide school voucher system was implemented. In this system, the government established a universal school voucher system that paid a flat, per-student subsidy to public schools and to private schools that did not charge tuition (private schools that did charge tuition received no vouchers and families paid tuition in full). Families were free to send students to the public- or private-voucher schools of their choosing. The universal voucher system paved the way for private sector participation in publicly financed education. By 1990, the proportion of students attending public schools had dropped from almost 80 to 60 percent and those attending private-voucher schools had increased to more than one-third. By 2014, 55.6 percent of school-age children were enrolled in private schools funded by government vouchers, 36.8 percent were in public schools, and 7.6 percent attended private-paid schools.

School voucher systems implemented around the world vary in terms of institutional design (West 1997; Patrinos 2002; Gauri and Vawda 2003), and these design specificities determine whether school choice improves outcomes (Epple and Romano 2012). Four institutional features are relevant in the Chilean case: the amount of the per-student voucher, rules about admission and expulsion of students, alternative sources of school financing, and teachers' regulations (Mizala and Torche 2012). At inception, the Chilean voucher was flat; that is, it did not vary with family socioeconomic resources (González, Mizala, and Romaguera 2004). Furthermore, private-voucher schools (but not public schools) were allowed to select students at will. No additional tuition funds paid by parents were permitted, but a change implemented in 1993 allowed primary and secondary private-voucher schools (and secondary public schools) to charge "add-on" fees to families to supplement the government voucher, under a withdrawal schedule that reduced the subsidy as parental fees increased. This system, known as "shared financing" (*financiamiento compartido*), expanded rapidly from 16 percent of the voucher sector enrollment in 1993 to about 80 percent in 1998, stabilizing thereafter. Over the past two decades, subsequent administrations have increased the real value of the voucher and targeted assistance on schools serving the most deprived populations. However, the central features of the voucher system have remained unchanged.

Critics of the Chilean voucher system argue that the institutional features of the system provide incentives for private-voucher schools to select socioeconomically advantaged students who have, on average, higher educational performance and are less demanding in terms of resources, rather than to increase their value added in terms of educational achievement. In fact, the studies that examine test score gains in voucher schools compared to public schools generally find positive but very small or insignificant effects (Mizala and Romaguera 2000; McEwan and Carnoy 2000; Anand, Mizala, and Repetto 2009; Lara, Mizala, and Repetto 2011). At the same time, the school choice policies implemented in Chile are associated with substantial socioeconomic inequalities in educational achieve-ment and socioeconomic segregation between school sector and across schools within sector (Torche 2005; Hsieh and Urquiola 2006; Mizala and Torche 2012; Valenzuela, Bellei, and de los Ríos 2013).

The cost of providing education depends not only on the cost of educational inputs, but also on the socioeconomic context in which education must be pro-vided. If students at a given school are likely to live in poverty, live in single-parent households, or have poorly educated parents, then obtaining a given performance level will imply higher costs. Schools need to be compensated for this additional cost to reduce incentives to "cream-skim" advantaged students as a competitive strategy (Duncombe and Yinger 2000; Reschovsky and Imazeki 2001). Indeed, the theoretical literature on voucher concludes that one way to ameliorate inequality and segregation is to design a voucher value as a function of family income, or to restrict the vouchers to poor families. For example, Epple and Romano (1998) claim that less-able students will need more financial assis-tance and vouchers will need to be income-dependent to avoid an increase in ability segregation. Hoxby (1996) argues that vouchers are particularly important for poor households, and that private-school vouchers should be means-tested. Bearse, Glomm, and Ravikumar (2000) state that if uniform and universal vouch-ers lead to more socioeconomic segregation, one obvious policy response is to use means-tested or targeted vouchers.

Following these insights, a major reform, known as "preferential school voucher" (*Subvención Escolar Preferencial*, or SEP), was implemented in 2008 in Chile. The reform amounts to transforming the flat voucher system into a means-tested one. It establishes an additional per-student subsidy for economi-cally disadvantaged students, designated as "priority students," and an extra sub-sidy for schools with a high proportion of disadvantaged students. When launched in 2008, the reform applied to pre-K through fourth grade, and it has expanded by one grade per year—to fifth grade in 2009, sixth grade in 2010, and so on—such that the policy reached all grades through the twelfth grade in 2016.

Schools' enrollment into the means-tested voucher program is voluntary. In 2008, the first year of the reform, as many as 93 percent of elementary public schools enrolled in the program and by 2011, 99 percent of public schools had enrolled. In contrast, only 51.7 percent of elementary private-voucher schools enrolled in the first year. More private-voucher schools joined the following years, and by 2014, 72.4 of them were enrolled in the program. The reform sub-stantially increased the value of the voucher for priority students, with schools receiving between 58 to 68 percent more funds for each priority student com-pared to their nonpriority peers, depending on the concentration of priority students in the school (Figure 1).

The intended objectives of the means-tested school voucher reform were to improve educational quality and to offer equal educational opportunity by focus-ing on the most vulnerable students. This analysis examines whether the reform resulted in an increase in students' scores on standardized achievement tests, whether this effect is concentrated among poor students or expands to their advantaged peers, and whether the effects on achievement change over time.

FIGURE 1
Value of the Means-Tested Voucher, 2005–2014

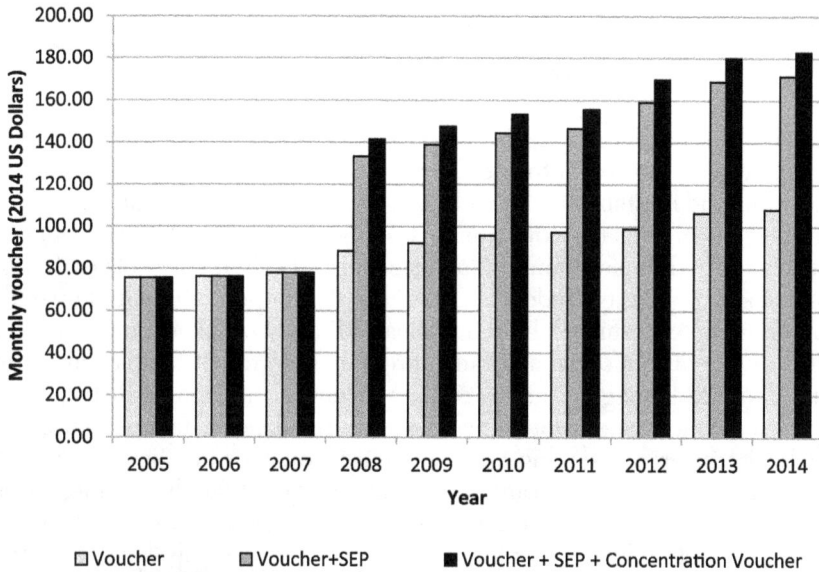

SOURCE: Ministry of Education.
NOTE: Value of the regular per-student voucher shown in light gray, value of the regular voucher plus the SEP means-tested voucher at an SEP school (Voucher+SEP) shown in dark gray, and value of the regular voucher plus means-tested voucher plus the maximum poverty concentration subsidy (60 percent or more priority students at the school) (Voucher+SEP+Concentration Voucher) shown in black. Values are for students in fourth grade in schools with full school shifts. US$ March 2014 (exchange rate Ch$563.84 per dollar).

Standardized test scores are relevant outcomes because they predict high school dropout, college entry, and freshman retention rates.

The following questions guide our analyses: What is the average effect of the means-tested voucher policy on student test scores in schools that took advantage of the policy? Does the effect vary by the socioeconomic characteristics of the school? Does the effect vary over time after uptake?

A central challenge in detecting the causal effect of the policy on the schools that took it is unobserved selectivity. Given that schools' enrollment in the program was optional those that enrolled can differ systematically from those that chose not to enroll. To alleviate bias emerging from unobserved selectivity we create a panel of schools between 2005 and 2014 and use fixed-effects at the school level and year. In this setting, we rely on within-school over-time variation to identify the effect of the means-tested school voucher policy on students' achievement. While most analyses using fixed effects consider only an average effect post–policy implementation, we empirically test the hypothesis that schools may have taken time to fully adjust to the new policy environment and realize its potential benefits (e.g., Rauscher 2016) by implementing time-distributed fixed effects (Dougherty 2006).

Means-Tested School Voucher

The main objective of the 2008 preferential school voucher reform was to transform a flat voucher system into one that varied according to the students' poverty level. To this end it establishes an additional per-student subsidy for economically disadvantaged students (priority students), roughly the poorest 40 percent of the student body, and an additional, much smaller, subsidy for schools with a high concentration of priority students. Criteria to define poor students targeted by the program are determined by the Chilean Ministry of Education and include family enrollment in a social assistance program targeted at families in extreme poverty; families belonging the lowest 33 percent of the income distribution by standard national socioeconomic classification regulations; families enrolled in public health insurance serving those without income; or families ranked below a cutoff based on a socioeconomic index including total family income, parents' education, rural residence, and the poverty level of the county of residence.

To enroll in the means-tested voucher program, schools have to sign an Equality of Opportunity and Educational Excellence Agreement (*Convenio de Igualdad de Oportunidades y Excelencia Educativa*), wherein they commit to enrolling all students who apply regardless of their prior or potential academic performance, not charging add-on fees to poor students, retaining poor students regardless of their academic performance, and achieving improvements in students' performance, especially for poor students. To fulfill this last condition, they are required to implement a four-year "school improvement plan" in exchange for the additional funds received. The extent of autonomy and support granted to enrolled schools by the Ministry of Education depends on the average test scores, adjusting for the socioeconomic status of the student body. The Chilean government classifies schools into five socioeconomic strata according to parents' education, parents' income, and the proportion of students deemed as "socioeconomically vulnerable" in the school. If the school performance is at or above the median for other schools with similar socioeconomic characteristics, schools are classified as "autonomous"; if performance is below the median for their socioeconomic group, they are classified as "emergent"; and if emergent schools fail to meet the quantitative goals required by the program within four years, they are deemed "in recovery." The agreement is valid for four years and can be renewable for a similar amount of time.

Schools that do not meet these requirements see the resources associated with the means-tested voucher partially or totally withheld. In extreme cases, they can also lose their public funding and administrators could be forbidden from participating in the management of private-voucher schools or public schools. Because of these requirements, the means-tested school voucher reform both increased school resources and enhanced accountability. When it was implemented, the means-tested school voucher was the only source of public funding for education that required schools to fulfill institutional goals and improve academic performance.

The value of the means-tested voucher depends on the grade attended by the priority student, with primary-level students receiving more funds, and it is calculated on the basis of the average attendance rate of the student during the prior three months. The additional poverty concentration subsidy depends on the proportion of poor students enrolled in the school. Schools start receiving an additional concentration subsidy when poor students make up more than 15 percent of the student body, and the concentration supplement increases with the proportion of disadvantaged students, up to 60 percent (Table 1).

The means-tested voucher reform substantially increased the funds that schools received for enrolling socioeconomically disadvantaged students. In 2014 the monthly voucher per pre-K–fourth grade student was US$108 for a nonpriority student. It rose to US$171 for a disadvantaged student attending a school with less than 15 percent disadvantaged students and to US$183 if the priority students attended schools with 60 percent or more disadvantaged students (Figure 1). In 2011, the policy was modified in several ways. Benefits were extended to secondary school students; the value of the means-tested voucher increased by about 20 percent (see Table 1), and schools were allowed to use the funds more flexibly, in particular by lifting restrictions in the use of resources for personnel expenditures such as hiring additional teachers, paying overtime to teachers, or financing professional development for school leaders. It is important to clarify that investments financed by SEP resources are not earmarked and could benefit both priority and nonpriority students.

Research suggests a positive effect of the reform on students' test scores (Correa, Parro, and Reyes 2014; Villarroel 2012; Carrasco 2014; Neilson 2013 Murnane et al. 2017). Correa, Parro, and Reyes (2014) use a difference-in-differences approach and a market-level analysis to identify schools that entered the program and received funds from 2009 to 2011 (treatment group) and those that chose not to participate in this program during this period (control group). Defining each municipality as an individual market, they also compare the changes in test scores after the implementation of the reform in a market where a different number of schools signed the agreement. Under both methodologies, they find a positive effect of the reform on private-voucher schools' academic results.

Villarroel (2012) combines matching methods with a difference-in-differences approach to compare test results of private-voucher schools that joined the program to those that did not participate between 2007 and 2010. Like Correa, Parro, and Reyes (2014) they consider two points in time. Valenzuela, Villarroel, and Villalobos (2013) follow up on this study and suggest that the effect of the SEP policy has been largely concentrated in schools with better performance and serving a large number of disadvantaged students. Using an interrupted time series approach, Carrasco (2014) compares trajectories of schools that joined the SEP program with different control groups during 2005 to 2011. He finds that treated schools experienced gains in standardized Math

TABLE 1
Monthly Value of the Means-Tested Voucher and the Additional "Concentration
Voucher" (2014 US$).

	Pre-K to 4th Grade	5th and 6th Grade	7th to 12th Grade
Regular voucher 2011	97.20[a]	97.20	116.06[b]
Regular voucher 2014	108.04[a]	108.04	128.56[b]
Means-tested voucher:			
Before 2011	52.29	34.74	17.55
After 2011	63.27	63.27	42.17
Additional voucher for concentration of priority students:			
Before 2011			
• Between 15% and 29%	3.66	2.43	1.23
• Between 30% and 44%	6.27	4.18	2.09
• Between 45% and 59%	8.37	5.57	2.80
• 60% or more	9.41	6.27	3.14
After 2011			
• Between 15% and 29%	4.41	4.41	2.91
• Between 30% and 44%	7.54	7.54	5.00
• Between 45% and 59%	10.05	10.05	6.69
• 60% or more	11.28	11.28	7.54

SOURCE: Ministry of Education data.
NOTE: The amount of the voucher is calculated using the value of the Unidad de Subvención Educacional of March 2014 (exchange rate Ch$563.84 per dollar).
a. This amount corresponds to the voucher for primary education.
b. This amount corresponds to the voucher for secondary education (ninth to twelfth grade).

and Language achievement test scores compared to the control groups. Both Neilson (2013) and Murnane et al. (2017) offer a general equilibrium analysis of the effect of SEP on overall test scores, test scores of poor students, and the income gaps in test scores. Both analyses show substantial increases in the test scores of poor students and a narrowing of the achievement gap between these students and the rest of the population. Given their focus on a general equilibrium outcome, they do not distinguish trends among schools that took SEP and those that did not.

These studies suggest that the means-tested voucher reform had a positive impact on students' test scores. However, comparisons between two discrete time-points preclude the understanding of effects of the reform over time. Furthermore, the aggregate effects captured may hide substantial heterogeneity in the effects of the policy, both in terms of socioeconomic status of the students served by the school, and in terms of time elapsed since uptake. We expand on these findings to assess the effect of the means-tested voucher on private-vouchers schools, its socioeconomic heterogeneity, and variation over time.

Data and Methods

We create an annual panel of private-voucher schools between 2005 and 2014. The panel combines information about standardized test scores in Math and Language for fourth graders obtained from the Measurement System of Educational Quality (*Sistema de Medición de la Calidad de la Educacion*, SIMCE) with information based on a survey to parents that accompanies standardized score testing, and with administrative data from the Ministry of Education. Administrative data include information about schools, their location, enrollment, number of "priority students," and the year in which schools took the SEP program. Given that virtually all public schools took the SEP program when it was launched in 2008, yielding minimal variation in the treatment in subsequent years, we focus on private-voucher schools, among which there is a more gradual entry into SEP.

The main objective of this analysis is to examine the effect of enrollment into the SEP program on average test scores at the school level. Given that schools that opted to take the program might be systematically different from those that did not in terms of unobserved factors, it is not possible to simply compare schools across treatment categories. For example, the decision to take the policy may be based on the socioeconomic composition of the school, competitiveness of the market where the school is located, or quality of school leadership. To alleviate the problem of unobserved selectivity, we implement a regression model with fixed effects for school and year, as follows:

$$Test\ Score_{mit} = \beta_o + \beta_1 SEP_{it} + X_{it}'\beta_2 + \alpha_i + \lambda_t + u_{it}, \qquad (1)$$

where $Test\ Score_{mit}$ identifies the mean school test score in subject m (m = Math, Language) for school i in year t. Tests are given in November of each year, which corresponds to the end of the school year. SEP_{it} is a dichotomous variable identifying whether school i joined the SEP program at the beginning of the school year t (SEP is effectively an absorbing state, as there have not been transitions out of the program). X_{it} is a vector of time-varying characteristics measuring the socioeconomic composition of the school. These include the school-level mean of total family income, and the mean of father's and mother's schooling. α_i captures school fixed effects, λ_t captures year fixed effects, and u_{it} is an idiosyncratic error term, assumed to be uncorrelated with the predictors. Estimation using a fixed effects estimator relies on variation in the predictors and outcome of interest that is within school and over time and thus accounts for all sources of unobserved selectivity at the school level that is time-invariant, as well as any period effect that is constant across schools. Because SEP was implemented in 2008, years 2005 to 2007 serve as pretreatment controls.

By design, the fixed effects estimator compares the average school-level test scores across all years before the policy was implemented to the average test scores across all years after implementation, making the implicit assumption that the effect of the policy is homogeneous over time after the absorbing state has been entered. This assumption is likely unrealistic. Developments such as adjusting to and gaining experience with the new policy, or optimizing the use of additional resources emerging from the policy, may result in an effect that changes over time. A flexible nonparametric way to assess the change in effects over time is known as time-distributed fixed effects (Dougherty 2006). This model replaces the treatment dummy SEP_{it} with a set of dummies SEP_{itp} where p is the number of years since uptake of SEP, yielding the following formula:

$$Test\,Score_{mit} = \beta_o + \sum_{p=0}^{n} \beta_1 SEP_{it}^p + \alpha_i + X_{it}' \beta_2\ \lambda_t + u_{it}, \qquad (2)$$

where n is the number of years postimplementation of the policy, which takes a maximum value of seven.

Findings: The Effect of Transitioning from a Flat to a Means-Tested Voucher on Achievement

Before moving to the core of the analysis, Table 2 compares the socioeconomic characteristics of schools that enrolled in the SEP program by year of enrollment with those that remained unenrolled. We examine the socioeconomic composition of schools based on mother's education, father's education, and family income percentile, all measured in 2006–2007 prior to the implementation of the policy.

Based on these indicators, schools that entered the SEP program in 2008, the year the program was launched, served families that were, on average, more disadvantaged that those attending schools that did not join the program. Schools that entered in subsequent years served gradually more socioeconomically advantaged populations. Still, the schools that had not taken the program by the last year of observation served significantly more advantaged populations than those that entered the program at any point. For example, schools that had not taken the policy by 2014 had a mean mother's years of schooling of 12.9 in 2006/07, compared with 11.5 years of schooling for those that entered in 2011–2014, 10.5 years for those entering in 2010, 10.2 years in 2009 and 10 years in 2008. In terms of family income percentile, schools that had not taken the program ranked in the 73rd percentile, compared to the 49th, 36th, 30th, and 28th percentiles for schools entering in 2011–2014, 2010, 2009, and 2008, respectively.

Table 2 also displays the mean standardized test scores in 2006/07 at the school level by year of entry into the program. The pattern is very similar to the socioeconomic composition. Schools that entered SEP in 2008 had the lowest mean test scores in 2006/07 with an average of –0.92 in Math and –0.96 in Language. Those entering over the following years have gradually better scores, and schools that are

TABLE 2

Private-Voucher School Socioeconomic Characteristics and Average
Fourth-Grade Test Scores, by Year of SEP Uptake

	2006–2007			2006/2007		2014	
	Mean Mother's Schooling (years)	Mean Father's Schooling (years)	Income Percentile	Math Scores	Language Scores	Math Scores	Language Scores
Entered 2008	10.02	10.10	27.9	–0.92	–0.96	–0.54	–0.48
Entered 2009	10.21	10.29	30.2	–0.99	–1.05	–0.65	–0.70
Entered 2010	10.47	10.65	36.4	–0.70	–0.77	–0.62	–0.55
Entered 2011–2014	11.52	11.60	49.4	–0.46	–0.56	–0.50	–0.41
Never	12.89	13.05	72.8	0.33	0.19	0.18	0.25
SD				1.22	1.18	1.11	1.05

not in the program have substantially higher scores with 0.33 in Math and 0.19 in Language. As a preliminary foray into the effect of the SEP program, average test scores are also presented for 2014, six years after the implementation of the policy. Even if disparities between schools based on year of entry into the program remain, the dispersion between schools had declined substantially, with the schools that entered the program earlier experiencing the most gains. The narrowing of disparities across schools is not a simple artifact of declining overall dispersion in test scores, as it can be seen, the test scores' standard deviation declines only marginally between 2006/07 and 2014. These descriptive findings suggest that the SEP policy may have had a positive effect on test scores, particularly for schools serving disadvantaged populations that were more likely to enroll in the policy early.

Moving to the first research question, Table 3 presents fixed effects models assessing the effect of SEP on fourth-grade Math and Language standardized test scores at the school level among private-subsidized schools. Model 1 includes school and year fixed effects only, and model 2 adds controls for socioeconomic attributes of the school (mean family income, father's schooling, and mother's schooling). Figure 2 presents the focal parameter estimates from Table 3, capturing the effect of the SEP program on standardized test scores, along with 95 percent confidence intervals. The main finding from model 1 is that SEP has a positive and significant effect on students' test scores. On average, schools gain about 0.14 standard deviations in both Math and Language fourth grade scores after taking the SEP. Adding controls for schools' socioeconomic composition in model 2 alters these parameter estimates minimally, suggesting that change in socioeconomic composition of schools triggered by SEP does not drive the effect of the policy (see Figure 2).

Is the effect of the SEP program large? To offer a benchmark, we can compare these effects with the effect of other voucher programs and educational interventions elsewhere. Rouse (1998) estimates that participation in the Milwaukee Parental Choice Program increased Math scores by 0.08 to 0.12 standard

TABLE 3
Effect of SEP Program on Fourth-Grade Math and Language Standardized Test Scores:
Fixed Effects Models, Private-Voucher Schools in Chile, 2005–2014

	Math		Language	
	Model 1	Model 2	Model 1	Model 2
λ2005 (reference category)				
λ2006	−.006	.053***	−.193***	−.136***
	(.017)	(.018)	(.018)	(.018)
λ2007	−.057***	−.001	−.121***	−.068***
	(.018)	(.018)	(.017)	(.018)
λ2008	−.098***	−.031	.070***	.133***
	(.022)	(.023)	(.022)	(.023)
λ2009	.081***	.049**	.082***	.048**
	(.023)	(.025)	(.023)	(.024)
λ2010	.041*	.011	.465***	.433***
	(.025)	(.026)	(.024)	(.025)
λ2011	.162***	.137***	.183***	.155***
	(.025)	(.026)	(.025)	(.026)
λ2012	.278***	.253***	.219***	.191***
	(.027)	(.029)	(.027)	(.028)
λ2013	.024	.088***	.007	.064**
	(.026)	(.030)	(.026)	(.029)
λ2014	.020	.076**	−.011	.038
	(.027)	(.031)	(.026)	(.030)
SEP	.135***	.136***	.138***	.141***
	(.023)	(.023)	(.022)	(.022)
Household income		−.000**		−.000*
		(.000)		(.000)
Mother's schooling		.141***		.130***
		(.012)		(.012)
Father's schooling		.058***		.062***
		(.011)		(.012)
Constant	−0.098***	−2.434***	−0.129***	−2.404***
	(0.015)	(0.150)	(0.015)	(0.147)
Observations	16,368	16,368	16,368	16,368

*$p < .10.$ **$p < .05.$ ***$p < .01.$

deviation each year. Evidence from the Tennessee STAR experiment indicates that cutting class size by one-third increased achievement by roughly 0.2 standard deviations (Krueger 1999; Chetty et al. 2011), while estimated standard deviations of achievement impacts across teachers and schools range from 0.1 to 0.2 (Chetty, Friedman, and Rockoff 2014; Angrist et al., forthcoming). Studies of

FIGURE 2

Effect of SEP Program on Fourth-Grade Math and Language Standardized Test Scores,
Fixed Effects Models, Private-Voucher Schools in Chile, 2005–2014

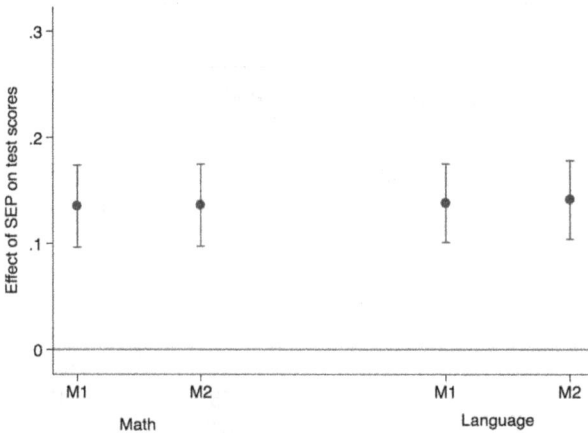

SOURCE: Table 3.

effective charter schools show annual score gains between 0.2 and 0.4 standard
deviations (Abdulkadiroglu et al. 2011; Angrist et al. 2012; Curto and Fryer
2014). For the Chilean case, we can compare the effect of SEP with two major
educational interventions. Bellei (2009) finds that the full–school day program
increases high school students' test scores by 0.05 to 0.07 standard deviations in
Language and by 0.00 to 0.12 standard deviations in Math. Contreras and Rau
(2012) assess the impact of a teachers' collective incentives program known as the
National System of School Performance Assessment (*Sistema Nacional de
Evaluación del Desempeño*, SNED) on students' academic performance; they
find an effect of 0.14 and 0.25 standard deviations in Language and Math test
scores, respectively. These figures indicate that the effect size of the SEP program is similar or larger than the effect of major educational interventions in
Chile and abroad.

The second research question addresses the socioeconomic heterogeneity of
the effect of participating in SEP. As mentioned, the explicit objective of the SEP
policy was to favor poor students and reduce achievement gaps. If the additional
resources are effective in improving test scores, we should observe that schools
at the bottom of the socioeconomic scale should experience larger benefits from
the policy. Alternatively, it is possible that schools serving more advantaged students benefit more from the additional SEP resources even without the additional "concentration supplement," if the socioeconomic advantage of the
population they serve translates into stronger management skills, or they are able
to hire or retain more capable personnel (e.g., Ladd and Fiske 2009).

To assess economic heterogeneity in the effect of SEP, we created a socioeconomic index based on the school's average household income, mother's schooling,

TABLE 4
Effect of SEP Program on Fourth-Grade Math and Language Standardized Test Scores,
by School Socioeconomic Quintiles: Fixed Effects Models, Private-Voucher Schools in
Chile, 2005–2014

	Math		Language	
	Model 1	Model 2	Model 1	Model 2
λ2005 (reference category)				
λ2006	−.007	.045°°	−.193°°°	−.145°°°
	(.017)	(.018)	(.018)	(.018)
λ2007	−.058°°°	−.010	−.121°°°	−.077°°°
	(.018)	(.018)	(.017)	(.018)
λ2008	−.113°°°	−.054°°	.055°°	.108°°°
	(.022)	(.023)	(.022)	(.023)
λ2009	.065°°°	.034	.066°°°	.032
	(.024)	(.025)	(.024)	(.025)
λ2010	.023	−.007	.447°°°	.414°°°
	(.025)	(.026)	(.024)	(.025)
λ2011	.145°°°	.118°°°	.166°°°	.136°°°
	(.025)	(.026)	(.025)	(.026)
λ2012	.265°°°	.237°°°	.206°°°	.174°°°
	(.027)	(.029)	(.027)	(.028)
λ2013	.013	.063°°	−.003	.038
	(.026)	(.030)	(.026)	(.029)
λ2014	.010	.052°	−.020	.013
	(.027)	(.031)	(.026)	(.030)
SEP°Quintile1	.426°°°	.390°°°	.442°°°	.409°°°
	(.039)	(.038)	(.038)	(.037)
SEP°Quintile2	.207°°°	.214°°°	.209°°°	.218°°°
	(.039)	(.039)	(.036)	(.036)
SEP°Quintile3	−.002	.016	−.015	.003
	(.041)	(.041)	(.038)	(.037)
SEP°Quintile4	−.070°	−.046	−.074°	−.050
	(.037)	(.036)	(.038)	(.037)
Sep°Quintile5	−.119°°	−.090°	−.089°°	−.059
	(.055)	(.055)	(.042)	(.042)
Household income		−.000		−.000
		(.000)		(.000)
Mother's education		.128°°°		.116°°°
		(.011)		(.012)
Father's education		.049°°°		.053°°°
		(.011)		(.011)
Constant	−0.097°°°	−2.188°°°	−0.129°°°	−2.146°°°
	(0.015)	(0.145)	(0.015)	(0.142)
Observations	16,368	16,368	16,368	16,368

°p < .10. °°p < .05. °°°p < .01.

FIGURE 3

FIGURE 3
Effect of SEP Program on Fourth-Grade Math and Language Standardized
Test Scores by School Socioeconomic Quintiles, Fixed Effects Models,
Private-Voucher Schools in Chile, 2005–2014

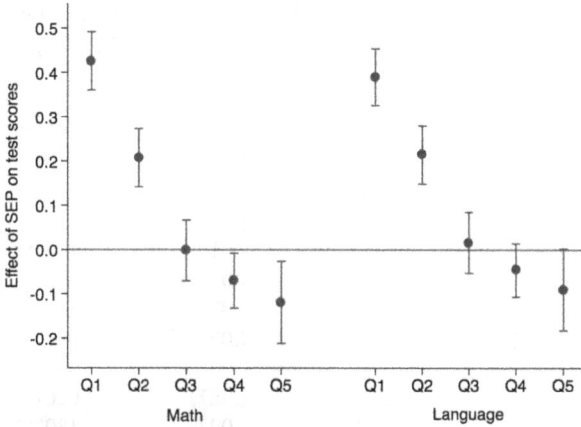

SOURCE: Table 4.

and father's schooling for all private-voucher schools in years 2006/07 (prior to
the implementation of the SEP program). These three indicators were combined
by means of principal component analysis, and the first component was extracted
to create the socioeconomic index. We then divided the index into quintiles, and
allowed the effect of SEP on test scores to vary by quintile. The analysis reveals
substantial variation in the effect of participating in SEP across socioeconomic
quintiles (see Table 4 and Figure 3). For Math, the positive effect reaches about
0.44 standard deviations among the poorest fifth of schools, 0.21 standard deviations for the second poorest quintile, and then becomes not statistically different
from zero for private-voucher schools serving more affluent families. The pattern
is similar for Language test scores. The positive effect reaches 0.41 standard
deviations for schools serving the poorest 20 percent of students, and 0.22 for
schools serving students in the next quintile, and is not significantly different
from zero among the private-voucher schools serving the remaining 60 percent
of the student population.

These findings show that the policy was particularly beneficial for the schools
serving the most disadvantaged students, an effect aligned with the objectives of
reducing socioeconomic achievement gaps. It is a concern, however, that no positive effect is found for schools in the top 60 percent of the socioeconomic distribution of private-voucher schools.

The fixed effects model captures an average effect of the policy by comparing
the school average test scores across all years after the SEP reform was implemented with the average across all years prior to the policy. However, the effect
of the policy is likely to evolve over time, driven by processes such as gaining

TABLE 5

Effect of SEP Program on Fourth-Grade Math and Language Standardized Test Scores across Years since Enrolling in the Program: Time-Distributed Fixed Effects Models, Private-Voucher Schools in Chile, 2005–2014

Variables	Math		Language	
	Model 1	Model 2	Model 1	Model 2
$\lambda 2005$ (reference category)				
$\lambda 2006$	−.007	.042**	−.193***	−.142***
	(.017)	(.018)	(.018)	(.018)
$\lambda 2007$	−.058***	−.015	−.121***	−.075***
	(.018)	(.018)	(.017)	(.018)
$\lambda 2008$	−.042*	.010	.105***	.161***
	(.022)	(.023)	(.022)	(.023)
$\lambda 2009$	.126***	.076***	.119***	.073***
	(.023)	(.025)	(.024)	(.025)
$\lambda 2010$	.048*	−.007	.464***	.415***
	(.026)	(.027)	(.026)	(.027)
$\lambda 2011$	.078***	.027	.130***	.085***
	(.027)	(.029)	(.027)	(.028)
$\lambda 2012$	.165***	.117***	.144***	.103***
	(.031)	(.033)	(.030)	(.031)
$\lambda 2013$	−.118***	−.078**	−.064**	−.011
	(.030)	(.034)	(.030)	(.033)
$\lambda 2014$	−.157***	−.118***	−.130***	−.077**
	(.034)	(.039)	(.032)	(.036)
SEP 1 year	.007	.006	.059**	.056**
	(.024)	(.024)	(.025)	(.025)
SEP 2 years	.062**	.083***	.071***	.090***
	(.027)	(.027)	(.027)	(.027)
SEP 3 years	.146***	.171***	.160***	.182***
	(.032)	(.032)	(.031)	(.031)
SEP 4 years	.333***	.351***	.262***	.277***
	(.035)	(.035)	(.035)	(.035)
SEP 5 years	.368***	.375***	.292***	.295***
	(.040)	(.040)	(.038)	(.037)
SEP 6 years	.411***	.382***	.266***	.232***
	(.043)	(.042)	(.041)	(.039)
SEP 7 years	.465***	.421***	.370***	.321***
	(.047)	(.046)	(.045)	(.044)
Household income		.000		−.000
		(.000)		(.000)
Mother's education		.130***		.125***
		(.012)		(.012)
Father's education		.047***		.057***
		(.011)		(.012)
Constant	−0.097***	−2.247***	−0.129***	−2.316***
	(0.015)	(0.150)	(0.015)	(0.149)
Observations	16,368	16,368	16,368	16,368

*$p < .10$. **$p < .05$. ***$p < .01$.

FIGURE 4

Effect of SEP on Private-Voucher School Average Fourth-Grade Math and Language Test Scores by Year since Enrolling in the SEP Program

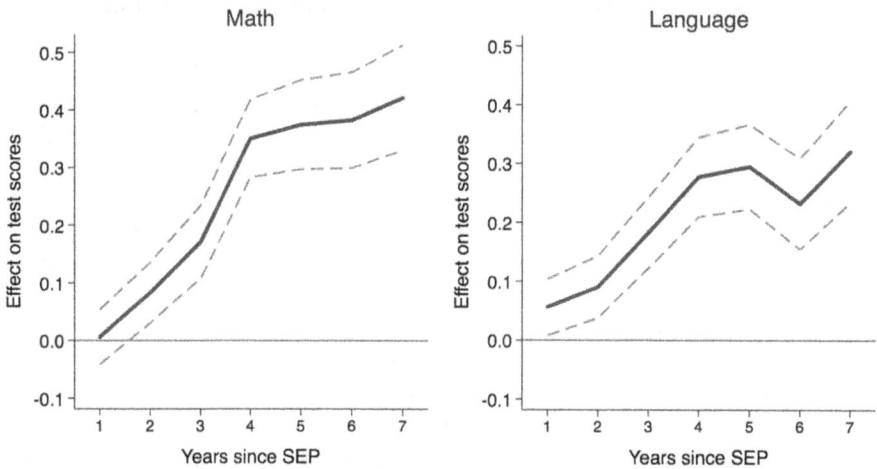

SOURCE: Table 5.

experience with the new policy environment, learning about how to allocate additional resources, or peer effects of the additional pedagogical support and training received by some teachers at the school level. We estimate a distributed fixed effects model that flexibly captures changes in effect across years since uptake to allow for temporal change in the effects. This model estimates the effect of the policy each year after uptake, using as a baseline for comparison the average test scores in the years prior to the policy.

Results from the distributed fixed effects models are reported in Table 5, and focal parameter estimates along with 95 percent confidence intervals are reported in Figure 4. As can be seen, the effect of the SEP policy increases substantially across years postimplementation for both Math and Language test scores. In the case of Math, the effect is consistently positive across years but insignificant for the first year post-treatment, then reaches 0.08 standard deviations in year two after the school enrolls in the means-tested program, 0.17 standard deviations in year 3, 0.35 in year 4, stabilizing around .40 standard deviations in subsequent years after policy implementation. Results are very similar for Language test scores, with an initial effect of only 0.06 standard deviations the first year, which increases to reach about 0.30 standard deviations in year four, stabilizing thereafter. This pattern of small improvements immediately after policy uptake followed by very large effects after a few years strongly suggests that schools need some time to fully adjust and realize the benefits of the policy.

Conclusion

Chile implemented a universal school voucher system in the early 1980s. In this system, the government paid schools a flat, per-student subsidy that did not vary by family socioeconomic status. Also, private-voucher schools—but not public-voucher schools—were allowed to select students at will and to charge add-on fees. These institutional features of the Chilean voucher system appear to have contributed to socioeconomic inequalities in educational achievement. In 2008, to improve educational quality and reduce socioeconomic stratification of achievement in the school system, a major policy change transformed the flat voucher system into a means-tested one, adjusting the amount of the voucher by the poverty level of the student and the proportion of poor students attending the school.

This analysis evaluates the impact of this means-tested voucher known as "preferential school voucher" (SEP) on test scores at the school level, how those effects evolved over time, and the heterogeneity across private-voucher schools that served students of different socioeconomic statuses in Chile. To alleviate bias emerging from unobserved heterogeneity among schools, we created a private-voucher school-level panel between 2005 and 2014, and a fixed effects model at the school level and year.

Findings indicate that private-voucher schools gain, on average, about 0.14 standard deviations in fourth-grade Math and Language scores after taking up the SEP policy. This effect size is similar or larger than the effect of major educational interventions in Chile and abroad. Moreover, this result is not affected when controls for schools' socioeconomic composition are included in the model, suggesting that change in socioeconomic composition of schools does not drive the effect of the policy. Our analysis also reveals substantial variation in the effect of participating in SEP across school's socioeconomic quintiles. For Math, the positive effect reaches about 0.44 standard deviations among the poorest fifth of schools, 0.21 standard deviations for the second poorest quintile, and then becomes not statistically different from zero for schools serving more affluent populations. The pattern is similar for Language test scores; the positive effect reaches 0.41 standard deviations for schools in the poorest quintile, 0.22 for those in the second poorest, and is not significantly different from zero among the schools serving the remaining 60 percent of the student population. This finding shows that the policy was particularly beneficial for private-voucher schools serving the most disadvantaged students, reducing socioeconomic achievement gaps. Findings from distributed fixed effects also indicate that the impact of the policy increases substantially across years postimplementation for both Math and Language test scores, with insignificant gains the year immediately after implementation and gains that reach about one-third of a standard deviation in both Math and Language scores after four years (a dynamic that might be obscured by methodological approaches that focus on time-averaged effects). This finding suggests that the educational system in general, and schools in particular, require some time to fully adjust to policy reforms and realize the benefits of the policy, and it may be generalizable to many educational policies that require organizational adaptation and mobilization of resources (e.g., Rauscher 2016). These results are consistent with the stated objectives of the reform, and show substantial gains from moving from a flat to a means-tested voucher in terms of overall achievement and equality of educational opportunity. These findings highlight the relevance of considering design when examining the consequences of voucher systems.

It is important to note that the outcome estimated is a treatment-on-the-treated effect, that is, the effect of joining SEP among schools that joined the program. This effect is different from a general-equilibrium approach in which the focus is on the effect of the policy on all students or all disadvantaged students, regardless of whether the school they attended took the program (e.g., Nielson 2013; Murnane et al. 2017). Both kinds of effects are relevant for policy-makers: Our analysis of schools that enrolled in SEP focuses on the gains or losses among the eligible population that took up the program and for whom effects of the policy are expected and intended. Given potential spillover and externality effects, the population-wide effect is also of interest, although its mechanisms are less immediately apparent.

Even if we had found uncontroversially positive treatment effects of a means-tested voucher among schools that took up the policy, it should be emphasized that this policy is not a panacea. First, some of the gains in test scores may have been due to an increase in low-performing students missing the test, as a school's strategy to respond to the new accountability regime (Quezada-Hofflinger and von Hippel 2017). Second, as suggested by the analysis by Valenzuela, Villarroel, and Villalobos (2013) and Dominguez (2014), making the Chilean universal voucher means-tested has not reduced socioeconomic segregation in the school system. One of the reasons is that schools serving more advantaged populations, and charging higher add-on family contributions, opted out of the SEP policy (see Table 2), thus reducing the choice set of more disadvantaged parents. If policy-makers wish to reduce socioeconomic segregation in the school system, policies prohibiting or substantially restricting the use of add-on funds might also be needed. In January 2015, an inclusion law was approved in the Chilean Congress that gradually eliminates add-on fees. These resources are being replaced by, among others measures, extending the preferential school voucher to middle-class students. Furthermore, given that school segregation is closely patterned to residential segregation—even in a school system that does not restrict enrollment to local catchment areas—addressing segregation requires looking beyond the educational system.

References

Abdulkadiroglu, Atila, Joshua Angrist, Susan Dynarski, Thomas Kane, and Parag Pathak. 2011. Accountability and flexibility in public schools: Evidence from Boston's charters and pilots. *Quarterly Journal of Economics* 126 (2): 699–748.

Alexander, Karl, and Stephen Morgan. 2016. The Coleman Report at fifty: Its legacy and implications for future research on equality of opportunity. *Russell Sage Foundation Journal of the Social Sciences* 2 (5): 1–16.

Anand, Priyanka, Alejandra Mizala, and Andrea Repetto. 2009. Using school scholarships to estimate the effect of private education on the academic achievement of low income students in Chile. *Economics of Education Review* 28:370–81.

Angrist, Joshua, Susan Dynarski, Thomas Kane, Parag Pathak, and Chris Walters. 2012. Who benefits from KIPP? *Journal of Policy Analysis and Management* 31 (4): 837–60.

Angrist, Joshua, Peter Hull, Parag Pathak, and Chris Walters. Forthcoming. Leveraging lotteries for school value-added: Testing and estimation. *Quarterly Journal of Economics*.

Bellei, Cristián. 2009. Does lengthening the school day increase students' academic achievement? Results from a natural experiment in Chile. *Economics of Education Review* 28:629–40.

Belley, Philippe, and Lance Lochner. 2007. The changing role of family income and ability in determining educational achievement. *Journal of Human Capital* 1 (1): 37–89.

Bearse, Peter, Gerhard Glomm, and B. Ravikumar. 2000. On the political economy of means-tested education vouchers. *European Economic Review* 44:904–15.

Carrasco, Rafael. 2014. Hacia una distribución más equitativa de las oportunidades educativas. ¿Cuál es el impacto de la política de subvención escolar preferencial en el mejoramiento de las escuelas que participan del programa? Paper presented at CIIE2014, 21–22 August 2014, Santiago Chile.

Chetty, Raj, John Friedman, Nathaniel Hilger, Emmanuel Saez, Diane W. Schanzenbach, and Danny Yagan. 2011. How does your kindergarten classroom affect your earnings? Evidence from project STAR. *Quarterly Journal of Economics* 126:1593–1660.

Chetty, Raj, John Friedman, and Jonah Rockoff. 2014. Measuring the impacts of teachers II: Teacher value-added and student outcomes in adulthood. *American Economic Review* 104 (9): 2633–79.

Coleman, J., E. Campbell, C. Hobson, J. McPartland, A. Mood, F. Weinfeld, and R. York. 1966. *Equality of educational opportunity*. Washington, DC: U.S. Government Printing Office.

Contreras, Dante, and Tomás Rau. 2012. Tournament incentives for teachers: Evidence from a scaled-up intervention in Chile. *Economic Development and Cultural Change* 61 (1): 219–46.

Correa, Juan, Francisco Parro, and Loreto Reyes. 2014. The effects of vouchers on school results: Evidence from Chile's targeted voucher program. *Journal of Human Capital* 8 (4): 351–98.

Curto, Vilsa, and Roland Fryer. 2014. The potential of urban boarding schools for the poor: Evidence from SEED. *Journal of Labor Economics* 32:65–93.

Dominguez, Patricio. 2014. School segregation in Chile: The impact of a targeted voucher for disadvantaged students on the socioeconomic composition of schools. MA thesis, University of California, Berkeley.

Dougherty, Christopher. 2006. The marriage earnings premium as a distributed fixed effect. *Journal of Human Resources* 41 (2): 433–43.

Duncombe, William, and John Yinger. 2000. Financing higher student performance standards: The case of New York State. *Economics of Education Review* 19:363–86.

Epple, Dennis, and Richard Romano. 1998. Competition between private and public schools: Vouchers and peer-group effects. *American Economic Review* 88 (1): 36–72.

Epple, Dennis, and Richard Romano. 2012. Economic modeling and analysis of educational vouchers. *Annual Review of Economics* 4:159–84.

Fryer Ronald, and Steven Levitt. 2006. The black-white test score gap through third grade. *American Law and Economic Review* 8 (2): 249–81.

Fuller, Bruce, and Prema Clarke. 1994. Raising schools effects while ignoring culture, local conditions and the influence of classroom tools, rules and pedagogy. *Review of Educational Research* 64 (1): 119–57.

Gauri, Varun, and Ayesha Vawda. 2003. Vouchers for basic education in developing countries. A principal-agent perspective. World Bank Policy Research Working Paper 3005, Washington, DC.

Glewwe, Paul, Eric Hanushek, Sarah Humpage, and Renato Ravina. 2013. School resources and educational outcomes in developing countries. A review of the literature from 1990 to 2010. In *Education policy in developing countries*, ed. P. Glewwe, 193–241. Chicago, IL: University of Chicago Press.

González, Pablo, Alejandra Mizala, and Pilar Romaguera. 2004. Vouchers, inequalities, and the Chilean experience. Occasional Paper Series No. 94, National Center for Study of Privatization in Education, Teachers College, Columbia University, New York, NY.

Hanushek, Eric. 1995. Interpreting recent research on schooling in developing countries. *World Bank Research Observer* 10 (2): 227–46.

Hanushek, Eric. 1997. Assessing the effects of school resources on student performance: An update. *Educational Evaluation and Policy Analysis* 19 (2): 141–64.

Hanushek, Eric. 2016. What matters for student achievement. *Education Next* 16 (2): 19–26.

Heyneman, Stephen, and William Loxley. 1983. The effect of primary-school quality on academic achievement across twenty-nine high- and low-income countries. *American Journal of Sociology* 88 (6): 1162–94.

Hoxby, Caroline. 1996. Are efficiency and equity in school finance substitutes or complements? *Journal of Economic Perspectives* 10 (4): 51–62.

Hsieh, Chang-Tai, and Miguel Urquiola. 2006. The effect of generalized school choice on achievement and stratification: Evidence from Chile's school voucher program. *Journal of Public Economics* 90:1477–1503.

Krueger, Alan. 1999. Experimental estimates of educational production functions. *Quarterly Journal of Economics* 114:497–532.

Ladd, Helen, and Edward Fiske. 2009. Weighted student funding for primary schools: An analysis of the Dutch experience. Sanford School of Public Policy, Duke University Working Paper SAN09-02, Durham, NC.

Lara, Bernardo, Alejandra Mizala, and Andrea Repetto. 2011. The effectiveness of private voucher education: Evidence from structural school switches. *Educational Evaluation and Policy Analysis* 33 (2): 119–37.

McEwan, Patrick, and Martin Carnoy. 2000. The effectiveness and efficiency of private schools in Chile's voucher system. *Educational Evaluation and Policy Analysis* 22 (3): 213–39.

Mizala, Alejandra, and Pilar Romaguera. 2000. School performance and choice: The Chilean experience. *Journal of Human Resources* 35 (2): 392–417.

Mizala, Alejandra, and Florencia Torche. 2012. Bringing the schools back in: The stratification of achievement in the Chilean voucher system. *International Journal of Educational Development* 32:132–44.

Murnane, Richard, Marcus Waldman, John Willett, María Soledad Bos, and Emiliana Vegas. 2017. The consequences of educational voucher reform in Chile. National Bureau of Economic Research Working Paper 23550, Cambridge, MA.

Navarro-Palau, Patricia. 2017. Effects of differentiated school vouchers: Evidence from a policy change and date of birth cutoffs. *Economics of Education Review* 58:86–107.

Neilson, Christopher. 2013. Targeted vouchers, competition among schools, and the academic achievement of poor students. Working Paper.

Patrinos, Harry. 2002. A review of demand-side financing initiatives in education. World Bank Working Paper, Washington, DC.

Quezada-Hofflinger, Alvaro, and Paul von Hippel. 2017. *The response to high stakes testing in Chile, 2005–2013: Legitimate and illegitimate ways to raise test scores.* Available from https://ssrn.com.

Rauscher, Emily. 2016. Does educational equality increase mobility? Exploiting 19th century U.S. compulsory schooling laws. *American Journal of Sociology* 121 (6): 1697–1761.

Reschovsky, Andrew, and Jennifer Imazeki. 2001. Achieving educational adequacy through school finance reform. *Journal of Education Finance* 26:373–96.

Rouse, Cecilia Elena. 1998. Private school vouchers and students achievement: Evidence from the Milwaukee choice program. *Quarterly Journal of Economics* 113:553–602.

Torche, Florencia. 2005. Privatization reform and equality of educational opportunity in Chile. *Sociology of Education* 78 (4): 316–43.

Valenzuela, Juan Pablo, Cristián Bellei, and Danae de los Ríos. 2013. Socioeconomic school segregation in a market-oriented educational system. The case of Chile. *Journal of Educational Policy* 29 (2): 217–41.

Valenzuela, Juan Pablo, Gabriel Villarroel, and Cristóbal Villalobos. 2013. Ley de Subvención Escolar Preferencial (SEP): Algunos resultados preliminares de su implementación. *Pensamiento Educativo. Revista de Investigación Educacional Latinoamericana* 50 (2): 113–31.

Villarroel, Gabriel. 2012. Mejoramiento en resultados académicos de la educación básica en Chile: ¿Primeros efectos de la ley de Subvención Escolar Preferencial (SEP)? MA Economics Thesis, University of Chile.

West, Edwin. 1997. Education vouchers in principle and practice: A survey. *World Bank Research Observer* 12 (1): 83–103.

Over the half century since the Coleman Report was issued, there has been an extensive debate among scholars, policy-makers, and the courts about the extent to which "money matters" in education. This article briefly reviews the relevant academic literature and then analyzes the forty state court education funding litigations that have considered whether there is a correlation between educational expenditures and improved student outcomes. I find that that there is now an overwhelming consensus that, of course, money matters—when it is used well. This result indicates that policy-makers and judges should shift from continuing a fruitless abstract discussion of whether money matters and concentrate instead on the significant accountability questions of what resources are needed to provide all students a meaningful educational opportunity and how these resources can best be used to maximize student success, especially for students from poverty backgrounds and students of color.

Keywords: education finance; educational policy-making; courts; money matters; Coleman Report

The Courts' Consensus: Money Does Matter for Educational Opportunity

By
MICHAEL A. REBELL

Since the issuance of James Coleman's 1966 report, *Equality of Educational Opportunity* (Coleman et al. 1966), there has been a continuing debate in the media, among researchers, policy-makers, and in the courts about whether increased expenditures for schools have a significant impact on educational opportunity and

Michael A. Rebell is professor of practice in law and educational policy at Teachers College, Columbia University, and an adjunct professor at Columbia Law School. He also was co-counsel for plaintiffs in Campaign for Fiscal Equity v. State of New York, *a case that is discussed in this article.*

NOTE: Esther Cyna, a doctoral student at Teachers College, and Aaron Rogoff, a third-year student at Columbia Law School, provided valuable research assistance for this article, and Jessica Wolff contributed her editing expertise.

Correspondence: Mar224@columbia.edu

DOI: 10.1177/0002716217732311

educational outcomes. Coleman's nuanced findings have often been misunderstood and distorted, but after 50 years of intense discussion of this issue, a clear consensus has emerged in both the academic literature and in the numerous court rulings on school funding that have considered the question: money does matter in education—if it is well spent.

Coleman summarized the findings of his historic report in the following terms: "Per-pupil expenditure, books in the library, and a host of other facilities and curricular measures show virtually no relation to achievement if the 'social' environment of the school—the educational backgrounds of other students and teachers—is held constant" (quoted in Mosteller and Moynihan 1972, 19–20). Although the report was interpreted in many quarters as saying that the academic performance of educationally disadvantaged students cannot be improved by spending more money on schools and providing additional educational resources, that is not what the report said.

What the report actually found was that the then-current school practices did not appear to overcome differences in students' backgrounds. It did not, however, preclude the possibility that the availability of additional resources beyond those included in the study and more effective and efficient educational practices could overcome the family-background factors identified in the report. Furthermore, in the years since the report was written, many researchers have identified methodological shortcomings stemming from limitations in the statistical analyses that were used and from the paucity of data on the full range of factors that affect student achievement (Mosteller and Moynihan 1972; Guthrie 1996; Biddle and Berliner 2002; Borman and Dowling 2010; Konstantopolous and Borman 2011; Hanushek 2016).

One could also validly interpret the findings of the report as indicating that because family-background factors profoundly impact educational outcomes, what is needed is substantially more investment in programs and services aimed precisely at compensating for and overcoming deficiencies in these areas experienced by students from disadvantaged backgrounds. Indeed, Coleman himself concluded that society needs to invest heavily in developing the kinds of "social capital" necessary to overcome the education deficiencies created by poverty and that "children and youth need to succeed in schools and as adults" (Coleman 1990, 339).

Not being aware of these nuances and of the methodological limitations of the report, many people who have a general awareness of its conclusions have interpreted the report to mean that providing schools additional funding would not lead to significant improvements in student outcomes. This simplistic interpretation has had a profound impact on the educational-policy debate among policymakers and in the media. "Dollar bills don't educate students," said President George H. W. Bush in 1991.[1] Nearly a decade later, the editors of the *Wall Street Journal* (2000) wrote, "Just as more money has not provided a remedy in the past, it will not miraculously do so in the future." More recently, New York governor Andrew Cuomo (2011) opined, "Not only do we spend too much, but we get too little in return"; and President Donald Trump declared that our "education system [is] flush with cash, but … leaves our young students deprived of all knowledge" (Klein and Ujifusa 2017, 18).

This debate about the relationship of funding to educational opportunities and outcomes has also been taken to the courts. In 1973, the U.S. Supreme Court denied relief to parents of school children in a poor Texas school district who claimed that per-capita spending on their children was only 60 percent of the amount spent on their peers in a neighboring wealthier district (*San Antonio Independent School District v. Rodriguez* 1973). The Supreme Court declined to consider these inequities because it held that education, not being specifically mentioned in the U.S. Constitution, is not a "fundamental interest" under the federal constitution. Uncertainty about whether additional resources would result in improved student achievement also clearly influenced the Court's thinking:

> [O]ne of the major sources of controversy concerns the extent to which there is a demonstrable correlation between educational expenditures and the quality of education—an assumed correlation underlying virtually every legal conclusion drawn by the District Court in this case. … The ultimate wisdom as to these and related problems of education is not likely to be divined for all time even by the scholars who now so earnestly debate the issues. (pp. 42–43)

For these reasons, the Court expressed reluctance to enter into this debate and indicated that the question of whether there is a correlation between expenditures and education quality is not one that the federal courts should consider.

Because the Supreme Court's ruling meant that the federal courts would not consider claims of inequities in educational funding, since 1973, aggrieved plaintiffs have brought their challenges to school funding systems in the state courts. In contrast to the federal constitution, most state constitutions do have provisions that guarantee some basic level of education to all students.[2] Substantial resource disparities between affluent and needy school districts exist throughout the United States,[3] and in many states, school funding levels in poorer school districts have been insufficient to meet students' basic educational needs. To address these inequities, lawsuits have been filed in forty-five of the fifty states in the past 40 years.

Overall, plaintiffs have prevailed in about 60 percent of these cases.[4] For the courts to rule in plaintiffs' favor in these cases, the judges had to find, explicitly or implicitly, a positive correlation between increased school funding and the quality of educational opportunities. In most of the cases in which the state defendants prevailed, the courts did not even consider the "money matters" question. Instead, the judges decided that the courts should not review legislative decisions about education funding, invoking separation of powers reasons or other purely legal rationales. The overwhelming consensus of the courts that have considered the question is that there is a definite correlation between educational expenditures and educational quality. In some of the cases, this general conclusion is accompanied by nuanced understandings that other factors also affect student performance and that to improve student achievement, the additional money has to be spent well (Rebell 2009).

The fact that plaintiffs in the education funding cases have generally needed to present expert evidence on the money matters issue has also spurred and supported a trove of academic research and writing on the subject. The close scrutiny that the issue has received has substantially lessened the controversy among scholars about the correlations between resource inputs and student outputs, and there is also now a basic consensus among scholars that there is a demonstrable correlation between educational expenditures and the quality of education—again, provided the money is spent well.

The Academic Debate

As Heather Hill's article in this volume, "The Coleman Report, 50 Years On: What Do We Know about the Role of Schools in Academic Inequality?" recounts, the Coleman Report led to a plethora of studies over the past half century that have analyzed the core question of the relationship between resources and student outcomes. Many of these studies have focused on potential correlations between specific resources such as reduced class sizes or preschool services and quantitative measures of school success (Konstantopoulos and Chun 2009; Schweinhart 2003). Rutgers University Professor Bruce Baker, after analyzing more than a dozen recent studies of correlations between specific resources and student achievement, concluded that the evidence demonstrates that "Schooling resources that cost money, including smaller class sizes, additional supports, early childhood programs and more competitive teacher compensation (permitting schools and districts to recruit and retain a higher-quality teacher workforce), are positively associated with student outcomes" (Baker 2016, 1).

Although many of these studies have indicated that the provision of certain types of resources has led to improved student outcomes, the evidence does not demonstrate that reducing class sizes or providing access to pre-kindergarten services will consistently and systematically improve outcomes. A key question that always needs to be considered is how effectively are the resources being used in any particular context and what countervailing variables must be taken into account in assessing the effect of providing specific additional resources.

Some of the most widely publicized studies of the correlation between resources and student achievement have involved broad meta-studies based on production function techniques that measure the effects of a range of resource inputs on specified student outcomes (such as student achievement, measured in terms of standardized test scores or graduation rates). In the 1980s and 1990s, Eric Hanushek, an economist at Stanford University's Hoover Institution, concluded on the basis of production function analyses that he undertook of 187 regressions involving 38 primary studies of the relationship between teacher/student ratios, teacher education, teacher experience, teacher salary, facilities and other such inputs, with outputs mostly in terms of standardized test scores (Hanushek 1991) that "key resources—ones that are the subject of much policy attention—are not consistently or systematically related to improved student performance" (Hanushek 1996, 20).

Hanushek's findings have had a substantial impact on the public policy debates regarding school funding issues. Other scholars have, however, questioned his findings because Hanushek may not have included all of the relevant studies that they believed should have been included under precise decision rules (Greenwald, Hedges, and Laine 1996), because his analyses do not adequately account for across-district variations in the costs of educational services, such as teacher salaries, and the proportion of students with special needs who require additional, more costly services. (Taylor 1997) and because production function analyses almost always measure outcomes solely in terms of standardized test scores, which are not complete and accurate measures of meaningful success (Card and Krueger 1992).

Hanushek's conclusions have resonated widely. However, Hanushek has never specifically said that "money doesn't matter," and in fact, he has specifically stated that "The research, of course, does not say that 'money never matters.' Nor does it say that 'money cannot matter'" (Hanushek and Lindseth 2009, 57). His point seems to be that for the time periods covered by his research, and under the educational conditions then in effect, additional funds had not yielded substantial increases in achievement. Hanushek left open the possibility that if utilized well, additional funds can make a difference. Indeed, in recent years, Hanushek himself has found that high quality teaching does increase student performance (Hanushek 2011; Hanushek 2016).

Another way of understanding Hanushek's position is that "the existing system of constraints and incentives [has] blunted the benefits of existing funds, with the result that more spending on schools has not translated into substantially better results" (Hanushek and Lindseth 2009, 57). For these reasons, he indicates that states should not increase their appropriations for education until and unless current educational practices and incentives are reformed in the market-oriented manner that he advocates. Although I do not agree with Hanushek's specific policy proposals, clearly, greater efficiency and improved educational practices are desirable, but the larger problem is that many of the schools attended by educationally disadvantaged students are so deficient in terms of basic resources that questions of efficiency and effectiveness cannot usefully be pursued. Schools with unqualified teachers, out-of-date textbooks, and excessive class sizes cannot substantially and systematically improve educational outcomes no matter how these scanty resources may be deployed, especially if its student population comprises mainly "educationally disadvantaged" students. This is essentially the implied conclusion of most of the state courts that have considered these issues and that have issued orders requiring states to increase their educational funding.

The Courts' View

In the overwhelming majority of school finance cases that have been litigated in the state courts, the relationship between educational expenditures, school quality, and student outcomes has been a central issue. Since a key question for the state courts in the education funding litigations is whether increased funding would provide better opportunities for students, extensive expert testimony has been presented on both sides in almost all of the trials that are held in these cases. Hanushek (who has testified as a witness for the defense in twenty-three of these cases) and other expert witnesses for both plaintiffs and defendants have presented "production function" and other statistical analyses on the correlations between increased educational expenditures and improved academic outcomes. Other experts have presented evidence demonstrating or denying correlations between specific resource inputs, including smaller classes, more qualified teachers, instructional materials, and more adequate facilities and improved educational outcomes.[5]

The New York Court of Appeals, New York's highest court, articulated the importance of these issues when, in its preliminary decision remanding the case for trial, it specifically stated that, to prevail, the plaintiffs must "establish a correlation between funding and educational opportunity ... [and] a causal link between the present funding system and any proven failure to provide a sound basic education to New York City school children" (*Campaign for Fiscal Equity, Inc. v. State [CFE] I* 1995, 667). When the case returned to the court years later after a long trial that included extensive testimony from experts on both sides of the issue, the Court of Appeals weighed that evidence and concluded:

> The trial court reasoned that the necessary "causal link" between the present funding system and the poor performance of City schools could be established by a showing that increased funding can provide better teachers, facilities and instrumentalities of learning. ... We agree that this showing, together with evidence that such improved inputs yield better student performance, constituted plaintiffs' prima facie case, which plaintiffs established. (*CFE* II, 2003, 340)

Persuaded by the evidence that additional funding would lead to improved school quality and better student outcomes, the New York court ruled the state's school funding system unconstitutional and ordered the state to remedy the violation of students' rights.

Similarly, in Kansas, after more than half a dozen experts on both sides of the issue presented detailed testimony, the court was persuaded that "there is a causal connection between the poor performance of the vulnerable and/or protected categories of Kansas students and the low funding provided their schools" (*Montoy v. State of Kansas* 2003, 49). Based on this finding, it held that "the funding scheme presently in place and as applied in Kansas by its underfunding in general and by its mid and large-school underfunding specifically, clearly and disparately injures vulnerable and/or protected students and thus violates both Article 6 of the Kansas Constitution and the equal protection clauses of both the United States and Kansas Constitutions" (*Montoy v. State of Kansas* 2003, 49). The Kentucky Supreme Court, in the school-funding adequacy case in that state, also found for the plaintiffs, writing that "achievement test scores in the poorer districts are lower than those of rich districts and expert testimony clearly established that there is a correlation between those scores and the wealth of the district" (*Rose v. The Council for Better Education 1989*, 197).

Although some legal scholars have argued that judges are "generalists" who do not have the scholarly background necessary to understand complex social science issues (Horowitz 1977), judges in many of these cases demonstrated sophisticated understandings of the complex statistical and methodological issues involved in these analyses. For example, Eugene W. Reese, a circuit judge in Alabama, expressed a nuanced understanding the evidence presented to him. Of the state's main expert witness, he wrote:

> Dr. Hanushek did not testify that spending can never positively affect student achievement on tests; his point was, instead, that to date experts have been unable to measure a systematic relationship between expenditures and achievement. He concluded that school money must be spent inefficiently (that is, in ways that do not improve achievement) in this state and elsewhere.

Judge Reese then went on to summarize the testimony of the plaintiffs' main witness, Ronald Ferguson, a professor of public policy at Harvard University:

> [Ferguson] found a systematic positive correlation between student achievement and certain expenditures (that is, money spent to secure smaller class sizes above a certain threshold, teachers with more experience, and teachers who themselves had better test scores). Dr. Ferguson's Alabama study was structured differently from that of Dr. Hanushek in several important respects: (1) Dr. Ferguson did not include all school expenditures in his analysis (eliminating, for example, spending on maintenance, school lunch, and transportation), but focused instead on those instructional expenditures that might be expected to affect student scores directly; (2) Dr. Ferguson used actual test scores, while Dr. Hanushek used only average test scores; (3) Dr. Ferguson used a methodology that simulated gains in achievement over time, while Dr. Hanushek reviewed only levels of achievement in a single year; and (4) Dr. Ferguson controlled for many more variables that could affect student scores (such as race, socio-economic status, and parental education) than did Dr. Hanushek.

Reese also expressed skepticism about using production-function analysis in the school-funding context:

> [T]he results of production function studies alone are in any case not an appropriate basis for concluding that additional funding for public schools is unnecessary or misguided. These studies—which … were designed for use in ordinary business and manufacturing contexts—are rightly controversial when applied to the education field, in which inputs and outputs are complex, data are limited, and some goals designed to be served by public education entirely escape analysis, such as socialization, the protection of public health and safety, the inculcation of moral and civic values, athletic achievement and aesthetic appreciation. (*Alabama Coalition for Equity v. Hunt* 1993, 139–14)

Reese found Ferguson's evidence more convincing and concluded that "there is a positive correlation between spending on education and student performance" in Alabama.

Overall, from 1973 through the end of 2016, the state courts throughout the United States considered the relationship between education expenditures and student outcomes in forty cases.[6] In thirty-four of them, the courts determined that there was a substantial correlation between expenditures and student outcomes. The determination of this correlation took a number of forms. In many of the cases, as in Alabama, Kansas, Kentucky, and New York, the courts explicitly addressed the expenditure/quality correlation in their findings and decisions. In other cases, the courts implicitly addressed the issue in concluding that specific resource inputs were critical to meaningful educational opportunity. For example, courts examined whether states had fulfilled the guarantee of an "equal" educational opportunity or of an "adequate" education in the state constitution's education article if children in certain districts were deprived of critical educational resources, such as certified teachers, small classes, up-to-date textbooks, computers, laboratories, and decent facilities (See, e.g., *Tennessee Small School Systems v. McWherter* 1993; *Lakeview School District N. 25 v. Huckabee* 2002). In some cases, courts held that additional resources were needed so that children could meet new, more challenging state and national standards (e.g., *Leandro v. State of North Carolina* 1997; *Columbia Falls Elem. Sch. Dist. v. State of Montana* 2005).

In all the cases in which the plaintiffs prevailed (thirty-two cases in twenty-two states—school-funding issues were revisited in some states on several occasions), the courts determined explicitly or implicitly that "money matters." By way of contrast, in most of the cases in which defendants prevailed, the courts did not discuss expenditure/education outcome correlations at all. In these cases, the courts upheld the defendants' position by applying separation-of-powers principles and holding that school-funding issues should be determined by the legislative and executive branches rather than by the courts (see, e.g., *Mc Daniel v. Thomas* 1983; *Bonner v. Daniels* 2009); evoking the tradition of local control of education (see, e.g., *Committee for Educational Rights v. Edgar* 1996); or determining that plaintiffs did not properly raise educational adequacy issues in their complaints (see, e.g., *Scott v. Commonwealth of Virginia* 1994).

When state courts decide cases on such purely legal or procedural grounds, there usually is no opportunity for the parties to submit evidence or for courts to consider the expenditure/quality issues. Defendants have generally prevailed in these cases on a motion to dismiss, which means that the court determined that the plaintiffs had raised no valid constitutional claims and, therefore, the case was not permitted to even proceed to a trial where evidence could be introduced and considered.

In a few of the cases in which the defendants won, however, there had been a trial. In two of them, the state's highest court reversed the judgment of the lower court for a variety of legal reasons, but these courts did not discuss or overrule the lower court's holding that the evidence indicated that greater expenditures result in better student outcomes (*Lobato v. State of Colorado* 2013; *Hancock v. Driscoll* 2004). For example, in the Colorado case, the trial court had held, "Studies performed throughout the United States, in states ranging from Massachusetts to South Carolina to California, demonstrate a strong relationship between resources and achievement" (*Lobato v. State of Colorado* 2011, 50). But the state supreme court reversed the lower court's decision because it held that the judge had applied an erroneous legal standard, and the high court did not consider it necessary to consider or comment on this specific finding (*Lobato v. State of Colorado* 2011, 213.) Because the higher courts did not comment on the specific finding that school funding was related to education quality, I have included this trial court ruling and the trial court's *Hancock* decision from Massachusetts in my categorization of courts that, after reviewing the relevant evidence, had found a significant correlation between expenditures and outcomes.

In six of the defendant victory cases, the state supreme courts did speak to whether money matters in education. In each of these cases, the higher courts expressed concern about limitations of the evidence or about the appropriateness of courts considering the expenditure/quality correlation issue or expressed some degree of skepticism about whether there is, indeed, any such correlation. None of them, however, held that there is no correlation between educational expenditures and student outcomes, and none of them explicitly stated that, in education, money does not matter.

The Supreme Court of South Dakota upheld a trial court decision in which the defendants had prevailed. It discussed at length the expert witnesses' testimony and concluded that the plaintiffs had not met their burden of establishing the existence of an expenditure/quality education correlation: "The testimony and evidence raise questions about the correlation between the level of funding and student achievement. On this record, the correlation between the school funding system and poor academic results is not readily apparent" (*Davis v. the State of South Dakota* 2011, 640). In *Lujan v. Colorado State Board of Education* (1992, 1018), the Colorado Supreme Court simply refused to enter into "the realm of social policy" in regard to "a raging controversy, that there is a direct correlation between school financing and educational quality and opportunity." Two other state supreme courts also overruled lower court decisions that had been in the plaintiffs' favor. In Rhode Island, the Supreme Court, citing only a single study, stated that, "Recent studies have indicated that educational achievement by students is most clearly a function of parental involvement," but it also opined that the extent to which expenditures are related to student achievement is "a complex problem involving the allocation of statewide resources [that] is not a proper arena for judicial determination" (*City of Pawtucket v. Sundlun* 1995, 63).

Although, on at least two previous occasions, the Texas Supreme Court had premised major school-funding decisions on a presumption that "[t]he amount of money spent on a student's education has a real and meaningful impact on the educational opportunity offered that student" (*Edgewood Independent School District v. Kirby* 1989, 393; *Neeley v. West Orange-Cove Consol. Independent School District* 2005, 788), in its most recent decision, the court considered this issue in greater depth and reversed the trial court's decision. In doing so, it expressed "uncertainty as to the correlation between more money and better education" (*Morath v. Texas Taxpayer and Student Fairness Coalition* 2016, 851). Taking note of the extensive trial testimony on this issue, and referring specifically at several points to the Coleman Report, the court concluded:

We do not question that a school system must spend money to accomplish a general diffusion of knowledge. Common sense says as much, as have we. Our financial efficiency doctrine presupposes that some good comes from equalizing access to funding. But here the trial court went much further, embarking on a quest to calculate the statewide dollar cost of an adequate education, and declaring the system unconstitutional because the Legislature had not provided funds to meet that threshold. What is not clear, given the current state of knowledge in the social sciences, is that spending a specific amount of additional money necessarily correlates to a better education as measured by objective outcomes. (p. 854)

In other words, although this court believed that in a general sense money matters, it was not persuaded by the evidence in this case that the specific increases that plaintiffs were seeking would necessarily lead to better student outcomes. An Arizona intermediate appeals court reached a similar mixed conclusion. It stated, "We assume that, as contended by the School Districts, focusing additional resources on at-risk students might very well be an effective method to improve the test scores of this category of underperforming students," but it also determined that, on the facts presented in this case, "the causal relation with respect to operations is murky at best" (*Crane Elementary School District v. State of Arizona* 2006, 24–25). The Pennsylvania Supreme Court also did not deny that added resources can contribute to better results, but it emphasized the complexity of the correlation, saying that "expenditures are not the exclusive yardstick of educational quality, or even of educational quantity. … The educational product is dependent upon many factors, including the wisdom of the expenditures as well as the efficiency and economy with which available resources are utilized" (*Marrero v. Commonwealth* 1999, 427).

In sum, then, in thirty-four cases (85 percent of the total cases) that have considered the expenditure/quality education correlation issue, the courts have clearly held that there is such a correlation. Although the other six cases (15 percent) expressed uncertainty or some degree of skepticism about the proposition, none of them definitively held that there is no such correlation. It can now be said that the numerous decisions and the extensive records in these forty state courts have largely resolved the question raised by the Supreme Court 44 years ago (*Rodriguez* 1973) when it questioned "whether there is a demonstrable correlation between educational expenditures and the quality of education." After wrestling extensively with the expenditure/education quality issue, the state courts by and large have demonstrated a sophisticated understanding of the nuances of the issue, and they have determined overwhelmingly that there is a demonstrable correlation between expenditures and educational quality that can overcome poverty and family background factors—when resources are used effectively.

Some recent cases have explicitly called for greater resource accountability (*Lake View School District v. Huckabee* 2002; *CFE v. State of New York* 2003), and other cases have required school districts to provide prekindergarten, health services, after school family support, and other programs and services that they believe can successfully offset the effects of poverty (*Abbott v. Burke* 2002, *Hoke County Board of Education v. State* 2004).

What Have These Litigations Accomplished?

There is no dispute that the courts' intervention in education finance has resulted in significant increases in the amount of educational funding in many states and in the equity of their resource distributions. In Kentucky, for example, litigation resulted in dramatic reductions in spending disparities among school districts, the redesign and reform of the entire education system, and a significant increase in that state's student achievement scores (Newman 2013, 81). In Massachusetts, enactment of the Education Reform Act of 1993 in response to that state's adequacy litigation also sharply reduced the funding gaps between rich and poor school districts (*Hancock v. Commissioner of Education* 2005).

In a number of instances, these additional resources have led to significant increases in student achievement. For example, in Massachusetts, the percentage of students achieving proficiency on state tests rose dramatically after implementation of the court order.[7] Decades of litigation in New Jersey on behalf of the largely minority, low-income students in thirty-one urban districts also resulted in significant increases in their achievement test scores (Goertz and Weiss 2009). Union City in New Jersey, a 92-percent Latino district that is the poorest in the state, has effectively closed the achievement gap between its students and non-urban students, and it may be the first urban district in the United States to sustain academic achievement into the middle grades (Kirp 2013).

In other instances, though, strong resistance from the governor or the legislature or both has delayed or impeded mandated reforms. In Ohio, for example, the legislature had partially responded to a series of court orders by, among other things, reducing funding inequities and improving school facilities following the declaration of unconstitutionality. The legislature's failure to implement the judicial orders fully, however, and the judges' unwillingness to confront the legislature led the state supreme court to retreat from the fray and terminate the cases before an appropriate remedy had been effectuated (Obhof 2005). In West Virginia, the legislature virtually ignored the courts' extensive orders throughout the 1980s but then implemented some limited reforms after another follow-up litigation was initiated in the mid-1990s.[8]

Although achievement gains do not always follow from judicial intervention, especially when courts do not steadfastly enforce their remedies, recent research has indicated that overall, the results of judicial interventions in this area have been impressive. A recent major study by the National Bureau of Economic Research (NBER), (Jackson, Johnson, and Persico 2014) considered the impact of state supreme court decisions in twenty-eight states between 1971 and 2010. It concluded that school finance reforms stemming from court orders have tended both to increase state spending in lower-income districts and to decrease expenditure gaps between low- and high-income districts. The authors also discussed the effects of court-ordered funding reforms on students' long-term success. They found that a 20 percent increase in annual per-pupil spending for K–12 low-income students leads to almost one more year of completed education. In adulthood, these students experienced 25 percent higher earnings, and a

20 percentage-point decrease in adult poverty. The authors posit that these results could reduce at least two-thirds of the achievement gap between adults who were raised in low- and high-income families.[9]

Similarly, in studying the impact of state aid increases on student achievement as measured by representative samples of scores on the National Assessment of Educational Progress (NAEP), Lafortune, Rothstein, and Schzenbach (2016, 1) found that the "reforms cause increases in the achievement of students in these districts, phasing in gradually over the years following the reform. The implied effect of school resources on educational achievement is large." Nguyen-Hoang and Yinger (2014) also found that increases in state aid in Massachusetts resulted in significantly higher student performance and Hyman (2014) found that students receiving additional funding were more likely to enroll in college and earn a postsecondary degree.

Conclusion

This article has provided an overview of the "money matters" debate that has been pursued in the academy and in the state courts for the past 50 years. This debate has advanced thinking beyond the simplistic conclusion that family background and peer influences preclude extra resources from improving the academic performance of educationally disadvantaged students—a conclusion that many had reached after the Coleman Report. This extensive exploration of the subject has shown a strong consensus that, of course, resources do matter—if they are utilized effectively and efficiently.

Therfore, courts and policy-makers should cease the fruitless discussion about whether "money matters." Instead, they should shift their attention to the more significant accountability questions of whether (1) the education finance systems in each of the states are providing all of their schools the basic resources that are a *sine qua non* for an efficiently run school "to do well" and (2) the school personnel are actually using those resources efficiently and effectively to maximize student success, especially for students from poverty backgrounds and students of color.

Notes

1. President George Bush, Address to the Nation on the National Education Strategy, April 18, 1991. Available from http://www.presidency.ucsb.edu/ws/?pid=19492.

2. The education clauses of virtually all of the state constitutions contain language that requires the state to provide all of its students "an adequate public education," "a thorough and efficient education," a "high quality system of free public schools," or a "sound basic education." See Georgia Constitution, art. VIII, s. 1, para. I; New Jersey Constitution, art. VIII, s. 4, para. 1; Florida Constitution, art. IX, s. 1; New York Constitution, art. XI, s. 1; *Levittown* v. *Nyquist* (1982, 368–69).

3. Substantial resource inequities have tended to prevail in most states between school districts located in areas that have high property wealth and therefore yield large property tax revenues for local school funding, and those living in property poor districts that were incapable of raising equivalent sums.

Ironically, in the United States today the children with the greatest needs by and large have the fewest resources provided to them. In most states, the highest-spending districts expend about twice as much per pupil as the lowest-spending districts; in some states, like California, the ratio is more than 3-to-1 (even excluding the top 5 percent of districts, spending ranged from $6,032 to $18,025 per pupil in California in 2009). See Excellence and Equity Commission (2013).

4. SchoolFunding.info, 2017, "School Adequacy Liability Court Decisions Map." Available from www.schoolfunding.info.

5. Lack of available data prevented the Coleman study from considering small class sizes, teacher effectiveness, school facilities, and, of course, computers and other technological resources that were not available 60 years ago.

6. A case was included in this compilation if it constituted a final decision of the state's highest court or ruling of a lower court that was not appealed. For a specific listing of these cases, see the "Court Cases" section of the reference list.

7. For example, on the fourth-grade English language arts examinations, the percentage of students.

8. *Pauley v. Bailey*, 324 S.E.2d 128, 135 (1984); *Tomblin v. West Virginia State Board of Education*, Civ. No. 75-1268 (2003).

9. The authors note, however, that the spending changes they analyzed occurred during a period in which average school funding levels were much lower than they are at present. It is possible, therefore, that increases in education spending could have diminishing marginal impacts, meaning that to obtain learning gains of the same magnitude, even higher increases in spending might be required.

Court Cases

Decisions in Which the Plaintiffs Prevailed

Abbeville Country School District v. the State of South Carolina, 767 S.E.2d 157 (S.C. 2014).
Abbott v. Burke, 575 A.2d 359 (N.J. 1990).
Alabama Coalition for Equity v. Hunt, 1993, aff'd, Ex Parte James, 713 So.2d 869 (1997).
Bradford v. Md. State Bd. of Educ., No. 94340058/CE189672 (Baltimore City Cir. Ct. 2000).
Brigham v. State, 692 A.2d 384 (Vt. 1997).
Campaign for Fiscal Equity, Inc. v. State, 655 N.E.2d 161 (N.Y. 1995) ("CFE I").
Campaign for Fiscal Equity, Inc. v. State, 801 N.E.2d 326 (N.Y. 2003) ("CFE II").
Campbell County Sch. Dist. v. State, 907 P.2d 1238 (Wyo. 1995).
Claremont Sch. Dist. v. Governor, 703 A.2d 1353 (N.H. 1997).
Columbia Falls Elementary Sch. Dist. No. 6 v. State, 109 P.3d 257 (Mont. 2005).
Conn. Coal for Justice in Educ. Funding, Inc. v. Rell, 990 A.2d 206 (Conn. 2010).
DeRolph v. State, 667 N.E.2d 733 (Ohio 1997).
Edgewood Indep. Sch. Dist. v. Kirby, 777 S.W.2d 391 (Tex. 1989).
Hoke County Bd of Educ. v. State (N.C. 2004).
Horton v. Meskill, 376 A.2d 359 (Conn. 1977).
Idaho Schs. for Equal Educ. Opportunity, 976 P.2d 913 (Idaho 1998).
Kasayulie v. State, No. 3AN-97-3782 (Alaska Super. Ct. Sept. 1, 1999).
Leandro v. State of North Carolina 488 S.E. 2d 249 (N.C. 1997).
Lake View Sch. Dist. No. 25 v. Huckabee 91 S.W.3d 472 (Ark. 2002).
McCleary v. State, 269 P.3d 227 (Wash. 2012).
McDuffy v. Sec'y of the Exec. Office of Educ., 615 N.E.2d 516 (Mass. 1993).
Montoy v. State, 120 P.3d 306 (Kan. 2005).
Neely v. West-Orange Cove 176 S.W. 3d 746 (Tex. 2005).
Pauley v. Bailey, 324 S.E.2d 128 (W. Va. 1984).
Robinson v. Cahill, 303 A.2d 273, 277 (N.J. 1973).
Roosevelt Elementary Sch. Dist. No. 66 v. Bishop, 887 P. 2d 806 (Ariz. 1994).
Rose v. Council for Better Educ., 790 S.W.2d 186 (Ky. 1989).
Seattle School District No. 1 v. State, 585 P.2d 71 (Wash. 1978).

Serrano v. Priest, 487 P.2d 1241 (Cal. 1971).
Tennessee Small Schools v. McWherter, 851 S.W.2d 139,144 (Tenn. 1993).
Tomblin v. West Virginia State Board of Education, Civ. No. 75-1268 (2003).
Zuni School District v. State of New Mexico, No. CV-98-14-ll (McKinley County Dist. Ct. Oct. 14, 1999).

Decisions in Which the Defendants Prevailed

Bonner v. Daniels, 907 N.E.2d 516 (Ind. 2009).
City of Pawtucket v. Sundlun, 662 A.2d 40 (R.I. 1995)1995.
Committee for Educational Rights v. Edgar, 672 N.E.2d 1178 (Ill. 1996).
Crane Elementary School District v. State of Arizona (Ariz. Ct. App. 2006).
Davis v. the State of South Dakota 804 N.W.2d 618 (S.D. 2011).
Hancock v. Driscoll, 2004 WL 877984 (Mass. Super, 2004); rev'd.
Hancock v. Commissioner of Education, 822 N.E.2d 1134 (Mass. 2005).
Ex Parte James, 836 So.2d 813 (Ala. 2002).
Levittown v. Nyquist, 439 N.E.2d 359 (N.Y. 1982).
Lobato v. State of Colorado, 304 P.3d 1132 (Colo. 2013).
Lujan v. Colorado State Board of Education 649 P.2d 1005 (Colo. 1992).
Mc Daniel v. Thomas, 285 S.E. 2d 156 (Ga. 1981).
Morath v. Texas Taxpayer and Student Fairness Coalition, 490 S.W.3d 826 (Tx. 2016).
Marrero v. Commonwealth 739 A.2d 110 (Pa. 1999).
San Antonio Independent School District v. Rodriguez, 411 U.S. 1. (1973).
Scott v. Commonwealth of Virginia 443 S.E.2d 138 (Va. 1994).

References

Baker, Bruce D. 2016. *Does money matter in education?* 2nd ed. Washington, DC: The Albert Shanker Institute. Available from http://www.shankerinstitute.org/sites/shanker/files/moneymatters_edition2.pdf.

Biddle, Brude J., and David C. Berliner. 2002. *What research says about unequal funding for schools in America.* Tempe, AZ: Education Policy Reports Project (EPRP).

Borman, Geoffrey D., and Maritza Dowling. 2010. Schools and inequality: A multilevel analysis of Coleman's equality of educational opportunity data. *Teachers College Record* 112 (5): 1201–46.

Card, David, and Alan B. Krueger. 1992. Does school quality matter? Returns to education and the characteristics of public schools in the United States. *Journal of Political Economy* 100 (1): 1–40.

Coleman, James S. 1990. *Equality and achievement in education.* Boulder, CO: Westview Press.

Coleman, James S., Ernest Q. Campbell, Carol J. Hobson, James McPartland, Alexander M. Mood, Frederic D. Weinfeld, and Robert L. York. 1966. *Equality of educational opportunity.* Washington, DC: United States Department of Health, Education, and Welfare and United States Office of Education.

Cuomo, Andrew. 5 January 2011. New York at a crossroads: A transformation plan for a *new* New York. State of the State Speech, Albany, NY. Available from https://www.governor.ny.gov/news/2011-state-state-transcript.

Equity and Excellence Commission. 2013. *For each and every child: A strategy for education equity and excellence.* Washington, DC: U.S. Department of Education.

Goertz, M., and M. Weiss. 2009. *Assessing success in school finance litigation: The case of New Jersey.* New York, NY: Campaign for Educational Equity, Teachers College.

Greenwald, Rob, Larry V. Hedges, and Richard D. Laine. 1996. The effect of school resources on student achievement. *Review of Educational Research* 66 (3): 361–96.

Guthrie, James W. 1996. Implications for policy: What might happen in American education if it were known how money actually is spent. In *Where does the money go? Resource allocation in elementary and secondary schools*, eds. Lawrence O. Picus and James L Wattenbarger, 253–68. Thousand Oaks, CA: Corwin Press.

Hanushek, Eric A. 1991. When reform may not be good policy. *Harvard Journal on Legislation* 28 (2): 423–56.

Hanushek, Eric A. 1996. The quest for equalized mediocrity: School finance reform without consideration of school performance. In *Where does the money go? Resource allocation in elementary and secondary schools*, eds. Lawrence O. Picus and James L Wattenbarger, 20–43. Thousand Oaks, CA: Corwin Press.

Hanushek, Eric A. 2011. The economic value of higher teacher quality. *Economic Education Review* 30:466–79.

Hanushek, Eric A. 2016. What matters for student achievement. *Education Next* 16 (2): 18–26.

Hanushek, Eric A., and Lindseth, Alfred A, 2009. *Schoolhouses, courthouses and statehouses: Solving the funding-achievement puzzle in America's public schools*. Princeton, NJ: Princeton University Press.

Horowitz, Donald, L. 1977. *The courts and social policy*. Washington, DC: Brookings Institution Press.

Hyman, Joshua. 2014. *Does money matter in the long run? Effects of school spending on educational attainment*. Ann Arbor, MI: University of Michigan. Available from http://www.edpolicy.umich.edu.

Jackson, C. Kirabo, Rucker Johnson, and Claudia Persico. 2014. The effect of school finance reforms on the distribution of spending, academic achievement, and adult outcomes. National Bureau of Economic Research Working Paper 20118, Cambridge, MA.

Kirp, David L. 2013. *Improbable scholars: The rebirth of a great American school system and a strategy for America's schools*. New York, NY: Oxford University Press.

Klein, Alyson, and Andrew Ujifusa. 2017. Trump calls nation's schools "flush with cash, failing." *Education Week* 36 (19): 18–19.

Konstantopolous, S., and Geoffrey Borman. 2011. Family background and school effects on student achievement: A multilevel analysis of the Coleman data. *Teachers College Record* 113 (1): 97–132.

Konstantopoulos, S., and V. Chun. 2009. What are the long-term effects of small classes on the achievement gap? Evidence from the Lasting Benefits Study. *American Journal of Education* 116 (1): 125–54.

Lafortune, Julien, Jesse Rothstein, and Diane W. Schzenbach. 2016. School finance reform and the distribution of student achievement. National Bureau of Economic Research Working Paper 22011, Cambridge, MA.

Mosteller, Fredrick, and Daniel P. Moynihan, eds. 1972. *On equality of educational opportunity*. New York, NY: Vintage Books.

Newman, Anne, 2013. *Realizing educational rights: advancing school reform through courts and communities*. Chicago, IL: University of Chicago Press.

Nguyen-Hoang, Phuong, and John Yinger. 2014. Education finance reform, local behavior, and student performance. *Journal of Education Finance* 39 (4): 297–322.

Obhof, L. J. 2005. *DeRolph v. State* and Ohio's long road to an adequate education. *Brigham Young University Education and Law Journal* 3 (1): 83–150.

Rebell, Michael A. 2009. *Courts and kids: Pursuing equal educational opportunity through the state courts*. Chicago, IL: University of Chicago Press.

Schweinhart, L. J. 2003. Benefits, cost, and explanation of the High/Scope Perry Preschool Project. Paper presented at the Meeting of the Society for Research in Child Development. Available from http://www.highscope. org/Research/PerryProject/Perry- SRCD_ 2003.pdf.

Taylor, Corrine. 1997. *Does money matter? An empirical study introducing resource costs and student needs to education production function analysis*. Madison, WI: Developments in U.S. Department of Education, National Center for Education Statistics, Developments in School Finance. Available from http://nces.ed.gov.

Wall Street Journal. 20 December 2000. More money? Editorial.

School Segregation and Disparities in Urban, Suburban, and Rural Areas

Much of the literature on racial and ethnic educational inequality focuses on the contrast between black and Hispanic students in urban areas and white suburban students. This study extends the research on school segregation and racial/ethnic disparities by highlighting the importance of rural areas and regional variation. Although schools in rural America are disproportionately white, they nevertheless are like urban schools, and disadvantaged relative to suburban schools, in terms of poverty and test performance. Native Americans are most affected by rural school disadvantage. While they are a small share of students nationally, Native Americans are prominent and highly disadvantaged in rural areas, particularly in certain parts of the country. These figures suggest a strong case for including rural schools in the continuing conversations about how to deal with unfairness in public education.

Keywords: schools; segregation; urban-rural; disparities

By
JOHN R. LOGAN
and
JULIA BURDICK-WILL

Schools vary widely in characteristics that are widely believed to be consequential for the students who attend them, including racial/ethnic composition, poverty concentration, and average performance of classmates. It is well known that these differences are patterned by

John R. Logan is a professor of sociology at Brown University. He is coauthor, along with Harvey Molotch, of Urban Fortunes: The Political Economy of Place *(University of California Press 1987). His most recent edited book,* Diversity and Disparities, *was published by Russell Sage Foundation in 2015.*

Julia Burdick-Will is an assistant professor in the Department of Sociology and in the School of Education at Johns Hopkins University. She is the author of "School Violent Crime and Academic Achievement in Chicago," published in Sociology of Education *(2013).*

NOTE: This research was partially supported by the Population Studies and Training Center, Brown University (R24 HD041020), and by the US2010 Project with funding from the Russell Sage Foundation.

Correspondence: john_logan@brown.edu

DOI: 10.1177/0002716217733936

space (e.g., the disparities between many central city school districts and those in the surrounding suburbs) and by the race and ethnicity of enrolled students (e.g., the disadvantages of schools attended by blacks and Hispanics in comparison to whites and Asians). In this study, we describe the nature and extent of these differences for public elementary schools across the United States in 2010–2011. We extend existing research in two ways. First, most studies of school segregation and educational inequality are limited to schools in metropolitan regions (note, for example, that a recent review of school segregation [Reardon and Owens 2014] cited no study including rural schools). We pay particular attention to rural schools, showing that rural schools have much in common with (as well as some large differences from) schools in central cities. Second, in addition to comparing average characteristics among urban, suburban, and rural zones, we also look within each of them, gauging racial and ethnic segregation across schools and disparities in the schools attended by students of different racial/ethnic backgrounds. We find substantial inequalities in all three zones.

This is a national study. We are aware that different patterns in different parts of the country could be obscured in the national averages. For this reason, we repeat our analyses separately by geographic region and again in those specific urban or rural areas where each racial/ethnic group is highly concentrated. Despite some variations, the area-specific analyses mainly replicate the national-level results.

Our emphasis on rural America is especially useful for highlighting disadvantages that receive little attention for two racial groups that are disproportionately found outside metropolitan areas—white and Native American children. Because whites are mostly found in relatively advantaged urban and suburban schools and are typically used as a point of comparison to black and Hispanic children in those contexts, their situation in rural schools is usually overlooked. Native Americans are rarely included in studies of metropolitan schools due to their small numbers. They are a tiny share of students at the national level (about 1 percent as shown below) and only 3 percent of students even in rural schools. But we find that in rural America these children are highly segregated from other groups in the same area, and consequently they attend schools that are disproportionately Native American (40 percent or more in some regions). The poverty level of their classmates is as high as in central city schools (more than 60 percent), and test score performance in schools that they attend is unusually low.

Segregation and School Disparities

American public schools remain highly segregated despite major changes in the 1970s, when court orders and new expectations eliminated de jure segregation (Clotfelter 2004; Logan, Zhang, and Oakley 2017). A primary consequence of segregation is the high level of inequality in educational opportunity between white or Asian children, and black or Hispanic children (Orfield and Yun 1999; Logan, Minca, and Adar 2012). Disparities appear as large differences in individual students' test scores (Stiefel, Schwartz, and Chellman 2008, 527) and dropout rates (Mickelson 2003). In this study, we focus not on these effects on individual students but rather on differences in the schools that they attend. Few studies have reported direct measures of school quality, although it is widely believed that minority students attend worse schools than non-Hispanic whites (Bankston and Caldas 1998; Roscigno 1998). There is evidence that minority children attend higher-poverty schools, partly because they are highly concentrated in central cities (Saporito and Sohoni 2007; Orfield and Lee 2005; Logan 2002). This finding is especially relevant in the context of this special issue focused on the anniversary of the Coleman Report, because that report (Coleman et al. 1966) concluded that racial differences in school outcomes were primarily attributable to socioeconomic differences between races. Coleman argued that predominantly white schools tended to enroll students from higher socioeconomic backgrounds, and it was for this reason that these schools' academic performance was better than that of predominantly minority schools. He found, in short, that apparent contextual effects were compositional (see also Hauser, Sewell, and Alwin 1976). If there were a contextual effect, in Coleman's view, it was the effect of class composition (for related evidence, see Chaplin 2002; Jencks and Mayer 1990; Gamoran 1996).

Rural schools may complicate the story because rural areas in most of the United States are disproportionately white, yet at the same time they suffer high poverty rates (Lichter and Brown 2011). Much of the literature on nonmetropolitan schools reflects on the poor employment prospects of rural youth and their implications for educational achievement and aspirations (Carr and Kafalas 2009; Irvin et al. 2011; Petrin, Schafft, and Meece 2014; Sherman and Sage 2011). Unfortunately, this research typically limits itself to the rural situation without making explicit comparisons to metropolitan areas. Some studies add dummy variables for urban, suburban, and rural locations to multiple regression models to test whether rural students are distinctive (Fan and Chen 1999). To our knowledge, however, there has been no national study of segregation and racial/ethnic disparities in nonmetropolitan areas; nor has there been a study comparing metropolitan and nonmetropolitan areas on these dimensions.

One partial exception is a study by Logan, Minca, and Adar (2012; see also Logan and Burdick-Will 2016) that included a national sample of schools. They conducted a cluster analysis to identify general categories of schools based on such characteristics as racial composition, poverty, test scores, and metropolitan location. They found that the major clusters did not neatly divide schools into urban, suburban, and rural categories. One cluster seems to represent typical suburban characteristics, with a large number of white students (87 percent on average), low levels of free and reduced price lunch eligibility (21 percent on average), and highly ranked schools (averaging at the 68th percentile on test scores compared with others in the same state). However, only 71 percent of schools in this cluster are in the suburbs. The others are split evenly between cities and rural areas. Two clusters have a plurality of schools located in central cities, and their characteristics approximate the usual stereotype of urban problems: they have high shares of minority children, around two-thirds of students are free-lunch eligible, and they are also the poorest performing schools on standardized tests. Yet both suburban and nonmetro schools are also well represented in these clusters. Even the cluster that was most likely to be found in rural areas (distinguished partly by overrepresentation of Native American students) included just as many suburban and central city schools as it did nonmetro schools. Hence there is overlap in characteristics across these three kinds of locations.

In related research (Burdick-Will and Logan 2017) we compared city, suburban, and rural schools. We found that inner-suburban schools are somewhat more like central city schools, while schools on the suburban periphery are more like rural schools. On average, these locational classifications identify very different kinds of schools in terms of racial/ethnic composition, poverty, and test scores. Yet in the current study, we must keep in mind that there are also important variations within geographic zones. Indeed, these variations are the source of disparities across racial/ethnic groups that attend different schools in the same zone.

There are also likely to be variations in patterns in different parts of the country. An important reason is that there is so much regional variation in racial/ethnic composition. Although whites have a major presence in most areas, the shares of other groups vary greatly. Black students are disproportionately found in urban areas, but they are a much smaller presence in the West than in the rest of the country, and they are also found in large shares in the rural South. Hispanics have historically been found disproportionately in the Northeast, in Florida, and in the Southwest, and Asians in the Northeast and West. But these predominantly immigrant groups are increasingly found in new destinations, including nonmetropolitan areas (Lichter 2012).

Research Design

Our overall purpose is to provide an assessment of variation in schools within and among urban, suburban, and rural areas for all public schools in the United States in 2010–2011. Our research design incorporates two critical choices. First, unlike most past research, we ignore district boundaries and focus solely on the location of individual schools, coded as central city, suburban, or rural. In many areas, especially in the South, school districts are organized at the county level, and they include both city and suburban schools. In other cases, schools that fall outside the boundaries of a metropolitan area (which we define as *rural*) are in the same district as schools within those boundaries. It could be of value to assess disparities by location within school districts. One might ask, for example, whether urban-rural differentials are smaller within districts (possibly due to choices about attendance zones or other school assignment policies, or possibly due to common curricula or teacher recruitment or budgetary resources). Our attention is focused on a broader pattern. What is the variation in school racial/ethnic composition, poverty, and test performance within and among urban, suburban, and rural areas? Where, overall, are conditions better or worse, more or less equal?

Our second major choice is to focus on elementary schools. They are smaller than other schools and are likely to draw students from a smaller catchment area, so we would expect to find clearer evidence of segregation and other disparities at this level. Because grade ranges in schools vary greatly across districts, we define an *elementary school* here as one that includes at least one grade between kindergarten and sixth grade. As far as possible we consider data only for children in these elementary grades.

Data

Data on all public schools in 2010–2011 are provided by the National Center for Education Statistics (NCES). NCES provides data on the student body of each school through its Common Core of Data (NCES 2012). Race/ethnicity is reported in the following categories: non-Hispanic white, black, Hispanic, Asian, and Native American/other races. NCES also reports, for most schools, the number of students who are eligible for free or reduced price lunches, which we use as an indicator of poverty. Eligibility for free or reduced price lunches is not separately reported by grade level, and therefore we assume that the share of free/reduced price lunch children is the same for elementary grade students as for the whole school. The Common Core of Data also include the total number of students and the precise geographic location of each school.

Testing data are calculated from the percent of students who meet state proficiency levels in reading and mathematics on tests administered by each state, reported to and made available by NCES (EDFacts 2013a, 2013b). We use fourth graders to represent the achievement levels of elementary students because this is the elementary grade level for which test scores are most often available. When test score data are not available for fourth graders, we use scores from fifth graders. If there are no fourth or fifth graders, we take the scores of third graders. The content and scoring of these tests vary widely across states. However, these are the most comprehensive testing data. The National Assessment of Educational Progress (NAEP) provides scores that are comparable across states, but these are available only for a sample of students within a small sample of U.S. schools. To make the state test scores more meaningful, we have recalibrated the percent passing scores as percentiles of school performance within the state (following the approach by Logan, Minca, and Adar 2012). A complication in using these scores is that in many cases NCES reported a score range (sometimes a range as large as 15 or 20 percentage points) rather than a specific score. For each reported range, we determined the average score among schools in the nation with reported specific scores in that range. We then use the imputed precise scores to calculate a percentile within each state. This creates a rank ordering within every state. From the perspective of a parent who is considering a range of school options, almost always within a state, these percentiles are meaningful. A school at the 20th percentile is much worse than one at the 50th percentile in any state, regardless of differences in the states' test content or proficiency cutoffs that we suspect are considerable.

Methods of Analysis

Our purpose is to understand differentiation among and within the traditional large census categories of urban, suburban, and rural. To do this we code every school based on its location using the school's geographic coordinates (reported by NCES). Geographic information systems (GIS) procedures were used to locate schools within principal cities of metropolitan statistical areas (MSAs), the suburban remainder of the MSA, or outside of an MSA using the U.S. Census Bureau's geographic definitions as of 2010. To study differentiation of rural schools within a delimited area, we introduce the concept of metro-plus zone, which is based on metropolitan regions and includes the rural schools that are located nearest to the outer boundaries of a given metro. We define *nearest* by using GIS software to find the nearest metropolitan principal city to every rural school. Rural schools are then considered to be part of that nearest principal city's metro-plus zone (see Burdick-Will and Logan 2017).

We also wish to make a distinction between different parts of the country. In the following analyses, this distinction is made in two different ways. The first is simply by census region (Northeast, Midwest, South, and West). We use standard census categories except for Texas. The census treats Texas as a southern state. Because its large Hispanic population makes it more like western states, we treat Texas schools as being in the West. The second is by racial/ethnic composition. Although whites are well represented in most areas, other groups tend to be highly represented in some metro-plus zones but relatively scarce in others. And a given group may be disproportionately represented in one portion of the metro-plus zone but not others. For example, as we have already noticed, Asians are generally underrepresented in rural areas, but Native Americans are overrepresented, especially in areas containing reservations. In our final analyses, we identify the metro-plus zones or portions of zones where each group is most highly concentrated, those in the top decile of group share. To be clear, in many cases the top decile for one portion (say, suburban) of zones does not include the top decile of another portion (say, rural) of the same metro-plus zone. We then focus on disparities within each of these locales where the largest share of members of a given group is found.

Table 1 provides information on the actual group share of total enrollment in the selected urban, suburban, and rural portions of metro-plus zones and in entire overrepresented zones. White presence is especially pronounced in schools in the most predominantly white rural and suburban portions, accounting for 94 or 95 percent of the elementary enrollment in these locations. There is somewhat more diversity in overrepresented urban areas, where whites average 83 percent of enrollment. Black students are nearly three-quarters of the enrollment in the most predominantly black urban areas and slightly more than half in their overrepresented rural areas. Their relatively small presence in suburbs, however, is reflected in the finding that even where they are most highly represented in the suburbs, they are only 31 percent of the total. Hispanics make up the majority of students in the top Hispanic zones, as high as 70 percent in urban areas, and 55 percent to 58 percent in suburban and rural areas. Asians and Native Americans are present in much smaller shares even in areas of high concentration. What most stands out is that Native Americans constitute only as much as 20 percent of enrollment in their most concentrated rural areas.

TABLE 1
Shares of Group Members among Students in the Top Decile of Locations (for Whole Metro-Plus Zones or Portions of Zones)

Racial/Ethnic Group	Total	Urban	Suburban	Rural
White	92%	83%	94%	95%
Black	41%	73%	31%	51%
Hispanic	60%	70%	55%	58%
Asian	9%	15%	8%	4%
Native American	10%	4%	9%	20%

Our analyses use standard measures of segregation and group disparities among schools within the same metro-plus area or within the urban, suburban, or rural portion of the area. One measure is the index of dissimilarity (D), which is used here to describe how similarly white students and students of a minority group are distributed across schools. If all schools contained the same share of white students and minority students, D would equal zero; D would achieve a maximum value of 100 if every school were either all-white or all-minority. In most studies of segregation, values of 60 and above are treated as "very high," values between 40 and 60 are considered more moderate, and values under 40 are considered "low." For other types of disparity, we use exposure indices, defined as the characteristic of the school that the average group member attends. *Group isolation* is the percentage of classmates who have the same racial/ethnic background. It is useful as a descriptive measure of segregation, but (because it evidently is greatly affected by the overall share of group members in a set of schools or in the nation) it should be interpreted in relation to that overall share. For example, we find (see Table 3) that the average white elementary student in the United States attends a school where enrollment is 73 percent white. This represents a high level of segregation because we also found (see Table 2) that only 51 percent of elementary students are white, so 73 percent is highly disproportionate. We also calculate three other exposure indices: poverty of classmates (share of classmates for the average group member who are eligible for free/reduced price lunches) and reading and math performance (the school's percentile on state reading/math tests in the school attended by the average group member). These measures refer to characteristics of children's schools, not their own likelihood of being poor or their own test performance.

Results

Urban, suburban, and rural schools across the nation

Table 2 reports simple descriptive statistics for schools in the nation and in different metropolitan locations. We note first that there are more students in suburban areas (13.5 million) than in urban or rural areas combined (12.2

TABLE 2
Characteristics of Elementary Schools by Metropolitan Location, 2010–2011

	All Schools	Urban	Suburban	Rural
Number of Schools	67,977	19,339	32,529	16,109
Elementary enrollment				
White	13,227,906	2,455,764	7,865,172	2,907,657
Black	4,016,028	1,960,722	1,609,862	443,974
Hispanic	6,246,869	2,847,098	2,905,605	495,455
Asian	1,200,429	519,348	637,717	42,009
Native American	288,515	64,007	97,485	126,850
Total	25,760,284	8,102,157	13,539,632	4,118,495
Area share of group national total				
White	100.0	18.6	59.5	22.0
Black	100.0	48.8	40.1	11.1
Hispanic	100.0	45.6	46.5	7.9
Asian	100.0	43.3	53.1	3.5
Native American	100.0	22.2	33.8	44.0
Total	100.0	31.5	52.6	16.0
Group share of area total				
White	51.4	30.3	58.1	70.6
Black	15.6	24.2	11.9	10.8
Hispanic	24.3	35.1	21.5	12.0
Asian	4.7	6.4	4.7	1.0
Native American	1.1	0.8	0.7	3.1
Free or reduced price lunch	51.5	62.5	42.9	58.0
Reading proficiency (percentile within state)	45.0	37.4	50.7	41.4
Math proficiency (percentile within state)	44.7	38.0	49.7	41.7

million). A little under one-third of students attend urban schools, and 16 percent attend schools in a rural area. Whites are barely a majority in all schools but still there are more than twice as many white students (13.2 million) as the next largest group (Hispanics, 6.2 million). Native Americans (less than 300,000) are greatly overshadowed by the other groups.

The overall differences in racial composition among area categories are large. Whites constitute just over half of overall elementary enrollment—less than a third of urban enrollment but a clear majority of suburban children (nearly 60 percent) and an even larger share of rural children (71 percent). The next largest group is Hispanic, reflecting the transformation of the minority population over recent years. Almost a quarter of students nationally are Hispanic. Hispanics now comprise the largest number of students in urban schools. There is nearly an equal number of Hispanics as whites in suburban schools, but Hispanics are underrepresented in rural enrollment. Black students are most likely to be found in urban schools (where almost half of them attend school), but they are almost equally underrepresented in suburban and rural schools (11–12 percent). Asians are found in much smaller numbers, also a larger share in urban schools and a much smaller share (only 1 percent) in rural schools. Native Americans, in contrast, are most highly represented in rural schools (where 44 percent of them are enrolled), but even here they are only 3 percent of the total.

Setting aside racial composition, suburban schools are greatly advantaged in comparison to both urban and rural schools. They have lower shares of students eligible for free or reduced price lunches (our indirect indicator of poverty)—43 percent compared to 63 percent in urban schools and nearly as high a share in rural schools (58 percent). Patterns of test performance also favor suburban schools, with reading and test scores lowest in urban schools and nearly as low in rural schools.

These patterns tend to favor white students, because a large majority of white students are suburban. At the same time, though, because whites are such a large share of rural students, they are also disadvantaged by the poverty and poor test performance of rural schools. Black, Hispanic, and Asian students are disadvantaged by their higher likelihood of attending urban schools. Native American students, in contrast, are disadvantaged by their much higher likelihood (44 percent) of attending rural schools.

Racial/ethnic disparities: An overview

Table 3 directly measures racial/ethnic disparities at a national level and within urban, suburban, and rural areas. Segregation is measured by the index of dissimilarity with whites and by the group's isolation in the metro-plus area (or the urban, suburban, or rural portion of the area) where the average group member is enrolled. Other indices (poverty of classmates and reading/math performance) refer to the school attended by the average group member (these group-weighted averages can also be described as exposure indices).

We find an average segregation (D) between whites and blacks at the national level of 63. This means that the average black student in the nation attended a school in a metro-plus area where segregation across schools was 63. This represents a high level of segregation, although reduced from the levels prior to 1970 when many districts operated separate schools for black students (Logan, Zhang, and Oakley 2017). In fact, it is about the same as the level of residential segregation across metropolitan area census tracts as reported in 2010 (Logan 2013). Black-white school segregation was highest in urban schools (62), moderately high in suburbs (54), but considerably lower in rural areas (44). Hispanics and Native Americans are modestly less segregated from whites. Hispanics, like blacks, are most segregated in urban areas and least in rural schools. However, the opposite is true for Native Americans. Their segregation is highest in rural schools, which is where they are also a larger share of the population. Finally, Asian students are moderately segregated in all portions of metro-plus areas.

TABLE 3
National Average Disparities among Schools by Students' Race/Ethnicity, Nationally and
within Urban, Suburban, and Rural Zones

	National	Urban	Suburban	Rural
Segregation from whites (D)				
Black	63.0	62.2	54.4	44.4
Hispanic	56.0	56.4	49.7	36.8
Asian	49.6	45.1	45.6	43.0
Native American	56.4	40.7	43.8	59.1
Group isolation				
White	72.8	56.5	74.6	81.8
Black	50.6	58.9	40.7	49.2
Hispanic	57.0	63.9	52.6	43.3
Asian	21.9	28.0	17.7	9.9
Native American	29.6	8.2	16.8	50.3
Poverty of classmates				
White	40.3	45.5	33.7	53.7
Black	69.3	75.6	60.1	75.0
Hispanic	64.9	70.4	59.7	64.0
Asian	40.4	50.0	31.8	53.1
Native American	64.2	64.2	54.5	71.8
School reading proficiency (percentile within state)				
White	53.3	51.8	57.1	44.4
Black	30.7	25.3	37.6	31.4
Hispanic	34.6	30.1	38.9	35.7
Asian	57.1	53.8	60.7	41.6
Native American	35.9	36.3	44.1	29.4
School math proficiency (percentile within state)				
White	51.5	49.7	54.8	44.3
Black	31.7	26.3	38.2	33.4
Hispanic	36.8	33.1	40.5	37.1
Asian	56.1	53.6	59.0	42.5
Native American	36.1	36.4	43.8	30.1

Measures of group isolation necessarily directly reflect the relative shares of group members in total school enrollment. Hence white isolation is very high in the average metro-plus area, and especially in the rural portion where they constitute the highest share of students. Isolation also is affected by segregation, and every group attends schools where they are a larger share of students than in the whole area. For example, we found nationally that black students are only about 16 percent of national elementary enrollment and Hispanics about 24 percent, but the average black and Hispanic students are both found to attend a school that is more than 50 percent black or Hispanic, respectively (see Table 3). The largest imbalance is found for Native Americans in rural schools. Nationally they are 3 percent of rural enrollment, but on average they attend rural schools that are 50 percent Native American. Hence a very small minority population can be a major component of students in certain areas.

The table shows that poverty of classmates differs greatly across groups and across metropolitan zones. Nationally the average white or Asian student attends a school where about 40 percent of students are eligible for free/reduced price lunches. The values for black, Hispanic, and Native American students are all above 60 percent, creating a 25- to 30-point differential with whites and Asians. For every group, there is also a differential, generally in the range of 10 to 20 points, between suburban schools and urban or rural schools. The disparity between urban and suburban schools is well known, but in fact poverty in schools attended by the average white student is highest in rural areas, and the same pattern holds for Asians and Native Americans. Poverty is almost the same in urban and rural schools for black students. And for Hispanics, both rural and urban schools are poorer than suburban schools, although poverty in urban schools is highest for Hispanic students.

The disparities in reading and math performance follow a similar pattern. Whites and Asians attend schools with the highest test scores, with Hispanics, Native Americans, and especially black students found on average in the worst-performing schools. Suburban schools again have a large edge over urban and rural schools for all groups. White and Native American students have the least favorable placement in rural schools, while black and Hispanic students are most disadvantaged in urban school placement.

To summarize, we find considerable segregation nationally and even within urban, suburban, and rural portions of metro-plus areas. This segregation is reflected in the composition of schools that each group attends, with especially high levels of isolation (in comparison with the group's share of total enrollment in the locale) in urban schools for blacks and Hispanics and in rural schools for whites and Native Americans. Segregation translates into disparities in school quality that strongly favor white and Asian students overall. But although researchers are familiar with the disadvantages of urban schools, especially for blacks and Hispanics, we show that rural schools are in some ways equally disadvantaged, especially for whites and Native Americans.

Variations by census region

We now replicate these analyses within each of the four major census regions of the country. Table 4 repeats Table 3 for the Northeast, Midwest, South, and West. While we expect and find many similarities between regions, we discuss here only the results for Native Americans and whites with an emphasis on rural schools. Most findings for other groups and settings are consistent with results in Table 3 and prior studies in metropolitan contexts.

Consider first the results for rural Native Americans, the least-known group in the least-studied portion of metro-plus areas. Nationally, 44 percent of Native American elementary students are in rural schools. The largest numbers are in

TABLE 4
Segregation (D) and Average Values of Other School Characteristics
by Census Region and Metro-Plus Location

	Northeast				Midwest			
	National	Urban	Suburban	Rural	National	Urban	Suburban	Rural
Segregation from whites (D)								
Black	73.6	70.1	61.6	40.3	72.8	68.7	61.6	44.4
Hispanic	66.8	62.2	57.2	38.2	57.2	56.8	47.4	36.2
Asian	52.9	52.2	45.3	36.5	50.8	45.1	45.1	49.5
Native American	65.4	55.9	63.6	66.1	60.3	44.9	41.7	63.4
Group isolation								
White	80.2	54.1	81.7	91.7	81.7	64.2	82.9	89.0
Black	49.1	59.7	34.2	12.1	57.2	67.0	44.1	12.5
Hispanic	47.5	55.1	40.1	20.4	41.8	52.4	35.0	30.0
Asian	25.0	35.4	18.2	3.0	14.1	20.1	10.8	3.9
Native American	8.3	2.5	6.0	26.4	27.9	14.5	3.4	45.8
Poverty of classmates								
White	28.4	53.9	22.1	43.1	39.0	48.4	31.7	48.3
Black	68.8	80.9	50.6	48.8	70.5	78.0	58.1	59.4
Hispanic	67.7	81.5	52.3	49.8	64.2	77.2	52.4	59.9
Asian	41.9	71.3	21.1	39.5	37.2	49.4	26.9	48.9
Native American	51.8	75.3	33.8	54.7	60.0	66.8	40.5	65.8
School reading proficiency (percentile within state)								
White	53.8	42.8	58.0	40.4	50.7	43.7	56.5	43.3
Black	26.8	21.6	34.9	36.2	24.1	18.4	33.7	36.4
Hispanic	29.8	24.4	36.1	34.0	30.3	23.0	37.5	32.7
Asian	55.0	47.0	61.3	43.0	52.2	43.8	59.9	41.6
Native American	38.7	29.8	48.3	30.3	31.3	26.0	48.1	26.4
School math proficiency (percentile within state)								
White	51.8	44.4	55.0	40.6	49.5	42.7	54.4	43.7
Black	26.9	22.1	34.3	35.9	24.6	19.5	33.4	36.4
Hispanic	31.4	27.4	36.1	33.1	31.0	24.7	36.7	35.0
Asian	55.9	52.6	58.7	41.8	49.8	41.2	57.4	41.6
Native American	39.4	32.0	46.2	35.6	30.8	26.6	47.4	25.4

	South				West			
	National	Urban	Suburban	Rural	National	Urban	Suburban	Rural
Segregation from whites (D)								
Black	57.5	58.6	49.7	44.0	59.0	58.9	53.6	45.9
Hispanic	48.3	48.4	44.7	34.9	55.7	57.4	50.1	37.1
Asian	45.5	34.9	43.4	42.9	49.2	45.3	46.5	40.7
Native American	45.5	34.2	38.2	43.0	58.7	42.6	47.0	64.8

(continued)

TABLE 4 (CONTINUED)

	South				West			
	National	Urban	Suburban	Rural	National	Urban	Suburban	Rural
Group isolation								
White	69.7	55.8	70.3	76.6	61.0	53.0	62.9	70.5
Black	56.4	67.0	47.4	55.0	26.1	30.3	21.0	19.1
Hispanic	36.4	36.3	39.1	22.6	66.2	70.8	62.3	57.6
Asian	10.8	8.4	12.4	2.5	26.5	30.4	22.4	20.7
Native American	26.9	5.2	17.7	39.2	34.5	7.8	21.3	63.5
Poverty of classmates								
White	49.8	48.6	43.9	62.7	39.4	39.8	35.6	53.0
Black	70.9	75.8	63.7	77.3	63.3	66.8	58.0	67.7
Hispanic	64.7	70.4	61.3	69.7	64.6	67.3	61.6	63.7
Asian	40.4	47.3	36.0	60.7	40.6	43.0	37.2	53.7
Native American	67.1	67.2	58.7	73.8	65.0	61.0	57.9	73.6
School reading proficiency (percentile within state)								
White	53.3	54.0	56.6	46.3	55.8	57.5	57.5	45.3
Black	32.3	27.4	37.6	30.7	37.8	33.8	43.7	35.6
Hispanic	40.7	34.4	43.6	39.7	34.6	31.6	38.0	35.1
Asian	57.0	52.6	59.4	47.7	59.3	58.6	61.3	37.1
Native American	43.1	42.4	48.8	39.1	32.2	38.7	38.8	22.0
School math proficiency (percentile within state)								
White	51.8	50.5	54.7	46.8	53.1	54.5	55.0	42.6
Black	34.1	29.0	39.3	33.2	37.5	34.1	42.7	32.4
Hispanic	42.1	35.0	45.0	42.7	37.4	35.1	40.3	35.6
Asian	55.1	49.3	57.9	48.0	58.1	57.3	60.2	39.2
Native American	42.9	41.4	47.1	40.1	33.0	38.7	40.0	23.0

the West (52,000 or 40 percent of those living in the West) and the South (47,000, 50 percent of the total). They are very highly segregated from whites in every region except the South. Their level of isolation is disproportionately high in all locations, but clearly highest in rural America. Native Americans attend schools that are 26 percent Native American in the rural Northeast and 39 percent in the South. More extreme values are found in the rural Midwest (46 percent) and especially the West (63 percent). These are areas where many live on reservations and attend predominantly Native American schools. They are also the locales where the disadvantages of their schools—though apparent in all settings—stand out the most. In the rural portions of Midwestern metro-plus zones, for example, the average Native American's school is 65 percent poor and scores only around the 25th percentile on reading and math tests. In the rural West, average poverty is even higher (73 percent) and test scores even slightly lower (22nd to 23rd percentile).

Let us turn now to the situation of whites in rural schools. There are 2.9 million white elementary students in rural areas. The largest number are in the Midwest and South, over a million in each region, comprising 27 to 28 percent of the total white students in those regions. The very high share of whites in these areas combines with a moderate degree of segregation to create quite high levels of isolation. The average rural white elementary student attends a school that is 70 percent or more white in the South and West and around 90 percent white in the Northeast and Midwest. In urban and suburban settings, segregation distances white students from the poverty experienced in schools typically attended by minority students. To some extent, this distancing also occurs in rural areas, since rural whites' schools have lower free/reduced price lunch levels than those of rural blacks, Hispanics, or Native Americans. But at the same time, rural schools in the South and West are where white students have the highest exposure to poverty (even higher than in urban schools), while in the Midwest their urban and rural schools are equally poor. Only in the Northeast do whites' urban schools have appreciably higher poverty than whites' rural schools.

A similar pattern appears in test scores. In the South and West, rural whites' schools have worse reading and math performance than the urban schools that they attend, and in the Northeast and Midwest they are about equally low performing. Segregation within the rural setting does shelter whites somewhat from the disadvantages of schools attended by minority children, but Table 4 shows that the differentials between whites on one hand, and blacks, Hispanics, and Native Americans on the other, are smaller in rural areas than in urban or suburban locales. More than in other areas, white students share the disadvantages of their schools with minority students.

Patterns in each group's areas of concentration

We now delve into the national-level patterns in another way, focusing on settings that are the most "typical" for a given group in the following sense—these are settings where group members are an especially high share of total enrollment. The "national" column in Table 5 reports the average values for group members in the metro-plus zones that are in the top decile of group concentration (the approximately 37 of the total 366 zones where they are the highest percentage of enrollment). The "urban" column selects for each group the urban schools in the metro-plus zones where the group has the highest share of urban enrollment, with similar independent selections for suburban and rural portions. How do these specific "ethnic pockets" compare with the average national situation of group members shown in Table 3? Again, rather than attempt to discuss all the results reported here, we focus on the case of rural Native Americans and rural whites.[1]

For Native Americans, levels of segregation (D) are similar in these overrepresented areas to the national averages. Isolation, necessarily, is higher because we have selected areas with the largest group presence. Yet in these specific metro-plus areas, Native Americans' presence is appreciable. In the metro-plus areas overall nearly half of the students are Native American in the school

TABLE 5
Average Segregation and Other School Characteristics in Metro-Plus Areas
Where Group Members are Overrepresented

	National	Urban	Suburban	Rural
White metro-plus areas				
White isolation	93.0	84.3	94.2	95.3
Poverty: whites' schools	48.7	47.6	41.3	55.4
Reading proficiency: whites' schools	45.9	46.7	49.3	42.8
Math proficiency: whites' schools	46.7	49.0	49.4	43.7
Black metro-plus areas				
Black segregation from whites	61.0	67.9	54.1	47.4
Black isolation	66.3	84.2	55.0	66.9
Poverty: blacks' schools	74.3	83.4	65.7	81.4
Reading proficiency: blacks' schools	29.6	21.7	35.4	28.3
Math proficiency: blacks' schools	32.0	23.3	38.4	30.4
Hispanic metro-plus areas				
Hispanic segregation from whites	56.0	56.6	54.7	46.1
Hispanic isolation	57.6	64.6	54.3	41.6
Poverty: Hispanics' schools	65.3	73.4	60.9	65.2
Reading proficiency: Hispanics' schools	36.6	31.5	39.4	35.4
Math proficiency: Hispanics' schools	38.9	35.9	40.5	37.3
Asian metro-plus areas				
Asian segregation from whites	51.0	50.4	47.6	37.8
Asian isolation	27.9	37.3	21.6	22.4
Poverty: Asians' schools	39.7	51.7	31.0	52.2
Reading proficiency: Asians' schools	58.7	56.2	61.1	35.6
Math proficiency: Asians' schools	58.3	57.6	59.5	38.9
Native American metro-plus areas				
Native American segregation from whites	58.0	37.0	40.7	63.1
Native American isolation	44.9	14.8	32.8	60.2
Poverty: Native Americans' schools	70.4	65.4	63.2	75.2
Reading proficiency: Native Americans' schools	32.5	35.5	41.7	27.5
Math proficiency: Native Americans' schools	33.2	35.8	42.1	28.4

attended by the average Native American, and they are among the larger groups in schools they attend in the suburbs (33 percent) and are a majority in their rural schools (60 percent). Although we anticipated that such a large presence might constitute a disadvantage, we find that poverty exposures and test performance for Native Americans are quite similar in Table 5 to the national averages found in Table 3.

Are white students' schools distinctive in the most predominantly white areas of the country? White isolation, of course, is much higher in these areas (reaching

93 at the metro-plus zone scale). Exposure to poverty ranges from 41 percent (suburban; 7–8 points higher than the national average) to 55 percent (rural; about the same as the national average). Reading and math performance of whites' schools is slightly lower in these areas, while scores in rural areas similarly lag those in the suburbs.

Discussion and Conclusion

Findings presented here reinforce previous studies that documented continuing segregation in metropolitan schools, inequalities between urban and suburban schools, and disparities between relatively advantaged white and Asian students in comparison to black and Hispanic students. These are the issues that motivated the Coleman Report decades ago, and we find cause for continuing concern.

We have extended the scope of segregation studies to include a systematic comparison to rural schools. We used the simple device of expanding metropolitan boundaries to metro-plus zones that include all of the rural schools that are closest to the metro area and designated these schools as the "rural portion" of the larger area. (These might be described as the *catchment areas* of major cities.) We can then compare these rural schools to schools in the nearest, most relevant urban and suburban schools. By ignoring district boundaries, we avoid having to consider how to measure segregation in districts that often have only one or two schools, and where the major differentiation is between rather than within districts.

The main finding in this respect is that rural schools—despite being disproportionately white—face similar disadvantages to urban schools. Big city schools naturally are more visible because of their larger size, but we would argue that rural schools, which enroll more than four million elementary children, also deserve a place on the policy agenda. The issues of concentrated poverty and poor test performance are similar in both rural and urban schools. Because of the smaller size of rural schools and the continuing issue of population loss in rural America, these schools may face unique problems of providing specialized classes, and teacher recruitment may be more difficult in low-density areas where the range of other job opportunities may be narrower. The charter school alternative that has been popular in some districts is uncommon in rural areas, perhaps obstructed by low densities, long travel distances, and difficult teacher recruitment. The obstacles to student success are possibly different in rural areas or where schools are majority white than in urban, predominantly minority schools. Therefore, it is not obvious whether the same policies that are traditionally proposed to support urban schools would apply equally to rural ones, but the question needs to be raised. There is much that we do not know because research on rural public education has often been pursued separately from research in metropolitan areas.

Taking rural schools into account profoundly alters the racial/ethnic component of the educational segregation/inequality discussion. Study after study has documented the large gaps between city and suburban schools, the associated differentials in their enrollment of black and Hispanic students, and the disparities experienced by black and Hispanic students both across the city-suburb divide and within both city and suburban contexts. Giving attention to rural America brings two other experiences into play. The first is the great challenges for Native American education, present but rarely documented in cities and suburbs but unavoidable in the rural context. We have shown that Native Americans are a large share of enrollment in schools that the average group member attends, and the class composition and academic performance of these "Native American" schools pose concerns very similar to those raised in discussions of black and Hispanic public schooling.

Second is the fact that in much of the country rural schools are overwhelmingly white. And though whites attend schools that are somewhat less poor and better performing in rural areas than do blacks, Hispanics, and Native Americans, their schools, too, are relatively poor and underperforming. What is generally recognized as white advantage is complicated by the disadvantage faced by whites who (like Native Americans) are disproportionately found in rural areas. In terms of absolute numbers, there are more white elementary students in rural schools (2.91 million) than there are black students (1.96 million) or Hispanic students (2.85 million) in urban schools. These figures suggest a strong case for including rural schools and the special situations of rural Native American and white children in the continuing conversation about how to deal with unfairness in public education.

Note

1. Because Asians are typically only a small share of students in much of the country, it is also interesting to note that in these selected areas Asians average as much as 28 percent of enrollment in the schools they attend, and as much as 37 percent on average in urban schools. Nevertheless, they maintain considerable advantages in terms of poverty concentration and school test performance.

References

Bankston, Carl L., III, and Stephen J. Caldas. 1998. Race, poverty, family structure, and the inequality of schools. *Sociological Spectrum* 18:55–76.

Burdick-Will, Julia, and John R. Logan. 2017. Schools at the rural-urban boundary: Blurring the divide? *The ANNALS of the American Academy of Political and Social Science* 672:185–201.

Carr, Patrick J., and Maria J. Kefalas. 2009. *Hollowing out the middle: The rural brain drain and what it means for America*. Boston, MA: Beacon Press.

Chaplin, Duncan. 2002. Estimating the impact of economic integration. In *Divided we fail: Coming together through public school choice*, ed. Century Foundation, 87–113. New York, NY: Century Foundation Press.

Clotfelter, Charles T. 2004. *After Brown: The rise and retreat of school desegregation*. Princeton, NJ: Princeton University Press.

Coleman, James S., E. Campbell, C. Hobson, J. McPartland, A. Mood, F. D. Weinfield, and R. York. 1966. *Equality of educational opportunity*. Washington, DC: U.S. Government Printing Office.

EDFacts. 2013a. *Achievement results for state assessments in mathematics: School year 2010–11*. Washington, DC: U.S. Department of Education. Available from https://explore.data.gov/Education.

EDFacts. 2013b. *Achievement results for state assessments in reading/language arts: School year 2010–11*. Washington, DC: U.S. Department of Education. Available from https://explore.data.gov/Education.

Fan, Xitao, and Michael J. Chen. 1999. Academic achievement of rural school students: A multi-year comparison with their peers in suburban and urban schools. *Journal of Research in Rural Education* 15 (1): 31–46.

Gamoran, Adam. 1996. Effects of schooling on children and families. In *Family-school links: How do they affect educational outcomes?* eds. A. Booth and J. F. Dunn, 107–14. Hillsdale, NJ: Erlbaum.

Hauser, Robert, William Sewell, and Duane Alwin. 1976. High school effects on achievement. In *Schooling and achievement in American society*, eds. William Sewell, Robert Hauser, and David Featherman, 309–42. London: Academic Press.

Irvin, Matthew J., Judith L. Meece, Soo-yong Byun, Thomas Farmer, and Bryan Hutchins. 2011. Relations of community, family, and school contexts to rural youth's educational achievement and aspirations. *Journal of Youth and Adolescence* 40:1225–42.

Jencks, Christopher, and Susan E. Mayer. 1990. The social consequences of growing up in a poor neighborhood. In *Inner-city poverty in the United States*, eds. Lawrence E. Lynn Jr. and Micahel G. H. McGeary, 111–86. Washington, DC: National Academy Press.

Lichter, Daniel T. 2012. Immigration and the new racial diversity in rural America. *Rural Sociology* 77:3–35.

Lichter, Daniel T., and David L. Brown. 2011. Rural America in an urban society: Changing spatial and social boundaries. *Annual Review of Sociology* 37:565–92.

Logan, John R. 2002. *Choosing segregation: Racial imbalance in American public schools, 1990–2000*. Albany, NY: Lewis Mumford Center. Available from http://www.s4.brown.edu/cen2000/SchoolPop/SPReport/SPDownload.pdf.

Logan, John R. 2013. The persistence of segregation in the 21st century metropolis. *City & Community* 12 (2): 160–68.

Logan, John R., and Julia Burdick-Will. 2016. School segregation, charter schools, and access to quality education. *Journal of Urban Affairs* 38 (3): 323–43.

Logan, John R., Elisabeta Minca, and Sinem Adar. 2012. The geography of inequality: Why separate means unequal in American public schools. *Sociology of Education* 85 (3): 287–301.

Logan, John R., Weiwei Zhang, and Deirdre Oakley. 2017. Court orders, white flight, and school district segregation, 1970–2010. *Social Forces* 95 (3): 1049–75.

Mickelson, Roslyn. 2003. When are racial disparities in education the result of racial discrimination? A social science perspective. *Teachers College Record* 105:1052–86.

National Center for Education Statistics (NCES). 2012. *Public elementary/secondary school universe survey data 2010–11*. Washington, DC: U.S. Department of Education. Available from http://nces.ed.gov/ccd/pubschuniv.asp.

Orfield, Gary, and Chungmei Lee. 2005. *Why segregation matters: Poverty and educational inequality*. Cambridge, MA: The Civil Rights Project at Harvard University.

Orfield, Gary, and John Yun. 1999. *Resegregation in American schools*. Cambridge, MA: The Civil Rights Project, Harvard University. Available from http://w3.uchastings.edu/wingate/PDF/Resegregation_American_Schools99.pdf.

Petrin, Robert, Kai A. Schafft, and Judith Meece. 2014. Educational sorting and residential aspirations among rural high school students: What are the contributions of schools and educators to the rural brain drain? *American Educational Research Journal* 51 (2): 294–326.

Reardon, Sean F., and Ann Owens. 2014. 60 years after Brown: Trends and consequences of school segregation. *Annual Review of Sociology* 40:199–218.

Roscigno, Vincent. 1998. Race and the reproduction of educational disadvantage. *Social Forces* 76:1033–60.

Saporito, Sal, and Deenesh Sohoni. 2007. Mapping educational inequality: Concentrations of poverty among poor and minority students in public schools. *Social Forces* 853:1227–53.

Sherman, Jennifer, and Rayna Sage. 2011. "Sending off all your good treasures": Rural schools, brain-drain, and community survival in the wake of economic collapse. *Journal of Research in Rural Education* 26 (11): 1–14.

Stiefel, Leanna, Amy Ellen Schwartz, and Colin Chellman. 2008. So many children left behind: Segregation and the impact of subgroup reporting in no child left behind on the racial test score gap. *Educational Policy* 21:527–41.

Learning in Harm's Way: Neighborhood Violence, Inequality, and American Schools

By
ELIZABETH PELLETIER
and
PAUL MANNA

Is a school's geographic proximity to violent crime related to characteristics of its student body and to students' academic performance? Our understanding of the educational impacts of students' exposure to violence has been constrained because of various technical and financial limitations that have made research in this area problematic. The work presented here leverages advances in the availability of geo-coded data on incidents of crime to overcome the limitations of prior research in this area, showing that a school's proximity to violent crime is associated with common measures of educational inequality and also with school performance. We discuss the implications of our findings for future research and public policy.

Keywords: education; inequality; schools; crime; violence; GIS

The relationship between schooling and students' exposure to violence often takes center stage in policy debates and the national discourse when whole communities are traumatized by a horrific event such as the shooting

Elizabeth Pelletier is a research associate in the Justice Policy Center at the Urban Institute, where she focuses on criminal and juvenile justice policy. She previously researched education policy as a Fulbright grantee at the University of Toronto.

Paul Manna is the Isabelle and Jerome E. Hyman Distinguished University Professor of Government at the College of William & Mary, where he chairs the Department of Government and is faculty affiliate in the W&M Public Policy Program. His work explores intergovernmental policy implementation, bureaucracy, education, and applied research methods.

NOTE: The authors acknowledge the Roy R. Charles Center at the College of William & Mary, and its donors, for supporting this project with a W&M Summer Honors Fellowship. In addition, we thank Salvatore Saporito, Melissa McInerney, Keenan Kelley, Rachel Brooks, Molly Michie, Rachel Lienesch, Rob Marty, Daniel Casey, Ashley Napier, Rachel Smith, and Andrew Saultz for helpful feedback and guidance.

Correspondence: pmanna@wm.edu

DOI: 10.1177/0002716217734802

at Sandy Hook Elementary School in 2012 (Peralta 2013). Yet tens of thousands of American children attend schools in dangerous neighborhoods where violence is an almost-daily occurrence (Osofsky 1999, 34; see also Bieler and La Vigne 2014; Stein et al. 2003; Richters and Martinez 1993a; Bell and Jenkins 1993). Research on how children's exposure to chronic violence affects schools and academic performance is substantial but severely constrained; our focus here is overcoming the limitations of prior work so that research in this area can speak directly and more powerfully to policy.

The Coleman Report—the landmark education study whose implications are the centerpiece of this collection of research—did not directly examine the links between students' exposure to violence and their academic success, but Coleman and his collaborators did highlight important links between the environmental conditions that students experience outside school and their classroom performance. In the report's opening pages, the authors encouraged readers who envision a child at school also to recognize that "home and total neighborhood are themselves powerful contributors to his education and growth" (Coleman et al. 1966, 2). Key findings moved the authors to conclude as such. Among those points were these specific arguments (Coleman et al. 1966, 319–25): that students who feel that they have a low sense of control over their immediate environment tend to struggle more in school, that a low sense of control is exhibited by students who believe that luck rather than hard work is associated with success, that the environment can intervene to prevent students from getting ahead, and that such people have fewer chances to succeed in life. A perceived inability to confront challenging home or neighborhood environments, combined with the lower performance in school that such a view prompts, can snowball over time and lead a student to believe, as the report noted, "that nothing he could ever do would change things" (Coleman et al. 1966, 321). That snowball effect is even larger, due to peer effects, when students attend schools each year where many others have similarly low senses of control over their environments due to the conditions they experience outside school.

The specific home and environmental factors that Coleman et al. (1966) studied did not include violence in the communities where children attend school. Still, the mechanisms that likely lead students to perceive that they have limited ability to control their environments, which Coleman described, are entirely consistent with subsequent bodies of research on child development and student academic success. The links between exposure to violence and the mental health, development, and educational achievement of children are now well documented. Scholars have found school and neighborhood violence to be associated with students having more trouble with school authorities; worse teacher ratings of student functioning; and lower grades, attendance, standardized test scores, graduation rates, and college attendance rates (Bowen and Bowen 1999; Henrich et al. 2004; Ozer 2005; Grogger 1997; Sharkey 2010; Burdick-Will 2013). What is important to note is that children need not personally experience violence to be academically affected by it. Carrell and Hoekstra (2008) found that an increase in the number of children in a classroom who lived amid violence at home was associated with lower peer math and reading scores and higher peer disciplinary infractions and suspensions.

Scholarship on Exposure to Violence and Its Policy Impact

Although a well-known literature exists on the effects of exposure to violence on the academic, social, and emotional development of children, that knowledge has not carried substantial weight in contemporary debates about education policy reform. We believe that there are two reasons why, and we elaborate on them in the sections below. The first is that the scope of how violence is conceptualized minimizes its ability to inform education policy development. The second is the challenge of scaling up methods to measure and incorporate violence into such discussions on a broader scale. Even as modern education data systems have become much better at tracking school characteristics and performance, data collection efforts on youth exposure to violence have operated on separate tracks. That prevents them from being incorporated into larger systems of educational measurement or school accountability.

This article argues for an approach that overcomes the problems of scope and challenges of scale that have prevented youth exposure to violence from having a more central part in discussions about education policy. We propose a method to measure violence exposure that leverages information available in geo-referenced datasets on schools and community violence. We show how this method is easy to implement and can be adapted to help policy-makers across levels of government answer important questions about the prevalence and con-centration of violence that bears on individual schools and the associated inequal-ities that manifest from those conditions. We believe that our method will prove to be nuanced, flexible, accurate, scalable, and an easy way to inform policy dis-cussions and advance research literatures on these topics.

We use the urban public school systems of Atlanta and Philadelphia to illus-trate our approach. In so doing, we answer several related research questions. How persistent is the problem of exposure to violence for schools in these two cities? Who attends schools where violence exposure appears to be a substantial problem? And last, what are the implications of violence for school performance and accountability policy? Our descriptive findings show that numerous schools in these cities operate in neighborhoods where dozens of violent crimes occur each month, sometimes at a rate of more than one per day. Further, students who come from economically disadvantaged backgrounds and students who are racial minorities are more likely to be exposed to violence in their neighborhoods. We also show that the intensity of violence around a school appears to be associated with a school's academic performance.

The Devastating Effects of Learning in Harm's Way

Prior research has documented powerful relationships between neighborhood characteristics and youth development (Bronfenbrenner 1979; Jencks and Mayer 1990; Kahne and Bailey 1999; Osofsky 1999; Leventhal and Brooks-Gunn 2000; Morales and Guerra 2006). Building on the classic work of Shaw and McKay

(1942), scholars have found strong associations between a child's exposure to community violence and numerous behavioral and cognitive outcomes. Neighborhood violence is related to mental health concerns such as increased depression and anxiety, increased perceptions of danger, and symptoms of post-traumatic stress disorder, even in children who have only witnessed one violent incident (Richters and Martinez 1993b; Aneshensel and Sucoff 1996; Margolin and Gordis 2000; Lyons 1987; Pynoos et al. 1987). Youth in dangerous neighborhoods are more likely to engage in assaultive behavior and to report carrying weapons (Patchin et al. 2006). They also may have parents who adopt more controlling and less warm parenting behaviors, often intended to protect their children, which, unfortunately, can negatively affect child development (Furstenberg et al. 1993; Chase-Lansdale et al. 1997; Hill and Herman-Stahl 2002).

Exposure to violence is also negatively related to numerous student academic outcomes. These include reduced likelihood of graduating (Harding 2009), children having lower self-confidence in their academic abilities (Nettles, Caughy, and O'Campo 2008), worse attendance and behavior at school (Bowen and Bowen 1999; Bryk et al. 2010), and lower test scores and grade point averages (Schwartz and Gorman 2003; Bryk et al. 2010).

Further, teachers have been found to alter their classroom approaches in communities with high rates of violence. Matsumura, Garnier, and Resnick (2010) found that some teachers in such schools were less likely to follow advice from instructional coaches who suggested teaching their lessons more interactively. The teachers feared that those more open-ended approaches could spark conflict and even fights between students. Teachers in such environments who have limited understandings about the impact of violence in students' lives can have more difficulty connecting to their students in the classroom (Dance 2002).

The large body of work on child development and violence exposure helps to expand on the Coleman Report's conclusions about educational inequality and disadvantage by identifying another specific environmental factor—exposure to violence—that can hinder a child's ability to succeed in school. Not only can violence devastate individual children and harm their life prospects, but when such children are concentrated in the same schools, the results are magnified and create huge barriers for children and teachers to overcome. As Coleman et al. (1966) also noted, these kinds of challenges are unequally distributed. Students most likely to suffer the consequences of challenging home or neighborhood environments are from disadvantaged economic backgrounds and are racial minorities.

Problems of Scope and Challenges of Scale

The literature we described above has not played a substantial role in contemporary education policy debates, especially debates that inform discussions of school accountability. Why? We see two reasons and call them problems of scope and challenges of scale.

By *problems of scope*, we mean that learning in harm's way is conceptualized relatively narrowly and in isolation from other important issues. This arises because many individuals who debate or help to formulate education policy conceptualize violence by focusing entirely or almost entirely on violent incidents occurring at school. For example, the No Child Left Behind Act (NCLB) incorporated concerns about violence into its many provisions when it required states to determine which of their schools were "persistently dangerous." Yet a minuscule number of schools across the country were ever identified as such, in part because NCLB gave states much latitude in carrying out the provision and, important for our purposes, focused attention on violent incidents within a school building rather than the larger neighborhood contexts in which schools reside (Hernandez 2007). Further, policies such as the federal School Emergency Response to Violence (SERV) program illustrate the problem of focusing primarily on high-profile violent events and ignoring the less headline-grabbing levels of persistent violence that challenge some schools each and every day. Funds from SERV are available to help school districts to recover from "a violent or traumatic event" (U.S. Department of Education 2014)—a noble objective—but funds cannot be used for more regular supports in schools where neighborhood violence is persistent.

A further problem of scope is that unlike the connections between violence and the success of individual students, the relationship between persistently violent contexts and overall school performance tends to remain unexplored in policy debates. As we just noted, existing research tends to focus on violence occurring at school during school hours (Robers et al. 2014; Johnson 2009; Henry 2009; National Institute of Education 1978) and occasionally that research relates those conditions to violence outside a school (Astor, Benbenishty, and Estrada 2009). However, the relationship between neighborhood violence and school performance is rarely measured. Given how data are collected, it can be difficult, if not impossible, to relate these two concepts. (An exception at the local level is Bryk et al. 2010). For example, the federal government's School Survey on Crime and Safety includes no questions about academic performance (Robers et al. 2014). Other independent surveys conducted by researchers sometimes ask respondents for their opinions about performance, but those surveys lack concrete student outcome measures (Binns and Markow 1999). As a result, the typical and most comprehensive data collection efforts on youth exposure to violence remain disconnected from academic performance at the school level, a topic that otherwise receives much attention. Contrast this, for example, with efforts to measure the number of students who speak languages other than English in the home. Those data do inform accountability policy, through various exemptions from state testing or the administration of tests in languages other than English for these students.

In addition to problems of scope, we also identify *challenges of scale*. The current popular techniques for assessing the degree to which children learn in harm's way tend to focus on particular locales and are not easily scaled up to more communities. Even if policy-makers wanted to make youth exposure to violence a central issue in education policy discussions or regular data reporting, it would be incredibly difficult, using current popular methods, to gather data on an annual basis across the thousands of school districts and schools in the United

States. This is because the two main techniques used in the aforementioned articles we have cited are incredibly expensive, time-consuming, and require large research teams. One popular method is to survey school personnel to gauge violence in schools or to survey children and their families about the violence that children are exposed to outside school. Surveys are expensive to conduct and, as used in these settings, also tend to ask people about their perceptions of violence. This can be limited because, as Coleman et al. (1966) suggested, such perceptions can vary depending on the relative conditions within particular communities. Scaling up the use of survey methods to gauge the degree to which children in all the nation's schools learn in harm's way would be impractical.

A second prevailing technique used to assess learning in harm's way incorporates survey methods, but also augments them with detailed on-the-ground investigations of the neighborhoods in which students live. An example is the landmark study on school improvement from Bryk et al. (2010). These authors studied Chicago elementary schools and found that more neighborhood violence was associated with worse reading scores, math scores, and student attendance. The researchers posited that exposure to violence is likely to undermine "neighborhood cohesion" (p. 174) and, thus, deprive schools of the community supports needed for success. The ability of Bryk et al. to demarcate the neighborhoods where children attended school and then to link those conditions to schools relied upon a time-consuming and careful ground-level assessment that involved their own observations and the input from people in the community. As a result, Bryk et al. developed a nuanced portrait of the neighborhood conditions confronting Chicago elementary school students and then related those conditions to school performance. Scaling up such an effort to assess learning in harm's way for all schools every year would be impossible due to the time and expense involved and the need to recruit high-quality research teams to explore every community.

Fortunately, the growing availability of geo-referenced datasets on education, crime, and community characteristics is making it possible to begin to overcome the problems of scope and the challenges of scale that we have discussed here. Those advances allow researchers and policy-makers, especially in urban areas, to develop regular and more comprehensive assessments of youth exposure to violence and to relate those measures to school operations and performance. The next section describes our method for measuring violence exposure.

Constructing Measures of Violence Exposure

Our approach to measuring student exposure to violence, which overcomes the problems of scope and challenges of scale that we just explored, relies upon leveraging several data sources that are currently available or becoming increasingly available to researchers and policy-makers. These data are education data that capture measures of school characteristics and academic outcomes, administrative data from school districts that demarcate school attendance boundaries, geocoded crime data from law enforcement agencies, and data on community characteristics from the U.S. Census Bureau. We demonstrate our method by focusing on Atlanta and Philadelphia during the 2009–10 school year. Descriptive information about schools in these cities is available and, importantly, their city police departments make available geo-coded datasets that measure crime at the individual incident level. That allows us to capture information about the location, offense category, date, and time of each crime that occurred. We use data from the school districts themselves and from the National Center for Education Statistics (NCES) to identify individual schools in our two cities.

We restrict our sample to traditional public K–12 schools, excluding magnet schools and charter schools. Since we measure exposure to violence in school neighborhoods, it makes sense to focus on schools where attendees live within a defined boundary, as is common in thousands of school districts across the country. Magnet and charter schools often pull children from wider geographic areas, sometimes the entire city, making it difficult to calculate neighborhood violence exposure for students in those schools. However, with our method we are able to employ attendance boundaries of different sizes. Therefore, one could identify the levels of violence in larger, nontraditional attendance boundaries (e.g., for magnet or charter schools) should they be available. Such a method could also explore violence in other geographic spaces, such as violence occurring within a certain distance of these nontraditional schools. Our focus in this article, though, is public schools with defined attendance boundaries.

We generate our measures of schools' proximity to violence by comparing geo-coded school location data to geo-coded crime location data. Using ArcMap, we plot school and crime locations using latitude and longitude coordinates and then project these coordinates into a common geographic coordinate system. We develop two different measures of a school's proximity to violent crimes. Each measure associates a school with a certain number of crimes based on a different definition of proximity.

For one conceptualization of proximity, we calculate a school's proximity to violence using a one-half-mile buffer radius drawn around each school. Scholars studying other policy areas, such as environmental science and public health, commonly use buffer radii, but the approach is absent from studies of school accountability (An and Sturm 2012; Green et al. 2004; Chakraborty and Zandbergen 2007). In education, though, public health researchers have used half-mile buffers around schools to study student obesity. Those buffer zones were designed to capture the number of fast food establishments in proximity to schools (Davis and Carpenter 2009).

The buffer radius is a useful way to capture, in a uniform way, neighborhood context defined as the immediate geographic area around the school. With the school buffer radii drawn and the crime point data plotted on the same coordinate system, we can easily aggregate information on crimes contained within the school's buffer radius. We discuss the aggregation procedure below where we explain how we tally crimes for each school.

Another conceptualization for creating a proximity measure takes advantage of datasets created by the School Attendance Boundary Information System (SABINS) project, and expanded by the U.S. Department of Education through the School Attendance Boundary Survey (SABS) (College of William & Mary and Minnesota Population Center 2011; U.S. Department of Education 2017). These efforts have accumulated shapefiles of school attendance boundaries, which define the geographic area from which a school draws its students. Because schools that serve multiple grades can have different attendance boundary files for each grade level, we chose to use 3rd-, 7th-, and 11th-grade boundaries to incorporate the maximum number of Atlanta and Philadelphia elementary, middle, and high schools into our analysis. As with the buffer zone calculation, we link the attendance boundary information to our crime data, which allows us to calculate the number of crimes within the attendance boundary.

We link the attendance boundaries to schools by matching each boundary's unique identification number to a crosswalk table published by the SABINS database, which in turn links the boundary with school identification numbers assigned by the NCES. Each school is usually associated with a single boundary in a one-to-one relationship, but there are two situations in which the relationship is not one-to-one. First, this can occur when a single school receives children from multiple attendance boundaries uniquely linked to that school (i.e., one-to-many). In this case, we sum up the crime counts from each boundary that serves the school. Second, multiple schools can be served by a single attendance boundary (i.e., many-to-one). In this case, we divide the crime measure by the number of schools served by the boundary, allocating an equal portion of the crimes in the boundary to each school that it serves.

We focus on crimes in Atlanta and Philadelphia that the Federal Bureau of Investigation (FBI) has designated Part I, "violent" offenses that occurred during the 2009–10 school year between the first day of school and the first date of state standardized testing. The "violent" category within Part I comprises homicide, rape, robbery, and aggravated assault, and we consider these crimes for two reasons (FBI 2013). The first reason is theoretical. The literature we use to develop our hypothesis focuses on how exposure to violent incidents influences children (Bowen and Bowen 1999; Henrich et al. 2004; Ozer 2005; Grogger 1997; Sharkey 2010; Burdick-Will 2013; Carrell and Hoekstra 2008; Harding 2009; Nettles, Caughy, and O'Campo 2008).

The second reason is methodological. Measurement issues arise in the official reporting of all crimes, which could lead some incidents to be underreported or overreported given variation in victims' willingness to report and the administrative incentives to which police officers respond as they characterize incidents in official documents (Wilson 1989). Police are not notified of all incidents, and even when authorities respond to crimes there may be definitional ambiguities that make situations difficult to classify. However, previous work has found official crime reporting systems to be more accurate for the most severe offenses (Gove, Hughes, and Geerken 1985).

We aggregate information on these violent crimes within each school's buffer radius and attendance boundary. To do this, we use U.S. Census Bureau block data for each city. We sum the population of all the blocks that have their center in each buffer radius or attendance boundary to generate a population measure for that area. For each buffer radius and attendance boundary, we use a simple sum of crimes occurring within the buffer radius or attendance boundary for each school, which we then weight by population. The following equation summarizes our approach:

$$CC_i = \frac{H_i + R_i + RWF_i + RNF_i + AAWF_i + AANF_i}{POP_i / 100}.$$

In this calculation, i denotes the polygon of interest associated with a school (either the buffer radius or attendance boundary). The formula produces a crime count (CC), which includes the count of homicides (H), rapes (R), robberies with firearm (RWF), robberies with no firearm (RNF), aggravated assaults with firearm (AAWF), and aggravated assaults with no firearm (AANF). That count is weighted by population (POP) measured in hundreds. For the attendance boundary measure in particular, transforming this variable into a "per capita" metric by weighting by population is essential to produce a meaningful measure. Since the buffer radii are of a uniform size, our per capita violent crime count measure is highly correlated with a raw count of violent crimes ($r = .78$ for Atlanta; $r = .84$ for Philadelphia). However, weighting by population makes a substantive difference in the attendance boundary measure; within the school attendance boundaries the raw count of violent crimes is not highly correlated with the per capita measure ($r = .18$ in Atlanta; $r = .13$ in Philadelphia). We use the weighted measures in most of our analyses below, but sometimes we report the raw count of violent crimes within the buffer radius (not weighted by population) to more clearly convey the actual number of incidents captured by the measure.

Figure 1 provides a visual example and sample calculations of our measures of school proximity to violence, depicting the buffer radius and attendance boundary for Herndon Elementary School in Atlanta. The circle in each panel of the figure traces the half-mile buffer radius around the school and the other line within each panel shows the school's attendance boundary. Each dot represents a crime that occurred during the 2009–10 school year before the first day of state standardized testing. The first row of Figure 1 presents a visual of all violent crimes and the adjacent table of numbers reports the two measures of violence exposure for Herndon that we calculated based on the buffer radius and attendance boundary. The remaining plots describe the presence of each type of violent crime captured in our overall measures of violence exposure, which demonstrates the versatility of our approach.

While the buffer radius and attendance boundary plots in Figure 1 cover similar areas, they are not identical. For some crimes, the polygons will capture the same number of incidents. Herndon's counts for rape and homicide are the same for the buffer radius and attendance boundary measures as each geographic area contains zero incidents of rape and one homicide. For other types of incidents, there are crimes within the buffer radius that are outside the attendance boundary, and vice versa. For example, as Figure 1 shows, Herndon had thirteen robberies without a firearm within the buffer radius and nineteen within the attendance boundary.

FIGURE 1
Exposure to Violent Crimes for Herndon Elementary School (Atlanta)

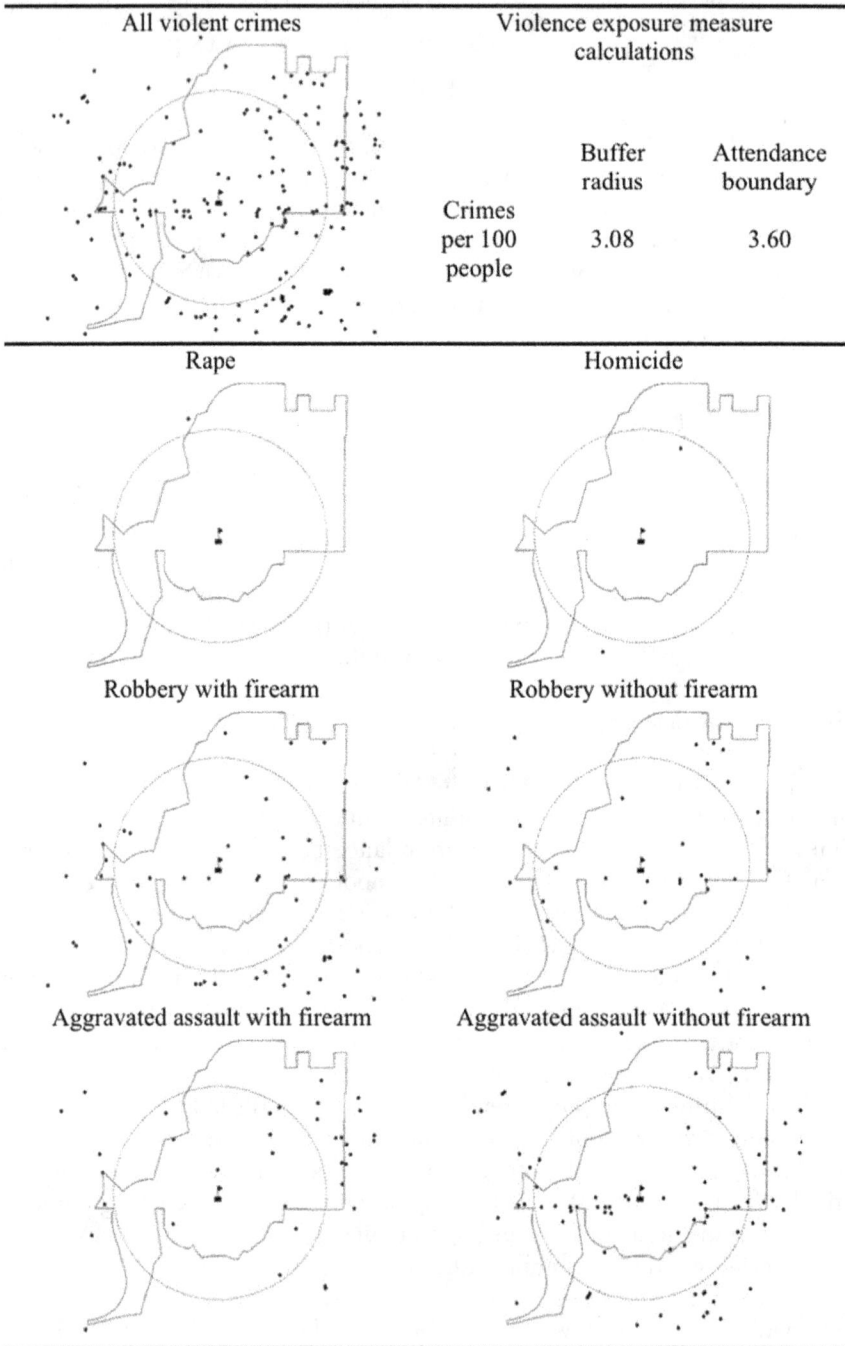

NOTE: Multiple crimes reported at the same address appear as a single dot but are analyzed as separate crimes in the statistical analysis.

Violence Exposure in Atlanta and Philadelphia

What does learning in harm's way look like in Atlanta and Philadelphia? In this section, we answer that question by using our buffer radius and attendance boundary measures to report three sets of findings. First are univariate results that describe levels of neighborhood violence for all schools in our sample. Second, we explore how other characteristics of students and neighborhoods relate to our measures of violence exposure. Third, we report bivariate and multivariate results, showing the association between our different measures of violence and school performance. Table 1 presents descriptive statistics for all variables, including our violence exposure measures, indicators of neighborhood poverty and student race, and other school-level variables for which we control in our multivariate models.

We begin by discussing the results within Figure 2, which plots a simple unweighted count of violent crimes near each school in our sample. Each bar represents the number of violent crimes within the half-mile buffer radius for an individual school. The results indicate extremely high variability across schools in each city. Some schools are in close proximity to very few of the most violent crimes, whereas others exhibit strikingly high levels of exposure to violence. For example, in Atlanta, three schools had zero violent crimes occurring within a half mile radius of the school, whereas one school had more than 100 such incidents. In Philadelphia, one school had three violent crimes occurring nearby, and another had 408. The striking variability in this simple measure reflects the dramatically different conditions under which children attend school. Even within the same city school district, significant inequalities are clearly evident.

The results in Figure 2 also reflect the failure of current policies to account for the presence of violence in and around the nation's schools (Klein 2007). For example, when NCLB was the law of the land it allowed parents to transfer their children out of schools deemed "persistently dangerous," a designation we described earlier. Despite the high levels of neighborhood violence around schools that Figure 2 describes, data reported by the Georgia and Pennsylvania state education agencies for 2009–10 show that the NCLB designation only identified seventeen schools in Philadelphia in our sample as persistently dangerous and not a single school in Atlanta as persistently dangerous.

Next we illuminate the characteristics of students who attend schools with higher proximity to violence by presenting bivariate relationships between our violence exposure measure and two other characteristics of schools: neighborhood poverty and student racial composition. This part of the analysis further explores one of Coleman et al.'s (1966) major findings about educational inequity. Students who are exposed to violence struggle to succeed in school, and Coleman et al.'s findings imply that such exposure is likely to be skewed more toward disadvantaged students.

As our measure of neighborhood poverty, we use the 2010 American Community Survey 5-year estimates of the percent of families with related children under 18 years whose income in the past 12 months is below the poverty

TABLE 1
Descriptive Statistics in the Analytical Sample

	Mean	SD	Min	Max
Atlanta variables				
% proficient or better in reading	86.19	7.85	67.60	100.00
% proficient or better in math	69.50	13.28	45.70	98.20
Buffer radius violence exposure	1.13	0.80	0.00	3.08
Attendance boundary violence exposure	1.20	0.69	0.09	3.60
% nonwhite students	91.75	20.73	23.82	100.00
% students with meal subsidy	83.82	25.55	8.03	99.52
Pupil to teacher ratio	13.06	1.77	8.78	18.03
Teacher experience, average years	10.73	2.41	5.58	16.37
% neighborhood poverty	35.59	19.21	1.40	77.20
Elementary school indicator variable	0.71	0.46	0.00	1.00
High school indicator variable	0.11	0.32	0.00	1.00
Philadelphia variables				
% proficient or better in reading	46.94	17.80	6.30	85.40
% proficient or better in math	54.78	21.48	2.20	92.20
Buffer radius violence exposure	0.84	0.42	0.05	1.82
Attendance boundary violence exposure	0.84	0.45	0.06	2.61
% nonwhite students	88.19	18.92	15.30	100.00
% students with meal subsidy	85.84	18.83	22.11	99.83
Pupil to teacher ratio	14.00	2.05	7.92	20.21
Average teacher degree attainment	4.40	0.10	4.13	4.79
% neighborhood poverty	32.12	17.82	1.40	85.40
Elementary school indicator variable	0.77	0.42	0.00	1.00
High school indicator variable	0.13	0.34	0.00	1.00

NOTE: N = 72 for Atlanta variables; N = 211 for Philadelphia variables. Philadelphia teacher degree attainment coded as 4 = bachelor's degree, 5 = master's degree, and 6 = PhD.

level. We find that our measures of violence exposure, encompassing incidents in both school attendance boundaries and half-mile buffers, are strongly positively correlated with prevalence of neighborhood poverty in both cities. The scatterplots in Figure 3 illustrate these relationships. Across Atlanta and Philadelphia, the correlations between neighborhood poverty and violence exposure are always positive and range from .67 to .73. Furthermore, schools with the highest levels of proximity to violence tended to have significantly higher neighborhood poverty rates when compared with the average for all schools in the city. Schools in the top quartile of our attendance boundary violence exposure measure in Philadelphia had an average neighborhood poverty rate of 47.5 percent. In comparison, the average for all schools in the city was 32.1 percent. Similarly, in Atlanta, the schools most proximate to violence had an average neighborhood poverty rate of 50.9 percent, compared with a citywide average of just 35.6 percent.

FIGURE 2
Violent Crimes within a Half Mile of Schools in Atlanta and Philadelphia

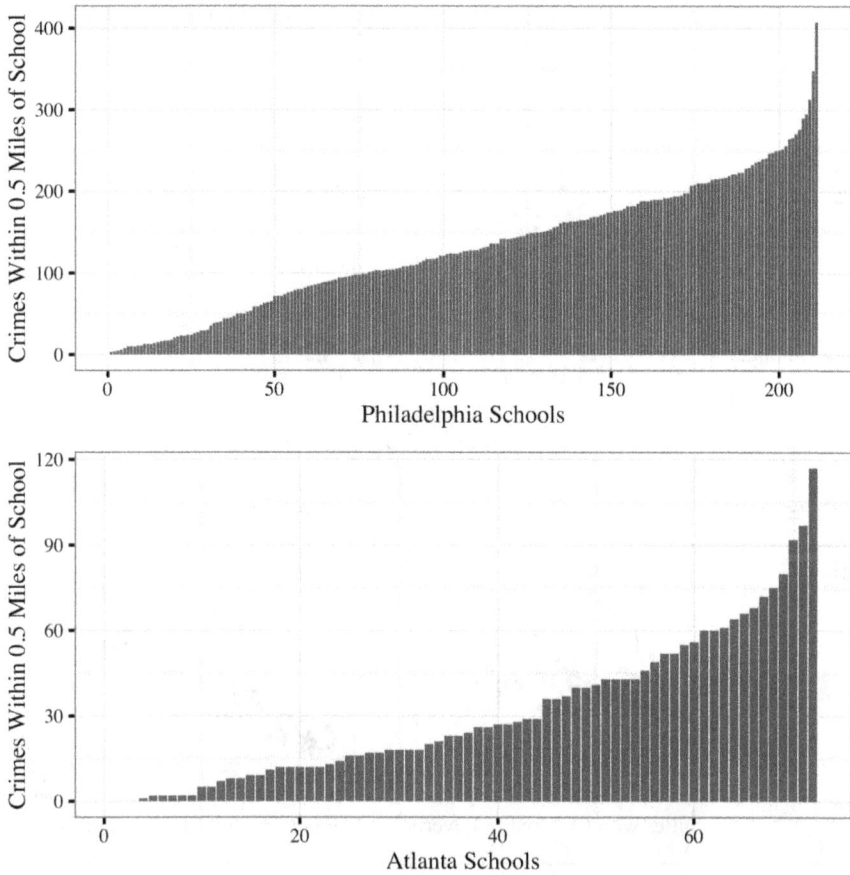

NOTE: Each bar represents an individual school. Counts for each school are not weighted by neighborhood population in these plots. N: Atlanta = 72 and Philadelphia = 211.

Next, we examine the relationship between our violence exposure measures and the percent of students of color in schools. We again find positive correlations between our violence exposure measures and the percent students of color, as the scatterplots in Figure 4 demonstrate. However, these relationships are not as strong as those between violence exposure and neighborhood poverty. This is due partly to less variability in the race measure given that a high number of schools, especially in Atlanta, clustered near 100 percent students of color. Still, the results show positive correlations ranging from .48 to .56 across both cities.

Taken together, Figures 3 and 4 suggest that school proximity to neighborhood violence tends to be disproportionately higher for students of color and students living in poorer neighborhoods. The challenges perpetuated by the violent

FIGURE 3
Relationship between Violence Exposure and Neighborhood Poverty

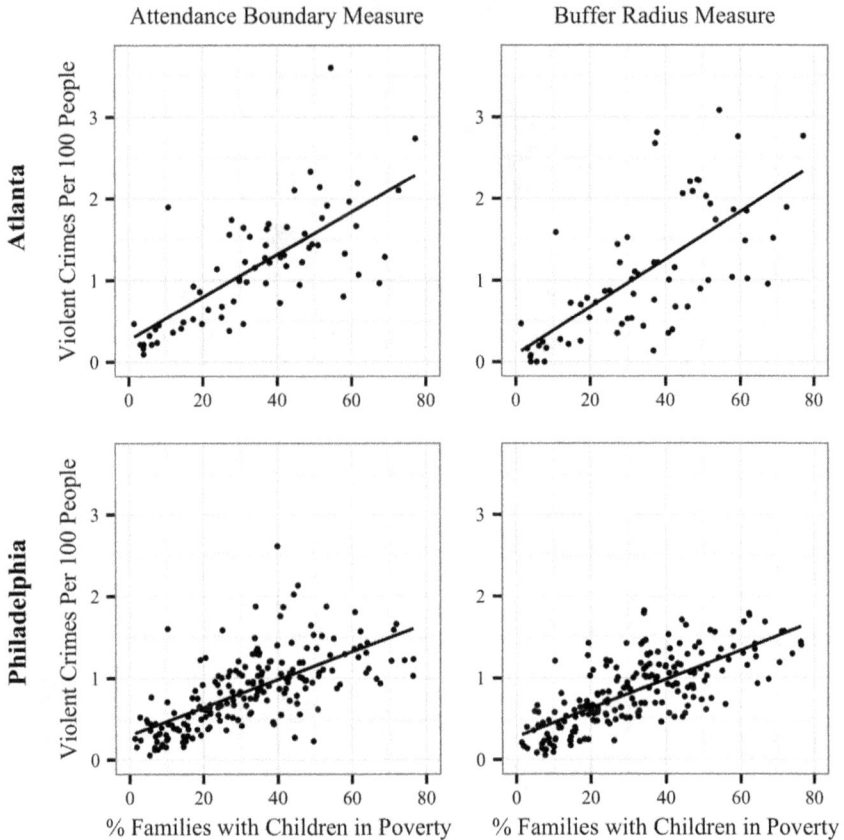

NOTE: N = 72 for Atlanta; N = 211 for Philadelphia.

contexts that we identify are layered on top of other dimensions of inequality, which Coleman et al. (1966) and many others since have documented. Just as students of color and economically disadvantaged students tend to find themselves in schools that have worse conditions, they also tend to attend schools that are disproportionately located in neighborhoods with persistently high levels of violence.

Next, we examine the relationship between violence exposure and school performance. Our first set of results appear in Figure 5, which includes scatterplots that illustrate the relationship between our violence exposure measures and academic performance metrics in both cities. Across all subjects and both cities, every correlation is negative. Despite that overall pattern, the plots also show that how one defines the neighborhood around the school affects the relationship between violence exposure and school performance. In Atlanta, the correlation

FIGURE 4
Relationship between Violence Exposure and Racial Composition of Schools

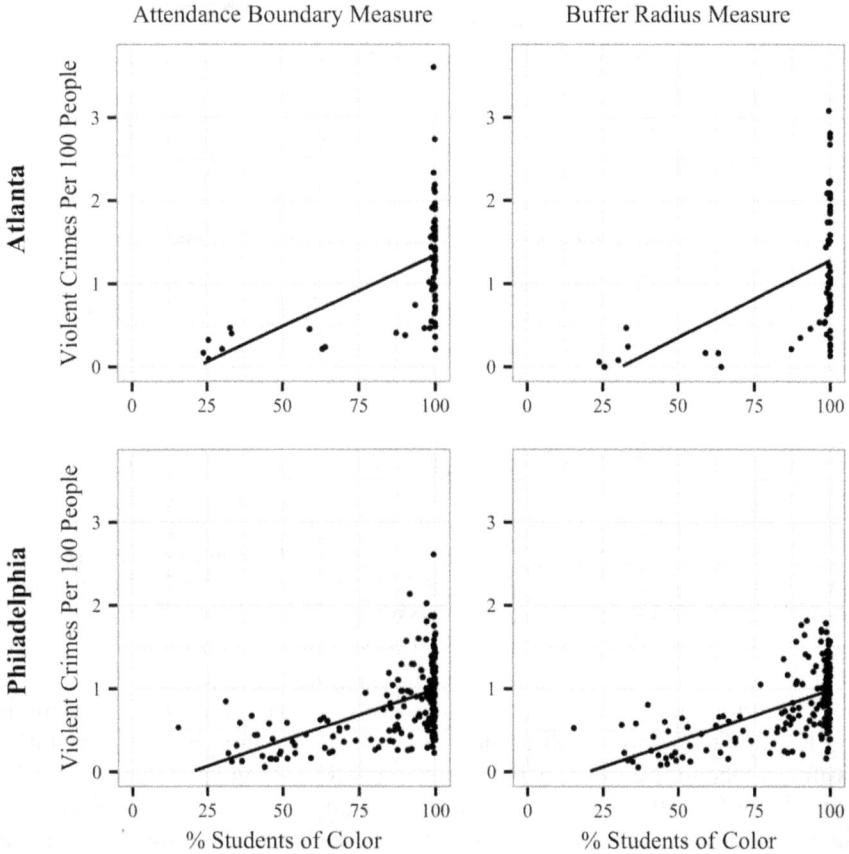

NOTE: N = 72 for Atlanta; N = 211 for Philadelphia.

between exposure to violence and proficiency percentages in reading and math is stronger for the attendance boundary exposure measure (–.51 for reading and –.63 for math) than for the buffer radius exposure measure (–.41 for reading and –.50 for math). In Philadelphia, however, the pattern is reversed; a stronger correlation exists between exposure and performance when the buffer radius measure is used (–.51 for reading and –.39 for math) compared to the attendance boundary measure (–.44 for reading and –.31 for math), a difference we discuss further below.

In addition, across both cities the strength of the correlation between violence exposure and test performance varies by academic subject. In Atlanta, violence exposure is more negatively correlated with math performance than other subjects. In contrast, in Philadelphia violence exposure is more negatively correlated with reading performance than other school subjects.

FIGURE 5
Relationship between Violence Exposure and School Performance Measures

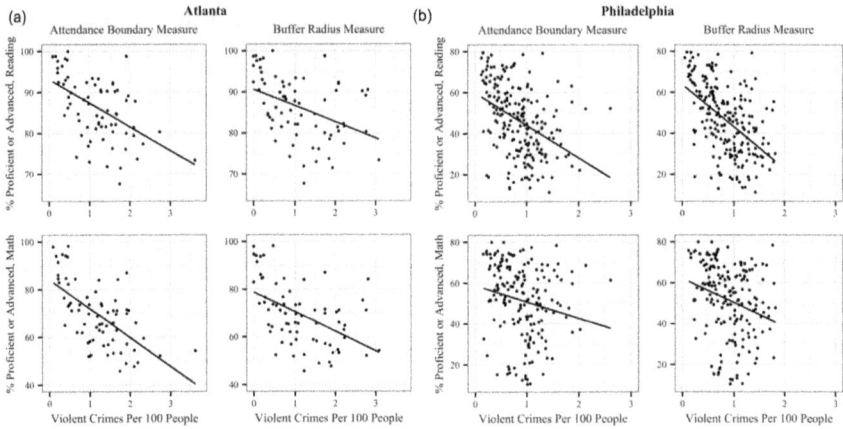

NOTE: N = 72 for Atlanta; N = 211 for Philadelphia.

A summary of key results from our multiple regression analyses appears in Table 2.[1] In each city, we examine the percent of students meeting or exceeding expectations on state standardized assessments in math and reading as our dependent variables. For each of the four school performance dependent variables (math and reading in Atlanta and Philadelphia), we estimate three models using the attendance boundary violence exposure measure and three models using the buffer radius. In all models, we control for the pupil-teacher ratio, a measure of teacher experience, the percentage of nonwhite students, and indicator variables of whether the school is an elementary or high school (middle school is the omitted category). To control for student socioeconomic status, we include multiple combinations of control variables in different models: (1) only the percentage of students with a meal subsidy; (2) only the percentage neighborhood poverty variable as described above; and (3) both the meal subsidy and neighborhood poverty measures, which correspond to the first, second, and third result for each group of three coefficients appearing in Table 2.

As Table 2 shows, the violence exposure measures are nearly always negatively signed, as predicted, even when we control for student and school characteristics. This is true in twenty-three of our twenty-four models. Further, eleven of the twenty-four coefficients that measure violence exposure are statistically significant at the $p < .10$ level or stronger. Interesting patterns also emerge when one considers different ways to measure violence and its relationship to performance across academic subjects.

How one defines the neighborhood around a school sometimes appears to influence the strength of the statistical relationship between violence exposure and school performance. Out of the twelve buffer models, zero of six in Atlanta and four of six in Philadelphia produce statistically significant results for the

TABLE 2
Regression Coefficients for Attendance Boundary Violence and Buffer Radius Violence
Measures for Atlanta and Philadelphia Models

	Attendance Boundary Models			Buffer Radius Models		
Atlanta—Math	1	2	3	4	5	6
Attendance boundary violence	−4.718°°	−5.098°°	−3.443			
	(−1.837)	(−2.307)	(−2.148)			
Buffer radius violence				−1.533	−0.755	0.242
				(−1.544)	(−1.924)	(−1.743)
Atlanta—Reading	7	8	9	10	11	12
Attendance boundary violence	−2.341°	−3.609°°	−2.593°			
	(−1.242)	(−1.546)	(−1.465)			
Buffer radius violence				−1.007	−1.479	−0.876
				(−1.021)	(−1.283)	(−1.189)
Philadelphia—Math	13	14	15	16	17	18
Attendance boundary violence	−5.092°	−1.614	−2.019			
	(−2.73)	(−2.99)	(−3.048)			
Buffer radius violence				−8.088°°°	−4.471	−5.076
				(−2.995)	(−3.428)	(−3.499)
Philadelphia—Reading	19	20	21	22	23	24
Attendance boundary violence	−8.043°°°	−3.987	−4.204			
	(−2.407)	(−2.602)	(−2.655)			
Buffer radius violence				−11.032°°°	−6.642°°	−7.001°°
				(−2.625)	(−2.974)	(−3.039)

NOTE: Regression model coefficients and standard errors in parentheses are reported. These results are excerpts, omitting control variables, from full regression models examining the relationship between neighborhood violence and school performance. All models contain controls for percent of minority students, pupil-teacher ratio, teacher experience, and indicator variables for whether a school is an elementary school or a high school (middle school is the omitted category). Within each group of three models reported here, the first contains an additional control for percentage of students on meal subsidy, the second contains an additional control for the percentage of people in the neighborhood in poverty, and the third contains both the meal subsidy and neighborhood poverty controls. Full results for all models are available from the authors.
°$p < .10.$ °°$p < .05.$ °°°$p < .01.$

violence exposure measures; for the attendance boundary models, statistically significant results accompany five of six in Atlanta and two of six in Philadelphia. In general, the boundary measure appears to be a more consistent predictor of school performance. One reason for this could be because it can better capture violence in the neighborhoods where children who attend particular schools live, and by extension can accurately account for peer effects on achievement, a finding that would be consistent with Coleman et al.'s (1966) conclusions. Still, in Philadelphia, the results are similar whether one considers buffer radii or attendance buffers; whereas for Atlanta, the definition of proximity matters substantially. This result could be due to the higher population density in Philadelphia, which contrasts with Atlanta's less dense patterns of development. Higher density in Philadelphia could, in practice, end up producing school attendance boundaries that more closely follow the buffer radii. This variation across cities underscores one of the virtues of considering proximity measured by both buffers and boundaries, which are easy results to produce given our method.

In addition to statistical significance, we also note that the relationships between violence and school performance in Table 2 are substantively important. Consider these illustrative examples. In Atlanta, a 1 standard deviation increase in the violence measure in model 1 corresponds to a 0.24 standard deviation decrease in math performance. A similar substantive relationship exists in model 7, where the same increase in violence is associated with a 0.20 standard deviation decrease in math performance. In Philadelphia, the results from model 13 show that a standard deviation increase in the violence measure is associated with a 0.11 standard deviation decrease in math performance. In model 19, a standard deviation increase in the violence measure in Philadelphia corresponds to a 0.20 standard deviation decrease in math performance.

Discussion and Policy Implications

Our analysis extends important insights of Coleman et al. (1966) about inequality and educational opportunity of the nation's children. Those opportunities vary depending not only on the conditions that children experience in school but also on the conditions in the neighborhoods where their schools reside. Our research contributes to the long body of work that has explored those topics by offering a new method for measuring exposure to violence and illustrating how that method can enhance understandings of contemporary inequalities confronting the nation's schoolchildren.

We recognize that no measure of any social science concept is perfect, and even though we find several virtues in our measures of violence exposure, a few limitations of those measures are worth mentioning for researchers applying them in future work. To overcome the challenges of scale that we described earlier, our measure sacrifices some methodological precision that could come with an analysis that takes advantage of specific local knowledge (Bryk et al. 2010). Both attendance boundaries and buffer radii are only approximations of neighborhoods around schools. Local experts may have different understandings of neighborhoods than those that our two measures define. Still, by providing a path forward for overcoming challenges of scale, our approach does increase the chance for violence exposure to become a more salient topic in state and national policy debates as others employ our methods to explore a broader range of communities.

Additionally, our attempt to overcome challenges of scale leads us to rely on police reports of violent incidents. These reports can only approximate the true level of exposure to violence that children experience. Like any administrative dataset, police incident reports reflect biases and incentives of agents recording information and may be incomplete. Our focus on the most violent crimes does help to attenuate those potential problems, although it does not eliminate them. Further, children may experience violent incidents in neighborhoods other than those where they attend school. Our measures would not pick up those additional incidents, whereas survey methods might. The trade-off, of course, is that survey methods are expensive to implement and difficult to scale up across many communities.

A final limitation to note emerges from our use of Census Bureau block data to help in our calculation of violence exposure by weighting our measures by population, and in our use of those data to help us design a control measure for neighborhood poverty. As time marches on past years in which the decennial census is conducted, researchers constructing these measures may sacrifice some precision as not all census geographies (i.e., census blocks) are available in intervening years. Additional methods of estimation will be needed to help ensure that subsequent measures of buffer or boundary populations and poverty rates are keeping up with population changes. One reason we chose the 2009–10 school year for our analysis was to eliminate the need to address that additional issue and to focus, instead, on demonstrating proof of concept for our method and two measures of violence exposure.

Before discussing additional conclusions, it is also worth addressing the possible presence of errors in our school performance data for Atlanta, given the well-known cheating scandal in that district during the academic year that we studied (Blinder 2015). The decision of district and school officials to alter answers on state exams, if affecting our results, likely would attenuate rather than accentuate the relationship between violence and school performance. Schools challenged by excessive neighborhood violence would have felt particular pressure to perform and, perhaps, to alter test scores (Meier and O'Toole 2006). The fact that we still found statistically and substantively significant relationships between violence and student performance in Atlanta could mean that efforts to alter student test scores cannot completely overcome the effects of violence. Alternatively, if the cheating were as widespread as some have suggested, the overall effect could have been simply to increase all scores by some amount (e.g., a shifting upward of school means), which could still enable us to observe the relationships that we observed.

Moving beyond our analysis, we believe that our method for estimating violence exposure helps to overcome the problems of scope and challenges of scale that we described. In so doing, the method provides a launching pad for other researchers interested in violence, school performance, and accountability. Others could extend our work, for example, by applying the method in other cities and for other years, or across multiple years.

Future researchers also might examine different approaches to weighting violent incidents that occur in proximity to schools. In analyses not reported in this article, we began to experiment with weighting violent crimes by their severity.[2] Violent crimes that are considered more severe in federal sentencing guidelines were weighted more heavily than those that were not. Additional use of weights might consider whether violent crimes occurring more closely to state testing dates have a stronger relationship to achievement than crimes occurring many months earlier. Recall that our analysis weights all crimes equally, but there may be reasons to try a different approach.

In communities where they are available, it also would be interesting to examine additional school-level administrative data that might show how schools react when they operate in communities with high levels of violent crime. Records might be able to show things like the number of lockdown drills, the level of school resources devoted to protecting the school from violence in the neighborhood, and the frequency with which students seek help from school personnel as they cope with the challenges of living amid neighborhood violence. The results could show the added resource burden that schools face as they spend money and devote personnel to address these pressing student needs.

In closing, we consider important policy implications that flow from our work. A first virtue of our approach from a policy perspective is that our measures of violence exposure are scalable, easily replicable at low cost, make transparent assumptions, and, perhaps most importantly, allow for comprehensive considerations of the violent environments in which schools operate. Although knowledge about violence within schools is certainly essential to help improve learning opportunities for children, alone it provides a very limited perspective. Given the growing availability of public, geo-referenced data on urban crime, generating high-quality measures of school proximity to neighborhood violence is becoming increasingly feasible.

Second, our work highlights the value of incorporating more nuanced interventions for school improvement into accountability frameworks. Current policies tend to rate schools based on standardized test results and prescribe remedies for schools deemed not making progress. To date, these policies have not accounted for neighborhood violence when passing judgments on schools. If high levels of neighborhood violence are undercutting student achievement, then accountability policies that ignore those conditions, as with firing the school's principal or staff or changing academic programs, are unlikely to solve the problem. Knowing that high concentrations of violence exist around schools should move policy-makers to consider a variety of interventions that attend to the consequences of violence exposure, specifically.

Last, perhaps a relatively basic, but nevertheless important, policy implication of our work emerges from the sobering school-level portraits that appear in our descriptive plots in Figure 2. Those results reveal that *every day hundreds of* children in Atlanta and Philadelphia attend school in neighborhoods with alarmingly high levels of violent crime. We suspect that one could produce similar plots by examining other cities. This is nothing short of a national tragedy. Federal, state, and local leaders and others interested in equality of educational opportunity and school accountability policy should take the reality of persistent neighborhood violence more seriously as they craft their proposals. Doing so will help schools to better meet the academic and mental health needs of children who struggle as they try to learn in harm's way.

Notes

1. Full results are available from the authors.
2. Available from authors upon request.

References

An, Ruopeng, and Roland Sturm. 2012. School and residential neighborhood food environment and diet among California youth. *American Journal of Preventive Medicine* 42:129–35.

Aneshensel, Carol S., and Clea A. Sucoff. 1996. The neighborhood context of adolescent mental health. *Journal of Health and Social Behavior* 37:293–310.

Astor, Ron Avi, Rami Benbenishty, and Jose Nuñez Estrada. 2009. School violence and theoretically atypical schools: The principal's centrality in orchestrating safe schools. *American Educational Research Journal* 64:423–61.

Bell, Carl C., and Esther J. Jenkins. 1993. Community violence and children on Chicago's South Side. *Psychiatry* 56:46–54.

Bieler, Sam, and Nancy La Vigne. 2014. *Close-range gunfire around DC schools*. Washington, DC: Urban Institute.

Binns, Katherine, and Dana Markow. 1999. *The Metropolitan Life survey of the American teacher, 1999: Violence in America's public schools—five years later*. New York: Metropolitan Life Insurance Company.

Blinder, Alan. 1 April 2015. Atlanta educators convicted in school cheating scandal. *New York Times*.

Bowen, Natasha K., and Gary L. Bowen. 1999. Effects of crime and violence in neighborhoods and schools on the school behavior and performance of adolescents. *Journal of Adolescent Research* 14:319–42.

Bronfenbrenner, Urie. 1979. *The ecology of human development: Experiments by nature and design*. Cambridge, MA: Harvard University Press.

Bryk, Anthony S., Penny Bender Sebring, Elaine Allensworth, Stuart Luppescu, and John Q. Easton. 2010. *Organizing schools for improvement: Lessons from Chicago*. Chicago, IL: University of Chicago Press.

Burdick-Will, Julia. 2013. School violent crime and academic achievement in Chicago. *Sociology of Education* 86:343–61.

Carrell, Scott E., and Mark L. Hoekstra. 2008. Externalities in the classroom: How children exposed to domestic violence affect everyone's kids. National Bureau of Economic Research Working Paper #14246, Cambridge, MA.

Chakraborty, Jayajit, and Paul A. Zandbergen. 2007. Children at risk: Measuring racial/ethnic disparities in potential exposure to air pollution at school and home. *Journal of Epidemiology & Community Health* 61:1074–79.

Chase-Lansdale, P. Lindsay, Rachel A. Gordon, Jeanne Brooks-Gunn, and Pamela K. Klebanov. 1997. Neighborhood and family influences on the intellectual and behavioral competence of preschool and early school-age children. In *Neighborhood poverty*, vol. 1, eds. J. Brooks-Gunn, G. J. Duncan, and J. L. Aber, 79–118. New York, NY: Russell Sage Foundation.

Coleman, James S., Ernest Q. Campbell, Carol J. Hobson, James McPartland, Alexander M. Mood, Frederic D. Weinfeld, and Robert L. York. 1966. *Equality of educational opportunity*. Washington, DC: National Center for Education Statistics.

College of William & Mary and the Minnesota Population Center. 2011. School Attendance Boundary Information System (SABINS): Version 1.0. Minneapolis, MN: University of Minnesota.

Dance, Lory Janelle. 2002. *Tough fronts: The impact of street culture on schooling*. New York, NY: Routledge-Falmer.

Davis, Brennan, and Christopher Carpenter. 2009. Proximity of fast-food restaurants to schools and adolescent obesity. *American Journal of Public Health* 99 (3): 505–10.

Federal Bureau of Investigation. 2013. *Crime in the U.S. 2012*. Available from http://www.fbi.gov/about-us/cjis/ucr/crime-in-the-u.s/2012/crime-in-the-u.s.-2012.

Furstenberg, Frank F., Alisa Belzer, Colleen Davis, Judith A. Levine, Kristine Morrow, and Mary Washington. 1993. How families manage risk and opportunity in dangerous neighborhoods. In *Sociology and the public agenda*, ed. William Julius Wilson, 231–58. Newbury Park, CA: Sage Publications.

Gove, Walter R., Michael Hughes, and Michael Geerken. 1985. Are uniform crime reports a valid indicator of the index crimes? An affirmative answer with minor qualifications. *Criminology* 23:451–502.

Green, Rochelle S., Svetlana Smorodinsky, Janice J. Kim, Robert McLaughlin, and Bart Ostro. 2004. Proximity of California public schools to busy roads. *Environmental Health Perspectives* 112:61–66.

Grogger, Jeff. 1997. Local violence, educational attainment, and teacher pay. National Bureau of Economic Research Working Paper #6003, Cambridge, MA.

Harding, David J. 2009. Collateral consequences of violence in disadvantaged neighborhoods. *Social Forces* 88:757–84.

Henrich, Christopher C., Mary Schwab-Stone, Kostas Fanti, Stephanie M. Jones, and Vladislav Ruchkin. 2004. The association of community violence exposure with middle school achievement: A prospective study. *Journal of Applied Developmental Psychology* 25:327–48.

Henry, Stuart. 2009. School violence beyond Columbine: A complex problem in need of an interdisciplinary analysis. *American Behavioral Scientist* 52:1246–65.

Hernandez, Nelson. 18 November 2007. "No Child" data on violence skewed. *Washington Post*.

Hill, Nancy E., and Mindy A. Herman-Stahl. 2002. Neighborhood safety and social involvement: Associations with parenting behaviors and depressive symptoms among African-American and Euro-American mothers. *Journal of Family Psychology* 16 (2): 209–19.

Jencks, Christopher, and Susan E. Mayer. 1990. The social consequences of growing up in a poor neighborhood. In *Inner-city poverty in the United States*, eds. L. E. Lynn and M. F. H. McGeary, 111–86. Washington, DC: National Academy Press.

Johnson, Sarah Lindstrom. 2009. Improving the school environment to reduce school violence: A review of the literature. *Journal of School Health* 79:451–65.

Kahne, Joseph, and Kim Bailey. 1999. The role of social capital in youth development: The case of "I Have a Dream" programs. *Educational Evaluation and Policy Analysis* 21:321–43.

Klein, Alyson. 20 June 2007. Panel: "Persistently dangerous" tag for schools needs to be reworked. *Education Week*. Available from http://www.edweek.org/ew/articles/2007/06/20/42safety.h26.html.

Leventhal, Tama, and Jeanne Brooks-Gunn. 2000. The neighborhoods they live in: The effects of neighborhood residence on child and adolescent outcomes. *Psychological Bulletin* 126:309–37.

Lyons, Judith A. 1987. Post-traumatic stress disorder in children and adolescents: A review of the literature. *Journal of Developmental and Behavioral Pediatrics* 8:349–56.

Margolin, Gayla, and Elana B. Gordis. 2000. The effects of family and community violence on children. *Annual Review of Psychology* 51:445–79.

Matsumura, Lindsay Clare, Helen E. Garnier, and Lauren B. Resnick. 2010. Implementing literacy coaching: The role of school social resources. *Educational Evaluation and Policy Analysis* 32:249–72.

Meier, Kenneth J., and Laurence J. O'Toole. 2006. *Bureaucracy in a democratic state: A governance perspective*. Baltimore, MD: Johns Hopkins University Press.

Morales, Julie R., and Nancy G. Guerra. 2006. Effects of multiple context and cumulative stress on urban children's adjustment in elementary school. *Child Development* 77:907–23.

National Institute of Education. 1978. *Violent schools-safe schools*, vol. I. Washington, DC: U.S. Government Printing Office.

Nettles, Saundra Murray, Margaret O'Brien Caughy, and Patricia J. O'Campo. 2008. School adjustment in the early grades: Toward an integrated model of neighborhood, parental, and child processes. *Review of Educational Research* 78:3–32.

Osofsky, Joy D. 1999. The impact of violence on children. *The Future of Children* 9:33–49.

Ozer, Emily J. 2005. The impact of violence on urban adolescents: Longitudinal effects of perceived school connection and family support. *Journal of Adolescent Research* 20:167–92.

Patchin, Justin W., Beth M. Huebner, John D. McCluskey, Sean P. Varano, and Timothy S. Bynum. 2006. Exposure to community violence and childhood delinquency. *Crime & Delinquency* 52:307–32.

Peralta, Eyder. 7 March 2013. Newtown, Conn. students are granted a waiver on exams. National Public Radio. Available from http://www.npr.org/sections/thetwo-way/2013/03/07/173726337/newtown-conn-students-are-granted-a-waiver-on-exams.

Pynoos, Robert S., Calvin Frederick, Kathi Nader, William Arroyo, Alan Steinberg, Spencer Eth, Francisco Nunez, and Lynn Fairbanks. 1987. Life threat and posttraumatic stress in school-age children. *Archive of General Psychiatry* 44:1057–63.

Richters, John E., and Pedro Martinez. 1993a. The NIMH community violence project: I. Children as victims of and witnesses to violence. *Psychiatry* 56:7–21.

Richters, John E., and Pedro Martinez. 1993b. The NIMH community violence project: II. Children's distress symptoms associated with violence exposure. *Psychiatry* 56:22–35.

Robers, Simone, Jana Kemp, Amy Rathbun, and Rachel E. Morgan. 2014. *Indicators of school crime and safety: 2013*. Washington, DC: U.S. Department of Education and U.S. Department of Justice.

Schwartz, David, and Andrea Hopmeyer Gorman. 2003. Community violence exposure and children's academic functioning. *Journal of Educational Psychology* 95:163–73.

Sharkey, Patrick. 2010. The acute effect of local homicides on children's cognitive performance. *Proceedings of the National Academy of Sciences* 107:11733–38.

Shaw, Clifford Robe, and Henry Donald McKay. 1942. *Juvenile delinquency and urban areas*. Chicago, IL: University of Chicago Press.

Stein, Bradley D., Lisa H. Jaycox, Sheryl Kataoka, Hilary J. Rhodes, and Katherine D. Vestal. 2003. Prevalence of child and adolescent exposure to community violence. *Clinical Child and Family Psychology Review* 6:247–64.

U.S. Department of Education. 2014. Project School Emergency Response to Violence (SERV) frequently asked questions. Available from http://www2.ed.gov/programs/dvppserv/faq.html.

U.S. Department of Education. 2017. School attendance boundary survey. Available from https://nces.ed.gov/programs/sabs/default.aspx.

Wilson, James Q. 1989. *Bureaucracy: What government agencies do and why they do it*. New York, NY: Basic Books.

Equalizers or Enablers of Inequality? A Counterfactual Analysis of Racial and Residential Test Score Gaps in Year-Round and Nine-Month Schools

By
ODIS JOHNSON JR.
and
MICHAEL WAGNER

Persistent racial/ethnic and residential disparities in test scores suggest schools fail to serve as society's great equalizers. Yet few studies have explored whether policies that adjust children's time in school are effective in reducing test-score inequality. We use ECLS-K data to compare children who attend year-round schools to those in nine-month schools, exploring (1) whether there were mean differences in the reading and math performance among first graders attending year-round and nine-month schools, (2) if racial and residential differences in children's test scores existed between the schooling types, and (3) if neighborhood effects related to academic performance strengthened or weakened as the children's exposure to schooling increased. Contrary to previous claims that schooling increases test-score inequality, we found no significant test-score differences among race-based groups of children according to neighborhood conditions in year-round schools. In contrast, we found prominent neighborhood effects and social class differences among children attending nine-month schools. We conclude with a discussion of the policy implications.

Keywords: race/ethnicity; residency; year-round; test scores; inequality

Whether U.S. schools exacerbate racial stratification has been a recurrent question since the Coleman Report (Coleman et al. 1966). If schools have functioned to increase racial/ethnic stratification (Burkham et al. 2004;

Odis Johnson Jr. is an associate professor in the Departments of Education and Sociology at Washington University in St. Louis. His research and teaching considers how neighborhoods, schools, and public policies relate to social inequality, youth development, and the status of African American populations.

Michael Wagner is a faculty research associate in the Department of African American Studies and a data analyst at the Center for Substance Abuse Research at the University of Maryland, College Park.

NOTE: This research is supported by grants from the National Science Foundation (#DRL-0941014) and the Spencer Foundation (#201000103).

Correspondence: o.johnson@wustl.edu

DOI: 10.1177/0002716217734810

Downey, von Hippel, and Broh 2004; Benson and Borman 2010; Johnson 2014), one might question how giving children more time in schools could be a helpful policy approach. This is indeed an important question to ask since the percentage of the U.S. school-age population enrolled in year-round schools, while low, has increased steadily from 3.5 percent in 2005 to 4.1 percent in 2012 (U.S. Department of Education 2013). To this question, year-round education (YRE) advocates might answer that while they are often described as "year-round," these schools usually provide instruction for approximately 180 days just like traditional nine-month schools. The difference in a year-round schedule is that the days that children attend are spread out within the calendar year, typically with cycles that include 60 days of instruction separated by 15-day intervals. YRE proponents, such as the National Association for Year-Round Education,[1] claim that these modified schedules have often led to less academic slippage than would have occurred during a typical summer recess, and a reduced amount of time that teachers must dedicate to review last year's lessons at the start of the traditional academic year (Cooper et al. 2003). Therefore, the potential benefits of YRE revolve around this "spacing effect," not just the amount of school exposure. A key question that we address in this analysis is whether spacing alters the growth of racial/ethnic gaps in test scores.

Unfortunately, research about the impact of YRE and spacing effects on learning and racial stratification is quite inconclusive. For example, Reece et al. (2000) tested more than 700 traditional and YRE students at the beginning and end of the summer in reading, math, spelling, and writing. While most of the estimates suggested summer knowledge retention was higher for year-round students, the analysis did not cover the school year to see if what children retained led to stronger academic year growth. In another study, von Hippel (2016) reported significant summer gains for YRE students in math and reading using data from the Early Childhood Longitudinal Study, Kindergarten Cohort (ECLS-K, 1999). After separating academic-year growth from summer growth, however, year-round children's rate of test-score growth appeared no better than their nine-month counterparts. Von Hippel's (2016) analysis offers mixed support for the spacing effect hypothesis in that the distribution of days that is typical of YRE led to less summer slippage, but failed to avoid an academic year lag in test scores that often follows lengthy summer recesses. Similarly, McMillen (2001) compared 106 year-round schools to 1,364 nine-month schools and found no overall significant benefit for YRE. Finally, the samples of McMillen and von Hippel lacked racial diversity. McMillen addressed this problem by using a white/non-white binary in his analysis. He concluded that inasmuch as racial categorization moderated YRE outcomes, white students in year-round schools had test performances about 0.04 standard deviation units stronger than their traditional school counterparts. There was no treatment dissimilarity for students of color.

Despite the official school schedule, some children in year-round schools do manage to experience more days of schooling. First, students who have performed less well during an instruction cycle often receive additional help during the intersession, in effect increasing the actual number of days that they attended school. Intersessions then give teachers an opportunity to meet the educational needs of children that would not have occurred during the traditional school year (Cooper et al. 2003). So while school dosage has been increased for students, the additional time is spent on remediation. Cooper et al.'s (2003) synthesis of evaluations suggested that little can be concluded about remedial time, since most of them did not include controls for the number of days of instruction to assess remediation's impact on racial stratification.

Second, there are year-round schools that extend the school year to include more than 200 days. Gandara and Fish (1994) examined extended-year effects for calendars that had approximately 223 days of school. Although the authors found extended-year benefits for children's learning and more positive parental perceptions of their schools, the benefits of increased school exposure were not easily distinguishable from the other significant changes that were implemented simultaneously, among them reduced class size and increased teacher salaries. Moreover, the description of the criteria and matching process has left unknown to what extent the control and experimental schools and the children within them were similar.

Third, an extended school-year is available to most children in the United States through summer school enrollment. Summer school is offered to address losses that occurred in the previous academic year, or to prevent anticipated losses in knowledge over the summer (Cooper et al. 2003). Summer school programs combat summer slippage by adding between three to six weeks of additional instruction, although programs typically have shorter school days and oftentimes meet four days a week. The most comprehensive summary of summer program effects reported that summer programs increased students' test scores by at least 0.14 standard deviation units, and possibly by as much as 0.25 (Cooper et al. 2000). Equally impressive effects have been found for young children in studies that assessed summer programs offered by community organizations and enrolled volunteers (Borman and Dowling 2006; Chaplin and Capizanno 2006; Borman, Goetz, and Dowling 2009), but the evidence is more mixed for the kind of summer programs that schools typically offer and are considered in this study. For example, Matsudaira (2008) finds that mandatory summer school participation in a large urban district is related to a 0.12 standard deviation unit increase in both math and reading test scores, falling short of the standard deviation range estimated by Cooper et al. (2000). Jacob and Lefgren (2004) in contrast found Chicago Public School students in grade 3 who attended summer school gained 20 percent of a year's worth of learning in reading and math. None of these studies, however, could provide evidence regarding racial/ethnic differences in summer school participation relative to nonparticipation as has this study.

Neighborhood Effects and School Dosage

The overrepresentation of African American and Hispanic children in resource-poor neighborhoods has led to a reasonable speculation that extending their time spent in school could reduce neighborhood contributions to racial test-score gaps. However, commentary that has weighed the importance of schools and neighborhoods to achievement ranges from suggestions that the two contexts are synonymous (Jencks and Mayer 1990) to claims that schools are more important than neighborhoods (Arum 2000). Rearranging or adding to the number of days that children are in school might be a beneficial policy option to the extent that the latter of these perspectives is more accurate than the former. That possibility was made somewhat uncertain by Johnson's (2012) review, which revealed that neighborhood effects tended to be larger than school effects in studies that attempted to consider both. Using Johnson's (2012) review as a point of departure, Rendon (2014) examined how neighborhoods and schools correlated to adolescents' odds of dropping out of school. Although she found that neighborhood conditions increased the odds of dropping out of school, these odds became greater once school characteristics were considered and remained significantly higher among African Americans. Rendon's observations implied that neighborhoods might in fact rely on school mechanisms to deliver a neighborhood effect net of school effects. If this neighborhood-school interaction were true for most schools, then lengthened school years might actually lead to more residential stratification in education rather than less as previously speculated.

In yet another model of neighborhood-school interactions, Johnson (2012) observed that neighborhood effects research has often assumed that neighborhood processes are static within the calendar year. He then borrowed from seasonal learning research (Entwisle and Alexander 1992) to propose a "faucet theory model of neighborhood-school relationships" to determine whether schools inhibit the "flow" of neighborhood influences into learning when in session, or if the flow subsides during cooler seasons due to a lull in the neighborhood's social activity (Johnson 2012, 491). Our analysis extends this line of thinking by observing how variation in children's amount of exposure to schooling or "dosage" corresponded to residential effects on test performances across seasons.

One study employing the faucet model estimated the impact of neighborhoods' economic and racial makeup in each season, finding that economic segregation was the most salient social background determinant of math and reading inequality during the summer but not in the academic year (Benson and Borman 2010). Yet this analysis was unable to tell us if these summer neighborhood effects would retain their significance for children who received some kind of summer instruction. Imposing variation in children's exposure to schooling during the summer, as our analysis has, clarifies whether summer test-score gains or losses extend from the absence of schooling or summertime changes in the neighborhood's social organization.

Testing neighborhood fluctuations is precisely why we examined the neighborhood dimension of social disorganization, or the breakdown of social control indicated by criminal behavior. Summer increases in crime, violence, and burglary have sadly become predictable (Lauritsen and White 2014), and with noted consequences for children. Sharkey and Sampson (2010), for example, have demonstrated the occurrence of a homicide in African Americans' census block within a week of their assessment reduces their reading and vocabulary performances by at least a half standard deviation unit. Johnson's (2014) analysis found seasonal fluctuations in which neighborhood problems with burglary had their strongest connection with reading during the summer and achieved a magnitude greater than any other social background characteristic. While others have investigated the temporal effects of neighborhood disadvantage in relation to dropping out and graduation within a counterfactual framework (Harding 2003; Wodtke, Harding, and Elwert 2011), we are not aware of a counterfactual study that has assessed the seasonal quality of neighborhood social disorganization effects related to test scores.

Research Design and Methods

We start our analysis with the general question: Does test-score growth differ among students in year-round and nine-month schools during the calendar year, nine-month academic term, and summer? To pursue this question, we constructed a research design that features three key components. First, we used a counterfactual approach, shown in Table 1, in which year-round and nine-month schooling represent two treatment conditions experienced by similar children; the former we refer to as the experimental and the latter the control. Examining both schooling schedules strengthens the causal inferences that we hope to make about school exposure's influence on test-score performance because the counterfactual, or alternative educational experience, is also tested. Second, we carried out this counterfactual approach within a seasonal learning framework where test-score growth within both treatments was measured for the calendar year, summer, and traditional nine-month academic year. The separate estimation of growth in distinct yearly, nine-month, and summer periods allowed us to understand at what point in the calendar year were test-score gains likely and if the magnitude of growth implied that any summer slowdown or spacing effect had occurred.

We also posed a second question regarding how race/ethnicity related to test scores across school schedules and seasons. More specifically, we asked a subset of related questions: Are there within-race/ethnicity test-score differences between the two school types, in which form of schooling is there less test-score inequality between racial/ethnic groups, and does growth in these within- and between-race/ethnic gaps differ in the nine-month academic term and summer? Again, the separate estimation of racial/ethnic differences in distinct periods permitted the addition of covariates that accounted for the type of summer educational experience that children in year-round school received (i.e., summer school or year-round school) and other social background factors.

Included among these other social background factors are residential dimensions. Hence, our third question reflects the nesting of the counterfactual design within residential areas (presented in Figure 1) and considers how residential

TABLE 1
Counterfactual Design

	In School Year-Round (Experimental)	In School Nine Months (Control)
Yearly growth	Yearly growth with year-round schooling	Yearly growth with nine-month schooling
Number of school days (% school days)	190.99 days (52.33%)	180 days (49.32%)
Summer growth	Summer growth with year-round schooling	Summer growth with nine-month schooling
Number of school days (% school days)	22.28 days (27.44%)	0 days (0%)
Nine-month growth	Nine-month growth in year-round schools	Nine-month growth in nine-month schools
Number of school days (% school days)	157.72 days (55.19%)	180.00 days (62.99%)

effects on children's test outcomes might correspond to the variation in school exposure found among schooling schedules and seasons. With this question, we addressed Johnson's (2012) speculation regarding the degree to which the residential effects (shown at the left of Figure 1) related to racial/ethnic test-score gaps (right of Figure 1) are negotiated by children's exposure to the various schooling calendars (shown in the middle of Figure 1). In estimating the neighborhood effect for the alternative educational treatment within the bottom middle block in particular, we were able to infer whether variation in children's scores is due to the absence of schooling or seasonal fluctuations in neighborhood activity. For example, in Table 1, summer test-score change is assessed in the presence and absence of schooling because 27.44 percent of experimental children's summer time is spent in school while control group children have no school days. Should summer losses occur for children who experienced no schooling rather than for those who did, we can then be more certain that those declines were due to the absence of schooling rather than summertime change in the social organization of neighborhoods, which is a potential confounder in existing studies of summer learning. Variation in the number of instructional days between year-round and nine-month schools is also exploited in estimating nine-month test-score growth, where experimental children are in school 22.28 days fewer than are their nine-month counterparts.

Data

Data from the ECLS-K are ideal for this study because they enabled the measurement of summer change in test scores and because, at the time of analysis, these data were the only ones of their kind that were linked to the census. The National Center for Education Statistics (NCES) collected data about the families, schools, neighborhoods, and activities of approximately 22,780 children, who were chosen at random

FIGURE 1
Nested Seasonal-Counterfactual Design

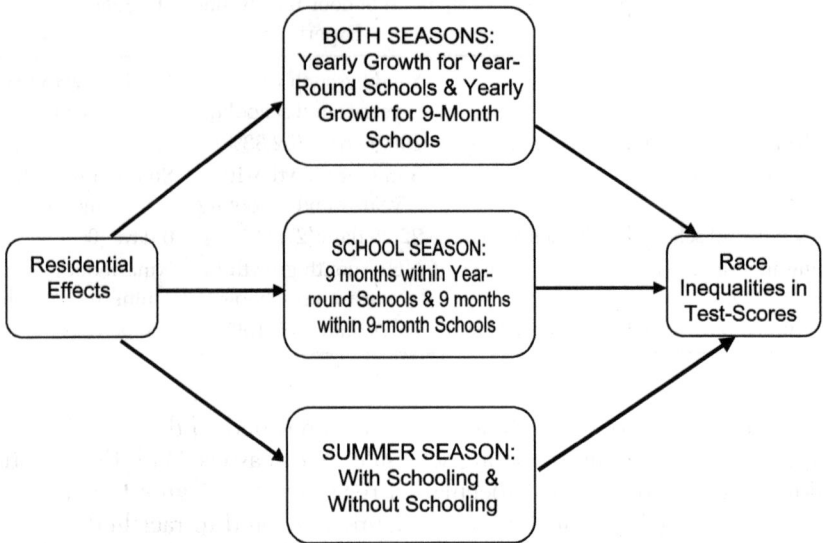

from 1,277 randomly selected public and private kindergarten programs.[2] Of this total sample, 30 percent were randomly selected to take assessments near the beginning and end of kindergarten and 1st grade. While this study's analysis was not limited to the children who participated in this subsample, only children in this subsample have a fall 1st grade test score. Similar to the strategy employed by Downey, von Hippel, and Broh (2004), we used the assessment dates and the beginning and end-dates of nine-month schools to calculate children's average rate of test-score growth between assessments.[3] Using this average rate of growth and under our valid assumption that growth between waves 3 and 4 was linear, we extrapolated for children who were missing scores what their test scores would have been at wave 3, the start of first grade. We focused on waves 2 to 4, which span from the end of kindergarten to the end of first grade, as the year-round schooling period because more than 35 percent of Hispanics did not take the fall kindergarten assessment in reading. Finally, before the matching process, we removed the cases that did not have parent data or any test scores; Native Americans, because fewer than twenty attended schools year-round;[4] and children who changed schools or neighborhoods during the study period.

Propensity score and matching process

Since we have not randomly assigned children to schools, reasons for their enrollment in either year-round or nine-month schools remain unknown and possibly related to their test scores. In truth, there may be many reasons why the test scores of children vary between the two conditions that would make conclusions about the relevance of educational exposure premature and possibly incorrect. To address these challenges and strengthen the causal inferences, we would like to make about school exposure, we matched children in YRE to those in nine-month schools by relying on propensity scores as child matching estimators. Propensity scores represent the predicted probability that individuals with certain qualities will experience a treatment when assignment is nonrandom. Using individuals' characteristics, we estimated a propensity score to identify those with a similar probability of choosing the experimental or control condition, irrespective of their true condition assignment. Once individuals with a similar propensity score were identified and compared, there would be enough similarity in their pretreatment characteristics to theoretically allow observed discrepancies between them to extend from the differing treatments that they experienced.

To start, no theoretical basis exists on how to select the ideal number of pretreatment dimensions for calculating matching estimators (Heckman et al. 1998). We reasoned that the qualities used to estimate our logit modeled propensity scores should span the multiple units of analysis and contexts examined in this study. Therefore, our initial calculation of matching estimators included all of the independent variables that we planned to use in the multivariate analysis. When these variables were applied in our matching process, they failed to produce year-round and nine-month school groups with insignificantly different baseline reading scores ($p. = .044$).

In our next attempt, we deleted independent variables from our full logit model one at a time until the propensity scores that were produced generated no significant mean differences in the analysis outcomes of the experimental and control group when applied in our matching process (math .51, $p. = .50$; reading $-.58$, $p. = .56$).[5] At the individual level, we included the traditional markers of social differentiation, namely, children's gender and their parents' social class and marriage status. Regarding their school experiences, we included kindergarten repeaters since studies have shown that they score lower in reading and math (Benson and Borman 2010), and school sector to consider variation in public and private school enrollment. Children's residency was accounted for in our matching approach by including children's city residency, the percentage of jobless males age 16 or older within the civilian labor force, and the percentage of minorities within children's residential zip code. Pretreatment characteristics' definition and measurement are discussed in greater detail in the sections that follow.

YRE was defined in this study as children's enrollment in a school identified as such by their school administrators or as having experienced summer school. Rather than viewing start and end-dates to make assumptions about the type of school, we relied on the variable F4YRRND to identify schools with year-round calendars. Year-round school participation was determined for 1,030 children, with nearly equal numbers attending summer school (520) or year-round schools (510). To pair these children with their counterparts in nine-month schools we express the general matching algorithm offered by Morgan and Winship (2007, 106) as:

$$\hat{\delta}_{TT,match} = \frac{1}{n^1} \sum_i \left[(y_i \mid d_i = 1) - \sum_j w_{i,j} (y_j \mid d_j = 0) \right],$$

where n^1 is the number of treatment cases, i is the index over experimental cases, j is the index over control cases, and w_{ij} represents the propensity scores that measured the distance between each nine-month school student (control case) and the target year-round student (experimental case).

There are numerous strategies that can be used in matching processes, and we have relied on several of them to increase the possibility of making successful matches and achieving balanced treatments. First, studies of YRE often control for race and social background, but controlling for race is different than ensuring that there is a balanced number of students of a given race/ethnicity in YRE versus nine-month schooling treatment groups. Therefore, we stratified our matching process according to race; that is, children attending year-round schools were matched, with the aid of propensity scores, to their coethnic/racial counterparts in nine-month schools. This maximized the likelihood that the schooling conditions would be experienced by comparable racial/ethnic groups. As shown in Table 2 the sample is roughly 12 percent African American, 14 percent Asian American, 32 percent Hispanic, and 42 percent white.

A second adjustment to our algorithm was needed because some inefficiency in the within-race matching process could arise if it limited possible matches to those of the same racial group when the true ideal match was of another race. To reduce the possibility that our matching strategy would yield less than ideal matches, our approach included a caliper match modification that bounds our matches to a maximum propensity score difference of .01 percent. For each year-round student w_i, the algorithm identified nine-month school students for whom $w_j = (w_i - .01, w_i + .01)$. If no nine-month match with a 1 percent or lower propensity score difference was found, the year-round case was eliminated from the analysis.

Third, we also carried out a one-to-one or "common-support" matching approach (Morgan 2001), using a lead-lag execution of our full-match algorithm (Hansen 2004). In this procedure, the algorithm identified a year-round case within the data file, and then alternated its consideration of the cases that preceded (lead) and followed (lag) the year-round case to identify the nine-month student with the proximate propensity score. Once the optimal match was identified for each year-round student w_{ij}, a corresponding flag variable was set equal to one for the matched control case and zero for all other control cases. All of the unmatched nine-month students with zero values and year-round students with no match were eliminated from the dataset, leaving us with a final sample of nearly 950 students in both year-round and nine-month schools, and nearly 1,900 children in total. This represents 92 percent of all possible matches. Inferences of the analysis are therefore limited to year-round students in 204 schools who have comparable counterparts in 246 traditional nine-month schools.

TABLE 2
Descriptive Statistics, Matched Full (N = ~1,896)

Variables	Mean	SD
Asian/Pacific Islander (1 = yes, 0 = no)	.14	.35
Black (1 = yes, 0 = no)	.12	.32
Hispanic (1 = yes, 0 = no)	.32	.47
White (1 = yes, 0 = no)	.42	.49
Social class quintile (1 = low, 5 = high)	2.75	1.42
Low social class (1 = yes, 0 = no)	.27	.44
Middle low social class (1 = yes, 0 = no)	.22	.41
Middle social class (1 = yes, 0 = no)	.19	.39
Middle high social class (1 = yes, 0 = no)	.17	.37
High social class (1 = yes, 0 = no)	.16	.37
Gender (1 = female, 0 = male)	.55	.50
Single parent (1 = yes, 0 = no)	.20	.40
Age in months (months at kindergarten start)	65.11	4.48
Sector (1 = public, 0 = private)	.19	.39
Repeated kindergarten (1 = yes, 0 = no)	.05	.21
Full-day kindergarten (1 = yes, 0 = no)	.48	.50
Preschool (1 = head start/center/day care, 0 = no)	.10	.30
Year-round school (1 = yes, 0 = no)	.24	.43
All-year (1 = summer school/year-round, 0 = nine-month)	.50	.50
City location (1 = yes, 0 = no)	.44	.50
Zip code average median family income	50,472.55	18,926.86
Zip code median family income – lower third	.42	.49
Zip code median family income – middle third	.31	.46
Zip code median family income – upper third	.27	.45
Zip code mean percent minority	36.48	32.53
Zip code percent minority – lower third	.23	.42
Zip code percent minority – middle third	.32	.46
Zip code percent minority – upper third	.46	.50
Zip code percent male jobless in civilian labor force	36.51	13.55
Neighborhood disorganization (1 = yes, 0 = no)	.16	.37
Months from kindergarten end to grade 1 start	2.62	0.28
Months from test 2 to kindergarten end	1.08	0.49
Months from grade 1 start to test 3	1.43	0.52
Months from grade 1 start to test 4	8.30	0.57
Months from grade 1 start to grade 1 end	9.45	0.36
Months from test 4 to grade 1 end	1.18	0.51
Reading score kindergarten end to grade 1 start	−0.03	9.37
Reading score kindergarten end to grade 1 end	31.95	16.88
Reading score grade 1 start to grade 1 end	31.85	16.00
Math score kindergarten end to grade 1 start	1.35	8.53
Math score kindergarten end to grade 1 end	25.25	12.19
Math score grade 1 start to grade 1 end	23.89	12.48

Analytical constructs

We have estimated growth in *reading* and *math* item response theory (IRT) scale-scores, not only under the two schooling conditions but also in time varying periods. We therefore report reading and math scores for the calendar year, the nine-month academic year, and summer. Regarding the latter two periods, assessments in these subjects occurred at times that did not coincide with the beginning and ending dates of the school year, resulting in the summer period having some days of schooling and the exclusion of relevant days of instruction from nine-month test-score estimates. This feature of the data was corrected by first estimating the time that elapsed between the test dates and the start and end dates of the nine-month school calendar, then calculating the amount of test-score growth that would have occurred during this time, and adding (to waves 2 and 4) or subtracting (from wave 3) the appropriate amount of test-score change. To establish a similar summer time frame in which to gauge test-score change between the two schooling types, we used the same elapsed-time approach described earlier to derive the test scores that year-round children would have had at the start and end of nine-month schooling.

In counterfactual modeling, you would not typically include as model covariates the dimensions that were used to match children. However, our stratified matching strategy allowed us to use these characteristics to select matches within racial groups while assuming that these dimensions would also vary across racial groups when estimated within a conditional multivariate model. These characteristics related to children's social background and their amount of exposure to school environments. Social background variables included race/ethnicity (*Hispanic, white, Asian-Pacific Islander, and African American*), coded as 1 = yes, 0 = no; and a composite measure of family *social class* that was segmented into equal-sized quintiles (e.g., *Low SES*, 1 = yes, 0 = no). This composite measure of family social class, provided by NCES, reflects the occupational status, educational level, and total household income of parents. We also considered children's *gender* (1 = female, 0 = male), *single parent* family structure (1 = yes, 0 = no), and their *age* in months at the start of kindergarten.

Another group of variables accounted for differences in the amount of children's exposure to school and the kind of summer education that they received. These measures included whether children attended a *full-day kindergarten* program (versus half-day), *attended preschool*, and *repeated kindergarten*, all coded 1 for yes and 0 for no. Regarding possible differences between year-round and nine-month schools, it must be noted that the experimental treatment included two forms of YRE: summer school and year-round school. We distinguished between these two arrangements by estimating differences in the *type of summer* instruction (1 = year-round, 0 = summer school) experimental students experienced.

To take advantage of the unique way both treatments inform questions of residential stratification, we used an NCES companion data file that linked ECLS-K children to characteristics of their zip codes. While the imperfections of census data as proxies for residential areas have been noted (Jencks and Mayer 1990), they present an objective appraisal of areas that complemented the more subjective parent reports of neighborhood conditions that we used in this analysis. These variables included zip codes' *median family income* and the *percentage minority*. To achieve a suitable distribution of incomes, we used a log transformation of the median income variable and converted those values into z-scores. For the sake of interpretation, Table 2 reports the original values of this variable. We combined measures of the proportion of African American and Hispanic individuals to create the zip code's *percentage minority* measure because those racial groups have the largest proportion of their populations located in hyper-segregated areas (Logan, Stults, and Farley 2004). Finally, the ECLS-K provided a location type variable to identify children who resided in *central cities* (1 = yes, 0 = no) and asked parents their perceptions of their neighborhood, which we used to create a composite indicator of neighborhood social disorganization. Parents were asked, *"How much of a problem is burglary," "violent crime,"* and *"selling/using drugs in the area?"* (1 = big problem, 2 = somewhat a problem, 3 = no problem). Our *social disorganization* composite was coded 1 for yes and 0 for no if parents indicated that any of these factors were a big problem. The descriptive statistics of these variables are listed in Table 2.

Estimation

Using HLM version 7.01 (Raudenbush and Bryk 2002), we specified a three-level model consisting of child test scores at level 1, between-child measures reflecting his or her social background and educational exposure at level 2, and residential dimensions at level 3. Given test-score change can happen in different periods of the year, test-score parameters were estimated separately for the nine-month school session, the summer, and the entire calendar year, yielding the combined level 1 equation:

$$Y_{tcn} = \pi_{0cn} + \pi_{1cn} \left(Spring\ kindergarten\ assessment_{tcn} \right) +$$
$$\pi_{2cn} \left(Fall\ 1^{st}\ grade\ assessment_{tcn} \right) +$$
$$\pi_{3cn} \left(Spring\ 1^{st}\ grade\ assessment_{tcn} \right) + e,$$

where test-scores Y_{tcn} was a function of an intercept representing reading and math for child c in neighborhood n, and her or his exposure to periods that span the spring kindergarten to fall first-grade test score (summer), the beginning and end score of first grade (nine-month), and the end of kindergarten to the end of first grade (year-round) at the time of test t. Test scores during these time spans were estimated for children who are enrolled in year-round and nine-month schools together in an unconditional analysis.

Within each time span, our counterfactual approach assumed that every individual had a potential outcome in both treatment conditions, even if each child could be observed in only one school treatment at any one time (Morgan and Winship 2007). We express this assumption as:

$$\delta_i = Y\frac{e}{i} - Y\frac{c}{i},$$

where Y_i = reading or math outcomes and e and c indicate whether test scores were of the experimental or control condition. The matching procedures that we described earlier addressed the fact that we could only observe child i in one treatment and not both, allowing us to continue with the specification of the causal effect on child i as an expected value of difference between Y^e and Y^c:

$$\overline{\delta} = \overline{Y}^e - \overline{Y}^c.$$

The average treatment effect is then the difference between these two estimated means as indicated by an *all-year* variable (1 = yes, 0 = no).

Other questions in our analysis concern variation in treatment effects across racial/ethnic groups, social background, and school dimensions. We therefore specified level 2 of the multilevel model in which test-score growth, π_{1cn}, was a function of children's age, gender, and single parent family structure; whether they repeated kindergarten; attended full-day kindergarten and a preschool program; the type of summer instruction; and their family social class quintile (with the middle quintile excluded), race, and city residency. The only way level 2 differed across the three periods is that the variable, summer program type, was withheld from the estimation of nine-month performances since there is no schooling for control group children. The full level 2 equation is as follows:

$$\begin{aligned}
\pi_{1cn} = \beta_{10n} &+ \beta_{1n}\left(Age_{cn}\right) + \beta_{12n}\left(Gender_{cn}\right) + \beta_{13n}\left(Single\ parent_{cn}\right) + \\
&\beta_{14n}\left(Repeated\ kindergarten_{cn}\right)\ \beta_{15n}\left(Full\ day\ kindergarten_{cn}\right) + \\
&\beta_{16n}\left(Preschool\ program_{cn}\right) + \beta_{17n}\left(Summer\ type_{cn}\right) + \\
&\beta_{1,8\text{-}11n}\left(SES\ quintiles_{cn}\right) + \beta_{1,12\text{-}15n}\left(Race_{cn}\right) + \beta_{116n}\left(City_{cn}\right) + a_{cn}.
\end{aligned}$$

Recall that children in our analysis are nested within residential areas. We therefore modeled "neighborhood-to-neighborhood" variation in residential characteristics with random intercepts in all three periods and both school conditions. Hence, test-score change in each time-span, β_{10n}, was a function of zip codes' median family income and percentage African American and Hispanic, both segmented into equal thirds and a social disorganization composite. We express this level 3 equation as:

$$\begin{aligned}
\beta_{10n} = \gamma_{100} &+ \gamma_{101,2n}\left(Median\ family\ income_n\right) + \gamma_{103,4n}\left(\%Minority_n\right) + \\
&\gamma_{105n}\left(Social\ disorganization_n\right) + r_{10n},
\end{aligned}$$

where the intercept γ_{100} represented the average test performance of a specific residential area for all areas in the sample, γ_{101n} through γ_{104n} indicated the estimated deviation from the area mean test performance associated with a point increase among those characteristics, and γ_{105n} represented the average point

TABLE 3

Unconditional and Difference Models of Reading and Math Test Score Mean Growth and Year-Round/Nine-Month Differences, Full Sample ($N = \sim1,900$)

	Reading				Math			
	Growth Model		Difference Model		Growth Model		Difference Model	
Yearly growth								
Intercept/SE	30.98°°°°	0.59	30.83°°°°	0.59	25.22°°°°	0.35	25.16°°°°	0.35
All-year/SE	—	—	−4.13°°°°	1.16	—	—	−2.58°°°°	0.70
Level 1 & 2 τ/SD	195.72°°°°	13.99	191.53°°°°	13.84	96.39°°°°	9.82	94.50°°°°	9.72
Level 3 τ/SD	53.91°°°°	7.34	55.22°°°°	7.43	16.29°°°°	4.04	17.06°°°°	4.13
Summer growth								
Intercept/SE	−0.49	0.35	−0.47	0.35	1.54°°°°	0.27	1.55°°°°	0.27
All-year/SE	—	—	0.52	0.64	—	—	0.76	0.52
Level 1 & 2 τ/SD	48.15°°°°	6.94	48.27°°°°	6.95	42.93°°°°	6.55	43.11°°°°	6.57
Level 3 τ/SD	18.04°°°°	4.25	17.81°°°°	4.22	10.50°°°°	3.24	10.12°°°°	3.18
Nine-month growth								
Intercept/SE	31.71°°°°	0.55	31.56°°°°	0.54	23.79°°°°	0.39	23.68°°°°	0.38
All-year/SE	—	—	−3.58°°°	1.13	—	—	−4.01°°°°	0.75
Level 1 & 2 τ/SD	169.27°°°°	13.02	169.43°°°°	13.02	94.91°°°°	9.74	92.85°°°°	9.64
Level 3 τ/SD	61.68°°°°	57.85	57.85°°°°	7.61	28.47°°°°	5.34	26.96°°°°	5.19

$°p < .10.$ $°°p < .05.$ $°°°p < .01.$ $°°°°p < .000.$

change in children's mean test performance associated with a residential area's identification as having those problems.

Analysis

Unconditional and difference analysis

Our first question asked whether significant test-score differences existed between year-round and nine-month school children, and if so, did they vary according to the season? Our analysis shown in Table 3 suggests the answer to both of those questions is yes. Table 3 shows estimates for children's reading and math test scores in all three time spans for the full sample analysis. The first column provides the mean test score, while the second column labeled "difference" includes the all-year variable, which represents the estimated difference of year-round test-score performances from the mean. For the calendar year, the first row of Table 3 shows that experimental group children accumulated 4.13 ($p = .001$) fewer test-score points in reading, leading to a gap between them and control group children of nearly 0.30 of a standard deviation unit. YRE students also accumulated about 2.58 ($p.$ = .001) points less than control group students in math, equaling a gap of about 0.27 standard deviation units.

In the second row, the same models are specified for summer test-score growth. The reading analysis reveals no significant test-score growth or loss for students in general (–0.47, $p.$ = .182) or year-round students in particular (0.52, $p.$ = .413). However, the math analysis shows that all children experienced summertime test-score gains (1.55, $p.$ = .001), and that this growth did not appear to vary significantly according to school type (0.76, $p.$ = .141).

Estimates of nine-month academic year learning are detailed in the final row. YRE children accumulated 3.58 ($p.$ = .002) points fewer than their nine-month counterparts in reading and 4.01 ($p.$ =. 001) points fewer in math. The magnitude of those losses (0.27 and 0.42 standard deviation units in reading and math, respectively) are as expected given that children in YRE received nearly thirteen fewer instructional days than did children in nine-month schools. It is also possible that summer school children are responsible for this slower YRE growth rate since struggling students are generally more likely to attend summer school and thus be included in our sample. We shed more light on this possibility in the multivariate analysis.

Moreover, these results present mixed evidence about the YRE spacing effect hypothesis (i.e., less academic slippage due to shorter summer breaks or a quicker resumption of learning than children in traditional nine-month schools) and the effectiveness of YRE in preventing unequal test performances. The finding that no losses occurred in reading while there were gains in math during the summer might indicate that less slippage occurred. We are nonetheless unable to state that test-score inequality between the two school conditions changed during the summer. Additionally, the nine-month growth estimates do not imply that YRE students experienced a quicker resumption of growth since the shortfalls between YRE and traditional schools during that period (0.39 and 0.45 points per month lower in reading and math, respectively) are larger than the yearly growth estimates (0.34 and 0.22). While finding less inequality in the calendar year than in the nine-month period might seem encouraging for YRE, the improvement over the nine-month gap is modest at just 0.05 points per month in reading and 0.23 points in math. At that rate, the calendar year would need to be extended by 10.19 months to totally offset the growth rate difference of 0.55 points between the nine-month and calendar year for YRE students.

Mixed multivariate linear models

We also asked whether there was variation in how race and residency related to test scores across seasons and school schedules. With this question, we addressed long-standing speculation within research about schools as sites where academic differences grow (Downey, von Hippel, and Broh 2004; Condron 2009), and where residential effects are mitigated (Johnson 2012; Rendon 2014). Pursuant to these interests, we specified conditional models for each treatment and time span and report the results in Tables 4 and 5. Addressing the racial concerns first, the reading results in Table 4 show that stratification along the

TABLE 4
Multivariate Models of Reading Growth, Year-Round and Nine-Month in First Grade

Reading	Year-Round Enrollment			Nine-Month Enrollment		
	Yearly	Summer	Nine-Month	Yearly	Summer	Nine-Month
Intercept	30.07°°°°	–0.06	30.16°°°°	33.35°°°°	–0.29	33.46°°°°
Age	0.51°°°	0.28°°	0.22	–0.10	0.15°°	–0.25
Gender	–3.54°°	–1.45	–1.15	–1.48	–1.03	–0.74
Single parent	0.14	–1.43	1.16	–0.27	1.40	–0.47
Repeated kindergarten	–5.27	–3.00	–4.56	–4.69	–3.12°°	–3.44
Full-day kindergarten	–0.03	–0.29	–0.99	–2.44°	–0.38	–2.04
Preschool program	3.61	2.90	–0.07	3.61	0.26	2.99
Summer type	1.57	1.61	—	—	—	—
Low social class	–3.15	–1.65	–0.75	–5.05°°	–0.92	–3.91°
Mid low social class	1.49	1.95	–0.79	–0.20	–0.32	–0.00
Mid high social class	–0.74	–0.93	0.66	4.49°	0.44	6.35°°°
High social class	3.54	–0.62	1.58	8.77°°°°	2.17	7.50°°°
Asian/Pacific Islander	2.56	–0.42	3.53	2.40	2.65°°	–2.22
Black	2.35	1.02	0.63	–0.98	–0.11	–1.40
Hispanic	0.80	–1.07	1.14	1.61	0.40	–0.77
City	1.95	0.31	1.30	3.37°	–0.74	3.85°°
Low area income	–2.66	–2.37°	–3.25°	–1.41	–0.62	1.00
High area income	1.25	1.57	0.11	–1.89	0.26	–1.44
Low minority percent	–1.26	0.01	–0.35	0.43	1.14	–1.83
High minority percent	–3.35	–0.15	–2.70°	–0.94	0.68	–3.05
Social disorganization	1.66	2.34	–0.18	–4.38°°	0.85	–5.27°°
Level 1 & 2 variance	149.72°°°°	68.82°°°°	84.78°°°°	201.72°°°°	35.01°°°°	213.49°°°°
Standard deviation	12.24	8.30	9.21	14.20	5.92	14.61
Level 3 variance	28.04°°°°	11.24°°°	73.55°°°°	47.90°°°°	12.93°°°°	65.08°°°°
Standard deviation	5.30	3.35	8.58	6.92	3.60	8.07

°$p < .10.$ °°$p < .05.$ °°°$p < .01.$ °°°°$p < .000.$

dimensions of race/ethnicity and social class appears unremarkable within year-round schools. So while year-round schools may not yield higher test scores than nine-month schools, we cannot say that the benefits they offer are not more uniform. Also, summer type is insignificant in both models, which is especially noteworthy for summertime growth since during that period there were approximately seven more days of instruction in year-round schools than in summer school.

The story is quite different in nine-month schools, where reading test-score gaps seem more prominent along the dimension of social class than race. Only

TABLE 5
Multivariate Models of Math Growth, Year-Round and Nine-Month

Math	Year-Round Enrollment			Nine-Month Enrollment		
	Yearly	Summer	Nine-Month	Yearly	Summer	Nine-Month
Intercept	24.08****	2.36****	21.23****	26.48****	0.93***	25.43****
Age	0.05	0.16°	−0.09	0.05	0.10	−0.14
Gender	1.69°	0.78	−0.03	1.56°	−0.18	1.69°
Single parent	−0.33	−0.86	0.03	−0.75	1.35°	−1.93
Repeated kindergarten	−4.13**	−1.63	−1.84	−4.88**	−3.62**	0.26
Full-day kindergarten	−2.57***	−0.84	−1.76°	−1.99°	0.58	−2.91**
Preschool program	0.37	−0.44	0.88	2.81	−0.78	2.60
Summer type	0.26	1.30	—	—	—	—
Low social class	−3.51**	−3.52***	1.55	−2.68°	−0.29	−2.02
Mid low social class	−0.22	−0.44	0.47	1.08	−0.60	0.39
Mid high social class	1.02	−0.61	1.89	2.73	−3.03***	4.75***
High social class	0.42	−0.53	1.15	3.24	−0.66	2.97
Asian/Pacific Islander	−1.96	0.72	−3.16	−2.96	1.56	−4.96***
Black	−0.57	1.40	−1.23	−2.99°	−0.74	−1.17
Hispanic	−2.21°	−0.43	−1.35	0.45	0.01	1.38
City	1.74°	−0.04	1.84	1.23	−0.59	1.71
Low area income	0.12	−0.40	−0.74	1.35	−0.86	2.19
Upper area income	0.10	1.06	−0.75	2.65	0.94	2.66
Low minority percent	0.02	0.61	−3.33	1.18	0.61	−1.17
High minority percent	−0.15	0.88	−1.25	−1.01	0.63	−1.92
Social disorganization	1.68	−0.07	0.99	−3.19**	−0.48	−2.99**
Level 1 & 2 variance	81.38****	47.99****	39.20****	89.33***	32.82****	112.02****
Standard deviation	9.02	6.93	6.26	9.45	5.73	10.58
Level 3 variance	3.04	7.94****	36.32****	27.12****	10.42****	31.70****
Standard deviation	1.74	2.82	6.03	5.21	3.23	5.63

°$p < .10$. °°$p < .05$. °°°$p < .01$. °°°°$p < .000$.

among Asian American/Pacific Islanders during the summer were test scores significantly higher (2.65, $p. = .039$) than average. For social class in contrast, inequality in test scores appeared to have increased as children's exposure to schooling lengthened. Children in the lowest social class accumulated fewer points (−5.05, $p. = .039$) while those in the highest social class experienced considerable gains (8.77, $p. = .001$). The total gap between the two social classes of 13.82 calendar year points almost amounts to a full standard deviation unit difference (−0.36 versus 0.62). Most of this yearly difference grew during the nine-month academic year.

The estimates of the math analysis shown in Table 5 were more varied, but mirrored the reading results in important ways. Growth estimates for year-round children were once again unremarkable along race/ethnicity. However, this time there were social class differences that left children in the lowest economic quintile accumulating roughly 3.50 points fewer during the summer, leading to a similar setback for the calendar year of .39 standard deviation units. Again, the summer type variable shows no significant difference in performance according to the form of year-round education. Nine-month schools in contrast had losses for Asian Americans (-4.96, $p.$ = .009) and gains for children in the moderately high social class (4.75, $p.$ = .009) that developed during the academic year offset by summertime growth rates, leaving the calendar year point estimates insignificant. In sum, the academic year of nine-month schools was the period in which math inequality grew as it was in reading. However, the summer months countered much of the academic year inequality in nine-month schools while it added to social class inequality in year-round schools.

Turning our attention to the subject of residential effects, the reading analysis displayed in Table 4 reveals no significant deviations from average rates of growth for YRE children among any of the neighborhood dimensions. In nine-month schools, however, large residential shortfalls in reading were related to neighborhood social disorganization during the traditional academic year (-5.27, $p.$ = .021, 0.36 standard deviation units). The magnitude of the disorganization effect weakened slightly once we considered nine-month school students' calendar year gains (-4.38, $p.$ = .044, 0.31 standard deviation units). Thus, in reading we have concluded that residential effects related to test scores were stronger in nine-month schools where children had the maximum percentage (62.99) of school days. These conclusions were reinforced in the results of the math analysis (Table 5). In math, the majority of the calendar year social disorganization effect (-3.19, $p.$ = .024, 0.34 standard deviation units) in nine-month schools accrued during the academic year (-2.99, $p.$ = .047, 0.28 standard deviation units). No significant neighborhood effects emerged for children enrolled in YRE.

Discussion

This study of race and residential effects in year-round and nine-month schools begins to answer the question of whether schools exacerbate or equalize disparities in children's test performance. This is a question worth answering, given that the United States has long-regarded education as the key to social mobility. There are gaps in the scientific literature regarding the usefulness of YRE as a viable policy option because we know little about what form it should take to secure the desired outcomes for children, and how it functions along race/ethnicity and residency lines. This analysis concludes that policies to reallocate instructional days to a YRE model or to extend instructional days through summer would neither worsen nor equalize test score gaps among racial/ethnic groups, but that such policies could reduce stratification that derives from children's exposure to social disorganization in their neighborhood of residence.

We show that children in year-round schools do less well than children in traditional schools and gain the least during the traditional nine-month period, casting doubt on the hypothesis that spacing noninstructional days differently in the year through YRE is beneficial. Yet smaller relative losses as children's learning is extended beyond the traditional academic year suggested that more time in school does improve test scores, but not significantly enough to make up the gap with traditional school children in just three months' time.

This analysis did not suggest any difference in the effectiveness between the modified calendar or summer school despite there being more instructional days in the former. That said, it would be erroneous to presume that the number of days is the only way in which these school programs differ. Indeed, we assume that differences in their social organization are not spurious and are in fact related to, if not caused by, the two treatments. Future research will need to illuminate to what extent their unique social organization contributes to differing impacts while accounting for variation in school dosage.

Our consideration of race/ethnicity explored whether there was variation in how these categories related to test scores across different forms of schooling and seasons. Our within-race/ethnicity matching strategy made it more likely that any differences that arose between the matched groups were due to the different schooling types that they had experienced. Our analysis revealed surprisingly few significant test-score differences between racial/ethnic groups related to the two forms of schooling. In fact, social class inequality often appeared more prominent than racial/ethnic differences, especially in nine-month schools. We nonetheless make no claims that YRE could reduce racial stratification in schools because our sample of YRE students is not representative of the average student in U.S. schools. Our conclusion about school effects is therefore similar to that reached by Haskins (this volume): YRE may not be adding to the problem of school-inspired inequality across racialized groups, but it also appears unlikely to solve the problem.

This study also produced insights into how residential effects were related to test outcomes given children's length of school exposure. The pattern of relationships found in the analysis of reading test scores suggested that traditional schools did not offset neighborhood effects as much as they functioned to relay them. The largest residential effects were of social disorganization, and occurred during the nine-month periods of traditional school—the period that offered the greatest number of instructional days. Within the summer when the percentage of instruction was lowest, neighborhood disadvantages were insignificantly related to test scores. There are a few conclusions that we have drawn about these residential effects.

First, the relationship of residential effects and traditional school dosage is not entirely counterintuitive since the former arises in large part through human interaction and schools are possibly the primary medium that facilitates the "effect-enabling" interaction for children. In contrast, the spacing of school dosage in YRE may periodically interrupt these effect-enabling child interactions with school intercessions. YRE schools may therefore be the schooling arrangement most likely to reduce neighborhood-based stratification in education.

Second, there is little evidence presented in this study that supports the presence of temporal fluctuations in residential effects in the way we imagined they might occur; they were not stronger during the summer as they appeared in the results of Benson and Borman (2010) and Johnson (2014). This study therefore offers the possibility that without schools, neighborhoods *of the kind in this analysis* would not function to directly impact children's test scores when all else is considered. Third, and consequently, we have concluded that the faucet theory of neighborhood effects may be more appropriately applied to the traditional academic season wherein stronger effects were present.

But there are some cautions related to research of this kind that we must mention. One caution is that counterfactual models address the bias of only observed characteristics that would be found in inferential studies and not unobserved ones. Another limitation is that our causal inferences pertain to year-round children that have nine-month matches. This analysis was based on the matched sample with the greatest number of experimental children to enhance generalizability, but we make no claims that it is representative of ECLS-K children or children nationally in year-round schools. These points together suggest that a fuller understanding of racial stratification in schools and of the Coleman Report requires additional studies that expand on the findings presented in this analysis.

Notes

1. See nayre.org.

2. This analysis uses a panel weight (C24PW0) to compensate for the unequal probabilities of selection inherent in the ECLS-K's stratified sampling design.

3. I used the beginning and end school dates supplied by school administrators and, when those dates were not provided, those given by parents.

4. NCES requires rounding to the nearest 10 when discussing the restricted use data sample sizes.

5. Our matching strategy also considered alternate methods, including adjustments to the caliper threshold and a multiple-match strategy that allowed any one year-round student to be matched with multiple nine-month students (Morgan 2001). The first alternate matching strategy imposed a more stringent caliper threshold of .005 in making one-to-one matches, and led to a matched sample of 1,094. The second alternate method was a one-to-many matching strategy, which yielded a sample of 3,818. Despite the larger size of this sample, it also resulted in a larger percentage of year-round students being unmatched and eliminated from the analysis. With both alternate matched files, we were able to generate racial/ethnic and residential estimates that mirrored the results we presented in this study. We are therefore optimistic that our findings are robust to alternative matching approaches.

References

Arum, Richard. 2000. Schools and communities: Ecological and institutional dimensions. *Annual Review of Sociology* 26:395–418.

Benson, James, and Geoffrey Borman. 2010. Family, neighborhood, and school settings across seasons: When do socioeconomic context and racial composition matter for the reading achievement growth of young children? *Teachers College Press* 112 (5): 1338–90.

Borman, Geoffrey D., and N. Maritza Dowling. 2006. Longitudinal achievement effects of multiyear summer school: Evidence from the Teach Baltimore randomized field trial. *Educational Evaluation and Policy Analysis* 28 (1): 25–48.

Borman, Geoffrey D., Michael E. Goetz, and N. Maritza Dowling. 2009. Halting the summer achievement slide: A randomized field trial of the KindergARTen Summer Camp. *Journal of Education for Students Placed at Risk* 14 (2): 133–47.

Burkham, David, Douglas Ready, Valerie Lee, and Laura Logerfo. 2004. Social class differences in summer learning between kindergarten and first grade: Model specification and estimation. *Sociology of Education* 77:1–31.

Chaplin, Duncan, and Jeffrey Capizzano. 2006. *Impacts of a summer learning program: A random assignment study of Building Educated Leaders for Life (BELL)*. Washington, DC: Urban Institute.

Coleman, James S., Ernest Q. Campbell, Carol J. Hobson, James McPartland, Alexander M. Mood, Frederic D. Weinfeld, and Robert L. York. 1966. *Equality of educational opportunity*. Washington, DC: U.S. Department of Health, Education and Welfare.

Condron, Dennis. 2009. Social class, school and non-school environments, and black/white inequalities in children's learning. *American Sociological Review* 74:683–708.

Cooper, Harris, Kelly Charlton, Jeff C. Valentine, and Laura Muhlenbruck, eds. 2000. Making the most of summer school: A meta-analytic and narrative review. *Monographs of the Society for Research in Child Development* 65 (1).

Cooper, Harris, Jeffrey C. Valentine, Kelly Charlton, and April Melson. 2003. The effects of modified school calendars on student achievement and on school and community attitudes. *Review of Educational Research* 73:1–52.

Downey, Douglas, Paul von Hippel, and Beckett Broh. 2004. Are schools the great equalizer? Cognitive inequality during the summer months and the school year. *American Sociological Review* 69:613–35.

Entwisle, Doris R., and Karl L. Alexander. 1992. Summer setback: Race, poverty, school composition and math achievement in the first two years of school. *American Sociological Review* 57:72–84.

Gandara, Patricia, and Judy Fish. 1994. Year-round schooling as an avenue to major structural reform. *Educational Evaluation and Policy Analysis* 16:67–85.

Hansen, Ben. 2004. Full matching in an observational study of coaching for the SAT. *Journal of the American Statistical Association* 99:609–18.

Harding, David. 2003. Counterfactual models of neighborhood effects: The effect of neighborhood poverty on dropping out and teenage pregnancy. *American Journal of Sociology* 109:676–719.

Haskins, Anna. 2017. Paternal incarceration and children's schooling contexts: Intersecting inequalities of educational opportunity. *The ANNALS of the American Academy of Political and Social Science* (this volume).

Heckman, James, Hidehiko Ichimura, Jeffrey Smith, and Petra Todd. 1998. Characterizing selection bias using experimental data. *Econometrica* 66 (5): 1017–98.

Jacob, Brian A., and Lars Lefgren. 2004. Remedial education and student achievement: A regression-discontinuity analysis. *Review of Economics and Statistics* 86 (1): 226–44.

Jencks, Christopher, and Susan Mayer. 1990. The social consequences of growing up in a poor neighborhood. In *Inner-city poverty in the United States*, eds. Laurence E. Lynn Jr. and Michael G. McGeary, 111–86. Washington, DC: National Academy Press.

Johnson, Odis, Jr. 2012. A systematic review of neighborhood and institutional relationships related to education. *Education and Urban Society* 44 (4): 477–511.

Johnson, Odis, Jr. 2014. Race-gender inequality across residential and school contexts: What can policy do? In *African American males in PreK-12 schools: Informing research, practice, and policy*, eds. James L. Moore and Chance W. Lewis, 345–76. Bingley, UK: Emerald Publishing.

Lauritsen, Janet L., and Nicole White. 2014. *Seasonal patterns in criminal victimization trends*. Report NCJ245959. U.S. Department of Justice, Office of Justice Programs. Washington, DC: Bureau of Justice Statistics.

Logan, John R., Brian J. Stults, and Reynolds Farley. 2004. Segregation of minorities in the metropolis: Two decades of change. *Demography* 41:1–22.

Matsudaira, Jordan D. 2008. Mandatory summer school and student achievement. *Journal of Econometrics* 142 (2): 829–50.

McMillen, Bradley J. 2001. A statewide evaluation of academic achievement in year-round schools. *Journal of Educational Research* 95 (2): 67–74.

Morgan, Stephen L. 2001. Counterfactuals, causal effect heterogeneity, and the Catholic school effect on learning. *Sociology of Education* 74:341–74.

Morgan, Stephen, and Christopher Winship. 2007. *Counterfactuals and causal inference: Methods and principles for social research*. Cambridge, MA: Cambridge University Press.

Raudenbush, Stephen, and Anthony Bryk. 2002. *Hierarchical linear models*. Newbury Park, CA: Sage Publications.

Reece, Jennifer, Carl Myers, Christy Nofsinger, and Reagan Brown. 2000. Retention of skills over the summer months in alternative and traditional calendar schools. *Journal of Research and Development in Education* 33 (3): 166–74.

Rendon, Maria G. 2014. Drop out and "disconnected" young adults: Examining the impact of neighborhood and school contexts. *Urban Review* 46:169–96.

Sharkey, Patrick, and Robert J. Sampson. 2010. The acute effect of local homicides on children's cognitive performance. *Proceedings of the National Academy of Sciences of the United States of America* 107 (26): 11733–38.

U.S. Department of Education. 2013. *Digest of education statistics*. Washington, DC: National Center for Education Statistics. Available from http://nces.ed.gov/programs/digest/d13/tables/dt13_234.12.asp.

von Hippel, Paul. 2016. Year-round school calendars. Effects on summer learning, achievement, parents, teachers and property values. In *The summer slide: What we know and can do about summer learning loss*, eds. Karl Alexander, Sarah Pitcock, and Matthew Boulay, 208–30. New York, NY: Teachers College Press.

Wodtke, Geoffrey T., David J. Harding, and Felix Elwert. 2011. Neighborhood effects in temporal perspective: The impact of long-term exposure to concentrated disadvantage on high school graduation. *American Sociological Review* 76:713–36.

Counting on Context: Cross-Sector Collaborations for Education and the Legacy of James Coleman's Sociological Vision

By
CAROLYN RIEHL
and
MELISSA A. LYON

Many localities across the United States are pursuing efforts to improve outcomes for children and youth through place-based, cross-sector collaborations among education, business, government, philanthropy, and social services agencies. In this article, we examine these place-based initiatives, investigating how they attempt to ameliorate educational inequity and how they might reflect the broader sociological vision of James S. Coleman. We draw from publicly available information on a set of 182 cross-sector collaborations across the United States and from in-depth case studies of collaborations in Buffalo, New York; Milwaukee, Wisconsin; and Portland/Multnomah County, Oregon. We find evidence that in some ways, cross-sector collaborations contribute to improving schools, offer interventions and resources to support families and communities, and attempt to revitalize localities with strong norms and social ties to support education and equity. However, these outcomes are not yet fully formed, widespread, or guaranteed to last over time.

Keywords: educational opportunity; Coleman Report; cross-sector collaboration; collective impact; social capital; socialization

Many localities across the United States are pursuing efforts to improve outcomes for children and youth through partnerships among

Carolyn Riehl is an associate professor of sociology and education policy at Teachers College, Columbia University. She is coeditor of A New Agenda for Research in Educational Leadership (Teachers College Press 2005). Her work has appeared in Educational Researcher, Sociology of Education, American Journal of Education, Review of Educational Research, American Educational Research Journal, and numerous edited volumes.

Melissa A. Lyon is a PhD student in the Politics and Education Program at Teachers College, Columbia University. Her research interests include urban education politics and the race, class, and interest group dynamics of social and educational policy. Prior to attending Teachers College, Melissa was a middle school teacher in Houston, Texas.

Correspondence: riehl@tc.columbia.edu

DOI: 10.1177/0002716217735284

education, business, government, philanthropy, and social services agencies. These place-based, cross-sector collaborations bring individuals and organizational agents together to develop shared goals and offer interventions, often along a "cradle to career" continuum. Some of these collaborations are long-standing and have their roots in educational programs such as community schools or in comprehensive community development initiatives (Henig et al. 2015; Riehl and Henig, forthcoming). Many new initiatives have taken inspiration from the "collective impact" approach to social change that was first articulated in the *Stanford Social Innovation Review* (Kania and Kramer 2011). Some are local, homegrown partnerships, while others are linked together in national networks that offer guidance and support—for example, the StriveTogether network that grew out of the Strive Partnership in Cincinnati and Northern Kentucky.

These collaborations can be seen as attempts to capitalize on the idea that an alignment of effort might gather together more resources and produce better results than a scattershot approach. They could be pragmatic acknowledgments that locally developed solutions are essential when assistance from state and federal sources is not guaranteed. In some cases, they may reflect an optimistic and forward-looking effort to shape new forms of civic cooperation in places where individuals and organizations have overcome past divisions of politics, economics, and race and are working together more productively than they once did. But they also may arise out of a sense of frustration and even desperation over low educational performance, poor employment prospects, and the ongoing effects of poverty, especially for children and youth of color.

In this article, we contribute to discussions of the ongoing legacy of James S. Coleman's landmark report, *Equality of Educational Opportunity* (EEO; Coleman et al. 1966), by asking: How, if at all, do cross-sector collaborations for education build on the contributions the study made to understanding and ameliorating educational inequity? Further, how might they reflect the broader sociological vision of James S. Coleman as it was expressed through EEO and other works?

A National Study of Cross-Sector Collaboration for Education

To explore these questions, we draw from two components of a comprehensive study of cross-sector collaborations for education in which we have been engaged.[1] The first is a national scan of collaborations around the United States. Our research team sought collaborations that were anchored in goals related to education, that involved the local K–12 school system and at least one additional sector (e.g., city government, social agencies, business, charitable foundations, higher education), and that operated at the level of a neighborhood, city, school district, or region (rather than being affiliated with just one school). We looked for programs that were currently in operation and had a presence on the Internet as of January 2015, using a broad keyword search strategy with additional efforts to locate collaborations in the one hundred largest cities and one hundred largest school districts in the country. We identified 182 collaborations and analyzed information presented on their websites, including links to published reports and other sources (see Henig et al. [2016] for further information about the scan methodology and findings).

The second component is a set of three intensive case studies of cross-sector collaboration for education. These include the Milwaukee Succeeds initiative in Wisconsin, affiliated with the StriveTogether network; Say Yes Buffalo in New York, one of several citywide initiatives across the country sponsored by the Say Yes to Education foundation; and the All Hands Raised partnership in Portland and Multnomah County, Oregon, another StriveTogether affiliate. For these case studies, we and other members of our research team visited the sites at least twice over the course of a year and conducted more than two hundred interviews, along with observations, document collection, and check-in conversations before and after the site visits. The analysis of these data is under way; in this article, we report preliminary findings.

The Coleman Report and What It Set in Motion

The release in 1966 of EEO, colloquially known as the Coleman Report, was a pivotal event that eventually became thought of as marking the beginning of a new federal role in research on schooling. Although the government had been collecting data about students, teachers, and schools and colleges since 1870, these data were mostly descriptive documentations of educational inputs and expenditures. A study a few years earlier, the Project Talent study shared many characteristics with EEO but did not have the same impact (Hutt 2016). The Coleman Report was notable for being comprehensive: it used a large, nationally representative survey database—more than 600,000 students in a 5 percent random sample of public schools (see Hill, this volume, for additional details). Methodologically, it was notable for using standardized tests as measures of student performance across elementary and secondary grades, and for employing statistical methods (primarily stepwise decomposition of variance) that, while inadequate by today's standards, linked contextual conditions and inputs in a production function analysis of outcomes. This approach took hold and a few years later the government began to monitor educational outcomes regularly through the National Assessment of Educational Progress and also began numerous longitudinal and cross-sectional survey research programs for purposes of correlational and causal analysis (Snyder 1993). The study did not draw from, articulate, or test a specific theory about how and why student academic achievement might vary across schools and students. Theory-based analyses of instruction and learning were not as well developed at the time as they are now, and the government's intentions behind EEO constrained Coleman to focus on statistical associations rather than theoretical elaboration. But the selection of measures included in the survey suggested a conceptual framework that linked student performance to individual and contextual background variables and to rudimentary features of the instructional program, and this led to new ways of thinking about educational productivity and equality.

The EEO acquired some notoriety before it was even released. Controversies erupted about the wording and intent of survey items, superintendents of prominent districts declined to participate, data were lost and surveys had to be readministered, and the project's advisory board refused to sign off on the report because of disagreements over the statistical analyses (Egalite 2016). Because its findings were in many ways unexpected and controversial, it spawned an extensive amount of examination, discussion, and reanalysis over the years (Hill, this volume; Mosteller and Moynihan 1972).

As consequential as it was for education research, the Coleman Report was a "fountainhead study" for those who more generally wanted to promote the use of evidence to inform policy (Hanushek 2016). It was commissioned in 1964 as Section 402 of the Civil Rights Act, tacked onto a bill that was known at the time mostly for its provisions regarding voting rights and public accommodations (Grant 1973). Initially, the bill called for the Commissioner of Education to "investigate … the extent to which equal educational opportunities are denied to individuals" (Grant 1973, 18), but the wording was changed to a less incendiary call for a survey to document "the lack of availability of equal educational opportunities for individuals by reason of race, color, religion, or national origin in public educational institutions at all levels" (Coleman et al. 1966, iii). The report itself contained no recommendations, but as the U.S. Commissioner of Education, Harold Howe II, wrote in his letter of transmittal, it was conducted in such a way as to be "useful to those concerned with public education in the United States" (p. iv).

As the study moved toward completion, Coleman and others in the Office of Education were well aware that it could impact policy in unintended and potentially undesirable ways. Hence, much attention was paid to crafting the executive summary. It was seen as so politically sensitive that three versions were prepared, none written by Coleman himself (Grant 1973). While the controversy swirled around the summary, Coleman "had barricaded himself in a motel in southwest Washington," with one change of clothing, working nonstop on the full report while meals were delivered along with daily analysis reports sent down from the computer center in Princeton via Greyhound bus (Grant 1973, 28). In the end, in the third and final version of the summary, the main finding was tucked beneath a deluge of tables and graphs: "It appears that differences between schools account for only a small fraction of differences in pupil achievement" (Coleman et al. 1966, 22). A few prominent newspapers reported the study's release. It garnered a short announcement, which included what might be the first public mention of the "achievement gap," on page 24 of the Saturday edition of the *New York Times* on July 2, 1966, under the headline "Negro Education is Found Inferior: U.S. Public Survey Confirms Racial Disparity." The article buried the lead that "the survey clearly showed that 'family background is more important than schools'" (*New York Times* 1966a).

For the next two years, nothing happened programmatically in the Office of Education because of the study. But at the same time, largely through the efforts of Daniel Patrick Moynihan, the report was pored over by Congress and eventually by the media and the public (Grant 1973; Hill, this volume). Senator Abraham Ribicoff of Connecticut accused the Office of Education of suppressing the report and asserted that "it should be subjected to exposure, argument and debate in every school board and PTA in the country" (*New York Times* 1966b). The report was invoked on different sides of education policy debates during the Johnson and Nixon administrations, as justification both for a doubling down on desegregation and for a proposed reduction in education spending for schools, which Nixon needed to offset costs of the Vietnam War. By 1970, the report was widely known, and Coleman was brought back to Washington as a consultant to the Cabinet Committee on Desegregation. This led eventually to a second Coleman Report (Coleman, Kelly, and Moore 1976) that documented extensive white flight from big cities following desegregation. This laid Coleman open to intense criticism and even vilification from his professional colleagues and eventually helped to fuel a subtle but pervasive retreat from desegregation as a core strategy for educational equity (Peterson 2010).

"Schools don't matter" was an immediate and frequently invoked summary of EEO's findings, but one that does not capture the full story. Whether this conclusion was just plain wrong or merely simplistic, the Coleman Report energized both those who wanted to refute this implication as well as those who accepted it. It ushered in a long era of attention to two sets of factors influencing student performance: policies, resources, and practices that could strengthen the ability of schools to make a difference for their students; and, conversely, policies and practices that bypassed the schools and were meant to help ameliorate the dampening effects of students' own backgrounds and the compositional effects generated by the social backgrounds of their peers.

Coleman's Legacy for Strengthening the Impact of the School

The Coleman Report found that school-related conditions such as teacher quality seemed to influence students from minority backgrounds more than white students, even if the effects were relatively small compared to other factors. Coleman and colleagues wrote: "It is for the most disadvantaged children that improvements in school quality will make the most difference in achievement" (1966, 22). This was heartening news to those looking to increase resources for schools. Since then, analysts and policy-makers have sought ways to increase the effect schools can have on equality of educational opportunity, in part by examining the many in-school factors the study did not measure, and by attending to the factors that the study did explore (like teacher quality), to make them more influential and equitable. Since Coleman was not a pedagogical expert and, as he admitted, he had only crude measures of school quality, many stones were left unturned in the study itself. The ensuing years have seen much research on the effects of curriculum content, pedagogical techniques, instructional pacing, academic tasks, class size and composition, and many other in-school factors on academic excellence and equity. Thus, in seeking to link cross-sector collaborations to the Coleman Report, we first ask: Do cross-sector collaborations extend the legacy of EEO in trying to bolster the ability of schools to make a difference for students?

Cross-sector collaborations: Extending the legacy for school improvement

There is evidence from our national scan that collaborations are attending to the condition of education in their communities. For example, of the 182 programs we identified in 2015, 44 percent presented data about student academic achievement, 35 percent showed high school graduation information, 17 percent provided measures of school attendance, 6 percent offered information about school discipline, and 5 percent tracked information about students' access to technology. The exact meanings of these indicators are ambiguous. Some likely represent broad outcomes for which the collaborations are pushing, and the public reporting may be intended to keep the community's attention focused on them. Others may reflect actual interventions in which the collaborations are engaged. It is possible that some are presented mainly because it is easy to get data on them; conversely, other programs probably did not present data on education simply because they could not obtain appropriate information.

Our three in-depth case studies give a closer, and more complicated, picture of how cross-sector collaborations can help to improve schooling. Two of the three collaborations arose specifically because of widespread civic dissatisfaction with current educational services and outcomes; the third was also concerned about education, though not boiling over with frustration. From these starting points, the collaborations have made only limited forays into the work of school systems. In Milwaukee, for example, the collaboration has supported a teacher development project to improve elementary literacy instruction. Implemented in a small but growing set of schools, this project directly addresses the issue of teacher quality in schools serving disadvantaged students. The collaboration sees it as a pilot project that may encourage further support for other teacher development efforts, but some in the community wonder how a small and relatively expensive project can be scaled up to make an impact for the whole city.

In Portland, Oregon, the All Hands Raised collaboration is also supporting small demonstration projects in selected schools, using a rapid improvement cycle to implement, review, and refine the approaches. One set of projects focuses on services for students with poor attendance; another provides summer programming to support student transitions from middle school to high school. This collaboration also hosts a subgroup that addresses the matter of racial inequities in school disciplinary action. In Buffalo, the initiative maintains close contact with the school system, and a number of district personnel participate regularly in the collaboration's meetings. Say Yes has assisted the district in organizing summer school programming. The collaboration also has arranged for a "family support specialist" to be assigned to every public, noncharter school. While the professionals in these positions are expected to work mostly with students and their families, their placement in schools makes it likely that occasionally they will assist with school-related activities, including attendance follow-up. But Buffalo program representatives are explicit in stating that the initiative is not promoting "education reform." This may be, in part, because an effort to get closely involved in the selection of a new school superintendent backfired and caused the collaboration to take a less activist role with the district.

Overall, the three cross-sector collaborations that we have studied do not seek to be chief architects or engineers of school improvement. They acknowledge that instruction is the purview of schools and school districts, and they seek neither to assign blame nor to fix major problems with schooling. While they have stepped carefully into some aspects of schooling, they have avoided engaging with thorny local problems of unequal distribution of resources across schools serving different populations, or policies and practices like tracking and school attendance zones that exacerbate segregation.

Nonetheless, the collaborations can be seen as helping to improve schooling in several ways. First, they are shining a light on educational issues and outcomes. This focuses attention and gives pertinent information to the community. When the collaborations choose to promote successful aspects of local education, this helps to counter long-standing narratives about endemic problems with urban school systems. Second, they are helping to soften aspects of the contentious political climates that swirl around education so that the school systems can focus on their core work. We are not claiming a strict causal pattern, but we think it is no accident that relationships between school superintendents, school boards, and teachers' unions in these cities have become somewhat calmer since the collaborations were established. At the very least, the cross-sector collaborations can model good working relationships across diverse partners, and they might provide a cushion of trust that makes contentious parties more willing to attempt to get along. Third, the collaborations feel they are doing school systems a big service by helping to address the out-of-school factors that impinge on students' academic success. In these ways, then, the cross-sector collaborations align with a "schools can matter" argument, but this alone does not provide an adequate explanation for the proliferation of collaborations and the range of services that they provide.

Coleman's Legacy for Addressing Family and Social Context Effects

The final paragraph of text in the Coleman Report offered a stark conclusion:

> Taking all these results together, one implication stands out above all: That schools bring little influence to bear on a child's achievement that is independent of his background and general social context; and that this very lack of an independent effect means that the inequalities imposed on children by their home, neighborhood, and peer environment

are carried along to become the inequalities with which they confront adult life at the end of school. (Coleman et al. 1966, 325)

Like the results about school effects, this finding has also been subjected to much scrutiny. EEO was not able to go very far in presenting a conceptual framework for explaining the impact of a student's background or the composite social background of a school's student population on achievement. For the most part, however, the impact of a student's own family and social background continues to hold up as "far more important than school social composition and school resources for understanding student outcomes" (Borman and Dowling 2010, 1202). Some have interpreted this to endorse the importance of families doing particular things to support their children's education and have sought strategies for enhancing family involvement (see Liu and White, this volume; Kraft and Monti-Nussbaum, this volume). Many interpreted it to mean that poverty was the culprit causing a negative family effect on academic performance. In response, direct poverty reduction strategies, urban community development, and school desegregation were employed as ways to improve the social backgrounds of students.

Others looked for ways in which social policy might help to provide some of the tangible benefits associated with family social class that seem to enhance student performance in school. For example, more advantaged students have access to health and social services that help to prepare and enable them to learn, early childhood education and out-of-school services that enhance their development, cultural experiences that enrich their studies, and assistance with the finances and logistics of moving from high school to higher education. This has led to policy initiatives for comprehensive or "wraparound" services to reduce disparities in what is available to advantaged and disadvantaged students (Egalite 2016; Rebell and Wolff 2011; Rothstein 2004). This also leads to our second research question: Do cross-sector collaborations help to ameliorate the impact of students' social backgrounds on school performance?

Cross-sector collaborations: Extending the legacy for family and social background

Cross-sector collaborations can be viewed as a legacy of Coleman's work with EEO to the degree that they seek to provide students with the services and resources for which the social background effect is a proxy. Many collaborations take a "cradle to career," "anything it takes" approach toward providing comprehensive resources for students, and they often place a special emphasis on rationalizing and aligning the many different services and service providers in their local communities.

In the national scan, we found collaborations that exist to address particular out-of-school conditions that help families and children; these include alliances of after-school providers and networks of early childhood care providers, and at least one initiative focused on health. Others had multiple social, health, and ancillary school-related services within their purview. Some took a community schools approach; others had received federal Promise Neighborhood funding to provide an array of services.

Of the 182 collaborations that we examined, 24 percent presented information on their websites about children's developmental progress toward kindergarten readiness, 17 percent tracked health indicators, 9 percent monitored pre-K enrollment, 8 percent followed indicators of children's safety, and 5 percent provided indicators of social-emotional development for children and youth. We believe these numbers are underestimates of the attention paid to nonschool services and resources for children and families, because data on these targets are not typically available from extant sources and are difficult for collaborations to gather on their own.

Many of the collaborations included on their websites information about the membership on their top governing boards. This is another indicator of the range of interventions in which cross-sector collaborations are engaged. Of the collaborations that presented such information in 2015, representatives from the medical/healthcare field were on 56 percent of the governing boards, early childhood representatives were on 29 percent of the boards, and 79 percent of the boards had representatives from social services agencies outside of the school district.

In the in-depth case studies, providing wraparound social services and other resources to ameliorate some of the inequalities associated with family background effects was a core component of the collaborations' missions and strategies. In Portland, All Hands Raised works with a long-standing community organization that provides support services for children in area schools. In Milwaukee, the Milwaukee Succeeds collaboration has had a focus on early childhood developmental screening and immunization as part of their kindergarten readiness goal, and they are developing a comprehensive focus on social-emotional health. Many local social service agencies are involved in this initiative.

Addressing students' social background needs is most clear with Say Yes Buffalo. The Say Yes to Education Foundation began as a charitable initiative to offer a college tuition incentive to a small cohort of students in a Philadelphia middle school. The benefactor learned fairly quickly that the scholarship alone was not sufficient to guarantee success for its recipients, and over time the theory of action for Say Yes evolved into a comprehensive menu of interventions and resources. With Say Yes Buffalo, the target population is the entire city. All students graduating from a traditional public or charter high school in the city are eligible for a college scholarship; and to support students along their educational pathway, the collaboration offers a comprehensive array of services for students and their families, including mental health clinics in schools, social worker services, school-based legal clinics, after-school programs, college counseling and help preparing financial aid applications, summer employment and internship opportunities, and mentoring programs.

In EEO, academic performance was related both to students' own social backgrounds and the compositional effects of the backgrounds of other students in the school. As we noted above, none of these collaborations is taking on the issue of student diversity and desegregation directly. However, leaders in Buffalo are optimistic that, with time, the initiative will address the school composition issue indirectly. Many anticipate that one of the long-term benefits of the Say Yes program will be that more affluent residents from the suburbs will move back into Buffalo to take advantage of the scholarship promise, but a change in the racial and socioeconomic status (SES) composition of the school district does not necessarily lead to diversity within schools or classrooms if, for example, practices such as tracking or ability grouping are in place. Still, if the high school completion rate rises in the city and more families reap the benefits of better employment prospects, the racial and SES composition of schools will change. Again, this is not a change that will happen quickly.

Coleman's Legacy for the Social Milieu and Collective Socialization

It is possible to interpret contemporary cross-sector collaborations as a legacy of the Coleman Report in a third way. To draw this through-line, we place EEO in the context of Coleman's broader sociological vision and body of scholarship. In much of his writing, Coleman was motivated by an interest in social institutions and systems. His approach was often structural-functionalist and Durkheiman in nature (Marsden 2005; Pallas 1999), exploring how social institutions could influence the actions of individuals and create a cohesive society. He saw this happening primarily through the social transmission of values, expectations, and motivations. In a seemingly sentimental analysis, which he repeated many times, Coleman extolled the family as the primordial social institution responsible for providing structure and socialization for the young. When economic activity was centered in family farms or small enterprises, children were watched over, educated, and prepared for their future social and economic lives within the household unit. Communities also served as socializing contexts for transmitting values and motivations, which were reinforced because community status hierarchies were congruent with them. To succeed, members of a community followed its norms and avoided its sanctions.

But these social forms have weakened over time, Coleman argued. Men's work migrated from the home to industrial organizations and businesses, and young people were sent to school to be prepared for those settings. Once women (especially mothers of young children) also sought work outside the home, the family as an institution was further "detonated" and "evacuated," "shrinking in size, function, and capability" and schools were relied upon for custodial care as well as education (Coleman and Hoffer 1987, 19). In some contexts, families and communities had become so buffeted by social and economic upheavals that the schools had to take over basic socialization functions for them. Some of Coleman's portrayals of these patterns sound downright alarming: Communities found themselves separating children from adults in their own households (now "emptied out during the day") and from the places where adults were to be found (Coleman 1961). As schools became remote sites for intellectual development, families had "an extremely variable ability to socialize children for achievement"

(Coleman 1971, 648). The family had turned into "a kind of backwater in society, cut off from the mainstream" (Coleman 1987, 33).

When family and community fail to perform their socialization functions, what happens to the schools? Coleman explored a version of this question in *The Adolescent Society* (1961). How, he wondered, were youth going to learn important social lessons that would motivate them to do well in school when their main relations were with each other and with large, impersonal social institutions like the school? In his analysis of the closed social system of peer group culture in high schools, he found that to some degree, students' attitudes about academic achievement and aspirations for college were responsive to adult value systems in the school—a "schools matter" argument. Community social class and values and students' family background also had some impact on student academic performance. But these socializing forces did not necessarily predict what was most important to the peer status culture or who would be in the "leading crowds" in schools, and adolescent peer culture became a "small society" on its own that was often at cross-purposes with educational values. Coleman implicated the wider social system in this analysis:

> It is the adult community that fixes the activities of the adolescent community. It does so by fixing the activities of the school—for example, by using high-school sports as community entertainment, and as contests between communities—and by restricting adolescent activities outside of school. The adolescent has little or no possibility of responsibility today; adults have shut him out of the job market—have told him, in effect, to go off to school and not bother them. (Coleman 1961, 305)

Coleman's *The Adolescent Society* (1961) preceded his massive study for the U.S. government by half a decade. Five years after EEO, he again took up the matter of socialization, and once again he saw a role for schools but also for the larger society. In "How do the young become adults?" (Coleman 1972), he once more noted that the home had become depleted as a site for socialization:

> In the family, the young remain, while the activities from which they could learn have moved out; in workplaces, the activities from which the young could learn remain, but the young themselves have been excluded. This exclusion places youth more on the fringes of society, outside its important institutions. …The young have no institutional base, they are a lumpen proletariat. (Coleman 1972, 433)

Coleman's proposed solution at this point became even more dramatic: attention to students' academic and intellectual work in schools needed to be supplemented by other efforts to enlist the "economic institutions of society" in giving all students opportunities to learn the knowledge and skills they would need to be well-rounded and productive citizens. Academic and vocational education had to go hand in hand; students should not be tracked into curricula emphasizing just one or the other.

In Coleman's early writings, these relationships among families, communities, and schools were described in sentimental and romantic terms, as essential elements of a tightly woven social fabric. Later on, he used a more hard-edged vocabulary to describe the same phenomena. Social relationships in value-rich "functional communities," especially those whose number, strength, and quality of ties created "intergenerational closure," created "social capital" that enhanced the ability to socialize the young and develop their human capital (Coleman 1988; Coleman and Hoffer 1987). Once again, he seemed provincial in blaming the loss of social capital and subsequent socialization problems on things like the structural deficiency of a one-parent household, the weakness of communities no longer held together by shared values and geographic proximity, and even "increasing psychic involvement of youth with mass media" (Coleman and Hoffer 1987, 230). But his point was that this long decline for families and communities will continue, and society must now look to the large institutions like schools to replace families and communities and to provide the norms and obligations that serve as socializing guides and motivations for the "engine of action" that young people would employ via rational self-interest (Coleman 1988, 1990). These large institutions cannot simply be more intensive versions of schools as we know them. Instead, children need to encounter not just the traditional demands, opportunities, and rewards of schooling, which are not motivating enough on their own, but also socializing features that could "induce the kinds of attitudes, effort, and conception of self that children and youth need to succeed in school and as adults" (Coleman 1987, 38). Whether these socializing features are engendered by adults manipulating the adolescent society in schools (Coleman 1961), or by using social capital in functional communities to transmit values (Coleman 1988), or by developing bonds between teachers and students around the shared expectation of being accountable for performance (Coleman et al. 1997), they turn schools into active agents of socialization, not just beneficiaries of the socialization accomplished through families and communities.

The strongest clue that socialization is what Coleman cared most about was in "A Vision for Sociology" (Coleman 1994), a reflection he offered late in his career, in which he reminisced about the watershed period for sociology in the 1950s. During this period, he explained, a shift was under way between, on one hand, sociologists' traditional interest in community studies—where the community was the unit of analysis and the goal was to examine the norms and values, status systems, and cleavages of social life—and, on the other hand, their burgeoning interest in survey research, which used systematic data and the statistical analysis of variables to develop causal accounts of individuals' actions and attitudes. In a more analytic piece on this same theme (Coleman 1986), he suggested that sociologists were unable to unify their "social theory" agenda with their "social research" innovations because they were interrupted by the government's need for applied social research that could provide guidance for programmatic interventions with specific social problems and populations. Their research pivoted to empirical studies with individuals as the unit of analysis.

In this so-called watershed moment, Coleman tried to bridge community studies and survey research by exploring the closed social system of high school and its impact on students. Although his data did not enable him to fully execute the intended analysis, this work became *The Adolescent Society* (1961).

Then, he had another chance with EEO. This time, he leaned more deliberately in the direction of the statistical analysis of individual outcomes. Given the intended aims of the government-sponsored study, Coleman focused on monetized resources in the school—the books, labs, debate teams, music programs, and well-trained and experienced teachers—that could be manipulated by social policy, and he examined their impact on academic outcomes for members of social groups defined by race. This was the analysis that galvanized the study's many audiences. It was empirical and policy-relevant, destined to become a landmark. But Coleman himself described it as a detour from his enduring interests (Marsden 2005).

As it turned out, however, the study did enable him to document at least some effects of a social system on individuals, because it included numerous measures of the social milieu of students' families and communities, including parent education, family structure, educational resources, and expectations for their children. These were factors that Coleman already believed produced variability in the socialization of youth toward academic performance. He also studied teachers' expectations for their students, and students' own self-efficacy or sense of control, two more indicators of the value climates in schools that could affect performance.

Presented as a production function analysis, EEO ended up bearing a close resemblance to classic sociological studies of social context, with the added bonus of measuring effects on individuals. Although it lacked an explicit conceptual framework and explanation of mechanisms (Sørensen and Morgan 2000), it led to the finding that mattered most to Coleman: that the "inequalities imposed on children by their home, neighborhood, and peer environment" are inequalities of socialization and social context, and they have a stronger effect on children and youth than the educational features of the schools themselves.

It also was the finding that Alexander Mood, the U.S. Office of Education official who brought Coleman in to direct the study, pointed to in his second version of the EEO executive summary, which never saw the light of day: "Thus these data suggest that the major source of variability among schools is not a result of the school effects, but of differences in the community that affect the children's receptiveness to the school" (Grant 1973, 26). And it probably was the finding that spurred Daniel Patrick Moynihan to pay so much attention to the report, because it seemed to resonate with his own controversial work, *The Negro Family* (Moynihan 1965).

In 1987, Coleman summarized the EEO findings about family background as follows:

> The outputs of education result from the interaction of qualities the child brings from home—which can be loosely characterized as attitudes, effort, and conception of self—with qualities of the school. As the social capital in home and neighborhood shrinks, school achievement and other growth will not be increased by replacing these resources with more school-like resources—that is, those that produce opportunities, demands, and rewards—but by replacing them with resources which produce attitudes, efforts, and conception of self—that is, those qualities that interact with the ones provided by the school. (p. 38)

Coleman understood full well the importance of the educational resources that schools provide. Indeed, in his biographical musings, he explained that he was motivated in this work by his own frustrations with dismal, stultifying, uninspiring schooling (Pallas 1999). But he cared even more that students have ample opportunities to develop the social values that would lead to their well-being and prosperity. Although EEO gave birth to a school effects industry that pursued more research evidence about, and practical development of, the inner workings of schools, and although EEO also ushered in equally ambitious efforts to understand and intervene around family/social background effects, what really interested Coleman was the school as a functional social system and how the social milieu affected youth. In this regard, EEO was not such a detour after all. This brings us to our final question: Do cross-sector collaborations lead to better social contexts and enhance the collective socialization capacities of cities?

Cross-sector collaborations: Extending the legacy for collective socialization

To serve as a legacy of EEO in this third sense, that is, to foster collective socialization, cross-sector collaborations would need to strengthen local normative beliefs and messaging about equity and education and strengthen the social ties among institutional and individual actors who can mobilize the social, human, and economic capital at their disposal to transmit those values and help to develop the human capital of children and youth. This would be, in other words, an effort to draw a new social contract around other people's children that redefines them as one's own. The unit of analysis becomes the city instead of the family, or small community, or school—but the fundamental question is the same: How can a social institution become a supportive environment for children?

There is evidence in our national scan that some cross-sector collaborations are at least attempting to move in these directions. First, we searched initiatives' websites for the meaningful use of terms such as "equity," "social justice," "racial justice," or "achievement gap," and found that 82 of the 182 collaborations use explicit language to promote the values of equity and educational parity. Thirty collaborations (17 percent of all collaborations) show one or more indicators disaggregated by race or socioeconomic status, suggesting a desire for transparency about disparate outcomes. Another way that collaborations in the scan have demonstrated a commitment to strengthening the social fabric of the community is through the participation and engagement of diverse community actors in their governance structures. Of the collaborations that present information on their top governing boards, businesses leaders, higher education officials, and superintendents or other school district representatives participate at the highest levels. However, representatives from religious organizations sit on 35 percent of the boards, minority organizations are represented on 29 percent of the boards, and neighborhood or community organizations are represented on 4 percent of the boards. Furthermore, a mayor sits on a quarter of the boards. Although there is not sufficient evidence to suggest that these collaborations are mobilizing and fully integrating grassroots level community members, it does appear that they are involving various sectors within the communities and building social capital together.

On the other hand, however, we also note that 63 of the collaborations we studied (35 percent of the full set of 182) used language about economic development in describing their missions and goals, incorporating terms such as "urban revitalization," "job growth," "economic growth," and "housing prices." For example, one collaborative writes, "We believe that education is the most important engine of individual opportunity and economic growth in our region." To be sure, promoting economic development and access to jobs could be an equity-focused approach, but it also could signal a desire for kinds of growth likely to benefit only some segments of the local population. Nearly half of the collaborations that wrote about equity also wrote about economic growth. The presence of both equity and economic language could indicate the collaborations were engaged in "split messaging"—the use of contradictory portrayals of a mission to different audiences, depending on racial or socioeconomic composition (Franklin 2010). To further explore this question, we examined the relationship between choice of language and city demographics. We found that, on average, collaborations that promote themselves using economic development language are in cities with 5 percentage points more white residents and 7 percentage points fewer black and Hispanic residents than collaborations that do not use economic development rhetoric. One might expect to find the opposite trend in the relationship between equity language and city demographics. This is not the case; we found that collaborations that use equity language are also in cities with more white residents. This is the case even though there is no significant relationship between the total number of words on the website and the percentage of city residents that are white. We wonder whether these findings suggest that cross-sector collaborations might be only symbolically promoting normative attention to equity, and whether they are doing so in contexts where racial and/or socioeconomic tensions are less dramatic and easier to discuss.

The in-depth case studies also shed some light on whether and how collaborations try to develop shared norms around equity and strengthen social ties that facilitate the provision of services for their most disadvantaged children. The stated mission of the initiative in Buffalo suggests a clear focus on citywide economic development, and much of the business community sees the initiative through an economic lens. However, the collaboration and its members orient much of their work around equity, and they are supportive of (though not leaders in) a civic racial equity roundtable that portrays local disparities in stark perspective. The Say Yes initiative is intentional in combining universal scholarships, which potentially benefit all social strata, with additional services specifically geared toward students with the greatest social needs. While their messaging around the city seems to stress the scholarship, they are quietly promoting the wraparound services as essential as well. And they are methodically drawing new partners into the collaboration, creating a growing network of relationships.

Milwaukee is another example of a city with a long-standing history of racial inequity, with numerous political and economic disparities and power struggles.

In some ways, it is apparent that while some in the city yearn for racial parity, the bread and butter issue for others is the economic health of the city and a renewal of the thriving economic hub that Milwaukee once was. Despite some leanings toward equity, business leaders in Milwaukee rationalize their participation in the education initiative as one of economic necessity. For example, one prominent member of the business community explained, "Never mind if I'm a good citizen or an enlightened citizen, forget about it, just the pure economics of it dictate that we want to help the community get this right, however that means. Milwaukee Succeeds, we're going to be in on everything, hoping something will move the needle faster than it is now."[2]

The situation is complicated by tensions across the public, charter, and private school sectors that have economic, political, and racial/social class overtones. Still, the staff of the Milwaukee Succeeds collaboration has increasingly brought racial equity issues into broader discussions and strategic planning. Their website now presents data disaggregated by race and socioeconomic status. And the collaboration has managed to keep a wide swath of community members engaged and talking across their differences.

The third case study, a county-wide initiative anchored in Portland, Oregon, is located in a context with a much stronger economic base than Buffalo or Milwaukee and a population that has lower proportions of persons of color. However, there are growing concentrations of low-income children of color in some areas of the county, partly a result of gentrification and displacement. Issues of race and social class are more muted here than the other study sites, and yet this is the collaboration that has been most explicit in raising issues about equity. Many local informants credit the All Hands Raised collaboration with enabling a racial educational equity policy to be adopted across the six school districts in the county. The policy calls for a set of racial equity strategies that include culturally responsive instruction, a culturally responsive workforce, and family and community engagement. While not all partnership members have made equal progress along these lines, it is a common focus. It might be tempting to dismiss this as an easy lift in a supportive climate. But even in this context, the collaboration has had to step gingerly around these issues. A few years ago, the collaboration's participants decided that the group was too large to have open and honest discussions about disparities and equity, so they formed a smaller group comprising only the local school superintendents and an equal number of representatives from what are locally known as "culturally specific" community groups. It has taken several years for this group to share and discuss district-level data about racial disparities in student discipline, and they have not yet formulated strategies for action on them.

It is clear from our study that the task of creating an invigorated normative environment around equity and education, building relationships of trust among a broad social network, and achieving concrete accomplishments is not easy, will not happen quickly, and could fall apart at any moment. Cross-sector collaborations are generally voluntary associations, based on value preferences instead of bureaucratic rules and on relationships between individuals instead of formal structures. Thus, although they may be "constructed organizations," in Coleman's terminology, they are also as fragile as the families and communities whose social-izing purposes they seek to augment.

Coleman was well aware of the challenges of urban renewal and he wrote about them in decidedly sociological terms as problems of values (Coleman 1977). Not all cross-sector collaborations are located in big cities, but Coleman's insights are relevant to many. He suggested the reason we do not rebuild our cit-ies is because we want to do other things more. One example he gave concerned the post-WWII housing loan guarantee programs, which many look back on as a prime factor leading to migration from cities to suburbs. These policies made it easy to buy new homes, most of which were in the suburbs, but not to purchase or upgrade older homes in the city. The postwar American polity apparently wanted to support the construction industry with jobs more than to preserve inner cities. As a result, urban housing stock declined in quality and disinvest-ment in cities followed. As Coleman argued (1977, 34):

> The conclusion of this examination of policy should be self-evident. It is that the rebuild-ing and strengthening of urban areas, the revitalizing of cities and metropolitan areas now undergoing decline, cannot be brought about by some brilliant plan which has so far eluded us. ... Only when we begin to recognize that the city declines simply because we actively pursue ends that bring about its decline will we have reached the sober point where serious discussion can begin about what will be gained and what will be lost by strengthening the city and its environs.

Conclusion

In a pragmatic sense, cross-sector collaborations for education aim to improve academic outcomes for children and youth in their locales. To the degree that they seek to do so by supporting schools and school systems in their efforts to improve, and by expanding and aligning comprehensive, wraparound social ser-vices and other resources for children and youth, they are pursuing strategies consistent with the EEO findings and are carrying forward Coleman's legacy.

We argue that cross-sector collaborations also have the potential to help real-ize James Coleman's deeper vision for social institutions that provide a consistent, nurturing, and normative context in which all children and youth can learn the values and habits that will enable them to thrive academically, economically, and socially. These collaborations set their sights on whole cities or, in some cases, regions defined by other boundaries. It is daunting indeed to imagine how a social context on that scale, in our era, can be a functional community, with cohe-sive values and strong social ties, that binds actors of many different backgrounds and with varying resources and disparate interests in a common pursuit on behalf of a diverse population of young people. It requires a level of political, economic, and educational acuity and will that was not present, for example, in many of the attempts to desegregate schools following the Coleman Report. The EEO was an empirical study that led to a solution embroiled in politics and culture. Cross-sector collaboration may be a newer solution, but one embedded in politics and culture as well. Coleman sought a social theory of the school because he thought the school was an institution of a scale that one could examine and understand in its entirety, and it was a target of policy efforts, always a compelling draw. Cross-sector collaborations invite thinking about a social theory of the city. If public policy looks for place-based solutions to the many problems connected to inequality, a social theory of the city might be just what James Coleman would prescribe.

Notes

1. The study was commissioned by The Wallace Foundation through a grant to Teachers College, Columbia University, with Jeffrey R. Henig as Principal Investigator and Carolyn J. Riehl as Co-Principal Investigator. In addition to a national scan and longitudinal case studies of three cities, the study also includes briefer case studies of five additional sites. We acknowledge the contributions of other members of the research team, including Jeffrey R. Henig, Michael A. Rebell, Jessica R. Wolff, Constance M. Clark, Iris Daruwala, and David M. Houston. Published reports from the study include an extensive literature review on the history, politics, and organizational dynamics of cross-sector collaboration (Henig et al. 2015), and a report of the national scan of collaborations (Henig et al. 2016). Reports of the case studies are forthcoming.

2. Interview, June 6, 2016, Milwaukee, WI.

References

Borman, Geoffrey, and Maritza Dowling. 2010. Schools and inequality: A multilevel analysis of Coleman's equality of educational opportunity data. *Teachers College Record* 112 (5): 1201–1246.

Coleman, James S. 1961. *The adolescent society: The social life of the teenager and its impact on education.* Westport, CT: Greenwood Press Publishers.

Coleman, James S. 1971. Conflicting theories of social change. *The American Behavioral Scientist* 14 (5): 633–50.

Coleman, James S. 1972. How do the young become adults? *Review of Educational Research* 42 (4): 431–39.

Coleman, James S. 1977. Can we revitalize our cities? *Challenge* 20 (5): 23–34.

Coleman, James S. 1986. Social theory, social research, and a theory of action. *American Journal of Sociology* 9 (6): 1309–1335.

Coleman, James S. 1987. Families and schools. *Educational Researcher* 16 (6): 32–38.

Coleman, James S. 1988. Social capital in the creation of human capital. *American Journal of Sociology* 94:S95–S120.

Coleman, James S. 1990. *Foundations of social theory.* Cambridge, MA: The Belknap Press of Harvard University Press.

Coleman, James S. 1994. A vision for sociology. *Society* 32 (1): 29–34.

Coleman, James S., Ernest Q. Campbell, Carol J. Hobson, James McPartland, Alexander M. Mood, Frederic D. Weinfeld, and Robert L. York. 1966. *Equality of educational opportunity.* Washington, DC: U.S. Government Printing Office.

Coleman, James S., and Thomas Hoffer. 1987. *Public and private high schools: The impact of communities.* New York, NY: Basic Books.

Coleman, James S., Sara D. Kelly, and John A. Moore. 1976. *Trends in school desegregation, 1968–73.* Washington, DC: The Urban Institute.

Coleman, James S., Barbara Schneider, Stephen Plank, Kathryn S. Schiller, Roger Shouse, and Huayin Wang. 1997. *Redesigning American education.* With She-Ahn Lee. Boulder, CO: Westview Press.

Egalite, Anna J. 2016. How family background influences student achievement: Can schools narrow the gap? *Education Next* 2:70–78.

Franklin, S. 2010. Situational deracialization, Harold Ford, and the 2006 Senate race in Tennessee. In *Whose black politics? Cases in post-racial black leadership*, ed. Andra Gillespie, 214–40. New York, NY: Routledge.

Grant, Gerald. 1973. Shaping social policy: The politics of the Coleman Report. *Teachers College Record* 75 (1): 17–54.

Hanushek, Eric A. 2016. What matters for student achievement: Updating Coleman on the influence of families and schools. *Education Next* 2:18–26.

Henig, Jeffrey R., Carolyn J. Riehl, David M. Houston, Michael A. Rebell, and Jessica R. Wolff. 2016. *Collective impact and the new generation of cross-sector collaborations for education: A nationwide scan.* New York, NY: Teachers College, Columbia University, Department of Education Policy and Social Analysis. Available from www.wallacefoundation.org.

Henig, Jeffrey R., Carolyn J. Riehl, Michael A. Rebell, and Jessica R. Wolff. 2015. *Putting collective impact in context: A review of the literature on local cross-sector collaboration to improve education.* New York, NY: Teachers College, Columbia University, Department of Education Policy and Social Analysis. Available from www.wallacefoundation.org.

Hill, Heather C. 2017. The Coleman Report, 50 years on: What do we know about the role of schools in academic inequality? *The ANNALS of the American Academy of Political and Social Science* (this volume).

Hutt, Ethan L. 2016. Surveying the nation: Longitudinal surveys and the construction of national solutions to educational inequity. *Ethics and Education* 11 (2): 240–58.

Kania, John, and Mark Kramer. 2011. Collective impact. *Stanford Social Innovation Review.* Available from http://www.ssireview.org/articles/entry/collective_impact.

Kraft, Matthew A., and Manuel Monti-Nussbaum. 2017. Can schools enable parents to prevent summer learning loss? A text-messaging field experiment to promote literacy skills. *The ANNALS of the American Academy of Political and Social Science* (this volume).

Liu, Zhen, and Michael J. White. 2017. Education outcomes of immigrant youth: The role of parental engagement. *The ANNALS of the American Academy of Political and Social Science* (this volume).

Marsden, Peter V. 2005. The sociology of James Coleman. *Annual Review of Sociology* 31 (xii): 1–24.

Mosteller, Frederick, and Daniel P. Moynihan. 1972. *On equality of educational opportunity.* New York, NY: Random House.

Moynihan, Daniel P. 1965. *The negro family: The case for national action.* A report for the U.S. Department of Labor, Office of Policy Planning and Research. Washington, DC: Government Printing Office.

New York Times. 2 July 1966 (1966a). Negro education is found inferior: U.S. public survey confirms racial disparity.

New York Times. 18 September 1966 (1966b). U.S. study finds racial inequality grows in school.

Pallas, Aaron M. 1999. James S. Coleman and the purposes of schooling. *Research in Sociology of Education and Socialization* 12:9–34.

Peterson, Paul E. 2010. *Saving schools: From Horace Mann to virtual learning.* Cambridge, MA: Harvard University Press.

Rebell, Michael S., and Jessica R. Wolff. 2011. *A proposal for essential standards and resources: A report on the task force on comprehensive educational opportunity.* New York, NY: Campaign for Educational Equity, Teachers College, Columbia University.

Riehl, Carolyn J., and Jeffrey R. Henig. Forthcoming. All together now: The apparent resurgence of locally based cross-sector collaboration. In *Shaping education policy: Power and process*, 2nd ed., eds. Robert L. Crowson, Douglas E. Mitchell, and Dorothy Shipps. New York, NY: Routledge.

Rothstein, Richard. 2004. *Class and schools: Using social, economic, and educational reform to close the black-white achievement gap.* Washington, DC: Economic Policy Institute.

Snyder, Thomas D. 1993. *120 years of American education: A statistical portrait.* Washington, DC: National Center for Education Statistics, Office of Educational Research and Improvement, U.S. Department of Education.

Sørensen, Aage B., and Stephen L. Morgan. 2000. School effects: Theoretical and methodological issues. In *Handbook of the sociology of education*, ed. Maureen T. Hallinan, 137–60. New York, NY: Kluwer Academic/Plenum Publishers.

Keywords: school; family; skill; academic

The findings in the Coleman Report (Coleman et al. 1966) were unusually expansive in their attention to factors beyond the school that affected academic inequality, challenging prevailing understandings of educational inequality and igniting fierce debates that have endured (and continue in this volume of *The ANNALS*). This volume provides a benchmark from which researchers and policy analysts can examine separate strands of research together, assessing the current state of educational inequality and informing the debates within. The articles in this volume focus on ideas that connect closely with the Coleman Report (school, family, and community effects), as well as issues that are increasingly relevant to our understanding of inequality (e.g., immigration, cross-national variation). In addition, the anniversary of the Coleman Report provides an opportunity to consider how contemporary researchers and policy-makers can incorporate insights and research findings of the last 50 years into the design of future studies and programs. This thought exercise raises several themes.

The State of Unequal Educational Opportunity: Conclusion to the Special Issue on the Coleman Report 50 Years Later

By
MARGOT I. JACKSON
and
SUSAN L. MOFFITT

Margot I. Jackson is an associate professor of sociology at Brown University. Her work focuses on social stratification and social demography, with an emphasis on inequality of educational opportunity, health, and children and families.

Susan L. Moffitt is an associate professor in the Department of Political Science and the Watson Institute for Public and International Affairs at Brown University. Her work focuses on state capacity to implement policy in the domains of public education and public health.

Correspondence: margot_jackson@brown.edu

DOI: 10.1177/0002716217734148

The "School vs. Family Background" Debate Is Not Useful

Much academic scholarship in the last several decades has justifiably worked to identify the independent effects of families, schools, and communities on children's skills and achievement. This body of research is essential for gaining a clear understanding of the social processes through which each institution affects children's achievement, and for providing sound evidence to inform the design of public policies and programs. An unfortunate result of the academic debate about effects, however, has been a tendency to concentrate on the relative impact of schools *versus* families or other contexts. This debate creates an artificial distinction between contexts that overlap closely and continually affect one other. Families create communities and schools through processes of neighborhood selection and school choice (e.g., Hill et al., this volume; Burdick-Will, Keels, and Schuble 2013; Sampson and Sharkey 2008). At the same time, the resources and communities within schools influence not only students' achievement, but also the future composition of surrounding families and communities.

Because each context has both independent and overlapping effects on student achievement, an important task for future research is to more closely examine the joint effects of families, schools, and other settings on students. For example, a burgeoning literature examines the costs and benefits of integrating students from low-income families and communities into higher-resource schools, motivated by the idea that the richer resources of that school context can better offset disadvantage at the family level (Crosnoe 2009; Kahlenberg 2001). Considering family, school, and community resources in concert will offer a richer approach to the reduction of academic inequality.

Neither Achievement nor Its Inputs Are Static

Several articles in this volume, and in the broader literature, highlight the importance of measuring children's environments and their achievement dynamically. While the Coleman Report and much subsequent research offered a cross-sectional perspective on the scope of academic inequality, more recent research (including work in this volume) has offered insight into the dynamics of academic inequality and its inputs. A dynamic approach has afforded both conceptual and methodological insights. First, examining children over time demonstrates the persistence of academic inequality, and in some cases the accumulation of disadvantage with age. Children living in disadvantaged environments are less likely to enter formal schooling adequately prepared (Heckman 2004), and these students then remain less likely to demonstrate strong performance throughout their schooling or attain key educational credentials (Heckman 2008; McLanahan and Sandefur 1994). Second, a longitudinal perspective has revealed how the degree and persistence of academic inequality depends on the developmental stage being considered, the duration and stability of children's environments, and the resources available to children across age and contexts. Researchers are increasingly focusing on how circumstances during critical and sensitive periods of development in early childhood contribute meaningfully to skill development and to the development of academic inequality (Shonkoff and Phillips 2000), and on how compensatory investments in families and schools may offset or reinforce previously existing inequalities (e.g., Grätz and Torche 2016).

Finally, the collection of longitudinal data has expanded the methodological toolkit available to researchers studying academic inequality. It is now possible to model stability and change in student achievement and to use temporal variation to identify stronger causal models of contextual effects on student achievement. Just in this volume, several articles model variation in children's family environment with age (e.g., Jackson, Kiernan, and McLanahan) and use statistical approaches appropriate for longitudinal data to better control for unmeasured sources of variation between children and schools (e.g., Mizala and Torche). In the broader literature, researchers are increasingly using longitudinal data to isolate the effect of an educational policy by comparing the progress of similar children who have different exposures to the policy (e.g., Rauscher 2016).

Skills Are Multidimensional

The articles in this volume focus on academic achievement as a marker of educational inequality. The focus on achievement is justifiable given the strong and lasting effects of students' cognitive skills and achievement on students' eventual social and economic outcomes (Heckman 2006). At the same time, a growing body of research links children's noncognitive or "soft" characteristics, including health, temperament, and behavior, to stratification processes over the life course, including family structure, children's academic achievement, and eventual labor market outcomes (Bowles and Gintis 1976; DiPrete and Jennings 2012; Hall and Farkas 2011; Jackson 2010; Palloni 2006; Reichman, Corman, and Noonan 2004). Future efforts to document the scope of educational inequality should examine the full set of skills implicated in patterns of educational inequality. An important feature of contemporary scholarship is its increasingly transdisciplinary perspective, as scholars in the social sciences incorporate insights from neuroscience, psychology, and other fields into their conceptualization and measurement of early life environments and their effects on the development of skills necessary for educational progression (Heckman 2006; Shonkoff and Phillips 2000).

Institutional Context Matters

The last 50 years have brought enormous changes in the educational landscapes of children in their families, schools, and communities. First, historic increases in income inequality in the United States in the last 40 years (e.g., Atkinson, Piketty, and Saez 2011) have dramatically altered the environments of children and families, with an increasingly differentiated opportunity structure for accessing high-quality housing, neighborhoods, and schools, and goods and services related to children's skill development (Duncan and Murnane 2011; Kornrich and Furstenberg 2013). A growing body of scholarship examines the implications of changes in the degree of economic inequality for the degree of inequality in children's skill development and academic progress (Kalil et al. 2016; Reardon 2011). What is clear, though, is the persistent impact of underlying structural determinants of children's environments, even as social and economic policies work to offset the effects of poverty and economic inequality. The need for research approaches that can connect to policy and practice remains as important as ever.

Second, the educational sector itself has changed in striking ways in the last 50 years, with an increasingly diversified school choice landscape that includes charter schools alongside public, private, and religious schools. These changes introduce major challenges to providing a comprehensive assessment of the state of educational inequality in the future, given the ways in which the educational sector can selectively alter the student composition of schools. A related challenge to studying the educational sector in its entirety is the substantial variation across states and districts in the provision of educational funding and the oversight of instructional designs. However, better teachers matter to students' long-term outcomes (Chetty, Friedman, and Rockoff 2014). Research has come a long way since Coleman in revealing ways to improve teachers' instruction. Promising evidence suggests that providing teachers with new curriculum and professional development opportunities to learn how to use that curriculum in meaningful ways can improve student outcomes (Roschelle et al. 2010; Saxe, Gearhart, and Nasir 2001). Yet how to take instructional improvement interventions to scale remains an open and uncertain terrain for both research and applied public policy.

Finally, it is important to inform the study of educational inequality with insights from other countries, where differences in educational systems alongside differences in demographic composition, cultural norms, and social service provision provide an opportunity to understand the generalizability of patterns observed in a particular country. It is important to understand whether findings observed in the United States can be generalized to other settings with more rigid educational tracking systems or more homogenous populations than the United States, as well as what the experiences of children in the educational systems of other countries (e.g., those undergoing rapid economic transitions or engaging in large-scale national reforms) imply for conceptual models of student skills and achievement.

References

Atkinson, Anthony B., Thomas Piketty, and Emmanuel Saez. 2011. Top incomes in the long run of history. *Journal of Economic Literature* 49 (1): 3–71.

Bowles, Samuel, and Herbert Gintis. 1976. *Schooling in capitalist America*. New York, NY: Basic Books.

Burdick-Will, Julia, Micere Keels, and Todd Schuble. 2013. Closing and opening schools: The association between neighborhood characteristics and the location of new educational opportunities in a large urban district. *Journal of Urban Affairs* 35 (1): 59–80.

Chetty, Raj, John N. Friedman, and Jonah E. Rockoff. 2014. Measuring the impacts of teachers II: Teacher value-added and student outcomes in adulthood. *American Economic Review* 104 (9): 2633–79.

Coleman, James S., Ernest Q. Campbell, Carol J. Hobson, James McPartland, Alexander M. Mood, Frederic D. Weinfeld, and Robert L. York. 1966. *Equality of educational opportunity*. Washington, DC: U.S. Government Printing Office.

Crosnoe, Robert. 2009. Low-income students and the socioeconomic composition of public high schools. *American Sociological Review* 74 (5): 709–30.

DiPrete, Thomas A., and Jennifer L. Jennings. 2012. Social and behavioral skills and the gender gap in early educational achievement. *Social Science Research* 41 (1): 1–15.

Duncan, Greg J., and Richard J. Murnane. 2011. *Whither opportunity? Rising inequality, schools, and children's life chances*. New York, NY: Russell Sage Foundation.

Grätz, Michael, and Florencia Torche. 2016. Compensation or reinforcement? The stratification of parental responses to children's early ability. *Demography* 53 (6): 1883–1904.

Hall, Matthew, and George Farkas. 2011. Adolescent cognitive skills, attitudinal/behavioral traits, and career wages. *Social Forces* 89 (4): 1261–85.

Heckman, James J. 2004. Lessons from the technology of skill formation. *Annals of the New York Academy of Sciences* 1038 (1): 179–200.

Heckman, James J. 2006. Skill formation and the economics of investing in disadvantaged children. *Science* 312:1900–1902.

Heckman, James J. 2008. Schools, skills, and synapses. *Economic Inquiry* 46 (3): 289–324.

Jackson, Margot I. 2010. A life course perspective on child health, cognition and occupational skill qualifications in adulthood: Evidence from a British cohort. *Social Forces* 89 (1): 89–116.

Kahlenberg, Richard D. 2001. *All together now: The case for economic integration of the public schools*. Washington, DC: Brookings Institution Press.

Kalil, Ariel, Kathleen Ziol-Guest, Rebecca M. Ryan, and Anna J. Markowitz. 2016. Changes in income-based gaps in parent activities with young children from 1988 to 2012. *AERA Open* 2 (3): 1–17.

Kornrich, Sabino, and Frank Furstenberg. 2013. Investing in children: Changes in parental spending on children, 1972–2007. *Demography* 50 (1): 1–23.

McLanahan, Sara, and Gary Sandefur. 1994. *Growing up with a single parent. What hurts, what helps*. Cambridge, MA: Harvard University Press.

Palloni, Alberto. 2006. Reproducing inequalities: Luck, wallets, and the enduring effects of childhood health. *Demography* 43 (4): 587–615.

Rauscher, Emily. 2016. Does educational equality increase mobility? Exploiting nineteenth-century U.S. compulsory schooling laws. *American Journal of Sociology* 121 (6): 1697–1761.

Reardon, Sean F. 2011. The widening academic achievement gap between the rich and the poor: New evidence and possible explanations. In *Whither opportunity? Rising inequality, schools, and children's life chances*, eds. Greg J. Duncan and Richard J. Murnane, 91–116. New York, NY: Russell Sage Foundation.

Reichman, Nancy, Hope Corman, and Kelly Noonan. 2004. Effects of child health on parents' relationship status. *Demography* 41 (3): 569–84.

Roschelle, Jeremy, Nicole Shechtman, Deborah Tatar, Stephen Hegedus, Bill Hopkins, Susan Empson, Jennifer Knudsen, and Lawrence P. Gallagher. 2010. Integration of technology, curriculum, and professional development for advancing middle school mathematics: Three large-scale studies. *American Educational Research Journal* 47 (4): 833–78.

Sampson, Robert J., and Patrick Sharkey. 2008. Neighborhood selection and the social reproduction of concentrated racial inequality. *Demography* 45 (1): 1–29.

Saxe, Geoffrey B., Maryl Gearhart, and Na'ilah Suad Nasir. 2001. Enhancing students' understanding of mathematics: A study of three contrasting approaches to professional support. *Journal of Mathematics Teacher Education* 4 (1): 55–79.

Shonkoff, Jack P., and Deborah Phillips. 2000. *From neurons to neighborhood: The science of early childhood development*. Washington, DC: National Academy Press.

THE IMPACT OF THE SOCIAL SCIENCES: How Academics and their Research Make a Difference

Simon Bastow, Patrick Dunleavy, and Jane Tinkler, *all from London School of Economics*

Foreword by Kenneth Prewitt, *Columbia University*

In the modern globalized world, some estimates suggest that around 40 million people now work in jobs that 'translate' or mediate advances in social science research for use in business, government and public agencies, health care systems, and civil society organizations. Many large corporations and organizations across these sectors in the United States are increasingly prioritizing access to social science knowledge. Yet, the impact of university social science continues to be fiercely disputed. This key study demonstrates the essential role of university social science in the 'human-dominated' and 'human-influenced' systems now central to our civilization. It focuses empirically on Britain, the second most influential country for social science research after the US. Using in-depth research, the authors show how the growth of a services economy, and the success of previous scientific interventions, mean that key areas of advance for corporations, public policy-makers, and citizens alike now depend on our ability to understand our complex societies and economies. This is a landmark study in the evidence-based analysis of social science impact.

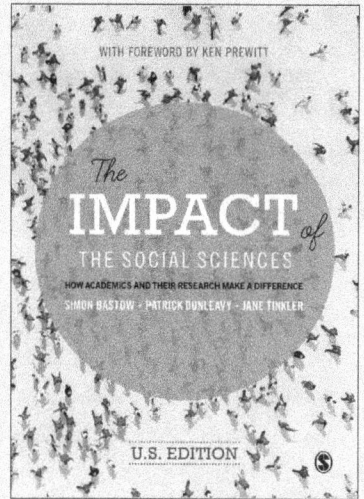

PAPERBACK ISBN: 978-1-4462-8262-5 • FEBRUARY 2014 • 326 PAGES

LEARN MORE AT SAGEPUB.COM!

0. STATEMENT OF OWNERSHIP, MANAGEMENT, AND CIRCULATION
   P.S. Form 3526 Facsimile

1. TITLE: ANNALS OF THE AMERICAN ACADEMY OF POLITICAL AND SOCIAL SCIENCE
2. USPS PUB. #: 026-060

3. DATE OF FILING: OCTOBER 1, 2017

4. FREQUENCY OF ISSUE: Bi-monthly
5. NO. OF ISSUES ANNUALLY: 6
6. ANNUAL SUBSCRIPTION PRICE:

   Institution $1,070.
   Individual $122.

7. PUBLISHER ADDRESS: 2455 Teller Road, Thousand Oaks, CA 91320
   CONTACT PERSON: Graeme Doswell, Head of Global Circulation
   TELEPHONE: (805) 499-0721

8. HEADQUARTERS ADDRESS: 2455 Teller Road, Thousand Oaks, CA 91320

9. PUBLISHER: SAGE Publications Inc., 2455 Teller Road, Thousand Oaks, CA 91320
   EDITOR:
   Thomas A. Kecskemethy, 202 S. 36th Street, Philadelphia, PA 19104

10. OWNER: The American Academy of Political and Social Science
    202 S. 36th Street, Philadelphia, PA 19104-3806

11. KNOWN BONDHOLDERS, ETC.
    None

12. NONPROFIT PURPOSE, FUNCTION, STATUS:
    Has Not Changed During Preceding 12 Months

13. PUBLICATION NAME: ANNALS OF THE AMERICAN ACADEMY OF POLITICAL AND SOCIAL SCIENCE

14. ISSUE DATE FOR CIRCULATION DATA BELOW: July 2017

15. EXTENT & NATURE OF CIRCULATION:

	AVG. NO. COPIES EACH ISSUE DURING PRECEDING 12 MONTHS	ACT. NO. COPIES C SINGLE ISSUE PUI NEAREST T FILING DAT
A. TOTAL NO. COPIES	518	55
B. PAID CIRCULATION		
1. PAID/REQUESTED OUTSIDE-CO, ETC	314	36
2. PAID IN-COUNTY SUBSCRIPTIONS	0	
3. SALES THROUGH DEALERS, ETC.	14	1
4. OTHER CLASSES MAILED USPS	0	
C. TOTAL PAID CIRCULATION	328	37
D. FREE DISTRIBUTION BY MAIL		
1. OUTSIDE-COUNTY AS ON 3541	18	1
2. IN-COUNTY AS STATED ON 3541	0	
3. OTHER CLASSES MAILED USPS	0	
E. FREE DISTRIBUTION OTHER	0	
F. TOTAL FREE DISTRIBUTION	18	1
G. TOTAL DISTRIBUTION	346	39
H. COPIES NOT DISTRIBUTED		
1. OFFICE USE, ETC.	172	15
2. RETURN FROM NEWS AGENTS	0	
I. TOTAL	518	55
PERCENT PAID CIRCULATION	95%	95

16. THIS STATEMENT OF OWNERSHIP WILL BE PRINTED IN THE NOVEMBER 2017 ISSUE OF THIS PUBLICATION.

17. I CERTIFY THAT ALL INFORMATION FURNISHED ON THIS FORM IS TRUE AND COMPLETE.
    I UNDERSTAND THAT ANYONE WHO FURNISHES FALSE OR MISLEADING INFORMATION ON
    THIS FORM OR WHO OMITS MATERIAL OR INFORMATION REQUESTED ON THE FORM MAY
    BE SUBJECT TO CRIMINAL SANCTIONS (INCLUDING FINES AND IMPRISONMENT) AND/OR
    CIVIL SANCTIONS (INCLUDING MULTIPLE DAMAGES AND CIVIL PENALTIES).

Graeme Doswell

Graeme Doswell   Date: 08/17/2017
Head of Global Circulation
SAGE Publications, Inc.

In compliance with GPSR, should you have any concerns about the safety of this
product, please advise: International Associates Auditing & Certification
Limited The Black Church, St Mary's Place, Dublin 7, D07 P4AX Ireland
EUAR@ie.ia-net.com